LAW WITHOUT NATIONS?

LAW WITHOUT NATIONS?

Why Constitutional Government Requires Sovereign States

Jeremy A. Rabkin

PRINCETON UNIVERSITY PRESS

PRINCETON AND OXFORD

Library of Congress Cataloging-in-Publication Data

Rabkin, Jeremy A.
    Law without nations? : why constitutional government requires
sovereign states / Jeremy A. Rabkin.
        p.   cm.
    Includes bibliographical references and index.
    ISBN 0-691-09530-2 (cloth: alk. paper)
        1. Sovereignty.   2. Constitutional law.   3. Globalization.   4. United States—
Foreign relations—Europe.   5. Europe—Foreign relations—United States.   I. Title.

    KZ4041.R328 2005
    341.26—dc22   2004046638

British Library Cataloging-in-Publication Data is available

This book has been composed in Sabon

Printed on acid-free paper. ∞

pup.princeton.edu

Printed in the United States of America

10 9 8 7 6 5 4 3 2 1

CONTENTS

LAW WITHOUT NATIONS?

CHAPTER ONE

INTRODUCTION: BY OUR OWN LIGHTS

FOR SOME MONTHS following the terror attacks of September 11, 2001, pundits affirmed that the event had irrevocably changed America and the world. Subsequent events proved that changes in America and changes in the world were far from symmetrical. Perhaps there was not even that much change.

Nations, like individuals, may respond in new ways when confronted with new challenges. But even new responses are shaped by old habits of thought and established patterns of conduct. American political ideals have often differed from those embraced by people in western Europe. Differing responses to the challenge of international terrorism simply highlighted the underlying divergence.

In the immediate aftermath of September 11, "the world"—speaking through the United Nations (UN)—condemned the attacks. But what could the "international community" do to catch the perpetrators or to ensure that such attacks did not recur? The "international community" offered condolences. America then had to summon its own resources to defend itself.

Working with Afghan resistance forces, the United States mounted a counterattack on the Taliban regime in Afghanistan, a principal host for the terror network that perpetrated the September 11 attacks. The Taliban regime was overthrown in less than four months. Hundreds of Islamist terrorists were captured and imprisoned. But the United States provided virtually all the outside military force to accomplish this result.

For most Americans, the experience offered a clear lesson: The nation must depend, in the end, on its own exertions for its own security. At home, police warn crime victims not to take the law into their own hands. The world as a whole, however, has no international policing capacity. When attacked, a nation must be able to take the law into its own hands because self-defense is the most basic right.

Most Europeans drew quite different conclusions. In the months after the Afghan war, the United States was scolded by the International Red Cross, by the UN Commissioner for Human Rights, and by many European leaders for refusing to accord prisoner of war status to captured Afghan terrorists. Their view was that even a justified war must be fought under international supervision, on terms acceptable to international authorities.

And on second thought, much of the world doubted that terror attacks could actually justify military responses. In April 2002, after hundreds of Israeli civilians had been killed by terrorist attacks on civilians in Israeli cities, the government of Israel sent troops into towns on the West Bank to seize terrorist leaders and dismantle the terrorist infrastructure. The United Nations issued fierce denunciations of Israeli "aggression" without making any reference to the terrorist attacks which provoked it. European leaders spoke of "massacres" and "war crimes"—on the evident assumption that even a conscript army of a democratic nation was quite capable of committing mass atrocities, unless constrained by international authority. The correct response to terror attacks, Europeans insisted, was to work with international authorities to defuse tensions and satisfy the grievances which provoke people into committing terrorist acts.

A year later, American and British troops invaded Iraq and overthrew the government of Saddam Hussein. The UN Security Council had demanded that Saddam's government demonstrate that it had dismantled all its programs for producing weapons of mass destruction. The same demand had been repeatedly reaffirmed since 1991, when it had been included in the truce terms ending that earlier Gulf War. In the previous war, a UN-authorized, American-led force had liberated Kuwait from Iraqi conquest but left Saddam in power in Iraq itself. By the spring of 2003, there was general agreement on the Security Council that Saddam was still not complying with disarmament obligations imposed in 1991. It was also widely understood that Saddam's government had developed friendly relations with international terror networks.

But the Security Council still would not authorize a second war to enforce its own demands. When the United States and Britain proceeded to war without formal authorization from the Security Council, the war provoked strong condemnation at UN Headquarters and in many capitals around the world. In Europe, the governments of France and Germany remained most adamant in their condemnations. Outside of Britain, European public opinion remained quite disapproving. American opinion generally supported the war.

For critics, the war showed that the United States was a dangerous "rogue nation," claiming the power to attack other countries on its own initiative.[1] For most Americans, it was hard to imagine who else, if not the American government, could decide when and where American military forces would be ordered into action. The United States had, in fact, secured endorsements of the war from some forty countries, many of which offered some degree of direct assistance to the military campaign. To critics, the war remained "unilateral" or in any case "illegitimate" because it was not sanctioned by the United Nations.

For most Americans, it remained strange to think that American defense efforts required authorization from the United Nations. The United States had fought many wars, large and small, since the founding of the United Nations in 1945. It had rarely sought or received UN approval for these efforts. How could the UN limit American defense efforts, when the UN had no troops to provide an alternate means of security? Criticism of American actions presumed, on the contrary, that no country would be safe unless international institutions were acknowledged to be paramount to the impulses of individual states.

Even as the United States was gearing up a bolder defense strategy in the months after September 11, European governments rounded up endorsements for a project which embodied this alternate view. A treaty establishing an International Criminal Court (ICC) had been negotiated in the summer of 1998, but it took some time to get the required sixty ratifications to put the plan into effect. The United States had, from the outset, sought revisions in the design of the project. European governments resisted these pleas and pressed forward with their efforts to see the court set up and running on the original plan. In the spring of 2002, the Bush administration announced its unalterable opposition to the court as now constituted. This stance provoked intense criticism.

The extent of the divergence in underlying attitudes was perfectly reflected in the differing perspectives on this new international project. The court would have jurisdiction to indict American soldiers for "war crimes" and could accuse higher officials of "command responsibility" for such "crimes," even for abuses they had neither ordered nor known about. Ultimately, according to the original plan, the court would also have jurisdiction to indict American leaders for the general crime of "aggression." Was it really to be expected that a government of the United States could submit itself to the judgments of such a court?

Europeans seemed convinced that only arrogance and selfishness could explain American resistance to this project. Why should America set itself above the rest of the world? The fact that China and Russia, India and Pakistan, Japan and South Korea, Israel and Egypt—in fact a majority of UN members—had also held back from the treaty did not receive so much attention. Certainly the recalcitrance of other states did not provoke so much criticism. European critics focused on the American stance: Why was the United States holding itself aloof from a project that aroused such hopes among democratic countries, western countries, peace-loving countries?

A short book by Robert Kagan offered an explanation which gained a good deal of attention in 2003: "Americans are from Mars, Europeans are from Venus."[2] The problem, as Kagan diagnosed it, was that Americans still felt the need to cope with serious threats out in the world, while Europeans imagined that a network of legal institutions could bring peace to the world, as it had to Europe. Such formulas seemed especially astute amidst intensifying debates over the war in Iraq.

But it was, in fact, only the most visible or the most recent round in a dispute that was much older and much deeper. Long before the dispute over Iraq, European governments had complained about American resistance to many other international undertakings. Before the United States provoked European scorn for repudiating the International Criminal Court, for example, it had provoked European resentment for backing away from the Kyoto Protocol on Climate Change. Those with longer memories could recall that the United States had backed away from a number of previous international environmental treaties, human rights conventions, and arbitration agreements. Those with a wider perspective would notice that European states had harnessed themselves to supranational authorities in the European Union (EU), establishing an elaborate treaty structure over their own national constitutions, in ways that would be unthinkable for Americans.

There was already a growing divergence between Europe and America in the 1990s, when everyone dreamed of enduring peace in a world finally released from Cold War tensions. At some level, the divergence reflected differing notions of what peace should mean. Years before September 11, Samuel Huntington had warned of a coming era characterized by "the clash of civilizations."[3] But even Huntington's pessimistic forecast took for granted that western Europe and the United States were part of the same cultural community—what he called "western civilization." But "western civilization" itself has competing strands. In some ways, the debate that emerged after September 11, like the trans-Atlantic disputes gathering momentum before that supposed turning point, reflected very much older divisions.

How can any nation hold to its own law and still have peace with its neighbors? The question has been posed—and answered in quite different ways—ever since the emergence of modern nation-states. It is a question that has shadowed the modern world.

In some ways, indeed, the underlying debate is still older. It goes back to some of the formative thoughts or formative experiences of western civilization. Certainly, the longing for some overarching political structure, encompassing all or many nations, is a very old dream. For many centuries, it was even an achieved reality.

UNIVERSAL EMPIRES

At the height of its power, the Roman Empire seemed to rule the whole of the civilized world. If there were different empires in China or India, they were impossibly remote, scarcely more than legends or rumors. At least within Europe, the boundaries of Rome appeared to be the boundaries of civilization. Within Europe, even barbarians, on the far side of this boundary, were awed by Rome's empire.

Rome was the source of wealth and luxury, of order and law, of political wisdom and saving religion. So the barbarians remained in awe of the empire. They remained in awe of Rome, even as they overran the empire and reduced it to chaos in the last stages of Rome's decline. Even then, after the complete disintegration of the empire, the memory lingered.

In the tenth century, German princes tried, with the blessings of a universal church, to revive the idea of a universal empire. These princes styled themselves rulers of an empire (*reich*) not only "holy" but "Holy Roman"—and claimed the title of *kaiser* to appropriate the luster of the ancient caesars. In the fifteenth century, after the Ottoman Turks conquered Constantinople, the last remnant of the Eastern Roman Empire, the rulers of distant Muscovy proclaimed themselves the final heirs of Roman glory—new caesars ("czars"), builders of a "Third Rome," which would be the ultimate and most enduring empire.

Centuries later, a different group of Russian rulers sought to build a new empire, again centered in Moscow, now seeking world dominance not as a "Third Rome" but as masters of a "Third International." By then, Germans were entranced with a new scheme for the German domination of Europe—a successor to the medieval revival of the Roman Empire, a "Third Reich," which would leave architectural monuments as grand and enduring as those left by ancient Rome.

Almost everyone now shudders at the horrors inflicted by these mid-twentieth-century efforts at restoring universal empire. But in their time, these projects inspired great hopes among millions of Europeans. People in France, in Belgium, in the Netherlands, and elsewhere in western Europe greeted the triumph of German arms in 1940 with relief. They hoped for peace. Relinquishing national sovereignty seemed a reasonable price to pay for the promise of peace.[4] Millions of people in conquered countries looked upon continued British resistance as an affront to peace. As late as the summer of 1943, the president of France, chosen by a freely elected parliament, insisted there could still be a general peace in Europe if only Britain were "not led by the fanatical Churchill and the United States by the Jews."[5]

There was reason, after all, to think that a triumphant empire could bring peace. While the Roman Empire lasted, it provided security from one end of Europe to the other—and good roads throughout. Medieval Europe, torn by endless feudal conflict and religious squabbles, longed for a revival of the Pax Romana—which it connected with the inner peace to be secured by a universally acknowledged faith.

There was more than a little yearning for peace in this sense, too, in western Europe, in the summer of 1940. Advocates of collaboration envisioned a Europe where harmony would reign between classes as between nations, where selfishness and petty interests would give way to common European structures, so encompassing as to preclude any possibility of future conflict. Europe's new leader voiced the ultimate promise of peace in this first modern effort toward European integration: "When National Socialism has ruled long enough, it will no longer be possible to conceive of a form of life different from our own."[6]

The victory of outside powers put a definitive end to this particular dream of assured peace through imposed unity. Millions of Europeans continued to embrace—or turned now to embrace—a rival vision of assured harmony. International socialism had defeated National Socialism in the east. Even in western Europe, hopeful followers assumed that the new faith had harnessed the irresistible tide of History. The underlying appeal was much the same. Communism, too, promised an escape from conflict—only this time, a more comprehensive escape. By eliminating private property, it would eliminate any impulse to distinguish "mine" from "thine" and allow all mankind to embrace a common humanity.

But contrary to the predictions of many European observers in the 1940s, the defeat of the Third Reich did not open the way for the triumph of the Third International in western Europe. Instead, postwar European governments pursued moderate social welfare policies. Prominent advocates spoke of the social welfare state as—inevitably—a "Third Way." This way would avoid the extremes of cutthroat capitalism and of bureaucratic socialism, providing a final synthesis that could be accepted by everyone.[7] To anchor this third way, Europeans began, in the 1950s, to build yet another overarching political structure, which would ensure that states in western Europe, like the classes within them, would no longer be drawn into conflict.

Perhaps there was more than a slight echo of the Pax Romana in this project, too. It was founded in 1957—by an agreement called, in fact, the Treaty of Rome.[8] The Italian prime minister at the time called attention to the "deep significance" attached to the launching of this new European Community "in Rome, this city which . . . has been recognized as the cradle of that European civilization which [the treaty] aims to advance . . . [and which] will help to make Europeans politically important in the world again."[9] Over the ensuing decades, the Community acquired more and more power and was finally given a new name in 1991, to emphasize that its bonds would be far stronger than those linking, say, "the Atlantic community."

Like the Roman Empire of old, today's European Union purports to provide Europeans with a common citizenship and a common legal system. Modern Europe also imitates ancient Rome in its submission to a governing scheme with republican (or parliamentary) trappings which still leaves almost all power with energetic administrators. Such arrangements are a considerable departure from the parliamentary form of government within each member state. But bureaucratic government is accepted at the European level as the price of "unity." Dominant opinion in Europe remains entranced with the idea of a universal authority and impatient with the claims of individual nations.

So European public opinion was strongly of the view that the United States must submit its war plans in Iraq to the approval of the United Nations Security Council. In practice, awaiting approval from the Security Council would mean leaving Iraqis under the murderous regime of Saddam Hussein. Europeans certainly deplored mass murder—at least in 2003. But as in the past, most Europeans held that peace must take priority over freedom. Peace could only be obtained by submitting to some higher structure, reigning above individual nations. It was well worth leaving Iraqis under a murderous tyranny if that were necessary to constrain American freedom of action.

There was much complaint in the aftermath that the United States was building a new empire in the Middle East or acting like an imperial power. When the United States insisted that it would withdraw from Iraq, after a new democratic government had been put in place, critics complained of hypocrisy and double standards, since the United States had "supported" so many dictatorships in other parts of the world. Was it really in the power of the United States to replace dictators with democracies around the world, without deploying military force on the scale that it did in its war against Saddam? Would the United States really secure more international support by sending troops around the world to establish new democracies, even where existing governments posed no threat to the United States or to other states? Even complaints about U.S. imperialism betrayed a longing for empire—but a better, more even-handed empire, which would assure peace and eliminate the need for hard choices.

Nations Apart

Longing for empire is not unique to Europeans any more than longing for peace and security is unique to people in western countries. If anything,

Europe was, compared with vast stretches of Asia, rather unusual in its inability to sustain stable empires after the fall of Rome. Long after the fall of Rome, millions of people lived for many centuries under emperors in China, or under caliphs and sultans in the lands of the Islamic conquest. These empires, too, experienced periods of convulsion and disarray. But again and again, new rulers succeeded in reviving and restoring these ancient empires. Empire was a matter of deeply ingrained expectation. Perhaps it satisfied some genuine hopes or longings for peace and order among subject peoples.

Europeans had much more difficulty restoring and sustaining a continental empire after the fall of Rome. Part of the reason is that reverence for empire is not the only tradition in western political thought. Perhaps it is not even the main tradition. The deepest roots of western culture have often been traced to Athens and Jerusalem—relatively small cities, intensely aware of their distinctiveness. The literature of the ancient Greeks and ancient Hebrews certainly shows awareness of empires and of the temptations of empire. Their most important literature reflects considerable distrust or outright hostility toward imperial schemes.

In his sprawling chronicle of the war between the Greek cities and the Persian empire, Herodotus depicts the conflict as a struggle between Greek freedom and Persian despotism. Even within Greece, Herodotus emphasizes the paradoxical way the Greeks drew strength from their divisions and the way their divisions reflected their civic freedom. "Greece was saved by the Athenians . . . who held the balance" and "having chosen that Greece should live and preserve her freedom, roused to battle the other Greek states which had not yet submitted [to the Persians]."

Most of the Greeks were discouraged by the prophecy given by the oracle at Delphi, urging the "doomed ones" to "fly" from "fire and the headlong God of War." The Athenian envoys insisted on seeking a second opinion from the oracle. A new prophecy suggested there would be security in "the wooden wall." To the "professional interpreters," this referred to an old thorn hedge around the Acropolis, where the Greeks might find refuge. Themistocles saw it as a reference to Athenian ships: "The Athenians found Themistocles' explanation of the oracle preferable to that of the professional interpreters, who had not only tried to dissuade them from preparing to fight at sea but had been against offering opposition of any sort."[10]

Under the leadership of Themistocles, the Athenians mobilized their navy and drove back the Persians after a great battle at sea. So Greece was saved in the end by the imagination and free spirit among the leading citizens of Athens, who dared to disregard the fatalism of other cities and the fatalistic advice of their own priestly authorities.

The Hebrew Bible begins with an account of Creation that emphasizes the oneness of God and the unity of His Creation. All human beings are shown to have a common father and a common mother. But humanity's first family is ruptured by its first crime—a fratricide, emerging from a dispute over which form of sacrifice is most pleasing to God. Human wickedness becomes so pervasive that God is provoked to drown almost all humanity in a great flood and start humanity over again from the righteous family of Noah.

But the opening chapters of the Bible make clear that restored unity has its own dangers. Only a few generations after the flood, a united humanity embarked on the building of a tower "with its top in heaven," in order to "make us a name, lest we be scattered abroad upon the face of the whole earth." God sees that "they are one people, and they have all one language" so "now nothing will be withholden from them, which they purpose to do." The building of the tower is halted when God confuses the builders by giving them different languages (Gen. 11:1–9). Immediately preceding this narrative, the Bible provides an extended series of genealogies (Gen. 10:1–32). This placement suggests that it was the "confusion of tongues" at Babel which rendered these different families into separate nations. The entire account suggests that this division of mankind was, in some way, necessary or providential.

What was the precise affront to God or the danger to man in the building of the tower? It appears to be a symbol of human over-reaching: The unity of mankind tempts men to think they can challenge the ultimate authority of God—to think that their own united strength allows them to displace the omnipotence of the One God. Ancient and medieval commentators saw a connection, which is not explicit in the biblical text, between the over-reaching ambition of the tower builders and the ambitions of Nimrod, mentioned earlier in Genesis as a "mighty one" and a "mighty hunter." So the tower was seen as the project of an ambitious tyrant; tyranny, in turn, was seen as the inevitable concomitant of imposed unity.

Milton's *Paradise Lost* gives a version of this view that may still resonate with readers in the English-speaking world. Given a glimpse of human history, Adam is told that after the great flood men will "spend their days in joy unblam'd, and dwell/ Long time in peace by Families and Tribes . . ."

> . . . till one shall rise
> Of proud ambitious heart, who not content
> With fair equality, fraternal state,
> Will arrogate Dominion undeserv'd
> Over his brethren, and quite dispossess
> Concord and law of Nature from the Earth;

Hunting (and Men not Beasts shall be his game)
With War and hostile snare such as refuse
Subjection to his Empire tyrannous:
. . .
He with a crew, whom like Ambition joins
With him or under him to tyrannize,
Marching from Eden towards the West, shall find
. . . that stuff they cast to build
A City and Tow'r, whose top may reach to Heav'n;
And get themselves a name, lest far disperst
In foreign Lands their memory be lost,
Regardless whether good or evil fame.

. . .

O execrable Son so to aspire
Above his Brethren, to himself assuming
Authority usurpt, from God not giv'n:
. . . Man over men
He made not Lord; such title to Himself
Reserving, human left from human free.
But this Usurper his encroachment proud
Stays not on Man; to God his Tower intends
Siege and defiance: Wretched man!

(12.22–74)

Immediately after it recounts the frustrated ambitions of the tower-builders, the Bible proceeds to describe the immediate ancestry of Abraham, the father of a particular nation, whose history is narrated through all the subsequent books of the Hebrew Bible. That special nation must hold fast to its own special law. Moses emphasizes this trust to the people of Israel in his last admonition: "this is your wisdom and your understanding in the sight of the nations, which shall hear all these statutes and say, Surely this great nation is a wise and understanding people" (Deut. 4:6).

Israel will be "a light to the nations"—not by its direct rule but by its example: "Kings shall see and arise, princes also shall worship, because of the Lord that is faithful" (Isa. 49:6–7). The prophets foresee an era of ultimate peace between nations but no prophecy foretells the merger of all nations into one. "The wolf and the lamb shall feed together" and yet "not hurt nor destroy" (Isa. 65:25). The vision is wondrous precisely because it assumes that wolves will still be, in some way, wolves and not merely lambs in wolf clothing.

Only God, it seems, can finally bring this wondrous reign of peace to the world. "They shall beat their swords into plowshares, And their spears into pruning hooks"—but only after "the Lord . . . shall judge between the nations, And shall decide for many peoples" (Isa. 2:4). As it waited for divine deliverance, Christian Europe still preserved the memory of the heroism and civic spirit of the independent Greek city-states. And it added to the biblical canon the record of the Maccabees, who rose against a Hellenistic empire to preserve their own worship in their own temple in Jerusalem.[11]

Almost from its origin, then, western civilization has wrestled with warnings against the all-encompassing empire. Imperial pretensions have been seen as threatening, both to freedom and to proper piety. Resistance to empire seems to rest, in the first place, on this insight: In a world where so many are led astray, boundaries are necessary to preserve the possibility of pursuing the true way. By living independently, a pious or righteous people can save themselves from the corruptions of others. By defending the independence of their own free states, free citizens can preserve their freedom.

The ancient aversion to empire also seems to rest on a deeper insight: all-encompassing power, in a geographic sense, inspires rulers with dreams of power that is boundless in other ways. An independent city or an independent nation must live with other cities, other nations that are near enough to be known—and may be known to be different. The different ways of others may raise some question about the rightness of what one has at home. The awareness of difference can be a stimulus to wonder and reflection and perhaps a spur to self-improvement.

That is a Greek idea, quite obvious in Aristotle's discussion of the relative merits of the different constitutions and different regimes in different Greek cities. This idea may not be altogether remote from the Hebrew idea, that a single people may be a model or an example to other nations.

In the course of western history, a succession of empires imagined themselves successors to Rome. But a number of nations have viewed themselves as, in some way, a new Israel—distinctive, luminous, faithful to some special destiny. In the seventeenth century, Puritans were particularly taken with the vision of a new Israel in England—or in New England. In the era of the American Revolution, clergymen preached sermons again urging Americans to see their country as "God's American Israel"—not a conquering empire but a special nation.[12]

At the outset of the Civil War, Abraham Lincoln spoke of Americans as an "almost chosen people." Later he sought to comfort a stricken people, by assuring them that their agonies would have significance for the whole world, by "testing whether this nation *or any nation* so conceived and so dedicated can long endure."[13]

STILL A SEPARATE NATION

Most Americans still cling to the belief that the United States remains a special country, that it is, in some way, different from others and has a right to continue in its different ways. Americans have retained many ways that have disappeared elsewhere. Americans even cling to the English system of weights and measures, long since replaced by the metric system in England itself.

And to the annoyance of Europeans, America clings to the idea that it can remain its own nation. The United States refused to participate in a range of global initiatives on the environment and human rights during the 1990s and set itself firmly against an international criminal court. And the United States continued to insist on its own right to defend itself against terrorist aggression.

In western Europe, the American stance appears selfish, obstinate, arrogant—indeed, stiff-necked. The association was irresistible to many Europeans. The foreign minister of France explained to the French National Assembly that the American resort to war against Iraq had been the work of a "Zionist lobby" in Washington.[14] Following what was by then a well-established rhetorical convention, Villepin proceeded to single out American officials in the Bush administration with Jewish-sounding names. Europeans were united in their desire for peace but Israel and America insisted on pursuing the path of conflict. With unerring rhetorical instinct, M. Villepin also scolded Britain's government for deserting Europe, adopting just the same tone of petulance as that displayed by French officials in the fall of 1940.[15]

Such complaints, of course, made little impact on American thinking. The United States owes its founding to an exodus of independent-minded people from Europe, seeking their promised land on a new continent, safely distant from the tyrannies and constraints of the Old World. The United States has often been out of step with prevailing currents of opinion in Europe. Still, Europeans have had reason to be grateful for American independence.

In the twentieth century, Europeans threw themselves into political schemes of boundless ambition—imposing total unity, seeking to build towers that would conquer Heaven by human will. And they brought death to millions and misery to hundreds of millions. More than once, the United States helped to save Europe from its own political frenzies. There was a time—a brief time, now some decades past—when many Europeans acknowledged that fact with appreciation.

Perhaps the United States retained the strength and decency to save Europeans from their own worst impulses, because Americans themselves had remained loyal to distinctive American ways. Perhaps there is some value, then, not only for Americans, but for the world at large, in allowing America to adhere to its own traditions.

Of course, many leaders and thinkers in other nations see the world differently. So long as they do not threaten violent attacks against the United States, American leaders might simply agree to disagree with leaders or governments of other nations. Is peace more likely by imposing a common stance or by accepting differences?

Europeans protest that the United States now behaves like an imperial power. They do not imagine that the United States will soon invade Portugal or Iceland or that it will drop bombs on Europe to force Europeans to participate in American "imperial adventures." Still, the United States inspires great fear and resentment in Europe. Is it more "imperial" to overthrow a particular dangerous tyranny—or to establish institutions which purport to judge all leaders of all nations? The charge against the United States is that it will not submit to global schemes of control which are strongly favored by Europeans. By asserting its own independence, the United States is disrupting projects for global law, which are supposed to achieve global peace. Apart from the actual consequences of any particular action which the United States may undertake, its overall stance looks to many Europeans as the moral equivalent of imperialism—now understood as asserting the right to differ. It follows, in a way, if one assumes that dissent from a universal faith must imply a design to impose a countering faith on the whole world.

Indeed, prominent thinkers in Europe warn that the United States remains in the grip of "religious fundamentalism." Jürgen Habermas, Germany's most prominent philosopher, shuddered in disgust at the idea of "a president who begins his daily business with public prayer and associates his momentous political decisions with a divine mission." In Europe, such a leader is "hard to imagine."[16] No doubt, a previous generation of German thinkers reacted with equal disgust at reports that President Roosevelt had implored "Almighty God" to bless the American troops embarking for the liberation of Europe or that General Eisenhower had implored the troops, themselves, to "beseech the blessings of Almighty God upon this great and noble undertaking."[17] It seems to have been forgotten in Europe that the victory of American arms in 1945 was not followed by forced conversion of Europeans to the dominant Protestant faith in America or even to Christianity. It seems almost unknown to Europeans that the most evangelical sects in America have been the most insistent defenders of religious independence from government.

But of course, actual American religious practice is not the point. Even if Americans do not seek to impose their faith by force, their self-confidence is seen as an obstacle to the reasonable common management of global problems. So European commentators persist in drawing bizarre parallels between religious "fundamentalism" in America and the kind of Islamic fundamentalism championed by Osama bin Laden.[18] The United States may not practice or applaud terrorist acts, but it remains terrifying because it is, in its own way, a powerful obstacle to plans for assuring peace and harmony in the world.

Assuring peace and harmony may prove rather difficult, however. War has cast its shadow through all of human history. Religious faiths are also very old. The new idea is that international institutions can bypass religion and establish perpetual peace. Or perhaps it is simply the new version of the very old idea of a universal empire—a plan which has not done very well, either, in securing universal peace in recent centuries.

Will it be easier to learn to live with differences by insisting that differences be negotiated away in common global standards—or by acknowledging that differences run deep? Apart from doubts about whether programs of universal agreement can ever be really voluntary, we might wonder whether people prepared to agree on so much can retain their own freedom or their own principles. So we might come back to the idea that distinct nations have a right to be distinct—that is, in old-fashioned terms, sovereign.

POST-MODERN CHALLENGE

Europeans scoff at sovereignty. Many scholars disparage thinking about it in the name of pragmatic adjustment. An increasingly influential school of academic writers assures us that, if we do let ourselves look at it, we will find that sovereignty is merely a word or at most a passing "social construction" with no necessary or inherently compelling logic.

It is the central insight of "post-modern" thought: there are no "essential" qualities to any social arrangement or to any standard or concept with which we "discourse" about the world. All our categories for thinking about international law or international authority—"internal" vs. "external," "domestic" vs. "foreign," "sovereign state" vs. "international organization"—are all mere social constructions, the outcome of power impositions over time.

It follows that we do not need to take these categories or distinctions very seriously. Old books made much of them but "we" now know better. Part of the appeal of post-modernism may lie precisely in this liberating dispensation. There is no longer any need to read old books or study old history with any care when one knows in advance that there is no "essential" point to grasp.

But probably the greatest appeal lies in the implication that everything is up for grabs, because there is no standard, no truth, no logic but only human willfulness. If all boundaries are socially constructed, all can be reconstructed on different lines. It is an enticing thought to intellectuals dreaming of worlds transformed.[19]

Many scholars thus seem to embrace post-modernism with the exuberance of adolescents, discovering that sex is a lot more appealing and a lot more available than they had realized as children. "Postmodernism exposes the smokescreens and the histories of the screens and the smoke, in brilliant, eye-opening ways," as one scholar exulted. But a "post-modern feminist method" applied to international relations would go beyond moral relativism, emphasizing "gender relations over time" and questioning the "gendered assumptions" that have been "encrusted in the field" of international relations. If some theorists envisioned a world of "postinternational relations," practitioners of feminist international relations theory protest that "gender relations persist untransformed, which must mean that important aspects of relations international did not change."[20] Dazzled by such demonstrations, which claim to strip away the protective covering of conventional assumptions, scholars proclaimed, as if it were a titillating discovery, that sovereignty has been "socially constructed."

In many ways, they were kicking down an open door. American independence began with a declaration asserting that "governments are *instituted* among men, deriving their just power from the *consent* of the governed," so it remains "the right of the people to *alter* or *abolish* [government] and to institute new Government . . . on such principles and . . . in such form, as *to them* shall *seem* most likely to affect their safety and happiness." The same John Locke who spelled out the doctrine of government by consent, on which the Declaration draws, published an *Essay Concerning Human Understanding* which argues that all abstract concepts are human constructions (book III, chapter v, paragraph 12).[21]

But, after all, no one disputes that the George Washington Bridge is a human construction. It could certainly have been constructed according to a different design. Many designs, however, would risk tumbling drivers into the Hudson river instead of carrying them safely to New Jersey. Not every construction is as solid or serviceable as any other[22]—a point one may also find in Locke's *Human Understanding* (III.x.26–31) as well as in his *Second Treatise of Government* (Paragraphs 161–66).

It does not matter, in the end, whether one views the pattern of the past as a social construction or an accident of history or a providential design. There remain strong reasons to welcome the division of the world into separate nations and to endorse the principal safeguard of this division—the sovereignty of independent states.

Certainly the world could be different. We know for sure that it can be worse—because it has been. In the modern world, sovereignty has been closely associated with constitutional government, at least in the sense that constitutional government has only been achieved in sovereign states. And it is only in the modern practice of constitutional government that guarantees of personal liberty have been combined with political structures capable of sustaining stable democracy.

It is fair at least to wonder whether contemporary disdain for sovereignty does not reflect (or at least encourage) an impatience with its historic counterparts—that is, with constitutional government, with liberty and democracy. It is fair to wonder whether disdain for sovereignty does not, in fact, reflect a disgust with all the "constructions" of modern liberalism. It is fair to wonder whether it does not reflect a longing for a world in which—as in the promised wonderland of communism—there are no longer real differences, hence no longer any need for legal boundaries protecting the right to be different.

Perhaps the clever insights of post-modern imagination lost some of their appeal in the aftermath of September 11 or in the subsequent bitter dispute over the war in Iraq. In contemporary academic literature, however, those who reject the visions of post-modernism are rarely concerned to defend constitutional government in its own terms. Instead, critics of post-modernism generally respond with "realism." They seem to counter grotesque "ideals" only with unpleasant "realities." Stephen Krasner, for example, does not defend sovereignty—in his book of that title—but rather depicts it as an "organized hypocrisy" (in the words of his subtitle) which simply must be taken into account, because it will not go away.[23]

It is surely better to be "realistic" (even in this sense) than fantastical. But these are not the only choices. Anyone interested in defending the American Constitution has to think in different terms. What sort of rule can we live with? That is not a cynical question, even if it excludes some fantastical answers at the outset. It is the sort of question that would naturally occur to a citizen, a statesman, a Framer of the Constitution—or anyone who wants to understand their choices.

This book is primarily about American ideas of constitutional government. It is not a study of international relations, as such. The book offers no advice about how to make peace or how to deal with other global challenges. Its aim is to explain why American constitutional traditions make it hard for the United States to embrace schemes of global governance which find so much favor in other countries, particularly in western Europe.

This book has other limitations which should also be acknowledged. Economics, sociology, and other social sciences may have much to say on

the viability of global schemes of governance. This book instead emphasizes trends or patterns in political thought. I believe that ideas and opinions are most decisive in structuring law and constitutions.

From some perspectives, the United States is simply a vast collection of
consumers and producers, preference-holders who might be better off
under global governance. That is not the grounding assumption of the
U.S. Constitution, however. And it is ultimately the Constitution that
makes the United States a nation.

To put it succinctly, this book aims to clarify the assumptions about the
world that led the American Founders to "construct" constitutional
arrangements as they did and to show why their grounding assumptions
remain hard to reconcile with new "constructions" in contemporary international politics.

As in the past, the American view differs from ideas prevailing in Europe. But difference can be the beginning of reflection. Aristotle's survey
of politics suggests that reflection can lead to moderation and sobriety. It
is at least a plausible claim.

The opening passage of *The Federalist* put it as a question: "whether
societies of men are really capable or not of establishing good government from reflection and choice or whether they are forever destined to
depend for their political constitutions on accident and force"? By linking "choice" with "reflection," this version of the question acknowledges
that choice has inherent limits. Random choice is not much different
from leaving matters to "accident and force." By posing the question as
one for "societies," *The Federalist* still acknowledges that choice can remain for some, even when others choose differently. It asks about the
possibility of acting by "reflection and choice," not whether the answer
can be guaranteed for all mankind. Framed this way, the question might
be decided, as *The Federalist* concluded, "by the people of this country,
by their conduct and example." The most important "example" was to
establish and adhere to their own national constitution.

That remains a plausible answer. This book is an extended effort to
show why it is a plausible answer. It is an answer that may have something to contribute to contemporary debates about "global governance."

CHAPTER TWO

GLOBAL GOVERNANCE OR CONSTITUTIONAL GOVERNMENT?

IN 1917, "WORLD WAR" was a new term. And it was still a somewhat hyperbolic term, even after the United States entered the "Great War" (as it had previously been called). The First World War remained largely centered in Europe and its environs.

By 1945, the Second World War had brought carnage and destruction to four continents. In this war, nations of the western hemisphere, too, had been drawn, much more fully than before, into a connected web of conflicts, raging simultaneously on opposite sides of the world. The experience of war on this scale spurred ambitious postwar plans for securing world peace.

The United Nations Organization was supposed to guarantee peace through ongoing consultation among the victorious powers and their allies. The UN Charter even contemplated that the major powers would prepare for joint enforcement of peace, by lending their own military chiefs of staff to a permanent, international Military Staff Committee.

To many advocates at the time, this treaty structure seemed barely a beginning. Serious people insisted that only a fully realized "world government" could ensure future peace. Some spoke of "world federalism," conceding that world authority must acknowledge the diversity of the world's peoples. Still, advocates of world federalism insisted that peace could only be maintained by delegating supreme military force to a worldwide authority.

Chapters of "world federalism" organizations sprouted up in all corners of the world. In the United States, the movement was embraced by scholars at distinguished universities, by members of Congress, by prominent judges.[1] Many advocates insisted that the United Nations Organization might prove to be the initial seed of a more established and ambitious structure, capable not only of preserving peace between nations but of protecting individuals within each nation under an International Bill of Rights, enforced, in the last instance, by an international supreme court. It seemed to many people entirely logical. The world had been brought to misery by letting brutal governments get out of control. A world organization would provide control on such governments, just as national governments control violent or lawless individuals within each nation.

Within a few years, of course, visions of perpetual peace gave way to a recognition of enduring conflict or at least of enduring Cold War. The Soviet Union, with its totalitarian ambitions, brushed off an American proposal for an international control of atomic energy. No one could seriously imagine that Stalin would subordinate his authority to that of a world peace federation. Few people in America warmed to the idea of sharing or subordinating American power under a world structure in which the Soviet Union and its satellites and adherents might eventually predominate. World federalism dwindled from a serious movement to a crank cause, like nudism or vegetarianism.

But in the 1980s, as the Cold War began to wain, "global thinking" returned to respectability. Arms control negotiations between the United States and the Soviet Union were suddenly broaching serious plans for massive reductions in missiles and warheads. Meanwhile, environmental advocates called attention to threats which could affect everyone, like the depletion of the ozone layer in the earth's atmosphere. International conferences spawned ambitious new treaties to address such threats through common policies. Advocacy organizations, organized to promote respect for human rights, seemed to be having real impact on tottering dictatorships. In Latin America, one military government after another gave way to restored democracy in the late 1980s.

Then, unexpectedly, the Soviet Union relaxed its hold on eastern Europe and communist regimes there gave way to new democracies. Shortly thereafter, the Soviet Union itself fell to pieces. Russia and other successor states struggled to establish their own forms of multiparty democracy. Even the white minority government in South Africa gave way to multiracial democracy. The "democratic wave" seemed to be a worldwide phenomenon.

New democracies eagerly sought outside investment and full participation in international markets. Even in China, where a nominally communist government retained its grip on power, liberalization seemed to be gathering momentum, tying China to world trade and a new worldwide web of communications. Talk of "global consensus" no longer seemed visionary or absurd but almost a matter of common sense.

If most states were already in general agreement, there was no need for international authority to compel states to live in peace. No one talked of world government in the 1990s. The vogue term of the new era was "global governance." The term was almost unknown at the start of the decade. By the dawn of the new century, it had become a ubiquitous catchphrase.[2]

The evasiveness of the term enhanced its charm. Ambiguity was central to its logic. The most obvious difference between government and governance is that governments deploy force. Advocates of global governance seldom talked about force.

If everyone agreed, however, there could be coordination without compulsion—something a bit less coercive or a bit less definitive than an actual law, enforced by an actual government. Governance could have broader scope than government. It could reach behind structures of governmental control to guide private activity in ways that no government on its own might do. It could be global. National governments would not have to surrender their sovereignty to a world government. Sovereignty would simply be transcended.

The vision presupposed a world already at peace. It looked a lot less compelling once Americans began to notice that not everyone was so inclined to peace. Global governance was not going to disarm Saddam Hussein or the crazed tyrant of North Korea, Kim Jong Il, or the angry mullahs of Iran. Historically, the right to resort to war was conceived as one of the defining prerogatives of sovereignty. Sovereignty began to look a good deal more relevant when people awoke to the realization that threats from terrorism and from terror-exporting states had survived the "democratic wave" of the 1990s. Sovereignty began to look especially relevant when national leaders discovered that other states did not at all agree on how to respond to such threats.

It also turned out to make a big difference that Americans could elect their own leaders and foreigners had no direct say in American electoral choices. Europeans expressed mounting fury at the new policies of President George W. Bush. Prominent Europeans voiced the kind of indignation which pious believers often feel toward those who openly defy the dictates of the faith. Believers were convinced that the world would have been able to proceed without force if only the United States had continued to uphold the new faith. Everyone might have agreed—if only the United States had agreed.

Perhaps, from a certain perspective, this was even plausible. Global governance could deliver perpetual peace without coercion if everyone would go along with new international standards without being compelled to comply. Force would not be necessary if there could be conversion. If everyone would cooperate with global governance, THEN there could still be peace.

Europeans and Americans tended to have quite different assessments of how reasonable it was to expect such a transformation. Those with the capacity to defend themselves by other means might not put much stock in such pious or desperate hopes. The pattern had been displayed within Europe in the past.

After trying repeatedly to appease Germany, Britain and France reluctantly went to war in 1939. They still had formidable military resources and calculated that they would be drawn into war, sooner or later, so they would do better to resist German aggression before it swelled with further conquests. Belgium, the Netherlands, Denmark, and Norway all tried to protect themselves by clinging to neutrality. As it turned out, that strategy did not work. But it is not altogether surprising that states with little capacity to resist aggression placed their hopes on the protections of international law.

The underlying question, however, is not merely a question of strategy. To talk of "national security strategy" is to brush aside the deepest question. Almost everyone prefers peace to war or even to the risk of war—in the abstract. The underlying question remains: peace on what terms? What will a government or a nation sacrifice to maintain the hope of peace? Finland was prepared to make itself a Soviet protectorate to maintain some degree of internal autonomy during the Cold War. What if peace requires concessions touching on domestic arrangements? What if the point of resorting to war is to ensure the capacity to maintain your own way of life, in your own nation? People who were prepared to defend their own institutions might not be so inclined to sacrifice them—even in the name of peace.

Or they might insist that peace must not demand such sacrifices. They might hold that peace cannot be reliably secured by entangling states in such a welter of international controls that no state can any longer hope to defend itself. They might rather insist that real peace will be assured when states learn to respect their differences with others.

Somewhere in the differences between the United States and its former allies in Europe there is a profound disagreement about how much independence a nation can reasonably be expected to sacrifice. The differences are not just rooted in differing hopes for peace. They reflect deeper differences about what any nation should expect to retain for itself, even in times of peace.

The International Criminal Court offers a prominent example. The ICC Statute defines a long list of offenses as international crimes. Some are so broadly defined that many actions by American officials might at some point be thought to violate them. The treaty allows national states to prosecute these offenses in their own courts. But it also empowers an independent international prosecutor to insist on a new international trial, when he regards judicial process at the national level as inadequate.

If it ratified this treaty, the United States would be obliged to extradite Americans for a new trial, even for crimes committed on American soil and even where the accused had been acquitted by an American jury or pardoned by the American president. The treaty thus establishes a new criminal justice system, superior to the system established in the Constitution—and not bound by procedural guarantees in the U.S. Constitution. The ICC, for example, makes no provision for trial by jury nor for a right to confront witnesses.

Is it constitutional for the United States to cooperate in such a venture? Many people assume—perhaps too optimistically—that Americans could never be hailed before the court because Americans would never be guilty of atrocities rising to the level of "crimes against humanity." But the list of crimes in the Statute can be expanded by the vote of other states participating in the treaty. If it agreed to participate, the United States could eventually find itself subject to much broader jurisdiction than for those "crimes" now set out in the ICC Statute. In fact, when the idea for such a court was first seriously discussed in the early 1990s, some proponents thought it would be a natural forum for trying international narcotics traffickers.

From a domestic constitutional perspective, an international criminal court of this kind would pose no greater difficulties than the version of the ICC that has now been established. If American participation in the existing ICC is constitutional, then a court with far broader jurisdiction could also be grafted onto the American legal system. So, if the procedural guarantees in the Bill of Rights make domestic prosecutions look too difficult, the government of the United States must have the option, for an open-ended range of crimes, to hand over Americans to international authorities who can implement more efficient justice.

Might there be, after all, some constitutional problems here? One need not stand in pious awe of the American Founders to think so. Constitutional courts in Germany, France, and Portugal all held that various provisions of the ICC Statute posed constitutional difficulties under their own national constitutions. In Europe, however, such difficulties could be readily resolved. National constitutions were speedily amended to remove these obstacles. Europeans already submit to a system in which national constitutional courts can be overruled by a European Court of Justice (ECJ). The practice long predates any thought of something so formal as an actual constitution to confine or control European regulatory schemes. European law is held to be superior to national law, even to national constitutional law.

Meanwhile, federal courts in the United States have opened their doors to civil suits based on a "customary international law of human rights."[3] The most publicized cases have concerned perpetrators of murder and torture in foreign countries.[4] More recently, however, cases have been brought against American corporations for complicity in lesser human rights offenses in other countries.[5] If one accepts the premise that a customary law of human rights is already binding law for American courts, there is no reason why such suits could not be brought against American officials for actions taken in the United States. A federal district judge indeed ruled in 2002 that an immigration law dispute should be settled by looking to an international convention which the United States had never ratified—on the grounds that so many other countries had ratified it that it had become part of customary international law.[6]

Human rights authorities at the United Nations have proclaimed, for example, that capital punishment is now contrary to the customary law of human rights at least for anyone under age eighteen. An American court could therefore order state officials to stop the execution of seventeen-year-old murderers—though the U.S. Supreme Court has ruled this to be consistent with our own Constitution and the Senate has never ratified any treaty provision curtailing capital punishment. Once started on such claims, international human rights law may turn out to have remarkably broad application. Many scholars and some courts now affirm that protections for labor and the environment already fall within the scope of international human rights law. The scope of this law can be readily expanded.

If courts can apply a free-floating international law of human rights, they have much more authority than we used to think. Fundamental elements of American domestic law would, in effect, be made in international forums or in other countries and then simply appropriated by American judges, expounding or applying this law in place of our own. Is this compatible with our Constitution?

Here again, though, the concern has little meaning for contemporary Europeans. The European Court of Justice has long made it a practice to impose new obligations or restrictions on European governments in the name of international law. The ECJ feels free to justify its rulings on the basis of international treaties which have no direct connection with the European Union, sometimes with treaties not even embraced by all the member states. When no treaty is available, the ECJ feels free to invoke "general principles of law"—a concept so general that it needs no referent to any treaty at all.[7]

Here is a third example. The Kyoto Protocol seeks to reduce the build-up of carbon dioxide in the earth's atmosphere, thought by many scientists to contribute to a global warming trend. The Kyoto treaty requires the more industrialized or affluent nations to reduce their emissions of carbon dioxide by specified percentages over a specified period. As carbon dioxide is released whenever fossil fuel is burned, compliance would require painfully large reductions in fuel consumption. To ease this pain, the treaty would allow some of the reduction to be accomplished by financing comparable reductions in other countries (where improvements in energy efficiency might be achieved at much less cost) or by planting new forests to act as "carbon sinks," absorbing carbon dioxide from the atmosphere.

There remain great uncertainties about how emissions should best be monitored and calculated, particularly when it comes to calculating credits for international trade in "emission rights" and for "offset" credits for expanding "carbon sinks." The treaty proposes to establish specialized administrative agencies to work out the details. With a venture of this unprecedented scale, even technical rulings would have vast economic consequences. Would the United States be bound by the rulings of these bodies? Would such implementing regulations be as binding as actual treaties—though never ratified by the Senate?

For the United States, this raises obvious and serious constitutional concerns. Americans are not accustomed to having their law made for them by free-standing international authorities. Commentators in the past were quite clear that delegation of American law-making capacity to foreign bodies was forbidden by the Constitution.[8]

For Europeans, again, the objection is almost unintelligible. The European Commission, a free-standing bureaucracy, regularly spins out regulations which are binding on member states of the EU. They take direct effect in national law without any separate action by national parliaments and can be enforced against recalcitrant governments by the European Court of Justice. Europeans call it "pooling sovereignty."

It does not capture much of the dispute between Europe and America to speak merely of differences over "international law." The dispute is not simply about whether international law can be relied upon to provide reliable security. It is, fundamentally, about whether international law can be conceived as a vehicle for global authority—in which all sovereignty might seem to be pooled. It is a dispute about whether "pooling sovereignty" is not simply a euphemism for surrendering sovereignty— and whether that matters.[9]

WHAT KIND OF INTERNATIONAL LAW?

Clearly, the Framers of the Constitution expected the United States to participate in some system of international legal understandings. The Constitution, itself, specifies that Congress, among its other enumerated powers, should have the power to enact legislation to "punish offenses against the law of nations."

Just as clearly, the Framers of the Constitution did not think that adhering to the "law of nations" could guarantee peace. The Constitution also gives Congress the power to "declare war" and does not limit this grant of power to circumstances in which war would be seen as lawful or proper by other nations. War presumes disagreement among nations and the Framers of the Constitution did not blink the fact. The first Congress under the new Constitution proceeded to establish an executive department to organize the military capacity of the United States. At the time (and until after the Second World War), it was called the Department of War.

The "law of nations," as the Founders knew it, was a body of background understandings regarding the rights and duties of sovereign states. The new term, "international law," which gained currency in the nineteenth century, did not imply anything more ambitious. Indeed, the point of the new term was to emphasize the peripheral character of this law.

The modern term was coined by the English legal reformer, Jeremy Bentham, in a book published in 1789, the very year, as it happens, when George Washington took office as America's first president.[10] Bentham was concerned that the older term, "law of nations," might suggest a body of shared understandings among all nations, which might constrain a government's policy toward its own citizens in its own territory. The new terminology would emphasize that this body of law could only deal with "mutual transactions between sovereigns." It could not reach into nations but would simply remain between them: it would be international. Within a few decades, the new term was embraced by legal commentators in all western languages—except, notably, among German writers.[11] Elsewhere, the point of the narrowing term seems to have been endorsed along with the phrase.

So far from mandating peace, international law assumed that war would be an ultimate means of redress when one state threatened the rights of another. Legal commentators tried to limit the permissible justifications for war. But it was hard to be very precise about limits to war when there was no means of enforcing such limits, except by successful defense against an improper or unauthorized attack. The difficulty was that in a world where states were left to decide for themselves, no other states were obliged to come to the rescue of a state which had been unjustly attacked.

It was often a matter of sincere perplexity to outside states to determine which side had been the aggressor, as wars were generally preceded by escalating tensions, with threats and provocations on both sides. At the same time, other states doubted that rushing to the defense of a particular threatened state would always make for a more enduring or reliable peace. Both sides in any war might (and often did) draw in allies or hope to reverse the results of the last war after gaining new allies for the next round.

Rather than trying to organize the world, so that the "international community" could speak with one voice, classical international law pursued a more modest course, which could be described as a liberal path. Treatises published in the eighteenth and nineteenth centuries emphasized the formal equality of sovereign states. Each state was supposed to have the right to determine its internal policy for itself. So, in principle, no state could extend its own law into the territory of another. Meanwhile, each state was left to decide for itself when and whether to resort to war. Much effort was invested in defining the rights of neutral states—particularly their right to trade on the high seas and their trade rights in situations of naval blockade, imposed by nations at war. Efforts were made to limit the scope of war, so that war prisoners and wounded combatants would be shielded from the fury of war, along with civilian noncombatants and civilian property.

By the end of the nineteenth century, a "peace conference" at the Hague had considerable success in securing agreement on a codification of rules for the treatment of war prisoners and other laws of war, which was further elaborated at a second Hague conference in 1907. The Hague conferences also established the first "permanent court of international arbitration," so that states could submit their disputes to arbitration as an alternative to war. Characteristically, the Hague conventions on the laws of war did not try to lay down standards to clarify when resort to war would be justified. And they stipulated that their code of constraints in the conduct of war would only apply when (and so long as) all states in a particular war adhered to the code.[12] The court of arbitration did not require any state to submit a dispute to its judgment, even if another state wished to pursue arbitration. Everything remained conditioned on the consent of every state which might be affected.

The world wars certainly shattered hopes for achieving enduring peace by such voluntary measures. But "collective security," supposed to be assured by new international organizations, did not prove any more successful. The League of Nations did nothing to restrain fascist aggression during the 1930s. Britain and France, the major powers still in the League in 1939, did not bother to summon the League to debate their peace policy at Munich in 1938 (at Czechoslovakia's expense) nor their ultimate decision for war a year later (ostensibly on Poland's behalf). By the same token, no other states felt bound to join Britain and France in their resort to war in 1939. A sizable coalition of states ultimately entered the war—but in almost every case, they waited until they had been attacked themselves.

In the course of the Second World War, Allied leaders had began to refer to the states in this coalition as "United Nations." The victors proceeded to give this name to the successor organization to the League. It seemed to have stronger powers than the League.[13] But, of course, it fared no better than the League in organizing the world for peace.

The UN endorsed a plan for the creation of separate Jewish and Arab states in Palestine in 1947. Six Arab states, despite having ratified the UN Charter, ignored both parts of the plan and set out to destroy the Jewish state by launching armies against it. The UN reengaged only to help negotiate a truce, which was ignored by all sides in later years, when it suited their purposes to ignore it. In 1950, the UN denounced North Korea's invasion of South Korea as unlawful aggression. Both communist China (not then seated in the UN) and the Soviet Union (a founding member, holding a permanent seat on the Security Council) ignored the UN's decision and did their best to secure North Korean victory. The United States, which had sought to mobilize international support for the defense of South Korea in 1950, ignored the UN in almost all its subsequent military actions, most notably in its long war in Indo-China from the early 1960s to the early 1970s.

American involvement in the Vietnam war aroused great controversy in the United States, as also in western Europe (where no country joined the U.S. war). Not even the most intense critics of the Vietnam war wasted much energy, however, in complaining about the absence of UN authorization for the American war effort. It was largely taken for granted that the UN was incapable of speaking for the international community, let alone summoning adequate force to ensure compliance with its decisions.

It was entirely in keeping with past practice and past experience, then, that the United States and Britain went to war against Iraq in 2003, without authorization from the Security Council. If nations were obliged to entrust their defense to international direction, they would be relying on bodies that, judging from all past experience, had no actual capacity to protect them. Instead, the UN would simply make their own defense strategy hostage to the calculations of others, who would not be nearly so concerned about the defense of any particular nation as that nation itself. Nations which feel threatened continue to look to their own resources for defense—at least if they have any choice.

The record of international law did not look nearly so hopeless, however, if one ignored the pathetic performance of collective security and focused instead on the classic concerns of international law, as it was known to the American Founders and developed by American and European statesmen in the nineteenth century. The underlying liberal tenet of the classical scheme of international law—that each state must decide for itself—proved compatible with a great deal of international cooperation. In fact, it proved compatible with a great expansion of international exchange among private citizens. States voluntarily dismantled barriers to commerce.

By the end of the nineteenth century, flows of foreign investment and foreign trade rose to levels not seen again (relative to gross national product [GNP]) until the 1990s.[14] Treaties between particular states helped to lower economic barriers but there was no international organization to supervise trade liberalization, much less any authority capable of enforcing it.

By the mid-nineteenth century, international agreements had established a worldwide postal system, so that letters and packages could be sent from any part of the world with a fair degree of assurance that they would be delivered at their intended destinations, all for the price of postage collected in the country of origin. A multinational treaty made the scheme work, with almost no permanent bureaucracy or standing administration to supervise its implementation.[15]

It was not only commercial freight and private correspondence that could move freely. Businessmen, scholars, missionaries, tourists could travel freely through most of the world in relative confidence. Again, no international authority protected them. Injury to a foreigner (at least, one who had entered the country lawfully) was conceived as an injury to his home state. By and large, nations refrained from gratuitous injury or interference with each other's citizens. Every now and then a powerful state might send warships to emphasize that this obligation was one to be honored.[16] But even powerful states were often willing to see disputes about treatment of each other's nationals settled by the payment of financial reparations, sometimes in accord with judgments rendered after agreed resort to arbitration.

Liberalization in these ways was related to another feature of a system which assumed the independence of sovereign states. In a world where resort to military retaliation was always a possibility, states worked out definite ideas about what would or would not be tolerated by other states. Interfering in the domestic affairs of another state was generally seen as a provocation, especially when it meant stirring rebellion. On the other hand, harboring guerrillas or plotters against another state could also lead to war. States were obliged to control their own territory as the price for getting others to respect their sovereignty. By the nineteenth century, colonization in Africa was justified on the grounds that a colonial power would perform a service to other states in assuring order in a colonized territory—which would mean, among other things, protection for foreign travelers.

Obviously, such claims were often quite self-serving. Still, it is notable that during the nineteenth century, the era of most extensive colonization, European powers were able to settle almost all colonial disputes through peaceful negotiation—that is, with other colonial powers. The extension of sovereignty to colonial territories was not seen as inherently threatening to other states and was often regarded as an advantage compared to leaving politically unorganized territories in a lawless state.

Even when the League of Nations tried to soften the appearance of colonial rule by characterizing some colonial acquisitions as "mandates" from "the international community" (that is, from the League, itself), such mandates always went to one particular power. The least one can say is that the underlying problem of lawless states—states without a reliable government—has not been solved by international peacekeeping missions, which, in many cases have continued to preside over murderous chaos. Serious threats have been contained, when they have been contained, by the intervention of outside military power, almost always delivered by a particular outside state with reliable command over a reliable military force.

In Afghanistan in 2001, that power was the United States. In Sierra Leone in 2000, it was the British army. In Cote d'Ivoire in 2002, it was the French army which turned out, not surprisingly, to be rather ineffectual in pacifying the country, since French commanders remained quite reluctant to expose their troops to serious risk.[17] But the "international community" has no means of its own to quell chaos in territories without states. When the United States withdrew from UN-sanctioned humanitarian intervention in Somalia in 1992, the country reverted to chaos. The world simply looked away as it had so often before, until the September 11 attacks refocused attention on the danger of leaving territories without some government for other states to hold accountable.

To see the classical scheme as a mere acquiescence to power politics is to take for granted that power is a uniform entity, only to be assessed by quantity. Again, the least one can say is that this view was not prevalent in the eighteenth and nineteenth centuries. It seems to have been encouraged rather by embittered power theorists who saw all liberal ideas as a mask for power—whether of "capitalists" or "imperialists." The classical scheme of international law assumed that states did have an interest in cooperating and that cooperation could be of mutual benefit. Trade was assumed to be, at least potentially, of mutual benefit, which is why most states did cooperate in agreements to facilitate trade.

One can see the point even in relation to the laws of war. Protection for wounded or captured combatants was justified not merely on humanitarian grounds but on the practical ground that soldiers no longer capable of fighting posed no threat to fighting forces. Both sides in a war could, accordingly, cooperate in humanitarian measures which did not affect their own military capacity. So, also, the notion that war measures must avoid harming civilians assumed that civilians had no necessary role in war. It made sense, if one thought of war as a contest between professional armies, instruments of a conflict between organized states.

Humanitarian restraints in war may have roots in medieval chivalry, as some scholars contend. But medieval warfare was not, of course, notable for humanitarian regard for civilians—rather the contrary. Modern efforts to codify such restraints made sense when governments accepted that civilians had no direct role in war or even in statecraft—when, that is, the state came to be seen as something removed from private life. Medieval theologians, who did not recognize private life as a distinct sphere, readily endorsed pillage, enslavement, and even rape as just punishment for those who supported the wrong side in an unjust war.[18]

The modern law of war assumed that war was an affair between states. The law presumed the characteristic modern distinction between state and society. It is, of course, a distinction at the bottom of classical liberal ideas, not only of international relations, but also of domestic authority. And it is at some level precisely about sovereignty.

Sovereignty is an attribute of states. To speak of a "sovereign individual" or a "sovereign corporation" is to engage in metaphor or in satire. A distinct idea of the state makes it possible to distinguish entities which are not the state. In particular, liberal societies distinguish "church and state," meaning that the state has different functions and a different character than religion.

At some level, the obvious basis of the distinction is that states are equipped to apply coercion. At least the point once seemed obvious. It no longer seems obvious once sovereignty is subsumed in some larger scheme of global governance.

To take a telling example, the laws of war now look rather different, once war is no longer conceived as the distinctive capacity of states or even of rebel forces aspiring to become states. Earlier codifications limited protections to lawful combatants, those who fought in uniform, under military command and obeyed the law of war, themselves.[19] The International Criminal Court adopts a broader perspective, supposed to apply to all "armed conflict." By design, it seeks to protect guerrilla forces, fighting without uniform and hiding in civilian enclaves. Failure of one side to obey the laws of war does not excuse the other side from obeying these laws—as, for example, by pursuing terrorists into civilian areas, even if this causes harm to innocent civilians or to civilian property.

One can think of this approach as more humane. It looks that way only if one abstracts from the logic of war. It is only humane if one thinks it is better to put up with guerrilla or terrorist attacks than to enforce peace. And of course, this approach only works to the extent that force can be replaced by moral appeals. The ICC itself has no army, it does not even have police to enforce its arrest warrants. It can speak of legal obligation but in practice it must appeal for voluntary compliance. Will such appeals work as well on terrorists as on liberal states?

The ICC came to seem plausible after decades in which advocacy groups had lobbied for international human rights conventions and then participated in international forums to extend and interpret those conventions. The conventions are not, of course, normal treaties between states, which depend for their enforcement on shared understanding between actual states which sign them—and the threat to withhold compliance if other signatories do not comply.

International human rights treaties cannot be enforced in this way, since no state will persecute its own citizens to force a foreign government to stop persecuting that government's own citizens. Human rights treaties generally provide no serious alternate mechanism for enforcement of their requirements. The normal means of "enforcement" in human rights treaties is for international monitors and private advocacy groups to cite the provisions of such treaties in hectoring pronouncements against states which fail to comply with them in full (which turns out to mean almost all states).

Are such pronouncements actual law? At best, they constitute a sort of shadow law, conferring shadow rights. For advocacy groups, they supply a kind of leverage—which may be nice for them but not easy to accommodate to normal liberal ideas about government by law. International organizations will intervene to protect rights—but not by coercion. And advocacy groups will ensure compliance—but not by coercion. And everyone will have rights—but not really. The scheme does not rest on a wider plan for world government. It only seeks global governance—though some analysts insist that "governance" is already nurturing a world constitution.[20]

The extension of this pattern to international commerce implies that advocacy groups can impose standards on private firms. So the UN sponsors a "Global Compact" in which firms are supposed to agree to live up to international notions of environmental rectitude and workers' rights, without reference to the actual law of the place where they operate.[21] In return, the UN or advocacy groups will refrain from attacking business or the particular firms that cooperate. It is not exactly law. It can not be reliably enforced. It is governance. But it is not so easily constrained as government. Many firms complain that it opens them to rather nasty sorts of moral blackmail or ongoing harassment.[22]

The argument for such practices is that corporate power will otherwise behave abusively. Who determines what is abusive? We know how to lay down laws and due process when states regulate business. How do we correct "market power"—and on a global basis?

Other critics think the problem is cultural power. So UN conventions insist that states must promote non-sexist thinking—even, it seems, in churches and religious institutions. Might there be some problem for a limited state in interfering in this way? Not to worry—it is not really law. At most it is "soft law," a category developed by international legal scholars to describe aspirational norms that are not quite binding.[23]

Again it is governance. So there is no need to worry about what these standards really require or how they would really be enforced.

Perhaps something is lost, after all, when we shrug off sovereignty. Much talk about global governance in the 1990s insisted that shrugging off sovereignty was both necessary and good.

SOVEREIGNTY MISCONCEIVED

Many scholars have come to regard sovereignty claims as an untenable anachronism in a globalizing world. Professor Louis Henkin, one of the foremost scholars of international law, serving at the time as president of the American Society of International Law, protested in the early 1990s that "sovereignty" has "grown a mythology of state grandeur and aggrandizement . . . a mythology that is often empty and sometimes destructive of human values." He contemplated "a campaign to extirpate the term and forbid its use in polite political and intellectual company or in international law. . . . Away with the "S" word!"[24]

It was a characteristic view of that era. Henkin did not envisage a world government replacing the claims of sovereign states, but simply a series of agreements among states to be "governed by norms and institutions" in what he described as a "social contract" among states—but with "few 'inalienable' state rights" withheld from the process. States would retain "sovereignty" only as an "internal concept, the locus of ultimate authority in a society." Henkin did not address the obvious question of how the state could retain "ultimate authority" within each "society" if the state itself were subject to "international governance" and could waive any retained "inalienable" right to reject or exit from "international governance."

Many scholars were quick to take the next step. New ventures in international control, they held, would indeed require that sovereignty be subordinated to international law and international institutions. Consent could no longer be the foundation of obligation. States were obligated to embrace larger structures by some higher necessity.

Seemingly quite different versions of this argument were developed in the 1990s. Some scholars advanced a moral claim: Sovereignty is incompatible with what we now understand as universal rights of human beings—human rights, perhaps rights to a safe global environment, rights to subsistence, etc. No state, it is said, should be able to resist these claims on pretense of sovereignty.[25] Others offered a pragmatic argument: No state can now govern effectively on its own, so "effective sovereignty" requires sharing of state powers in some scheme of supranational governance.[26]

These seem to be entirely different arguments from entirely different perspectives. On one side: moralistic, selfless, doctrinaire—Kantian, as is often said. On the other side: hard-headed, self-interested, calculating—merely pragmatic or utilitarian. This seems to cover the ground. Everyone seems to agree—except the old-fashioned constitutionalists. And that is not suprising. It is much easier to presume world consensus if the premises of liberal constitutional government are rejected at the outset.

The moral challenge may seem particularly powerful. If states have the last word on what happens in their own territory, then rulers are free to impose any level of torment on their own citizens without fear of outside intervention. It seems a powerful argument—until one thinks about what, if anything, follows from this moral challenge.

The traditional view was that even sovereign rulers were morally bound to fundamental principles of natural law or moral law. No doubt, this left much room for abuse. But what exactly do we substitute by proclaiming that moral law is now really law, if we do not add reliable enforcement for that law? Prior to the mid-twentieth century, it hardly seemed credible that modern governments would resort to mass murder of unresisting populations. The moral depravity of twentieth-century Europeans provoked legal analysts to coin a new term—"genocide"—to define a horrifying new practice as a distinct "crime." Perhaps it required the mentality of twentieth-century Europe to imagine that evil on this scale could be deterred by calling it a "crime," as if people prepared to perpetrate such horrors could be deterred by name-calling. But international organization has no better or more reliable means of enforcing international denunciations of mass murder than do sovereign states.

In the extreme, a brutal government may provoke a revolt and outside powers may assist the rebels. That is how America gained its independence. The practice was quite as well known in the eighteenth and nineteenth centuries as it is today. But a state which intervened on behalf of rebels could not expect other states to take its humanitarian professions at face value. And, of course, that is still the case. Vietnamese forces ended the horrifying murder regime of Pol Pot in Cambodia—and Vietnam was denounced by almost all other states for then installing its own favored rebels as the new government of Cambodia. The United States and Britain certainly overthrew a murderous tyranny in their war against Saddam Hussein in 2003—and states around the world refused to accept that the horrors of Saddam's rule could justify this intervention.

What is new in the claim that human rights are now superior to states is not that states are in general more reliably bound by international standards. Instead, the change is that moral limits which were once thought to apply only to the most extreme outrages are now thought to apply to a vast range of ordinary policy. Again, the initial thought may seem quite plausible. Even a state that refrains from mass murder may still repress basic freedoms in ways that seem morally intolerable. But the contemporary world is no closer to agreeing on what sorts of repression are intolerable. When the United States implemented relatively mild detentions in the wake of the September 11 attacks, the practice was denounced by human rights organizations as abusive of human rights. How one evaluates such things depends on how one assesses the security risks in the particular circumstances. Even informed observers may differ in such assessments.

The sad truth is that there is no agreement on how to define human rights—or even on what constitutes inexcusable terrorism. Barely a year after the September 11 attacks, Libya, a longtime sponsor of terrorism, was elected to chair the UN Human Rights Commission. It was joined there by Sudan, Syria, Iran, and other prominent sponsors of terrorism. Also elected were representatives from China, Cuba, Pakistan. The Human Rights Commission is, in fact, a rogue's gallery of brutal and repressive regimes. And they bring their outlook to the Commission.

The world's most brutal governments take their places at the Human Rights Commission because other states, voting in UN councils, have chosen these states to serve as monitors for human rights in the world. There is not even great conflict between brutal tyrannies and democratic states at the Commission. States from western Europe agreed that terror attacks on Israeli cities should be lauded, for example, while also agreeing that the actual condition of human rights in China should not even be studied by the Commission.[27]

A reasonable inference from this pattern is that the majority of UN members do not care very much about human rights or at least they do not care very much about human rights in other countries. Why would anyone think that human rights would be more secure if left to be defined or protected by such bodies?

One can argue, very reasonably, that even a sovereign state must respect the rights of its citizens. But that has always been the American understanding. It was the British understanding before it was the American understanding. It has, intermittently, been an understanding shared by various states in Europe and Latin America and elsewhere.

It does not follow that because sovereign power must be limited by the rights of citizens that the state is not sovereign—anymore than it follows that because a sovereign power must respect the rights of other sovereigns, it is not sovereign within its sphere. The idea that states must submit to limits on sovereignty in the name of human rights is not at all a new idea, except if one assumes that those limits must be defined and enforced by international authority. But why suppose that international authority would be more respectful of our rights than our own government? Moralism about rights does not answer the question. It merely disguises a long train of questionable assumptions about how the world works or ought to work by resorting to the rhetoric of the moral imperative.

The second way of deriding sovereignty seems to avoid this moral dogmatism. Instead of burying or disguising practical concerns, it highlights them. The argument is that in an interdependent world, sovereign states can no longer exercise enough control to deal with their problems. Therefore, it is said, "effective sovereignty" requires international institutions. Some critics tell us that the sovereignty of nation-states is obsolete because it cannot deal with the pressures of global trade flows. Others say sovereignty must be revised because it cannot deal with pressures from foreign cultural influxes, eroding national cultural traditions. Still others emphasize global environmental problems.

But there is nothing in the concept of sovereignty that prohibits international cooperation. States have cooperated on many matters without imagining they were sacrificing their sovereignty. The United States and czarist Russia signed several treaties in the early twentieth century to foster common conservation measures in the Bering Sea. No one imagined they were yielding up their sovereignty in doing so. The issue is what to do when states do not agree—as when Japan in recent years has rejected limits on whaling. The actual answer is that the world does not even now have any reliable international mechanisms for imposing cooperation on states which do not want to cooperate.[28]

The attraction of formulas like global governance is to suggest more consensus than there really is. A succession of international conferences have persuaded many environmentalists that the world faces extreme weather shifts if we do not agree on means of reducing emission of greenhouse gases. Surely, we can all agree on common responses to this common threat? Well, no, actually, we can not. Nations will not be equally affected by climate change and they do not evaluate the costs of preventive or ameliorative measures in the same way, either. Poor countries, which are most dependent on local agriculture and have least infrastructure to cope with weather emergencies, would be most affected by warming. This fact does not make poor countries more eager to embrace limits on their own fuel consumption. It makes them all the more eager to develop their own economies now, using as much fuel as they need to do that, without worrying about possible climatic consequences many decades from now. Many decades from now they may hope to be much wealthier and much better able to handle whatever consequences may follow from climate change.[29]

Perhaps this reasoning appears short-sighted. Only environmental enthusiasts with very short memories should be surprised that governments which feel most threatened do not place most trust in long-term (therefore, speculative) international remedies. Nuclear war is a far more terrible prospect than global warming. The risk that future wars might be fought with nuclear weapons was apparent from the moment the first nuclear weapons were used in 1945. That did not mean all states could agree on how to control these weapons. Even today, almost all states acknowledge, in the abstract, that terrorist groups with nuclear weapons would pose a terrible menace to international security. That does not mean there is much agreement among states on how to prevent this terrible prospect from emerging as a terrible reality.

True, in a world of interdependence, states face many challenges to policies they might prefer. But that is not a recent development. New technologies and new patterns of trade and investment may generate new uncertainties and new pressures for governments. But what new technology can compare with the advent of the printing press or the telegraph, in altering expectations of citizens? What change in trade in the late twentieth century can compare with the advent of railroads and steam shipping in the nineteenth century?

The communication and transportation revolutions of the nineteenth century brought remote farms, plantations, and factories into touch with new cities in Europe and America and then brought these cities in touch with much of Africa and Asia. Urban centers in Europe and America, and then throughout the world, could now sustain, for the first time, not tens of thousands of people but millions of people. By the middle of the nineteenth century immigration across national borders and then across oceans swelled to encompass millions of people in each decade.

It seems plausible to think that government is now more constrained only because late twentieth-century expectations of government are so much higher. Governments have never been able to ensure that products of their country would find adequate export markets or that economic changes in the world outside would not require adaptations at home. Even the Soviet Union, at the height of its totalitarian power, could not prevent annual crop failures—always blamed on poor weather. Not even a convention on climate change will provide "weather sovereignty,"[30] however, nor prevent ill-conceived government policies from failing on other grounds.

The seemingly pragmatic appeal has this in common with the moral appeal against sovereignty: Both presume that sovereignty implies something like total control or complete self-subsistence. Starting from this exaggerated idea of sovereignty, any limitation on a state's authority may then be seen as a limitation on sovereignty. The idea of limiting sovereignty can then be passed off as something inevitable. It is the equivalent—or more literally, the extension—of the favorite arguments of socialists against mere "bourgeois" rights: Robinson Crusoe might make his own choices, but the "right to choose" guarantees nothing amidst market pressures, so real rights require a powerful government to supply the benefits that people really seek. Even a constrained choice remains a choice, however. And how one chooses to deal with the constraints of one's situation may make an immense difference over time. That is why socialist economies have turned out to be so unproductive and so unsatisfying. People want choices precisely because they do need to interact with other people, but do not want someone else to tell them exactly how and why and where.

Looking at sovereignty from a collectivist or globalist perspective, arguments for global governance obscure the liberal premises of the historic understanding of sovereignty. Naturally, those who embrace the collectivist perspective then proceed to illiberal conclusions or at least to recipes for something that is quite removed from liberal, constitutional government.

The world must make some provision for governance that extends beyond the reach and methods of constitutional government—that is the central premise of global governance. A lot needs controlling and mere governments can not do it. But there is no need to worry because we all agree.[31] We all agree on human rights. We all agree on saving the environment and on how to do it. We all agree, in fact, that business must be directed toward the greater good. We do not need to set down the precise obligations of business firms in national laws, because we all agree on what they are or should be. We can have a global compact. Agreed? Well, yes, business firms may complain, but they are not really part of "global civil society."[32]

CONSTITUTIONAL CLAIMS

Classic works on liberal constitutional government started from the opposite presumption. People do not naturally agree. In the state of nature—that zone without government—no one can get another to obey his will. At best, people can maintain peace by refraining from all but voluntary interactions, resorting to force or compulsion only in self-defense. Even then, peace may be fragile, because not everyone accepts this natural rule or interprets its limits in quite the same way.

In consenting to a common government, a particular group of people in a particular territory might make their rights more secure. A common government could establish legislation to clarify, with some precision, the rights and duties of individuals. A common government could establish a power to ensure reliable enforcement of that law. In relation to those outside this political community, however, the members—or the government itself—would remain with the original, natural rule: apart from non-interference, the only obligations arising between them would be those mutually agreed upon. Resort to force would likely be met by forcible resistance.

This account may sound impossibly quaint. It did offer an account of how constitutional government might arise by consent. If there are questionable assumptions packed into the classical liberal account, there are, to say the least, many more questionable assumptions built into the vision of a post-sovereign world. A world which is equipped to sustain global governance is a world that does not need constitutional government—and probably can not tolerate it. There are many reasons to doubt that this is a more compelling picture of the world we actually inhabit or even a picture of a world we would like to inhabit.

Sovereignty is, to begin with, a legal concept.[33] Sovereign power is the right to make binding law in a particular territory. As Blackstone remarks, "Sovereignty and legislature are indeed convertible terms; one cannot subsist without the other."[34]

It is easy to miss the point, however, if one simply associates legislation with laws and laws with rules. Counties and towns make laws, professional societies and even school clubs make rules. God gives Law. The legislation of a sovereign state is not Law in that sense. But it is something more than rules. A sovereign state makes law which cannot be appealed—at least on earth. If it does not have the supreme authority of God's Law, the legislation of a sovereign state still has a unique dignity. Lawyers speak of "the majesty of law."[35]

The "majesty" of the law made by a sovereign authority reflects its special force. It is not to be trifled with. It is law that can and will be enforced. Locke defined "political authority"—for which he might well have used the term "sovereignty"—as the "*right* [original emphasis] of making laws with penalties of death and consequently all less penalties."[36] What is distinctive about a state is that it can back up its rules with ultimate force. Even states that have abolished capital punishment can arrest and imprison in ways that no private organization is now allowed to do.[37] A state, as Max Weber put it, maintains a "monopoly of the legitimate use of physical force."[38] Legal systems still recognize the point in restricting state liability for "sovereign acts"—those involving coercive force.[39]

There are, to be sure, complications in the organization of national legal systems. Most states permit local or regional authorities to make rules and enforce them. Federal states guarantee certain governing prerogatives to the members of the federation. But the sovereign government retains ultimate force and legal supremacy. Federal law in the United States is "supreme law of the land" and, when challenged, federal authority is equipped with force to uphold that supremacy.

Over time, federal entities, almost everywhere, have expanded their control over subordinate entities in federal states. That is hardly surprising. Even where there are constitutional courts to establish limits on federal authority (in the interest of subordinate units), such courts are almost always creatures of the federal authority. A genuinely sovereign entity can resist encroachments in ways that a subordinate unit in a federal structure cannot. A sovereign state may resist legal claims from outside— by renouncing a treaty structure or, in the last analysis, by deploying force against those who make contrary claims.

It does not quite capture the point to reduce sovereignty either to force or to law, however. Pirates of old or terrorists today do not exercise sovereign power, even if they can force captives to obey their commands in a particular setting. Weber's qualification, "legitimate" force, captures something of the difference. A sovereign authority is one that can make law with the expectation of compliance, partly because it can wield enough force to enforce its law, but still more because it is generally accepted that it will do so.

International law and international practice has long recognized this feature of sovereignty: The government in actual control of the territory is the government held accountable by foreign states and generally the government recognized by foreign states.[40] But controlling territory is assumed to be more than a mere exercise of power, though it is sometimes not much more. Control rests, in some degree at least, on acceptance.

Inherent in the idea of sovereign authority is that it is constituted authority. That notion is already a considerable step toward the liberal idea of constitutional authority. At the least, it is a reminder that behind the legal formula is a political question or a political challenge: What sort of government can claim such compliance from citizens?

It is commonplace in contemporary discussions to assume the answer is democracy. But democracy is not exactly an agreed concept. The election in 2000 reminded Americans that the Constitution allows a president to take office even when more citizens voted for the rival candidate. The electoral college scheme, so rarely relevant to the outcome, turned out to pose complicated constitutional questions about the proper way of counting votes. The Constitution provided a means of resolving these questions: Rulings of the U.S. Supreme Court are supreme over the determinations of state courts. It is a lot more complicated, after all, than rule by the majority. Some partisans were enraged. Most Americans took the result in their stride.

The acquiescence of the American people in this instance should not have been surprising. The Constitution does not enshrine majority rule as the highest imperative. Under the Constitution, each state elects two senators to the Senate, even though the states vary enormously in population. So a very distinct minority of the voters can choose a majority of senators and block the preferences of the majority from becoming law. Even if a measure has such broad support that it musters concurrent majorities in the House and the Senate, the measure can still be blocked by presidential veto, unless the House and Senate can summon two-thirds majorities on its behalf. It is far from majority rule, but it is the scheme set down in the Constitution.

If the Constitution were being written from scratch today, Americans might favor a different scheme, one which allocated governing authority more equally or more democratically, so government would be more receptive to majority opinion. But there has been no great clamor to amend the Constitution in such ways. The procedure for making formal amendments to the Constitution, as set down in Article V, is, by design, quite cumbersome. But there has been no great demand to streamline the very cumbersome process for amending the Constitution, set down by the original Framers.

The crucial point is not that the system is perfectly democratic but that it establishes a system which is constitutional. The claim is not a mere tautology. The Constitution constitutes a system of government which is accepted by citizens. Congressional enactments have the authority that they do because the Constitution, as a scheme of government, has great authority. Of course, the Constitution imposes limits on the power of Congress. The Supreme Court can sometimes enforce such limits. The institutional system of checks and balances, built into the Constitution, provides other and perhaps more reliable restraints.

The constitutional scheme certainly does not guarantee that everyone will approve of every law or even that the majority of citizens will approve of every law (and all the various compromises with recalcitrant, opposing interests, built into most laws). What the Constitution has done for more than two centuries is to supply a fairly reliable mechanism for securing acquiescence to coercion. We submit to laws we may not like, on the assumption that laws which emerge from our constitutional process are generally tolerable. We trust that even a bad law can be improved or repealed in time. We can acquiesce even to a law based on disturbing premises, trusting that checks and balances will prevent it from smoothing the path for more intolerable exactions in the future. It is not that we all agree because we are citizens of the same nation. Rather the contrary. We accept an elaborate constitutional arrangement of powers on the assumption that we do not ordinarily or spontaneously agree.

The very idea of a legislature—with the power to make and unmake laws at will—is a modern idea, not much older than the seventeenth century. In fact, the idea of a legislative power arose at almost the same time as the idea of sovereignty because the ideas are closely linked. Both ideas acknowledge that there are choices to be made.[41]

In John Locke's classic account, establishing a legislative authority is the heart of civil authority—the essential guarantee for constitutional government and the rule of law:

the *first and fundamental positive law* of all commonwealths is *the establishing of the legislative* power. . . . This *legislative* is not only the *supreme power* of the commonwealth, but sacred and unalterable in the hands where the community have once placed it; nor can any edict of any body else, in what form soever conceived, or by what power soever backed, have the force and obligation of a law, which has not its *sanction from* that *legislative* which the public has chosen and appointed: for without this the law could not have that, which is absolutely necessary to its being a law, *the consent of the society* over whom no body can have a power to make laws but by their own consent, and by authority received from them; and therefore all *obedience*, which by the most solemn ties any one can be obliged to pay, ultimately terminates in this supreme power, and is directed by those laws which it enacts: nor can any oaths to any foreign power whatsoever, or any domestic subordinate power, discharge any member of the society from his obedience to the legislative, acting pursuant to their trust. (*Second Treatise,* par. 134) (original emphases)

Global governance rests on the quite different premise that legislative consent to law is not so important to the authority of law. After all, in the perspective of advocates for global governance, there are no great choices left to make. Judges must embrace international standards, most notably in the realm of human rights, because what most nations have affirmed (or at least what many advocacy groups have asserted) is something approaching an inescapable moral truth. So, too, global governance encourages the delegation of rule-making powers to international organizations, in which the agreement of national representatives—representatives of the national executive—can bind whole nations to new international regulatory standards. Systematically left out is the power of a legislature to determine a state's own law.

Undermining and constraining the authority of legislatures is bound to have policy consequences. To imagine that downgrading the authority of legislatures has no consequences, one must imagine that legislatures are merely ornamental or ceremonial institutions. Given the expense and effort that party activists and private contributors put into campaigns for legislative office, the assumption does not seem very plausible.

Even if one thinks of legislative authority as a symbol, it symbolizes concerns that are crucial to the historic understanding of constitutional government. There are usually hundreds of representatives in a legislature (651 in Britain's House of Commons and another 692 in the House of Lords). Any executive authority, even if one associates the term with a cabinet of ministers rather than a single chief executive, is extremely compact, by comparison. The executive is meant to be more unified, so that it can be more decisive. In legislative bodies, as *The Federalist* remarks, the "differences of opinion and the jarring of parties . . . though they may sometimes obstruct salutary plans, yet often promote deliberation and circumspection and serve to check excesses in the majority." And tempering first impulses is all the more essential in legislative debate, since opposition "must be at an end" when the legislative body comes to a resolution: "That resolution is a law and resistance to it is punishable."[42]

In democratic countries, a legislature literally "embodies" the diversity of the nation, so that representatives of many different localities, different interests, and different opinions, can claim, in the end, to speak as one body with authority to decide for the whole. A legislature is an institutional monument to differences among voters as well as to their willingness to be bound, in the end, by a common rule.[43] Global governance not only thwarts or distorts the policy impulses of legislatures, but denigrates the principle that stands behind legislative authority—that a diverse electorate will accept the results of an ultimate legislative decision so that "we" can be governed in common.

On the premises of global governance, "we" are little different from "them." All peoples share the same moral intuitions regarding human rights. All peoples understand that national policies must be coordinated to deal with global economic and environmental necessities. On this view, it seems hardly necessary to bother with elections. Perhaps different nations need to choose executive authorities to provide bargaining agents at international forums. But choosing a supreme executive for the nation might as well be done by plebiscite which, in purporting to decide everything, decides nothing in particular. None of this will seem troubling, if one assumes it is, deep down and even near the surface, basically one world, anyway.

In practice, what global governance actually means is that those who may be in a minority in one country can enhance their political leverage by associating their claims with stronger forces in other countries. That also makes sense, once one thinks of the relevant decision forum as international or transnational. What the majority of other countries do (or a majority of some selected group of other countries do) is then the democratic thing. The Council of Europe advanced this claim quite explicitly in 2001: In continuing to impose capital punishment, the Council scolded, "the United States is out of step with other democracies . . . and in this aspect 'undemocratic.' "[44] It is a convenient notion in Europe, where small countries are bullied into compliance with policies preferred by the largest countries, France and Germany. Fortunately, this is democratic, as well as proper. Those who disagree are selfish or at least idiosyncratic.

The obvious way to resist such pressure is to appeal to fellow citizens: Is this what *we* really want? It is, of course, what a legislature might determine. But the whole logic of global governance subverts the claim of a legislature to make its own decisions for its own constituents. Global governance requires us to acknowledge that "we"—the constituents of a particular legislative authority—do not have different interests from the others, so *we* don't really need distinct institutions to define these interests. Of course, there can still be legislative action in local matters, if such decisions do not threaten the larger scheme.

Europeans have an entire doctrine to deal with this challenge: The doctrine of "subsidiarity" holds that matters which can be decided locally should be decided locally.[45] And in the decades since this reassuring doctrine began to be propounded by the European Community, more and more and more matters just happened to gravitate to European-level authorities and away from local authorities. The doctrine presumes that it is not for local authorities themselves to decide what is best determined at the local level. Subsidiarity, in other words, is a very poor substitute for sovereignty.

It is true, of course, that even sovereign states, even constitutional democracies, even the United States, cannot always insist on the supremacy of legislative authority. In times of crisis, particularly in times of war, executive authority may sometimes claim extraordinary powers. In war time, presidents are accorded broader powers to deal with extraordinary challenges—to meet, as people say, pressing necessities.

The European Union has no executive authority of this kind. And global governance, which is in so many ways an extension of European governing practices into the wider world, makes no provision for an executive authority. Such schemes presume a world at peace, so they may seem entirely opposed in principle to the extraordinary powers sometimes accorded to executive authority in time of war.

In effect, though, global governance presumes extraordinary pressures which make it impossible for individual states to decide differently—or individual legislatures to debate matters. The point seems paradoxical: the shadow of peace instead of the shadow of war. In fact, it is not so paradoxical. The thought in the background of global governance is that if nations insisted on their own rights, there could not be peace. Perhaps the idea appeals to contemporary Europeans. One can doubt that it is a basis for constitutional government.

After all, at the bottom of the American constitutional tradition is the right of the people to make a revolution. Another paradox, it may seem.

Actually, it follows quite logically. The image of humanity that is presupposed by enthusiasts of global governance is of people who are helpless, supine, needy, and ready to obey anything offered up to them as "help"—so global managers can secure peace if only given enough scope. In the background of the American tradition is the image of the Minuteman, ready to assert his rights by his own action—unless given some assurance that his rights will be respected. It has almost been possible to provide such assurance of security under the American scheme of government. We have this much in common—our common willingness to protect our rights under a common system of government.

It does not follow that we have the same things in common with the world at large. Again, the truth is almost the reverse. The world is not organized to protect or defend "us"—certainly not to the same extent as our own government, certainly not to the same extent as the national constitutional arrangements that define and limit the powers of our own government.

It hardly needs saying that not every country is in quite the same position as the United States. No other nation has remotely as much military power at its disposal. No other nation has such a well-established constitutional tradition. Many countries do not really aspire to maintain liberal institutions at home. Many countries do not even aspire to maintain their independence in international affairs.

But Americans happen to be citizens of the United States. Global governance implies the abolition of American independence. It implies the denigration or erosion of many things that make the United States relatively distinctive. The result would surely be a world in which Americans were less free.

It would also be a world in which there would be less freedom for many others, in many other lands, who now aspire to freedom and constitutional government or might do so in the future. Americans who believe in their own political traditions have reason to believe they are not simply acting in a selfish way when they insist upon their right to continue to govern themselves under their historic principles. Certainly Americans are not being idiosyncratic or selfish when they insist upon their own principles.

Strange as it may now seem, American ideas were European ideas before the United States ever existed.

CHAPTER THREE

THE CONSTITUTIONAL LOGIC
OF SOVEREIGNTY

FOR ENTHUSIASTS OF global governance, sovereignty seems an annoying anachronism. And when it comes to dismissing anachronisms, the older the better. So, many people assume that sovereignty must be connected with medieval notions of kingship.

But it isn't. The term only gained wide currency in the seventeenth century—that is, at the outset of the Enlightenment. And it is closely connected with Enlightenment thought.

Many people assume that sovereignty is connected with claims to total power. It isn't. Its central meaning, historically, is the power to enact and enforce laws. This is precisely the power that a modern state exercises in regulating free individuals, whose persons and property are otherwise conceived as their own. The medieval overlord ruled by granting and withholding lands on conditional terms and neither exercised nor claimed "legislative power."

It is true, of course, that "sovereignty" has been invoked by tyrants to justify all manner of brutal oppression. But communist regimes have called themselves "republics" and "democracies." Their bizarre usage has not discredited these terms.

Many people assume that sovereignty is not, at any rate, relevant to American constitutional thought. But it is. The term (or a close paraphrase) appears in the Declaration of Independence, in the Articles of Confederation, and in the Northwest Ordinance of 1787—three of the four founding texts of the American constitutional tradition.[1]

True, the word does not appear in the text of the federal Constitution. The Framers did not want to call attention to their repudiation of sovereign powers in the states. But the meaning and location of sovereignty was a central theme in the debates over the federal Constitution.

In the text of *The Federalist Papers*, for example, the terms "sovereign" or "sovereignty" appear more often than "freedom," more often than "republic" or "republican," far more often than "moral" or "morals." That favorite term of the Enlightenment, "reason," appears more often—but not much more often.[2] "Sovereignty" appears so often because it is extremely central to the argument.

[handwritten margin note: not even a remotely good argument]

"Government," as *The Federalist* observed, "implies the power of making laws." What is it that gives authority to "laws"? *The Federalist*, which was not afraid to use Professor Henkin's "'S' word," was not afraid to speak bluntly about the necessary premise of law:

> It is essential to the idea of a law that it be attended with a sanction; or in other words, a penalty or punishment for disobedience. If there be no penalty annexed to disobedience, the resolutions or commands which pretend to be laws will, in fact, amount to nothing more than advice or recommendation.[3]

We might usefully compare this with the famous definition offered by Thomas Aquinas in the mid-thirteenth century:

> the definition of law . . . is nothing else than an ordinance of reason for the common good, made by him who has care of the community, and promulgated.[4]

Compared to the Thomistic definition, the account in *The Federalist* may seem shallow or crass. In fairness, it does not purport to be a comprehensive definition or catalog of everything that might be relevant to "the idea of a law." But in insisting on the means of enforcement, *The Federalist* emphasizes something which is glossed over in the Thomistic account, with its emphasis on the moral authority of law and its appeal to the "reason" of those whom the law directs.

Enforcement is, of course, related to force. In emphasizing the question of enforcement, then, *The Federalist* calls attention to the first question in politics: Who gets to wield the force to enforce? The question looms large because it is not simply about what I, as an individual, would approve. It is about what will be accepted by others. As even that great modern moralist, Immanuel Kant, conceded, it may seem quite naive—or quite dangerous—to rely on a law which others will not respect.[5] If there are competing laws, laid down by competing authorities, which will prevail? One might care less in this setting about which law was most in accord with "reason" than which was most likely to receive compliance from others. If "international governance" can promulgate new "norms and institutions," for example, who gets to enforce their dictates and what happens if many others fail to go along?

To press these questions is not to reduce law to force but, on the contrary, to raise the most basic questions about the control of force. *The Federalist* was, after all, defending a constitution, not a limitless enforcement power. To ask about the connection between law and enforcement is the beginning of sovereignty but also the beginning of constitutional government.

Notions of "law" floating free of any reference to a constitutional framework for reliable enforcement are not something new, however. They are, in truth, medieval—as the Thomistic definition of law (which conveniently evades any questions about constitutional authority) reminds us. Reviving this thinking in the contemporary world is not a natural extension of liberal thought but a repudiation of it.

To see why this is so, it is worth a look at the pre-modern world. It was precisely to escape medieval patterns that doctrines of sovereignty were initially advanced. We can then turn to some of the landmarks of classical liberal thought, where the same concern for sovereignty appears in much the same light. American notions of constitutional government rest on the premise of national sovereignty. A full understanding of these notions requires a look at how and why they developed.

MEDIEVAL STRUGGLES: THE WORLD BEFORE SOVEREIGNTY

Scholars dispute whether the ancient world had a distinct notion of sovereignty. For different reasons, neither ancient republics, where citizens ruled directly, nor ancient empires, where rulers claimed divine authority, were inclined to define governmental powers in precise terms. They did not make clear distinctions between "state" and "society." Nor were they anxious to make clear distinctions between independent states, on one side, and client states or dependencies, on the other. But whatever the ambiguities of ancient practice, medieval Europe surely could not sustain any notion of sovereign states.

To start with, feudal conditions made it impossible to distinguish sovereign powers from other kinds of authority. Roman notions of governing power were impossible to sustain amidst successive waves of invasion by Germanic tribes, then by Magyars, Huns, Saracens, and Vikings in the centuries that came to be called "the Dark Ages." Kings could not maintain standing armies and gave lands to their warrior chiefs, on condition that these vassals would maintain fighting men, available at the king's call. Vassals then gave lands to subvassals who often retained subvassals of their own. Vassals came to regard their fiefs as a kind of property which could not be taken back—and they usually had the military strength to resist what they regarded as arbitrary seizures. They also could call other vassals to their aid. Many a vassal was more than a match, in military terms, for his nominal overlord, which meant that overlords usually declined to intervene in local wars—over honor, land claims, or sheer plunder—between their own vassals.

In principle, however, land was still conditional on feudal loyalties, conceived in quite personal terms—land was held "of" another lord, who might have a still higher lord "of" whom he held his land. In principle, land could not be transferred without the permission of the higher lord, because control implied personal loyalty and not outright ownership. Even "inheritance" of lands and titles required higher approval or had to follow customary practice.

At the lowest level, lords ruled over serfs who were obliged to stay on the land and render prescribed service to their local lord and pay the local lord for such privileges as operating flour mills. Like the obligations of vassals to overlords, such obligations congealed into customary law. As local lords inherited governing powers, their subjects or dependents expected earlier concessions or accommodations to follow with the inherited powers. Such local customary practices were, in most circumstances, the only kind of law people could imagine. A legislative power to override custom seemed a power without any limit at all.

In this setting, ownership could not be readily distinguished from office. "Dominium" could mean either property in land or "domain," in the sense of governing jurisdiction; a "dominus," either an owner or a ruler.[6] A duke or an earl, a count or baron "owned" his titles as much as he "owned" the lands and governing prerogatives associated with these titles. Local lords were anxious to control their own lands and would not easily accept intrusions of royal authority into their own dealings with their own vassals or their own serfs. They made their own deals with towns on their territory, granting self-government in return for payments—in effect, "selling" governing rights.

The second obstacle to any notion of sovereignty followed from these feudal practices. As kings had no very well-defined authority over their vassals, kingdoms were very vague. There were different peoples, speaking different languages, but no distinct nations or territorial states to define their boundaries. The same king might have vassals and territories in widely separated places. The same vassal might have territories requiring him to pay homage—and supply fighting men—to rival kings. Nobles came to regard themselves as a hereditary caste, having more in common with nobles elsewhere than common people in their native lands. A modern historian has described the feudal monarchies as "holding companies, composed of many subsidiary corporations"[7] and there was no sense that these conglomerates required territorial contiguity or demographic coherence.

By late medieval times, ambitious kings in some places had developed treasuries and court systems to give institutional force to royal authority. But even as other administrative services were developed, no medieval king had a "foreign ministry." Kings certainly conducted negotiations, signed treaties, and even exchanged emissaries with other powers. They did not have "foreign ministries" because they could not readily distinguish negotiations with these "foreign" powers from negotiations with their own nominal vassals.[8]

Symptomatic of this confusion, and aggravating it in some ways, was the looming presence of the Holy Roman Empire. By the ninth century, the warrior chief Charlemagne had managed to restore some measure of order and authority across much of western Europe. So Pope Leo III eagerly crowned him a successor to the emperors of Rome. Though the Carolingian empire was short-lived, in the following century, German kings claimed to be its successors and had themselves crowned as such by popes in Rome. Down to the sixteenth century, popes crowned the emperors in a ceremony by which the emperor swore to keep the peace of Christendom and uphold the authority of the Church. The emperor thus seemed to have a kind of predominance over all kings.

Yet it was characteristic of medieval conditions that no one could say with confidence what this predominance entailed or how far it extended. At various times, emperors claimed to exercise some form of authority over England and France, Denmark and Sweden, Hungary and Spain,[9] but emperors could rarely exercise reliable control even in the base territories of the empire in Germany and northern Italy. Emperors were constantly at war with their own nominal vassals and by no means always successful in these wars. Emperors usually had no very secure lands to provide revenue and troops for their imperial ventures.

Yet few princes were willing to assert complete independence of the Holy Empire. Modern scholars, noting resemblances between medieval Europe and periods of "feudal" rule in China, India, and Japan, have noted the presence of a "ghost empire" in all these historical episodes: Local warlords were often quite eager to associate themselves with a crumbling empire, which lent a certain prestige to their own rule without seriously constraining their power.[10] In medieval Europe, the appeal of the "ghost empire" had considerable grip on the popular imagination. As late as the fifteenth century, Swiss cantons affirmed their loyalty to the Empire, even while asserting their independence from the Habsburg princes who had come to monopolize the imperial throne.[11]

The prestige of the Empire derived from its special connection with the Church, which was what made it a Holy Empire and not merely a restoration of the ancient Roman Empire. But the Empire's dependence on the Church was also its central weakness—and another great obstacle to the assertion of clear notions of sovereignty. The Holy Emperor had special status as the protector of the Church. But it was a source of endless dispute whether this implied that the papacy had ultimate authority over the emperor or the emperor had ultimate authority over the popes. Early emperors claimed—and in some cases, successfully exercised—the power to unseat a pope and choose his successor. Popes also claimed and sometimes exercised the power to unseat emperors—and proved they could do it, by inciting feudal vassals of the emperor to revolt against him. One way or another, medieval emperors were continually embroiled in Italian wars and continually facing rebellions of German princes in their rear.

There was certainly nothing like a comprehensive imperial constitution to clarify lines of authority.[12] Amidst so much fundamental dispute, there could not be such a thing. The disputes were less about powers of control than ultimate rank. But power and rank could not be readily separated in a world where so much political authority was necessarily indirect and dependent on prestige more than institutions. It was an age when metaphors about the sun and the moon, legends about the will of the Emperor Constantine in the fourth century, genealogical tables, proving descent of modern kings from Homeric princes, were regarded as serious political arguments.[13] All "constitutional" disputes were in some way metaphors for deeper metaphysical disputes—and conducted on the plane of metaphor. Even anti-papalist writers, like Dante and Marsilius, in the fourteenth century, advanced arguments for the emperor as a guarantor of universal peace: Only such a universal authority could compete with the universalistic claims of the papacy.[14]

But no emperor could actually establish universal peace. The most ambitious military ventures of the medieval period, the Crusades to the Holy Land, were not proclaimed by the Empire nor by national monarchs. It is not even correct to say that they were ordered by the popes. They had to be preached by popes and local bishops. For the most part, the Crusaders were volunteers. Accordingly, they claimed for themselves whatever lands they could conquer in the Levant and organized their holdings on characteristic feudal lines. Nor could the Church, the emperor or local kings do much to limit the penchant of Crusaders for pillaging Jewish communities in their marches across Europe.[15]

Even when Muslim forces succeeded in expelling Christian knights from the Holy Land, Spanish "crusaders" continued their wars against Muslims in Spain. German knights continued with "crusading" conquests of Slavic lands, where Christianity had deviated from the Roman faith of the west. Along with lesser wars, to suppress heresies in western Europe, these crusades were also authorized by the popes. But the relation of these conquests to the Empire (or to local kings) remained quite obscure.[16]

How Europe settled into territorial states is a long and complicated story. The pattern was different in different places. But in most places in the west, the subordination of lesser feudal lords by successful kings was connected with an emerging sense of an ongoing community with rightful claims to its own law. As Charles McIlwain put it, "The chief historical prerequisite to the growth of a conception of sovereignty is the existence of a 'nation,' with a governmental organ competent to *make* true law." The emerging conceptions "of sovereignty" and "of the responsibility of the ruler" are "closely related" with "nationality": They all imply a community that can regulate itself without the approval or direction of higher powers outside the community.[17]

It came first and most fully in England. It was the one country where a representative body—the Parliament—survived into the modern era. A large part of the reason for Parliament's durability was that, from the outset, it was understood to represent the whole nation and not merely a regional or provincial division, which a centralizing monarch could play off (as centralizing monarchs did elsewhere) against the claims of other regions.[18] England was also the one kingdom which succeeded, early on, in establishing a standardized, "common" law, backed by reliable common authority. For this reason, English-speaking countries still rely on this "common law" rather than revised versions of Roman law introduced by modernizing princes in continental countries at a much later time. When English barons revolted in the thirteenth century, they did not try to replace the royal courts or the emerging common law but only to protect them from royal abuse.[19]

Even in England, however, the kings—and their emerging legal system—faced challenges from without. The revolt of the barons against King John in the early thirteenth century was stirred, in part, by a papal interdict, designed to punish the king for interfering with Church revenues. After John was forced by rebellious barons to sign Magna Carta—a promise to respect existing legal privileges, seen in later centuries as the foundation of English liberty—the king threw himself on the mercies of Pope Innocent III. John agreed to make himself the Pope's vassal and the Pope absolved him from honoring his pledge to the barons to observe Magna Carta. The barons forced John's successor, Henry III, to reaffirm Magna Carta, which helped greatly to stabilize English law in later times. But Parliament did not repudiate the kingdom's special vassalage to the Pope—with whatever nominal meaning it might have—until late in the following century, when a much weakened papacy had fallen under French control.[20]

England's King Henry VIII, when he denied the pope's authority in England, still thought it necessary to repudiate any obligation to the Holy Empire, as well. For centuries, emperors had unique claim to the title "majestas" ("majesty"): Henry VIII was the first king to claim the title for himself—not in a bid to displace the emperor but to seat himself firmly on his own throne. His example was soon followed by kings in France and Spain and eventually by all kings.[21] They no longer claimed to be local embodiments of a universal authority but mere national rulers, however aggressive they might be in their territorial claims.

Yet even this trend did not quite imply what the modern world understands by national sovereignty. Decades later, Henry's daughter, Queen Elizabeth, was denounced by the pope for heresy and her advisors were in constant fear that Catholic nobles would implement the pope's explicit authorization to kill her and seize her throne. Next door in France, Catholic nobles organized a military "league" to suppress the Protestant heresy—acting without the king's approval and sometimes over the king's objections. Protestant nobles organized their own military forces. France experienced not simply civil war between unofficial armies but the slaughter of Protestant civilians, as in the notorious St. Bartholomew's Day Massacre of Protestants in the towns—a kind of wholesale "private" violence reminiscent of the Crusades. In Germany, the Holy Roman Emperor spent the first part of the sixteenth century in endless wars with princes who rallied to the Protestant faith. By the early seventeenth century, most of the powers in Europe were drawn into a still more ferocious series of inter-German conflicts about religion and the empire, conflicts which came to be known as the Thirty Years War.

Thomas Aquinas, perhaps the most widely esteemed thinker of medieval Europe, wrote hundreds of pages on law and political authority. One can study these pages without gleaning any hint of what he thought about the status of the Holy Roman Empire or of feudal dependencies. He was concerned with universal truths, pitched at such a high level of abstraction that such questions did not intrude. Sovereignty came into the world as a powerful doctrine when political thinkers and political men began to focus on more mundane questions or to give priority to such questions in political thought.

The Original Theory: Jean Bodin

The growth of feudal monarchies, and with them the outlines of modern nation-states, was a long process. The Protestant Reformation gave further impetus to the development, by weakening surviving notions about the unity of Christendom, whether under popes or emperors. In much of Europe, wars of religion gave way to claims of territorial princes, claiming to rule by a divine right of their own and demanding absolute authority.[22]

But that is not the way sovereignty started as a doctrine or a theory. In medieval times, courts or councils which claimed to give final judgment had sometimes been characterized as "souverain." That status was necessarily a matter of degree, however, with popes or emperors in the background. To emphasize their authority, medieval kings often adopted formulas like *rex in regno suo imperator est*—the king is emperor in his own kingdom—which acknowledged the emperor's moral supremacy in the very act of distancing the local monarch from the emperor's jurisdiction.

The impulse to independence did not become a doctrine—claims to local supremacy did not become "sovereignty"—until a general theory of sovereignty was developed in the early modern era. The first writer to advance a theory of sovereignty was Jean Bodin, whose monumental treatise, *Six livres de la république*, was first published in his native French in 1576. Though the work straggles through some 800 pages of dense argument and staggering displays of erudition, it was quickly translated into all major European languages and reprinted in numerous editions, achieving a towering prestige that lasted into the mid-seventeenth century.[23]

Amidst the religious civil wars in France, Bodin associated himself with the "politiques" who defended royal authority against religious factions (whose champions were known as "fanatiques"). In this sense, the title of Bodin's famous treatise is misleading: The first English version of his work, published in 1609, rendered "république" as "commonweale" rather than "republic."[24] But Bodin was only a defender of monarchy in a secondary way. He sought to provide a general account of political authority, transcending ancient distinctions between monarchy, aristocracy, and democracy: "la république" might just as well be translated as "the state."[25]

Every properly constituted "republic" or "commonwealth," according to Bodin, requires a strong sovereign power to hold it together. The most famous element of Bodin's theory of sovereignty is his insistence that the sovereign power cannot be divided. To modern readers, this claim seems highly dogmatic or simply baffling. Bodin, himself, acknowledges that the sovereign power may rest in the hands of a number of men (constituting an aristocracy) or indeed in the hands of a multitude (a democracy). His point is not that sovereignty must have the unity of a single human being. Even when discussing monarchy, he notices the importance of counselors and actually endorses a permanent institutional role for counselors, organized as a senate—so long as it is understood to be an advisory and not a binding authority.[26]

On the other hand, Bodin is quite attentive to the fact that, even in a monarchy, sovereign power must be exercised by various subordinate "magistrates" because no king can really make every decision himself. Bodin even urges kings to dissociate themselves from magistrates hearing cases which directly concern the personal interests of the king, so that law retains credibility as an impartial rule.[27] But the sovereign is the necessary power behind the law.

Bodin's doctrine of an indivisible sovereignty is aimed, in part, against the ancient notion of a mixed or balanced regime—the notion that ultimate authority can be shared between the nobles, the common people, and the monarchy. He does not deny that different elements of the community can share distinct roles in "government." He even endorses such arrangements, so long as they are understood as subordinate to the common sovereignty.[28] But he denies that sovereignty, in itself, can be shared. It is in one set of hands or it is in another. So Bodin's sovereignty is something distinct from the community as a whole: It is not one part of the community ruling the rest but a higher authority over all. More importantly, perhaps, outside powers like the Church have no part in the sovereignty of an individual commonwealth.

The plausibility of this view depends, in turn, on Bodin's insistent identification between sovereignty and force. The wielder of force is the sovereign. If there are rival powers with authority to wield force, there is not a commonwealth but a prescription for continuous conflict.[29] Bodin readily acknowledges that towns, merchant guilds, universities, and other institutions can have their own internal organization, with their own internal rules. He even acknowledges that feudal lords may retain some governing powers that have come to be regarded as hereditary—though such powers, he insists, cannot be regarded as true personal property. All these governing powers must, in any case, be understood as operating by authorization of the sovereign power and distinctly subordinate to it.[30] The same logic holds for outside authorities like the Holy Empire and the Church. French kings are sovereign because they have always refused submission to these outside powers and always had the support of the French people in so doing.[31]

To see this theory as a celebration of force is to miss the point. It is instead an insistence on the primacy of security against force—from aggressors outside the community and within it. Tyrants and usurpers have no proper claim to sovereignty and may therefore be rightly resisted. There can be treaties and certain agreed rules of conduct between fellow sovereigns but not between sovereigns and mere robber bands.[32] Bodin acknowledged in an earlier work, the *Methodus*, that the rules which guide fellow sovereigns—and indeed fellow citizens—in their dealings with each other might well be deduced from reason, except that "reason [by itself] constrains no one."[33] Only a sovereign power can provide real security. Acknowledging the obvious dangers in hereditary monarchy, Bodin still defends it as the most likely to achieve stability.[34] But his emphasis is on stability and security rather than monarchy per se.

Bodin was trained as a lawyer and served for a time as a provincial judge (as well as a royal advisor, diplomat, and delegate to the Estates General). His political analysis is generally expressed in legal categories. So Bodin's doctrine of sovereignty is, in many ways, a doctrine about lawful authority and Bodin's sovereign is constrained by constitutional norms. The central power is the power to make laws.

From the power to make and unmake the laws, it follows, according to Bodin, that the sovereign must also have the power to settle legal disputes and grant pardons. The sovereign must have the power to declare war and control the army and establish the value of coinage. Bodin sets out the "marks" of sovereignty (as he calls them) like so many provisions in a constitutional charter—and all of these "marks," as it happens, are among the enumerated powers of the federal government, set out in the U.S. Constitution.[35]

Bodin insists on certain restraints, as well. The sovereign cannot change the laws of succession in a hereditary monarchy nor arrange for the succession of a daughter where female rule is forbidden. The sovereign is bound by constitutional norms that establish his own authority. He must even honor formal pledges made to his own citizens.[36]

Perhaps the most important limit is that a proper sovereign does not have power over private property. Bodin acknowledges that in some commonwealths the ruler claims a "lordly" power over all that the subjects possess. He distinguishes such "lordly monarchy" from true "royal monarchy." The earliest rulers probably exercised "lordly" powers—gained by plunder and aggression. But in contemporary Europe it survives only in Muscovy and Turkey. Bodin clearly regards these as unacceptable models, impossible to sustain in the rest of Europe, where the subjects will revolt against such "tyrannical" impositions.[37] In these countries, governing power comes from the sovereign, but property in land or goods is genuinely private. Bodin goes so far as to say that sovereign authority is "chiefly established to yield unto every man that which is his own and to forbid theft." Because a royal sovereign cannot take the property of his subjects, he cannot impose taxes without the subjects' consent. Such consent can only be secured from a positive vote of a representative assembly.[38]

But if the sovereign has command of force, why should he obey such limitations? Bodin emphasizes that the sovereign is bound by the laws of God and the laws of nature (which he sometimes combines, in Jeffersonian fashion, in speaking about the precepts of "Nature's God").[39] Respect for private property, for example, is "commanded by the word of God who will have every man to enjoy the property of his own goods." But Bodin does not mention Christian teaching when he discusses the abolition of slavery in western Europe: it was abolished, he says, by kings who were fearful of slave revolts.[40] Bodin frequently invokes the law of the ancient Hebrews, sometimes explaining them with Talmudic glosses.[41] He rarely invokes authority from the New Testament. He mentions Maimonides more often than Thomas Aquinas and Machiavelli more often than either—though usually to express disapproval of Machiavelli.[42]

Bodin's own religious beliefs were a matter of much dispute in his own time. His views were certainly unorthodox. In speaking of the "God of Nature," for example, he suggests that human rulers can model themselves on God's example as much as revealed law, so that traditional notions of "providence" may be helped along by human calculation.[43] Bodin continually emphasizes the importance of religion. But his appeals to the laws of Israel and his reliance on rabbinic interpretation allow him to endorse some notion of ultimate divine authority, while pointing away from any human institution claiming political authority in God's name, whether in Rome or Geneva. It is not religion, as such, that Bodin seeks to subdue but political authority acting in the name of religion—and in opposition to the sovereign.[44]

Whatever his own ultimate beliefs, Bodin was a "forthright advocate for religion toleration." In Bodin's account, sovereignty is entirely compatible with religious toleration—and indeed well served by it. In the *République*, Bodin affirms that there is only one completely true religion, but as the question has provoked so much violent strife, he will not give his view on which one that is. He does say that a sovereign should not try to coerce religious belief because doing so will only promote cynicism and ultimately, atheism. He continually laments that religion has become an excuse for persecution and plunder, calling attention to the expropriation and expulsion of Jews from various kingdoms which he attributes to greed on the part of the expropriators. If there are religious differences among people, he says, it is better to have several religions than risk chronic strife from the opposition of only two rival faiths.[45]

Just as he dismisses the need for a common religion, Bodin dismisses the importance of kinship or close association among citizens. He explicitly disputes Aristotle's claim that a proper commonwealth should be small enough for citizens to know each other; a larger commonwealth, Bodin argues, will be more stable and less vulnerable to tyrannical impositions.[46] He also disputes Aristotle's notion that nobles or citizens who take part in ruling are more properly citizens than others. Bodin insists that acceptance of a common sovereign is what defines citizens, so even slaves may be considered citizens. Every nation has distinctive ideas about nobility but most of them, Bodin suggests, are self-serving or simply irrational. Certainly descent in itself is no claim to rank.[47] In his earlier work, the *Methodus*, Bodin goes to some trouble to dispute notions that any European nation can claim a pure ancient lineage giving it precedence over others. Linguistic evidence, he says, proves that Europeans have been jumbled together for many centuries.[48]

Bodin's assumptions about the limited claims of sovereignty are equally evident in his attitude toward foreign trade. He says that God has scattered the world's resources in different parts of the earth, so that men will have incentives to deal peacefully with each other. Treaties on trade can be maintained, he claims, even with enemies. Trade, he says, is a source of income for a commonwealth and far more honorable than plunder.[49] He was, as J. N. Figgis put it, "a free trader in an age of bureaucracy."[50] Once political authority is well-established, private commerce can be left to find its own way.

But not entirely. Bodin was sufficiently interested in trade to publish a separate study of gold supply and inflation, which is regarded as one of the first contributions to the modern study of economics.[51] Maintaining the value of coinage, according to Bodin, is one of the prime duties of sovereign authority and debasing the coinage one of the worst offenses, one which contradicts the Law of God—because it is stealing.[52] To hold down prices, he advises, governments should try to break up monopolies in trade and discourage the price-fixing schemes of the craft guilds. But limiting exports, he says, will only impoverish the kingdom and hurt poor people the most by denying them access to cheap imports and opportunities for employment in export industries. Characteristically, he notes that while Plato and other Greek thinkers were hostile to foreign trade, for fear of its corrupting influence, the Law of Moses imposed no obstacles to foreign trade.[53]

So, the first theorist of sovereignty defended constitutional limitations, private property, consent for taxation, religious toleration, and free trade. To see him as a forerunner of classical liberalism does not require any leap of imagination. By reducing the aims of political authority, Bodin's doctrine of sovereignty sought to assure that much else in life—spiritual, economic, "ethnic"—could be removed from political contention and tolerated as matters for individual or private decision.[54] At the same time, the doctrine promised a more stable and secure government: "the less the power of the sovereign is (the true sovereign powers still reserved) the more it is assured."[55]

Bodin, a true Renaissance man in his mastery of ancient languages and literatures, was also extraordinarily cosmopolitan in his eagerness to acquire knowledge of the legal and institutional variations among European governments of his time.[56] He found much to admire even in the Islamic empire of the Turks.[57] He regarded a clear doctrine of sovereignty as compatible with—and even a safeguard for—broad tolerance, wide curiosity, and extensive international exchange in private life.

Within a decade of the appearance of Bodin's treatise, an English lawyer published the first extended argument for the sovereignty of Parliament. Modern scholars believe that the argument was adapted from Bodin's theory.[58] A few decades later, the great Puritan poet, John Milton,

published a plan to establish a religiously tolerant republic in England—
in which he invokes Bodin's authority for the conclusion that a supreme
parliamentary council will establish "one united and entrusted Sovrantie."[59]
By the late nineteenth century, Frederick Pollock, a distinguished legal
historian, could say of Bodin's theory: "to an English lawyer it needs a
certain effort of imagination to conceive that people ever thought otherwise."[60]

Sovereignty in the Liberal State

If the first theorist of sovereignty was something of a liberal, the most influential theorist of liberal constitutionalism, John Locke, was also a
strong proponent of sovereignty. Certainly he was seen this way by his
successors, including the American Founders, a century later.[61]

At first sight, the association between Locke and a strong doctrine of
national sovereignty may seem strange. Locke is famous for proclaiming
natural rights, including rights of religious freedom and private property.
The priority of individual rights certainly is a more central theme in
Locke's work than it is in the works of Bodin or indeed of any previous
exponents of "natural law." Locke is so readily associated with a universal doctrine of individual rights that legal scholars routinely cite Locke as
the forerunner of the contemporary human rights movement. Some
scholars even suggest Locke's theory would justify supranational institutions to protect natural rights.[62]

Yet Locke's "commonwealth" is not, in the end, so distant from Bodin's
"république." To start with, we should notice that Locke's doctrine denies
toleration to those who preach religious intolerance. It also denies toleration to those who give their civil allegiance to foreign authorities—by
which he clearly means Catholics who accept papal supremacy over the
civil authority. To guarantee religious freedom, the civil authority must
first establish its own civil supremacy over any particular religious authority. On the other hand, Locke denies toleration to those who preach
atheism or immorality; like Bodin, he assumes that even a tolerant government requires certain residual notions of moral restraint among its citizens and among its own officials.[63]

In his *Second Treatise of Government*, Locke speaks the language of
sovereignty: "in a Constituted Commonwealth, standing upon its own
basis, and acting according to its own nature, that is, acting for the
preservation of the community, there can be but one supreme power,
which is the legislative, to which all the rest are and must be subordinate"
(par. 149).

At the same time, Locke indicates that the executive power should be separated from the legislative. And he acknowledges a "prerogative" in the executive "to act according to discretion for the public good, without the prescription of the law and sometimes even against it" when circumstances require (par. 160). The legislative power may retain a supremacy, insofar as it can remove an executive who abuses this power. But the very fact of prerogative emphasizes that the law itself is not quite supreme. Locke's executive power retains the "federative power" to deal with foreign powers—that is, to manage external force. And the same executive then wields force to uphold laws at home (par. 147). So, far from concealing the element of force in this, Locke emphasizes it by treating judicial power (as we would now call it) as a mere incident of executive power (par. 143): judicial decisions are compulsory because they are backed by the force of the community.

The essence of "political community" or "civil society," then, is a common submission to these established powers. Each person must "part also with as much of natural liberty in providing for himself as the good, prosperity and safety of the Society shall require: which is not only necessary but just, since the other Members of the Society do the like" (par. 130). Anyone who has "given his Consent to be of any commonwealth is perpetually and indispensably obliged to be and remain unalterably a Subject to it" (par. 121). Mere treaties or contracts in the state of nature do not have the same force as law (par. 14)—because, it seems, they cannot be reliably enforced. Only a properly constituted commonwealth provides the authority of a fully compelling law.

What, then, of the right to revolution? Locke insists that "there remains still in the people a supreme power to remove or alter the Legislative" as "the Community perpetually retains a power of saving themselves . . . and to rid themselves of those who invade this fundamental, sacred and unalterable law of self-preservation, for which they entered into society."[64] But if the community "may be said in this respect to be always the supreme power," it is so only in an extra-legal sense and "not as considered under any form of government, because this power of the people can never take place till the government be dissolved" (par. 149).

If Locke looks more favorably on revolution than Bodin,[65] he is also more attentive to the preconditions for successful revolution—a degree of national unity among the people of a commonwealth, enabling them to act together in moments of revolutionary crisis. Revolution, in Locke's account, is an act of the whole people or at least of most people, who must retain some coherence to establish a new government. So Locke says that political communities arise, in the first place, among those with special affinities: "those who liked one another so well as to joyn into society, cannot but be supposed to have some acquaintance and friendship together and some trust in one another; they could not but have greater apprehensions of others than of one another" (par. 107). Here he speaks about "the beginning of things" amidst a "simple poor way of living." But if larger, wealthier communities need more formal institutions, the appeal to some residual sense of community seems to remain.

Thus the "Grecian Christians," after centuries of subjection to the Turks, may have the capacity—as they retain the right—to revolt against foreign tyranny and reconstitute themselves as an independent nation (par. 192). In his most philosophical work, the *Essay Concerning Human Understanding*, Locke emphasizes the way in which different languages create different communities of understanding, so there is, after all, some basis in nature—or rather, in the "custom" and "fashion" of different societies— for a sense of nationality.[66]

But apart from the extreme circumstance of outright revolution, the legislative authority, once established, is "sacred and unalterable in the hands where the Community have once placed it; nor can any Edict of any Body else, in what Form soever conceived, or by what Power soever backed, have the force and obligation of a Law, which has not its Sanction from that Legislative which the publick has chosen and appointed" (par. 134). Indeed, once the legislative power is fixed, "*the legislative can never revert to the people* [original emphasis] whilst that government lasts" (par. 243). For the "legislative" is "the soul that gives form, life and unity to the commonwealth" by which the "members have their mutual influence, sympathy and connexion" (par. 212).[67]

It follows that the transfer of authority to "a Foreign Power," even if authorized by the existing "legislative" power, is "certainly a change of the Legislative and so a Dissolution of the Government"—that is, a justification for revolution. Locke does not make the objection turn on whether the "foreign power" acts against natural rights or acts abusively. The transfer to a foreign power is itself the objection: "For the end why People entered into Society, being to be preserved one intire, free, independent Society, to be governed by their own Laws; this is lost, whenever they are given up to the Power of another" (par. 217). National independence is the first bulwark of personal rights.

The whole theory appears, a few decades later, in William Blackstone's *Commentaries on the Laws of England*, which became the principal legal authority for the American colonists. For Blackstone, it is simply a self-evident truth that "there is and must be in all [governments] a supreme, irresistible, absolute, uncontrolled authority, in which . . . the rights of sovereignty reside."[68] Yet he also affirms that "the principal aim of society is to protect individuals in the enjoyment of those absolute rights, which were vested in them by the immutable laws of nature": these "absolute rights" are "life, liberty and property."[69]

Blackstone does not regard the claim of sovereignty as a contradiction of the claim about rights but rather as a corollary: "the community should guard the rights of each individual member and (in return for this protection) each individual should submit to the laws of the community; without which submission of all it was impossible that protection could be certainly extended to any."[70]

For Blackstone, "sovereign power" is "the making of laws; for . . . all the other powers of the state must obey the legislative power in the execution of their several functions, or else the constitution is at an end." Fortunately, "the constitutional government" of England is "admirably tempered and compounded" by the balancing of king, lords, and commons in Parliament—and should the structure of the legislature be changed "from that which was originally set up by the general consent and fundamental act of the society, such a change, however effected is according to Mr. Locke . . . an entire dissolution of the bands of government; and the people would be reduced to a state of anarchy, with liberty to constitute to themselves a new legislative power."[71]

The seeming extremes of this account—from the "irresistible, absolute, uncontrolled authority" of Parliament to the "absolute rights" of individuals—are brought together in Blackstone's defense of criminal laws against papists who "acknowledge a foreign power, superior to the sovereignty of the kingdom" and therefore "cannot complain if the laws of that kingdom will not treat them upon the footing of good subjects."[72] Blackstone acknowledges that these restrictions "are seldom exerted to their utmost rigor" and "are rather to be accounted for from their history and the urgency of the times which produced them," when Catholic authority was invoked on behalf of rival contenders to the throne, in Queen Elizabeth's day and even in the early eighteenth century on behalf of the deposed Stuart dynasty. In a future time, "perhaps not very distant, when all fears of a pretender [to the throne] shall have vanished and the power and influence of the pope shall become feeble, ridiculous and despicable," such laws can be removed.[73]

But historically, the alliance between "overgrown lords" and "pontifical power" threatened both the British Constitution and the rights of British subjects—"until it vanished into nothing, when the eyes of the people were a little enlightened and they set themselves with vigor to oppose it." Once enlightened, the people grasped the fundamental point:

> So vain and ridiculous is the attempt to live in society, without acknowledging the obligations which it lays us under; and to affect an intire independence of the civil state, which protects us in all our rights and gives us every other liberty, that only excepted of despising the laws of the community.[74]

By the 1770s, Americans were invoking the "self-evident" truths of Locke's treatise against the sovereignty of Parliament, yet in terms that still echoed Lockeian notions about sovereignty. The Declaration of

Independence could speak in very vague terms about "one people" acting "to dissolve the political bonds which have connected them with another"— neatly skirting the question of how Americans came to be "one people." But only two years before, Jefferson's *Summary View of the Rights of British America* tried to answer the question. Americans had always been governed by their own local legislatures, hence they were always a distinct people (or at least, thirteen distinct peoples).[75]

The Americans were driven to argue not that particular parliamentary enactments were abusive but that any parliamentary enactments reaching inside America were improper, because Americans had always been, in effect, sovereign people (or peoples) and were merely allied to the British nation by common cooperation with a common figurehead. In other words, the Americans insisted on a theory of the British Empire which, in later times, was thought to be entirely compatible with Canadian or Australian independence.

When the newly independent American states tried to regularize their relations with each other, they claimed, in the Articles of Confederation, to retain their sovereignty despite their "perpetual union." By the earlier theory, this would seem inconsistent. And that is precisely what advocates of the new Constitution argued.

FOUNDING DEBATES: FEDERALISM AND SOVEREIGNTY

Critics of the new Constitution complained from the outset that the powers accorded to the federal government would violate the sovereignty of the state governments. "Cincinnatus," for example, rebuked defenders of the Constitution: "read Mr. Locke, in whom you will find that sovereignty consists in three things—the legislative, executive and negociating powers, all which our [proposed federal] constitution takes absolutely away from the several states."[76]

A critic in Virginia protested that "under the proposed constitution each state will dwindle into the insignificance of a town corporate." He rejected the notion that sovereignty could be equitably shared between the federal government and the states, since "two sovereignties existing within the same community is a perfect solecism . . . if the word means anything at all, it must mean that supreme power which must reside somewhere" as "the united powers of each individual member of the state collected and consolidated into one body."[77] If this power were lodged in the federal government, it could not also be preserved in the states.

Even the procedure for ratifying the new Constitution raised objections from Antifederalist critics. If the states were sovereign under the Articles of Confederation, then the Articles were akin to a treaty or alliance and could only be changed with the consent of the sovereign states, them-selves. By leaving it to newly elected ratifying conventions to decide whether to impose a new authority over the states, the ratifying proce-dure in the Constitution seemed to treat the states as passive bystanders to their own fate. It seemed to assume that citizens were thrown back into the state of nature, free to do as they liked.

But the truth, Luther Martin protested, was that, "once the people have exercised their power in establishing and forming themselves into a State government, [that power] never devolves back to them, nor have they a right to resume or again to exercise that power until such events take place as will amount to the dissolution or alteration of their State government."[78] This was sound Lockeian doctrine, too—if the state gov-ernments were viewed as sovereign entities.

Defenders of the Constitution did not dismiss such arguments as mere technicalities. They responded with rather technical, legal arguments in the same vein—contesting only the initial premise regarding the sover-eignty of the states. To refute Martin's reasoning, James Wilson invoked the Declaration of Independence to show that the colonies became inde-pendent "not *Individually* but *Unitedly*." Even the terms of the Articles of Confederation left the states "wholly incompetent to the exercise of any of the great and distinguishing acts of Sovereignty." In relation to any foreign "sovereign" the individual states were "deaf, dumb and impo-tent" and if the delegates to the Confederation Congress should vote to declare war, even against the instructions of the states, the United States would still be at war: "This remark proves the states are now subordinate corporations or Societies and not Sovereigns." The same argument was belabored at the Constitutional Convention, in substantially the same terms, by Alexander Hamilton and Rufus King. The force of the argu-ment derives, of course, from its premise that the fundamental attributes of sovereign power are not divisible, but necessarily in one set of hands or another.[79]

In appeals for public support, during the ratification debates, James Wilson contended that the American people, as a whole, were the real sovereign and could therefore delegate different powers to the state and federal governments.[80] Some Federalists, however, defended the notion of a sovereign federal government in quite unapologetic terms. Charles Pinckney put it this way:

I apprehend the true intention of the States in uniting is to have a firm national government, capable of effectually executing its acts and dis-pensing its benefits and protection. In it alone can be vested those pow-ers and prerogatives which more particularly distinguish a sovereign state. The [states] are to be considered merely as parts of the great

whole and only suffered to retain the powers necessary to the administration of their State system. The idea which has been so long and
falsely entertained of each being a sovereign State must be given up; for
it is absurd to suppose there can be more than one sovereignty within
a Government.[81]

Most Federalists tried to assuage Antifederalist concerns by emphasizing
the powers retained by the states. In *The Federalist* No. 44, Madison
struggles to demonstrate that the constitutional scheme is only partly that
of a consolidated national government and remains "partly federal" (in
the original sense of a confederation of otherwise sovereign states). There
was enough in this argument, at least in Madison's mind, for him to revert to this analysis decades later, in trying to calm the passions of South
Carolina nullifiers.[82]

Still, what is most striking about the argument of *The Federalist* is the
extent to which, in general, it meets the complaints of Antifederalists on
their own terms by embracing the logic of sovereignty—as well as the
term. The critics of the Constitution seek things "repugnant and irreconcilable . . . at sovereignty in the Union and complete independence in the
members. They still in fine seem to cherish with blind devotion the political monster of an *imperium in imperio*."[83]

The Federalist argues, quite bluntly, that federal laws and treaties—
and the federal Constitution itself—must have the status of sovereign law
if they are to have any real authority at all. Federal authority cannot simply be superimposed on state governments. It must reach into the states,
directly binding citizens in a true national community. The mere provision
for legal supremacy, in Article VI of the Constitution, is not sufficient.
Federal authority must be empowered "to address itself immediately to
the hopes and fears of individuals; and to attract to its support, those passions, which have the strongest influence upon the human heart."[84]

Without this direct control over citizens, a confederation of the state
governments would have no more force than a treaty or series of treaties.
History shows "how little dependence is to be placed on treaties which
have no other sanction than the obligation of good faith, and which oppose general considerations of peace and justice to the impulse of any immediate interest or passion." To go beyond this requires the logic of sovereignty: "If there be no penalty annexed to disobedience, the resolutions
or commands which pretend to be laws will, in fact, amount to nothing
more than advice or recommendation."[85] Like Bodin, *The Federalist* is
extremely insistent on the difference between "advice or recommendation" and the "coercion of the magistracy." *The Federalist* says, "The
majesty of the national authority must be manifested through the
medium of the Courts of Justice."[86] "Majesty" is the English equivalent
of Bodin's Latin term for sovereignty—"majestas."

But, as it is, the state governments have "one transcendent advantage" over the federal authority: The states retain "the ordinary administration of criminal and civil justice" which is "the most powerful, most universal and most attractive source of popular obedience and attachment," since these laws affect "those personal interests and familiar concerns to which the sensibility of individuals is most immediately awake."[87] *The Federalist* does not hesitate to enlist nationalist rhetoric on the side of the Union:

> Providence has been pleased to give this one connected country to one united people. . . . This country and this people seem to have been made for each and it appears as if it was the design of Providence that an inheritance so proper and convenient for a band of brethren, united to each other by the strongest ties, should never be split into a number of unsocial, jealous and alien sovereignties.[88]

But such pious or sentimental appeals are not sufficient, either. In the same paper in which we hear about the "transcendent advantage" of the states in retaining "the most attractive source of popular obedience and attachment," *The Federalist* claims that an ambitious federal government would disdain to meddle with "the mere domestic police of a State." Control of such local matters would "contribute nothing to the dignity, to the importance, or to the splendour of the national government."[89] To sustain its authority, the federal government needs to assert some distinctive "dignity," "importance," "splendour" on behalf of the whole nation.

The Federalist proceeds to review the history of past confederacies, showing that they all failed to maintain themselves because they lacked strong central authority. The paper on the German Empire (which, in the eighteenth century, was still officially the "Holy Roman Empire of the German Nation") is particularly eloquent, speaking with almost visceral disgust of the Empire's fate: "a nerveless body; incapable of regulating its own members; insecure against external dangers; and agitated with un-ceasing fermentation in its own bowels." In its weakness, the Empire is a perpetual prey to the intrigues of "neighboring powers": rather than per-mit constitutional changes that "would give to the Empire the force and preeminence to which it is entitled," outside powers pursue a "policy of perpetuating [the Empire's] anarchy and weakness." A somewhat less contemptuous account of the Swiss confederacy (which tracks very closely with Bodin's account, as it happens) emphasizes the weakness and isolation of the cantons and their ultimate dependence on rival foreign protectors, perpetuating divisions between Catholic and Protestant cantons.[90]

The inference is hammered home in paper after paper: The effective-ness of the national government in assuring constitutional authority at home is dependent on its effectiveness in standing up to foreign powers. Foreign powers will stir up dissension and intrigue among the states if the federal government cannot maintain its own authority. And "respect" for the federal government at home depends on its success in demonstrating its "respectability" in the world:

> How is it possible that a government half supplied and always necessitous, can fulfill the purposes of its institution—can provide for the security, advance the prosperity, or support the reputation of the commonwealth? How can it ever possess either energy or stability, dignity or credit, confidence at home or respectability abroad?[91]

Or again:

> An individual who is observed to be inconstant to his plans, or perhaps to carry on his affairs without any plan at all, is marked at once by all prudent people as a speedy victim of his own unsteadiness and folly. His more friendly neighbors may pity him; but all will decline to connect their fortunes with his; and not a few will seize the opportunity of making their fortunes out of his. One nation is to another what one individual is to another. . . . [So, lacking a strong national government] America . . . finds that she is held in no respect by her friends; that she is the derision of her enemies; and that she is a prey to every nation which has an interest in speculating on her fluctuating councils and embarrassed affairs.[92]

A strong version of sovereignty is required for a respected national government and an effective national government is required for a stable constitutional order. The appeal is not just to security—an argument for organizing sufficient force at home to meet dangers from abroad. The appeal is, as importantly, to national self-respect—to a sense of collective honor in dealings with outsiders.[93] If Americans want to be self-governing, they must organize themselves to sustain a respectable government: Independence requires a degree of national solidarity which can only be sustained by a constitutional discipline.

THE AMERICAN IDEA OF SOVEREIGNTY

Through most of American history, anyone who talked seriously about sovereignty took for granted the historic understanding: only a government of limited aims can aspire to be sovereign—within those limits. The question in America was how or where that limited power should be assigned.

Whatever the text of the Constitution, whatever the explanations in *The Federalist*, that question was not entirely settled by the ratification of the Constitution. For decades thereafter, many prominent politicians insisted that the Constitution was really a pact among states, by which states delegated some of their sovereign powers to a federal government but still retained ultimate sovereign authority. On this theory, eleven states claimed a legal right to secede from the Union after the election of Abraham Lincoln.

Lincoln's response did not evade the question of sovereignty: "What is a 'sovereignty' in the political sense of the term? Would it be far wrong to define it 'A political community, without a political superior?' Tested by this, no one of our states . . . ever was a sovereignty. . . . The Union, and not themselves separately, procured their independence and their liberty."

Lincoln also thought it "worthy of note" that in "the government's hour of trial," Army and Navy officers "in large numbers . . . proved false to the hand that had pampered them": they deserted their posts and joined the Confederate forces. But "the most important fact of all, is the unanimous firmness of the common soldiers and common sailors" who "understand, without an argument, that destroying the government, which was made by Washington, means no good to them."[94]

Not only the "common soldiers" but the common voters of the North sustained the Union through four years of terrible war. So they vindicated, as Lincoln later put it, "government of the people, by the people"—*the* people of one "political community."

Lincoln's rhetoric continually appealed to one of the historic arguments for sovereignty—that it preserves the claims of the whole people against the political ambitions of the few. The Framers of the Constitution seem to have anticipated that ambition of this sort would seek foreign support: They included an express prohibition not only on the granting of domestic "titles of nobility" but also on federal office holders accepting "Office or Title of any kind whatsoever from any King, Prince or foreign State."[95] The prohibition is not aimed at secret intrigues but precisely at the public flaunting of international honors, which might imply that outside powers can confer prestige and elevate the influence of favored office-holders in the United States.

Looked at in this way, sovereignty might seem to be simply a safeguard of governing authority within the country. This perspective, however, does not fully capture the historic American view. Well into the twentieth century, British legal theorists had no difficulty identifying Parliament as the repository of ultimate, sovereign authority, but they were puzzled about American institutions. Since acts of Congress could be overruled by the Supreme Court, perhaps the Supreme Court should be regarded as ultimate sovereign. Or perhaps sovereign power lay with the three-quarters of state legislatures empowered to overturn Supreme Court rulings by amending the Constitution.[96]

One American answer is that the Constitution in itself is the sovereign authority. In becoming American citizens, immigrants swear an oath of allegiance that commits them to support, not the president or Congress (as such), but the Constitution. American military officers and civilian office-holders take a similar oath of allegiance—to the Constitution.[97] If sovereignty is understood as a definite human authority, then we might say the sovereign is the people—but in the constitutional sense: "We the People" who "ordain" the Constitution and may change it, but only by procedures prescribed in the Constitution, itself.

The ambiguity about whether the Constitution itself is supreme—or the organs it creates or the people who ordain it—may seem a unique complication, by which Americans evade the historic logic of sovereignty. But some ambiguity of this kind is finally inseparable from the concept. Sovereignty was always a theory that tried to unite legality or legitimacy with command of force. Would the British Parliament remain sovereign if it empowered a foreign prince to exercise its powers? Would this foreign power still be entitled to claim obedience from British subjects? Blackstone and Locke emphatically denied the possibility. Even Bodin's sovereign is bound by certain constitutional requirements, preserving the terms by which he acquired sovereign power. A force with no limits and no constraints is hard to conceive as a rightful force—and rightful force was what the doctrine of sovereignty always aspired to establish.

Sovereignty, then, is not just about restraining ambition but, more fundamentally, about securing loyalty. As a doctrine, it implies some clarity about the conditions under which people will obey or should obey. It depends on some prior agreement on how a particular people will let themselves be governed. Liberal theorists called this the social contract. Americans might call it the Constitution. But the premise of such agreements is that quite a lot of people are independent-minded, ambitious, assertive—and cannot simply be overawed without some reasonable assurances about the power to which they submit.[98]

Is it consistent with sovereignty to be bound by international or supranational authority? In the United States, at least, the traditional view was that the Constitution prohibits delegations of governing authority to foreign bodies and therefore also to international bodies. One way of understanding this prohibition is that such delegations would blur lines of authority and make it harder for rightful, domestic authority to assert itself.

Perhaps this concern is not chimerical, even now. We have, for example, much dispute about the best ways of addressing racial and ethnic conflicts, which sometimes burst into violence. Would it be helpful to let UN human rights organs, for example, guide us in sorting out charges of police misconduct? Would it help to assure good relations between "Anglo" and "Chicano" to let the Court of Human Rights, under the Organization of American States, address such disputes and settle for us the proper standards for police conduct? Or would it provoke more tension and conflict, as ambitious political leaders posture as upholders of higher law, higher than the domestic or constitutional law which assigns such decisions to domestic authorities?

The question is not just about immediate effect. The international authorities offering to decide such disputes have no real capacity to enforce the standards they proclaim. Still less can they protect Americans from the consequences of following their standards, should this lead to further conflict or violence. International human rights authorities are not organs of an accepted government with the full range of governing powers. They exercise a moral or spiritual authority, not connected to any particular community that is organized to support or implement their decisions. International authorities of this sort thus seem to exercise the sort of "ghostly" authority claimed by the Holy Roman Empire or by the universal Church (which in some parts of Europe, they continued to claim, in fact, down to the nineteenth century).

Can new, secularized versions of such ghostly authority be placed on top of the American constitutional system? For many "crusaders"—who conceive themselves to have broader and nobler aims than their fellow citizens—such ghostly authority has much appeal. Not the least of its appeal is that which inspired medieval crusaders and feudal lords: International authority offers the prestige of a higher cause, without exerting much actual control over those who act in its name.

Increasing disorder, however, might not be the greatest danger in this trend. And allaying "disorder" was not the only purpose which sovereignty doctrines were meant to serve. Many countries have gotten accustomed to submitting themselves to international authorities. Most peoples through most of history have been ruled by foreign empires or local despots. People learn to accommodate irresistible power. In the long run, then, perhaps the greater danger is that, if international authority can establish itself over our own constitutional structures, the resulting erosion of sovereignty will get Americans accustomed to extra-constitutional authority—resting on no particular people, no particular constitution, no established organization of power. Medieval "governance" rested not only on the power of local lords and their distant spiritual sanctions, but also on the passivity and resignation of common people who did not dare to question their subordination—or could not imagine any way of rejecting it but riot and plunder.

Sovereignty is the first bulwark of constitutional government—as it implies the right to say no to outsiders. Without that, it may be hard to say no at all, because it becomes so hard to determine who has the right to utter the no and in whose name. A world in which sovereign states can be intimidated from asserting their own rightful powers is a world where most individuals can be intimidated from claiming their own constitutional rights. It is a world where conflict is "managed," because authority drained from sovereign states does not quite establish international governing powers with anything like the sovereign power once exercised by actual, national governments.

If the power of national governments rests on their respect for certain constitutional standards and limits, undermining those governments almost necessarily puts at risk the authority of those standards and limits. Power cannot be measured or limited and rights cannot be so well-asserted—because everything may run back to moral arbiters with official status but no firmly constituted powers, whose authority has no clear boundaries.

Along with sovereignty, our notions about individual rights and government by consent are at risk. They all rest on a constitutional arrangement of powers and limits that we have learned to operate as our own. It requires a great deal of trust or faith to think that ghostly empires will do as well. Sovereignty—like all our related notions of constitutional government—was premised, from the outset, on the opposite view: It is not wise to trust very much to good faith, without sovereign powers in the background.

CHAPTER FOUR

THE ENLIGHTENMENT AND THE LAW OF NATIONS

IN A WORLD where sovereign states are fully sovereign, there might seem to be no room for international law. If each state makes its own law for its own territory, how can there be a law that embraces all states? At least since the seventeenth century, scoffers have pressed such skeptical arguments with much intellectual force. Even governments committed to the rule of law at home have often given at least one ear to these arguments.

The American Founders did not embrace this skeptical view, however. They endorsed a different view in the very act of asserting American sovereignty. The American Declaration of Independence begins and ends with an appeal to a law that transcends the law of any one state. The very first sentence appeals to "the Laws of Nature and of Nature's God": when it becomes "necessary" for "one people to dissolve the political bands which have connected them to another," these "Laws" entitle them "to a separate and equal station."

Or, rather, as the Declaration carefully stipulates, these "Laws" entitle each nation to an equal station "among the powers of the Earth." God is above all nations. If every independent nation has, in some way, a claim to an equal station, each stands directly accountable to God for its conduct. There can be no ultimate or reliable intermediary between an independent nation and the "Supreme Judge of the world" (to Whom the signers of the Declaration appeal in the last paragraph "for the rectitude of our intentions").

If every nation stands open to judgment, it must be possible for every nation to know the law by which its actions will be judged. That law, it seems, is the "law of Nature and Nature's God," invoked in the opening sentence—a law that might be discerned from the study of nature or from reflection on "the course of human events."

The full text of the Declaration does not leave the matter at such pious speculations. The penultimate sentence, in summing up the argument, returns to the notion of a law that is higher than the will of any one state. This time, however, the Declaration elaborates the implications of that law with lawyerly care. In joining the ranks of "free and independent states," the Declaration concludes, the United States can now claim "full Power to levy War, conclude Peace, contract Alliances, establish Commerce and to do all other Acts and Things which Independent States may of right do." The Declaration thus seems to take for granted that there is something like a pre-existing law, determining the rights of independent states, with some degree of precision.

The claim may seem strange to contemporary readers. Can we really speak of a whole scheme of international law, implicit in God's Creation, laying down what each independent state "may of right do"? Yet even today, most Americans remain quite persuaded by the Declaration's famous appeal to the "self-evident" truths "that all men are created equal, that they are endowed by their Creator with certain unalienable rights," that "governments" derive "their just powers from the consent of the governed." These phrases also appeal to a higher law, or at least, to a set of principles which are of higher authority than the law of any particular state.

The Declaration itself indicates underlying connections between the natural rights of individual human beings and the rights of sovereign states. If "all men are created equal," then any government, "instituted" by any particular people, must be "entitled" to an "equal station" in relation to every other government—otherwise some men will seem to have a superior title to "institute" governments. If governments derive "their just powers from the consent of the governed," then each government must have a "separate station"—otherwise outside powers can interfere with a government's accountability to "the governed."

The framers of the Declaration were, of course, quite aware that outside powers did regularly interfere in the internal affairs of sovereign states. They were equally aware that governments often ignored the "unalienable rights" of individuals and ruled without "consent." In laying down standards for the excercise of "just powers," the framers of the Declaration did not mean to deny the existence of unjust powers in the world. They were, after all, in the midst of a revolution against unjust power.

The argument of the Declaration is that, as unjust exertion of domestic power lays the basis for revolution, unjust exactions by one state upon another may lay the ground for war. By their own lights, the framers of the Declaration were engaged in such a war against a foreign power. The higher law of the Declaration sets out the basis for peace. As the British have been "deaf to the voice of justice," Americans must "hold them, as we hold the rest of mankind, Enemies in War, in Peace Friends."

What if people prefer to give in to a foreign power? Perhaps this is not altogether different from the question of whether people are free to consent to tyranny. To the latter question, the Declaration acknowledges the "dictate" of "prudence," that a "long established" government "should not be changed for light and transient causes." But when a "long train of abuses and usurpations . . . evinces a design to reduce them under absolute Despotism," it is not only the "right" of a people "to throw off such Government," but "it is their duty" to do so. Perhaps nations, too, have not only a right to a separate and equal station, but a duty to assert this right, when it is in danger of being overwhelmed.

In the meantime, however, nations have strong reasons to respect each other's rights—to remain, "in Peace Friends." If the rights of nations can be reduced to certain agreed rules or standards, each state would gain a better understanding of its obligation to respect the "separate and equal station" of every other state. To the extent that such rules were observed, states could maintain peaceful and friendly relations. The Declaration seems quite open to the idea.

We might infer then, simply from a close reading of the Declaration, that the American Founders would have been sympathetic to international law, so far as international law corresponded to this vision. But it is not necessary to rely on inferences drawn from a close reading of the Declaration. We know, from a wealth of sources, that the American Founders were quite familiar with an account of international law which fit this description. It is an account that tracks very closely with the arguments and assumptions of the Declaration itself.

The founding perspective of the United States was not at all hostile to international law. It was, however, insistent on a certain understanding of what international law should be. It is hardly an exaggeration to say that a certain understanding of international law was seen as a necessary complement to the American understanding of liberal or constitutional government at home. To grasp the connection it is useful to look back at the development of European thought on this subject. The leading works illuminate the assumptions in the American Declaration of Independence and the notions which the Framers of the U.S. Constitution had in mind when they referred to "the law of nations."

Origins of the Modern Law of Nations

As U.S. secretary of state, James Madison published a long pamphlet, arguing that British blockade practices were in violation of the law of nations. Madison began with a learned review of relevant legal writings on the subject. And the first of these was the treatise of Grotius, because, as Madison cautiously phrased it, Grotius "is not unjustly considered, as in some respects, the father of the modern code of nations."[1] Within a few generations, these qualifications had disappeared: The American delegation to the Hague Peace Conference of 1899 organized a Fourth of

July ceremony at the tomb of the great jurist, expressing "reverence and gratitude" to the "memory of Grotius" from "the United States of America."[2]

The reputation of Grotius rests on his greatest work, *De jure bellum ad pacis* (The Law of War and Peace), first published in 1625.[3] This bulky treatise is hardly a stirring manifesto. It is a highly intricate book, displaying the vast learning of a humanist scholar, which Grotius assuredly was. The book also displays the cautious distinctions of a practicing lawyer, which Grotius had been as well. *De jure* also includes much to make later generations cringe, such as its defense of slavery and despotic government as lawful institutions. But the work's appeal to later generations remains understandable. The appeal starts with *De jure*'s unhesitating endorsement of state sovereignty.

Medieval writers generally assumed that kings and princes were—or should be—answerable to some higher human authority. Popes were proclaimed to have jurisdiction over the whole world or at least over all Christendom. Even anti-papalist writers often projected a notion of the Holy Roman Emperor as an ultimate authority for the whole world. Both claims persisted for a long time. Less than a decade before the appearance of Grotius's treatise, the great Spanish theologian, Francisco Suarez, thought it necessary to offer extended arguments against the notion of a universal empire—while still insisting that the Pope must have authority to depose sinful kings, like the Protestant (therefore, "heretic") King James I of England. Suarez wrote a whole separate treatise to establish the latter point.[4]

Grotius, a Dutch Calvinist, started from the opposite premise: Governments of independent states answer to no higher human authority—that is Grotius's basic definition of sovereignty. It is not a claim about power or resources but about legal authority: A sovereign power is one whose actions "are not subject to legal control of another, so that they cannot be rendered [legally] void by the operation of another human will" (book I, chapter iii, section 7, paragraph 1). Grotius then goes to some length to refute claims to rule or to make war on behalf of a universal empire or a universal church (II.xxii.13–14).

Grotius did not claim to have invented this notion of sovereignty. He indeed gave respectful notice to Jean Bodin, as to other writers who were already citing Bodin's work. But Grotius was the first writer who, even while accepting the premise of sovereignty, sought to provide a systematic account of a law constraining sovereign states in their mutual relations.[5]

De jure did this by emphasizing the rights of states in the context of a legal theory in which rights, for the first time, became the central focus of inquiry. Grotius launched the idea of "subjective rights"—the right

(Latin: *ius* or *jus*) seen from the perspective of the person who may claim it on his own behalf ("my right" as opposed to "what is right"). He speaks of a "right" as a "faculty" or "moral quality of a person, making it possible to have or to do something lawfully" and insists that this is "a legal right properly or strictly so called" (I.iv.5). If he did not invent this notion, Grotius certainly gave it a degree of clarity and vividness which it did not have in earlier works. Nearly a third of *De jure* expounds the Roman law governing private disputes—regarding property, contract, and injury—from this perspective, which Grotius then applies to the rights of states. An early English translation of the work plausibly rendered the title as "The Rights of War and Peace."

What gave force to the argument was the claim that rights can exist without being promulgated because they have a natural logic. Grotius was the first writer to make "natural rights" a theme of legal and political discussion. He did not use the later expression "state of nature" but his argument suggests the notion: "Natural rights" are the claims that could be justly advanced in the absence of any higher authority. So, they are rights that sovereigns can claim against each other, even though there is no international legislator to promulgate these rights.

While giving special prominence to the notion of natural rights, Grotius also reduced the claims of natural law. Medieval thinkers had associated natural law with aspirations to human perfection or the common good, treating "natural law" as a body of eternal principles against which human law might be judged. Grotius insists that "law, properly so called" must be distinguished from personal ethics or claims about distributive justice (in relation to civic honors or public benefits) (Prolegomena, sec. 8–10). In the strict sense, law refers only to duties that correspond to the rights of another. So natural law, in the Grotian account, is reduced to respecting the natural rights of others.[6]

In fact, it is often much less than that. In the Grotian version, natural rights are not unalienable. As an individual may consent to give up his property to someone else, a whole people, according to Grotius, might well consent to give up all their rights to an absolute ruler. The ruler would then be bound by no limitation, not even a moral obligation to rule for the benefit of those he ruled over (I.iii.8). In the Grotian version of natural law, a ruler has no inherent obligation to those he rules over and Grotius declaims at considerable length against the notion that people have an inherent right to rebel against unjust authority (I.iv.2).

On the other hand, Grotius conceded that a people might insist on yielding power to a ruler only under certain limiting conditions. In that case, the ruler might be obliged to respect these limits—and revolution might be justifed to enforce them (II.xiv.12). In the Grotian account, "consent" seems to allow wide leeway for varying approaches. Natural law is only, as he says, the "great-grandmother of municipal [that is, domestic] law" (Prolegomena, sec. 16). The extreme flexibility of this doctrine appealed to seventeenth-century English Whigs, who cited Grotius in their arguments against royal authority (given the special limitations which, they claimed, the English people had always insisted upon as the condition for their consent to royal rule).[7]

But the main point, of course, was to make credible the idea that one sovereign should not interfere with the rights of another and to make the outline of these rights clear enough to seem compelling—without resort to disputed religious or metaphysical claims. Grotius tried to disentangle the argument from medieval disputes by pointing at universal agreement as a sign of natural justice. He therefore drew most of his examples from the practice of pre-Christian Rome or other ancient cities. He was among the first writers to claim that treaties with Turks should be binding on the same terms as treaties with Christian powers.[8]

Grotius did speak of sovereign states as forming a kind of community or "great society" among themselves. But he seems to have intended far less by this phrase than modern scholars have sometimes attributed to it. From what is actually presented in *De jure*, sovereign states do not owe very much to each other. A modern critic, defending the Thomist version of natural law, complained that Grotius emphasized "sociability" almost to the exclusion of a "political" nature in men.[9] And the point has force. Grotian "society" does not seem to aim at much more than some restrictions on the violence of war.[10]

Grotius acknowledges, for example, that some practices, such as incest, may be universally recognized as evil. It follows that perpetrators deserve to be punished—that they have a "right" to be punished, as Grotius puts it—and, if civil laws do not provide otherwise, anyone has a natural authority to administer the merited punishment (II.xx.2). Following medieval doctrine on "just war," Grotius acknowledges that outside powers may justly attack and enslave whole peoples who commit such evils (or simply allow such evils to be perpetrated in their midst).[11] On this basis (again following medieval theologians), Grotius endorses the Spanish conquest of the Americas as just punishment for the crimes of the American natives (II.xx.40).

But Grotius then carefully limits the basis for such claims. Incest may justify "punitive" conquest (II.xx.42), but (contrary to the claims of some Spanish theologians) refusal to embrace Christianity cannot, since this is not universally recognized as evil (II.xx.48). Grotius offers what is a virtual parody of the medieval argument, insisting that only a general obligation to piety is universally acknowledged, so punitive war against the impious is only justified when a people disdains its own god or gods (rather than the god embraced by outsiders).

It also turns out that slavery and tyranny are not universally recognized as evil. These practices cannot therefore be classed among the "crimes" that would justify outside intervention. Wars of liberation are not justified (II.xxii.11; II.xxiv.6). In the main, the "society" of states has very limited aims when it comes to sustaining "social" or "communal" norms.[12]

Still, the "society" of states can maintain some rules, according to Grotius. The last book of *De jure* is devoted to the laws of war. So, far from prohibiting war, the Grotian scheme relies on war as the ultimate means by which a sovereign state enforces its rights. And by natural law, Grotius concedes, a victor in a just war may punish the people of the enemy state, along with enemy soldiers, killing them all or reducing them all to slavery (III.iv).

But Christian states have agreed to limit the ferocity of war and conventions of restraint can become binding law by the consent of all or almost all states. The concluding chapters of *De jure* are devoted to an enumeration of restraints (against sacking towns or killing prisoners or enslaving the defeated) which have now become accepted among European states (III.x–xii). In some cases, natural law can even be suspended in the interest of the society of states. Ambassadors may deserve to be punished for crimes committed in a host state but the practice of states reflects an overriding convention of immunity for diplomats (II.xviii).

In the course of expounding the laws of war, Grotius launched two doctrines of great importance in the subsequent development of the law of nations. Both reveal much about the character and basis of that law. First, *De jure* treats, concisely but with considerable moral dexterity, the rights of neutral powers (III.xvii.3). Grotius was indeed the first writer to make this a theme of inquiry.[13] The underlying assumption is that states are not obliged to come to the aid of the just side in war but may rightly look to their own interests and stay on the sidelines. A belligerent may seek to restrict neutral aid to an enemy state but cannot expect neutrals to cooperate with a blockade that is not enforced.

For similar reasons, no power has the right to claim dominion over the high seas, because no power can expect to enforce sovereign rights over such vast areas (II.iii.4 and 13). The "freedom of the seas" is another Grotian theme that became quite important in the subsequent development of international law. As with his analysis of neutral rights, the arguments Grotius offered for freedom of the seas are not very inspiring.[14] *De jure* tries to show that both doctrines are already implicit in existing practice, because the alternatives are widely recognized as too difficult to maintain. Both doctrines did, in fact, have enough support, even among major naval powers, to become well established in international practice over the next century. But the basis for this agreement remained somewhat obscure, even in the Grotian account.

In later generations, one school of self-avowed Grotians emphasized positive agreement among states as the sole basis for international law. Looking only to long-observed restraints as the sign of agreement, such writers as Bynkershoek, in the early eighteenth century, found only a few reliable legal norms in a few areas of international practice.[15]

Those writers who emphasized natural law also tended to interpret Grotius as offering a very restricted notion of the relevant law. In the late seventeenth century, the German scholar and diplomat, Samuel Pufendorf, tried to restate the rules of international law as pure deductions from a modernized version of natural law. His scheme was presented, quite explicitly, as a synthesis of Grotius and Hobbes, with no acknowledgment that there was anything incongruous in blending these two different authorities. In many ways, in fact, Hobbes seems to predominate in the synthesis, as Pufendorf continually stresses the self-interest of sovereign states.

So Pufendorf criticized the notion of universal crimes and repudiated Grotian justifications for Spanish conquests in the Americas. While acknowledging that states may use military force to coerce or intimidate other states, he denied that there can be, in the strict sense, "punishment" by one sovereign against another or by one sovereign against the subjects of another. He grounded this conclusion on the very Hobbesian premise that punishment implies a prior law and there can be no law laid down by one sovereign on those outside his own sovereignty.[16] Pufendorf even repudiated the notion that treaties need be observed, if the other party no longer has any strong incentive to honor its promise.[17] Yet Pufendorf was seen in his time as "the son of Grotius."[18]

CLASSICAL SYNTHESIS: VATTEL'S LAW OF NATIONS

In the mid-eighteenth century, the Swiss diplomat, Emmerich de Vattel, offered a seeming compromise between "naturalist" and "positivist" schools. His treatise was initially published in French in 1757, as *Le droit des gens, ou principes de la loi naturelle, appliqués à la conduite et aux affaires des nations et des souveraines* (The law of nations or the principles of natural law, applied to the conduct and affairs of nations and of sovereigns).[19] The title itself illustrates the somewhat complacent tone of the work in which natural law rests easily with "the conduct of affairs."

In almost every point of consequence, Vattel follows the new natural rights doctrines propounded by John Locke. Vattel's treatise won instant admiration in Britain where it was immediately translated into English and reprinted in successive editions for over a century.[20] It also won a great following in America. A new edition of Vattel's treatise was produced on the eve of the American Revolution. Its Dutch editor not only passed the work along to the first American envoys in Europe but became, himself, a journalistic champion and diplomatic agent for the struggling new nation across the Atlantic.[21] Vattel's treatise, itself, is thought to have inspired certain phrasings in both the American Declaration of Independence and the French Declaration of the Rights of Man and the Citizen.[22]

Vattel follows Locke most closely in attributing the authority of government to the consent of the governed. He scolds Grotius and Pufendorf for allowing a sovereign to alienate his authority to another prince, as if he were the owner and not merely the governing agent of his people (book I, chapter v, paragraph 61). He praises the constitutional arrangements in Britain where the king is restrained by an elected legislature—and where restraints on royal power have been enforced by popular revolution, as Vattel notes with warm approval (I.iv.51 and 54).

Vattel begins his international doctrine with a firm insistence on the equality of states, drawing out Lockeian premises in an argument which would later be given more succinct expression in the American Declaration of Independence:

Nations are composed of men who are by nature free and independent and who before the establishment of civil society lived together in the state of nature. . . . [S]uch nations or sovereign States must be regarded as so many free persons living together in the state of nature (I.iii.4). . . . It follows that nations are by nature equal and hold from nature the same obligations and the same rights. Strength or weakness, in this case, counts for nothing. A dwarf is as much a man as a giant is; a small Republic is no less a sovereign State than the most powerful Kingdom. (I.vii.18)

Meanwhile, Vattel gives an entirely Lockeian argument for repudiating any notion of an international community, above the authority of sovereign states:

It is essential to every civil society (civitas) that . . . there should be some authority capable of giving commands, prescribing laws and compelling those who refuse to obey. Such an idea is not to be thought of as between Nations. Each independent state claims to be and actually is independent of all the others. (Preface, 9a)

What there is instead is a law of nature. Locke's *Second Treatise of Government* had posited a "law of reason" in the state of nature, obliging "every one . . . as much as he can, to preserve the rest of mankind"—but only "when his own Preservation comes not in competition" (par. 6). So, according to Vattel, each nation "should contribute as far as it can to the happiness and advancement of other Nations" (I.vi.13). But Vattel immediately acknowledges that a nation's "duties to itself" clearly prevail over its duties toward others:

> the society of nations can not continue unless the rights which belong to each by nature are respected. No Nation is willing to give up its liberty. . . . In consequence of that liberty and independence it follows that it is for each Nation to decide what its conscience demands of it, what it can or can not do; what it thinks well or does not think well to do; and therefore it is for each Nation to consider and determine what duties it can fulfill towards others without failing in its duty toward itself. (I.vi.14 and 16)

How can these doctrines sustain a law of nations that is really law? Vattel distinguishes sharply between two kinds or categories of law. There is an internal law of nations, based on the fundamental principles of natural law, which is binding on the conscience of sovereigns. As such, Vattel calls it the "necessary" law. But it is "necessary" only in the sense that it derives from moral or logical necessities. There is, on the other hand, an "external law" which Vattel sometimes describes as "the positive law of nations." Its most important branches are a "customary" law of positive practices, to which nations have given "tacit consent" by continual repetition and a "conventional law" based on treaties to which nations have given "express consent."

When there is a conflict between the "necessary" and the "external law," Vattel endorses the latter. There is, for example, a natural duty to make commerce available under the necessary law. Under the external law, however, each state has an accepted right to impose monopolies and restrict access of other states to its own ports, if it so chooses (II.ii). Quite a few commentators have complained that Vattel covers harsh realities with soothing or sentimental rhetoric.[23]

Yet his treatise had an immense influence for well over a century.[24] In regard to the conduct of actual governments, it was far more influential than the treatises of Grotius or Pufendorf or any previous writer on the subject. It was the first work on international law to be widely consulted and cited by diplomats and government officials in the ordinary course of negotiations. It was widely cited, as well, by national courts facing disputed questions of international law. No single work has ever achieved as much prominence.

The success of Vattel's treatise at the time may be attributable, in part, to the wider range of diplomatic practices that it described, compared with previous works. Vattel had a good deal of diplomatic experience (though no formal training in law) and used his experience to good effect. But the success of the treatise was also a matter of style or outlook. Vattel's version of natural law has the optimistic tone of the eighteenth-century *philosophes*. Vattel edifies readers with frequent appeals to the obligations of "virtue" or "self-perfection." He tends to gloss over tensions between such moral claims and the underlying demands of self-interest, for which he always makes allowances.

Though Vattel acknowledged and often praised the work of his predecessors, no reader can escape the sense that Vattel was addressing a different world. Grotius and Pufendorf did not try to conceal the harsh logic of war. Both largely relied on examples from ancient histories to prove the enduring force of their arguments, which meant that the ferocity of ancient war was always in full view. Vattel wrote much more about commerce and diplomacy and drew almost entirely on modern examples, which gave his treatise a kind of worldliness and allowed him to treat the progress of more recent times as an irreversible achievement. Vattel no longer struggled to give philosophic credibility to his underlying claim, that a world of entirely sovereign states is still a world that can sustain certain sorts of restraints or courtesies in their interactions. By the mid-eighteenth century, the claim did not greatly trouble most of his readers because it already seemed to be confirmed by experience.

Major European wars were less devastating in the eighteenth century in large part because they were conducted more professionally. Drilled armies carried their own supplies and tried to avoid the sorts of depredations that would turn localities against them. Only a few years after the first appearance of Vattel's treatise, Adam Smith noted that local farmers and merchants in many places regarded the appearance of foreign armies as a potential source of profit and therefore welcomed the advent of war as a promise of economic advantage.[25] Kings calculated their interests more closely, so that nations switched alliances from one decade to the next. They thus tried to preserve diplomatic niceties, even with current enemies, since today's enemies might be a valued ally in the next round.

The laws of war, as they had come to be accepted in the eighteenth century, had roots in medieval chivalry. The underlying aim was to make war less destructive, but not necessarily less frequent. Gentlemen officers thus accepted each other's "parole"—their word as gentlemen—not to escape when captured by an opposing army. On that basis, officers were often allowed to move freely in the towns to which they were taken as prisoners of war. The practice was still recognized, as late as 1907, in the "rules of land warfare," agreed to at the Hague Peace Conference.[26]

So, too, it was generally accepted by the eighteenth century that in war at sea, naval forces of the belligerent powers must respect the rights of neutral commerce. Seizures of ships and cargoes were a standard part of naval warfare, but owners of seized property could appeal to national prize courts for compensation, if property had been taken in violation of the accepted rules. Protection in war time was also accorded to property that had already been delivered to a foreign territory. Treaties commonly specified that, at the outbreak of war, a merchant from an enemy state should be accorded a six-month grace period to sell his inventory, so that war would not become a pretext for outright expropriation.[27]

War was surrounded with courtesy and ritual and restraints, which regulated many aspects of war—but not the ultimate decision on whether to resort to war. Vattel suggests that minor disputes should be submitted to arbitration, so as to avoid unnecessary conflict. He acknowledges, however, that nations will not submit their most vital interests to outside determination, so the decision to go to war will remain, in the last resort, a national decision (II.xviii.334).

From a later perspective, one might see the pretense of law or rules in this setting as sheer hypocrisy, providing a civilized face on a brutal reality. The eighteenth-century version of the law of nations did provoke great disgust among some serious thinkers at the time. They voiced objections that are still heard. What the dissenters did not provide, in the view of the American Founders, was a plausible alternative.

EIGHTEENTH CENTURY DOUBTS—AND CONFIRMATIONS

The most famous voice of protest was raised by Jean-Jacques Rousseau. Of course, Rousseau was indignant about much more than the laws of war. He was, in some ways, incensed against the whole spirit of the Enlightenment. But Rousseau's most famous work, *The Social Contract*, is described in the opening pages as merely one section from a larger work that was not completed. That larger work, it is thought, was intended as a reply to Vattel's treatise.

Several pages that Rousseau prepared for the *Social Contract* were not included in the published text, but have been preserved in another form.[28] In these pages, Rousseau seems to attack sovereignty from both directions. In the name of safeguarding property within each state, sovereign authority actually perpetuates extremes of inequality. In the name of ordering relations between states, sovereignty becomes a shield for calculated aggressions. Both at home and abroad, doctrines of sovereignty offer a pretense of legality to what is really unbounded selfishness:

> I open the books on right and on ethics . . . and moved by their ingratiating discourses I deplore the miseries of nature, I admire the peace and justice established by civil order. . . . Fully instructed about my duties and happiness, I close the book, leave the class-room and look around me; I see unfortunate people groaning under an iron yoke, mankind crushed by a handful of oppressors, starving masses overwhelmed by

pain and hunger, whose blood and tears the rich drink in peace. . . . I raise my eyes and look afar. I see fires and flames, countrysides deserted, towns sacked. . . . I see a scene of murders, ten thousand men slaughtered, everywhere the image of death and dying. So this is the fruit of these peaceful institutions! . . . Ah, barbarous philosopher! read us your book on a battlefield!

In Rousseau's account, the law of nations is a fraud. Appealing to calculations of self-interest among sovereign states, it cannot restrain sovereigns who find a larger interest in aggression. And because it rests so directly on the spirit of self-interest, the law of nations does not even exert a genuine moral force, because it has no genuine moral appeal:

> As for what is commonly called the law of nations, it is certain that, for want of sanction, its laws are nothing but chimeras even weaker than the law of nature. This latter at least speaks to the heart of individuals, whereas the law of nations having no other guarantee than its utility to the one who submits to it, its decisions are respected only as long as self-interest confirms them.[29]

Rousseau acknowledges, however, that "the perfection of the social order consists in the union of force and law"—that is, in a just notion of "sovereignty." In the just order, "law must guide force" rather than allowing "force alone [to] speak . . . in the guise of law."[30]

The *Social Contract*, in its published version, gives one way of achieving this order. To ensure that there is no gulf between the demands of justice and the temptations of interest, sovereignty must remain entirely in the hands of the citizen body—and it must be all-encompassing. In this radical version of the social contract, all private property and all personal rights are initially ceded to the collective body and only returned to individuals on terms approved by the sovereign. And what is done by the sovereign, according to Rousseau, cannot be unjust, because the sovereign expresses the general will of the entire citizen body, to which each individual citizen has submitted his own will.

The American Founders rejected such an extreme notion of sovereignty. James Madison defended constitutional checks on democracy on the grounds that "no Society ever did or can consist of so homogeneous a mass of Citizens" as "theoretic writers . . . assume or suppose" in contending for a "simple Democracy or a pure republic." Among other things, the "diversity of the faculties of men" is "an insuperable obstacle to a uniformity of interests," but "protection of these faculties"— "from which the rights of property originate"—is "the first object of government."[31]

Defending a notion of natural rights against sovereignty at home, the

American Founders could acknowledge some force to limits on sovereignty from abroad: Both domestic property rights and the competing claims of other sovereigns could appeal to some notion of natural rights apart from the will of any one sovereign. By contrast, Rousseau's *Social Contract* never explains how the sovereign will of one body of citizens can be restrained—as a matter of law—in its dealings with another. If each state must acknowledge legal limits in its dealings with other states, then the citizens of each state must acknowledge that some law is not the product of their own general will. But Rousseau is extremely insistent that all law must emanate from the general will of the citizens—the citizens of each individual state, who can think of the law as an expression of their own wills, because they have identified so closely with their own community. From this doctrine, there seems no path to international law.

The very last chapter of the *Social Contract* acknowledges that a full account would "buttress the State" with expositions of "the law of nations" and "the law of war and conquests . . . treaties, etc." But Rousseau concedes, "all this forms a new object too vast for my short sight."[32]

In a subsequent work, when Rousseau returned to the theme of uniting force and law in relations between states, he dropped this entire account of sovereignty and law at home. In commenting on the proposals of the Abbé St. Pierre, he seemed to endorse the idea of a European federation, guaranteeing each state against territorial aggression and domestic rebellion. He may have treated the proposal with more respect than he felt, because he had taken up the editing of St. Pierre's work at the request of the abbe's family. Still, Rousseau's *jugement* insists that the scheme is entirely in the interest of existing princes and would succeed if only it were tried.[33] He says nothing about the scheme's inherent problems from the standpoint of his own prior work on citizen sovereignty.

The omission was not lost on later readers worried about the requirements of republican government. James Madison was again among the most trenchant critics in an essay published in 1792 on the theme of "Universal Peace." By affording guarantees equally to oppressive monarchies and genuine republics, Madison protested, Rousseau's scheme would have the "tendency" to "perpetuate arbitrary power wherever it existed." Insofar as it could guarantee security to every government, it would "cut off the only source of consolation remaining to the oppressed"—that is, the hope of sucessful rebellion, helped along, perhaps, by military aid from outside powers in a larger war. Heir to a successful revolution, Madison did not miss the connection between war and revolution—and therefore did not miss the threat that, for oppressed people, a guarantee of universal peace might mean "extinguishing the hope of one day seeing an end of oppression."[34]

Meanwhile, Rousseau's contemporary and one-time patron, the Scottish philosopher David Hume, offered a more general argument against an international guarantor of peace. Hume's position was, in effect, an endorsement of the mid-eighteenth-century version of international law or at least of its grounding assumptions. The arguments are of particular interest because Hume was a thinker often cited—and with approval—by the American Founders (and one who, in his last years, expressed sympathy with the American rebellion).

Born and educated in Scotland, when Scottish independence was still a living memory and a stirring cause for many Scots, Hume had also enjoyed years of travel and study in Europe. He was not at all an extreme nationalist. He deprecated wars based on national hatred or ancient grievances. Nonetheless, Hume devoted one of his famous political essays to an emphatic defense of a foreign policy aimed at "preserving" a European "balance of power." Such a policy, he argued, was "founded so much on common sense and obvious reasoning" that its underlying "maxim" must always have been recognized. He thought voluntary, defensive alliances—the staple of British statecraft in the eighteenth century—could prevent any one power from gaining complete ascendancy in Europe. True, the Roman Empire had once maintained such ascendancy, but that was in an age when "mankind were generally in a very disorderly, uncivilized condition." In modern conditions, Hume argued, vast empires would be "destructive to human nature" and "their downfall . . . never can be very distant from their establishment."[35]

So Hume expected Europe to remain divided into separate nations and he regarded this division of political authority as highly beneficial. He did not expect independent nations to retreat behind sealed borders. He strongly commended the benefits of international trade and disparaged contemporary concerns about maintaining a favorable "balance of trade." Britain, he insisted, would not be impoverished by the growing wealth of its neighbors but enriched by the greater opportunities for trade.[36] His writing on trade was elaborated by his friend and disciple Adam Smith.

While defending private trade across boundaries, however, Hume still defended national independence—and presented exchange and independence as, in effect, two sides of the same coin. In his essay on "Progress in the Arts and Sciences," he lauded the benefits of a continent divided into many states: "The emulation which naturally arises among those neighboring states, is an obvious source of improvement: But what I would chiefly insist on is the stop which such limited territories give both to *power* and to *authority*" (original emphasis).[37] Hume was an early advocate of the idea that competition leads to "progress."

Hume was quite aware that "progress" in some areas may cast a dark shadow in others. In his essay on "Refinement in the Arts," Hume notes that in the fifteenth century, the king of France exhausted all his revenues in a campaign into Italy with 20,000 men, while French kings of the eighteenth century deployed twenty times as many men under arms. The "difference . . . in the power and grandeur of . . . kingdoms . . . can be ascribed to nothing but the increase of art and industry."[38]

But Hume did not question "progress" because it allowed for the financing of longer or wider wars. He emphasized instead the connection between material progress and freedom: "progress in the arts is rather favourable to liberty and has a natural tendency to preserve, if not produce a free government." He argued that gains in productivity had allowed the peasantry of another era to "become rich and independent" and allowed for "tradesmen and merchants to acquire a share of property"; over time, these effects of economic progress delivered "authority and consideration to that middling rank of men, who are the best and firmest basis of public liberty."[39] Hume thus endorsed arrangements that gave governments an incentive to foster trade—to increase their own strength—and then gave participants in trade the means to restrain their own governments with "free constitutions."

Such arguments did not satisfy those with higher moral ambitions— or higher hopes for "progress." Only a few decades later, the Prussian philosopher Immanuel Kant resounded Rousseau's protest against a world in which war remained a plausible remedy for national grievances. Like Rousseau, whom he follows in so much of his moral philosophy, Kant dismissed the great exponents of international right as mere apologists for power. In his famous essay, *Perpetual Peace*, Kant specifically mentions Grotius, Pufendorf, and Vattel as "sorry apologists."[40] Their doctrines still leave sovereign nations in a state of nature with each other, where war will be a constant temptation to gain advantage or even a seemingly rational response to insecurity. Only an international federation, which can outlaw war by guaranteeing members against invasion, will ensure lasting peace.

Like Rousseau—indeed like all sovereignty theorists beginning with Bodin and Hobbes—Kant acknowledges that a peacekeeping federation must unite force with law. It is not enough to sign treaties or conventions against war. It is necessary to put force at the disposal of the peacekeepers. Hence, there must be a federation of states which has more force at its disposal than any one member.

Kant himself acknowledges that this plan may seem hopelessly visionary. So he turns to Hume's insight regarding trade and then turns it on itself: By enriching nations, commerce makes war more costly because it extends the resources at the disposal of competing states. Citizens dependent on commerce will not tolerate the financial costs of war. So over time, progress makes for peace because, "The spirit of commerce . . . cannot exist side by side with war."[41] At least, the needs of commerce will constrain resort to war if the citizenry has any say in the matter. Kant thus stipulates that lasting peace depends on the advent of republican governments, accountable to their people, at least to some extent.[42]

Yet the insistence that peace depends on republican government points to a different problem: How is republican government in each state consistent with ultimate control in the federation? Kant acknowledges the underlying problem. A republic draws on the loyalty of its citizens to what is their own. A higher federation undermines this sense of loyalty. It poses the danger of a "soulless despotism" where, instead of the competitive energy of Hume's balance of power, citizens are passive—or rebellious: "laws progressively lose their impact as the government increases its range, and a soulless despotism, after crushing the germs of goodness, will finally lapse into anarchy."[43]

Kant's answer is to insist that the federation will have control only over questions of war and peace but not over internal matters. One gets a sense of this from his preliminary articles of peace—a sort of transition to the federation. There is a "cosmopolitan right" of "hospitality" that echoes Pufendorf in truncating the notion to the most minimal obligation: Nations should not kill those who are shipwrecked on their shores—but they have no obligation to take in outsiders and certainly have no wider obligation to assist those in distress in other nations.[44] There is not even a suggestion that the international community (or the ultimate federation) will guarantee or define republican government.[45]

Kant insists that his proposed federation "would not be the same thing as an international state." The "federation does not aim to acquire any power like that of a state, but merely to preserve and secure the *freedom* [original emphasis] of each state in itself . . . this does not mean that [states belonging to this federation] need to submit to public laws and to a coercive power which enforces them, as do men in a state of nature."[46] Men in the state of nature require an actual government to clarify, in detail, what they can and cannot do. States do not require a superstate to govern their own activities, but merely some limited structure to maintain peace.

Not the least of the utopian elements in Kant's vision is the notion that an international federation can be endowed with sufficient power to ensure peace but then somehow be constrained from interfering in the internal affairs of the member states. Kant, himself, expresses hesitation or ambivalence about whether such a federation would actually be sufficient to maintain peace. The restricted authority of the peace federation would not be full sovereignty, yet full sovereignty, Kant acknowledges, might be the only way to peace.[47]

A limited peace federation remains the best hope, Kant concludes, because individual states will not cede their own sovereignty to a federation of all states. Since a peace federation might be feasible, statesmen must act on the belief that it will be accomplished. Acting otherwise, Kant insists, would be a betrayal of moral duty. Kant launched a form of moralism which still inspires many advocates today—and still remains very hard to reconcile with responsible statesmanship.

The vision held out by Kant was not unknown to the Framers of the American Constitution. They could not have read Kant's actual essay, published in German (a language few of them had mastered) eight years after the Philadelphia Convention. Yet the American Founders were not indifferent to the hope embraced by Kant. Quite explicit consideration is given to this vision, in fact, in central passages of *The Federalist*.

The Federalist defends the role of the federal government as a peacemaker among the states. It also defends the constitutional guarantee of "a republican form of government" in each state, as a necessary condition for peaceful and stable relations among the states. In the central paper of the whole series, No. 43, *The Federalist* raises the possibility of civil war within a state.

In such circumstances, "the representatives of the confederate States," because they were "not heated by the local flame," could offer the "impartiality of judges," yet as members of the same confederacy, they could still "unite the affection of friends." The thought is so pleasing that it leads immediately to a larger reflection: "Happy would it be if such a remedy for its [sic] infirmities could be enjoyed by all free governments; if a project equally effectual could be established for the universal peace of mankind."

It says something about their philosophic assumptions that the American Founders could see the appeal of a "project" for "universal peace." It says more that they did not take it very seriously. Immediately after this passage, *The Federalist* takes up the question of "an insurrection pervading all the states"—that is, an insurrection against republican government—and replies without hesitation that such a calamity "would be without the compass of human remedy." It is "a calamity for which no possible constitution can provide a cure." The argument dismisses out of hand any possibility that an international structure could somehow provide guarantees for the maintainence of republican government within each nation.

A later paper (also by Madison) explains why: "a power independent of the society may as well espouse the unjust views of the major as the rightful interest of the minor party and may possibly be turned against both parties."[48] If Americans cannot devise a constitutional scheme of their own to ensure republican government, they cannot trust to outside powers to assure it for them.

As to "projects for universal peace," Madison himself (the author of No. 43) addressed the issue, as we have seen, only a few years later in a newspaper article on the subject. War, he acknowledges, "contains so much folly, as well as wickedness, that much is to be hoped from the progress of reason"—but not enough to assure a "universal and perpetual peace," which, "it is to be feared . . . will never exist but in the imaginations of visionary philosophers, or in the breasts of benevolent enthusiasts."[49] The reason why this is so, evidently, is that, in the last resort, independent republics cannot trust to others to determine their rights, without forfeiting their independence.

The same paper of *The Federalist* that raises the "happy" dream of universal peace through international arbitration ends with a reminder that without a federal Constitution to establish a common force, the American states will have nothing more reliable to hold them together than a treaty. This is insufficient, *The Federalist* argues, because a treaty can be repudiated by any signatory which regards others as having violated its terms. There are no reliable contracts in the state of nature, where there is no common sovereignty to enforce them.

So "universal and perpetual peace" is not likely to arrive until there is a universal power to enforce the conditions of peace. And *The Federalist* takes it for granted that Americans will not agree to submit to such a power. Probably the American Founders also took for granted Hume's contention, that at some point, government on a vast scale could not be sustained. Probably they accepted Kant's own worry, that a world-state would degenerate into a "soulless despotism." At any rate, the need to keep international law within bounds was a central topic of concern in the debates over the new Constitution.

Founding Debates

At the outset of the Philadelphia Convention, Edmund Randolph of Virginia presented a plan to replace the existing confederation of the states with a strong national government. Supported by Madison and others in the Virginia delegation, it became known as "the Virginia Plan" and dominated almost all subsequent deliberations. The gist of the plan was to firmly establish the sovereignty of the national government, so that the national government could not only impose peace in the quarrels between states or within states, but also enforce state compliance with national standards. The plan would even have authorized the national legislature "to negative all laws passed by the several States, contravening in the opinion of the National Legislature the articles of Union."

Randolph offered many arguments to justify this plan. The striking

fact is that nearly half of his arguments rested on international considerations. Only a strong national government could stand up for the United
States in disputes with other nations. As it was, Randolph complained,
the confederation could not impose a common tariff and could not develop effective "counteraction of the commercial regulations of other nations." Since the confederation lacked effective control over the states,
moreover, it "could not cause infractions of treaties or of the law of nations, to be punished."[50] Substantially the same argument was repeated
by many defenders of the new Constitution in subsequent ratification debates. It is also the theme of the first four papers of *The Federalist*
(following the introductory remarks in No. 1).[51]

The text of the Constitution, as it finally emerged from the Philadelphia Convention, does indeed provide Congress with the power to "define and punish offenses against the law of nations" (Art. I, Sec. 8). The
supremacy clause, in Article VI, provides that, along with the Constitution itself and federal laws, treaties shall be "the supreme law of the
land; and the judges in every state shall be bound thereby, anything in the
Constitution or Law of any State to the contrary notwithstanding."

In a general way, these provisions were supposed to ensure that the
United States, as a sovereign power, would be able and willing to take
part in international transactions on a plane of equality with other sovereign powers. The United States could make treaties and ensure that
they were respected by its own states and citizens—and therefore demand
that other parties to treaties do the same. The United States could also
ensure compliance with its own obligations under the customary or
unwritten law of nations and therefore demand that others fulfill their
obligations to the United States.

But how far could such obligations extend? Toward the close of the
Convention, the delegates debated the precise wording of the provision
on "offenses against the law of nations." Should the provision give Congress power to "define" such "offenses" or merely to prescribe standards
for American efforts "to punish" these "offenses"? James Wilson—
subsequently a justice of the Supreme Court and author of the first extended survey on American law—admonished his fellow delegates that
"the law of nations . . . depended on the authority of all the Civilized Nations of the World." For the United States "to pretend to *define* the law
of nations" on its own "would have a look of arrogance that would make
us look ridiculous." But Gouverneur Morris noted that the relevant law
was "often too vague and deficient to be a rule." The Convention voted,
by a slim majority, to leave Congress with power "to define" as well as to
"punish." So the United States would punish only its own version or its
own understanding of "offenses against the law of nations."[52]

Antifederalists were not slow to turn this ambiguity around. Was it not true that the "law of nations" accommodated many exceptions? A critic at the Virginia ratifying convention noted, "It is part of the law of several Oriental nations to receive no Ambassadors and to burn their prisoners. It is a custom with the Grand Seignoir [the Turkish sultan] to receive but not to send Ambassadors. It is a particular custom with him to put the Russian Ambassador in the seven towers." In response to the assurance of a Federalist delegate, that there could not be a "particular law of nations" unique to particular states, the Antifederalist delegate pressed home his challenge: "I beg leave to tell him that the United States are entering into a particular law of nations now."[53] No assurance, therefore, could be drawn from the general law of nations. Smaller nations in Europe had made many concessions by treaty, which seemed contrary to the general law of nations. "Cannot Congress give up the Mississippi also by treaty, though such cession would deprive us of a right to which, by the law of nations, we are unalienably and indefeasibly entitled? I lay it down as a principle, that nations can, as well as individuals, renounce any particular right."[54]

The critics thus centered their fire on what seemed an open-ended treaty power. Patrick Henry raised the case of the Russian ambassador to England in the early eighteenth century. When he was improperly arrested by an English police official, the Czar demanded that the official be sent to Russia for immediate execution. Queen Anne personally wrote to the Czar that such a thing could not be allowed under the laws of England and the laws of England therefore prevented her from complying. But with an open-ended treaty power in the new Constitution, what would prevent the president of the United States from currying favor with a foreign power by handing over Americans?

> We may be told that we shall find ample refuge in the law of nations. When you yourselves have your necks so low that the President may dispose of your rights as he pleases, the law of nations cannot be applied to relieve you. Sure I am if treaties are made, infringing our liberties, it will be too late to say that our constitutional rights are violated.[55]

The argument was pressed with a more recent example from British practice. The king was not authorized to dismember the empire by simple treaty. It had required a parliamentary measure, equivalent to a constitutional amendment, to acknowledge the independence of the American colonies. How, then, could the Americans leave to the president or the president and Senate an unrestricted treaty power? Other critics noted that treaties in Europe had tied countries to respect a particular succession in their monarchies and particular concessions of other kinds. What would prevent the treaty power from being exercised in ways that would subvert the American Constitution?

Defenders of the new Constitution dismissed such concerns. Federalist delegates at the Virginia ratifying convention insisted that treaties would have to be consistent with the Constitution. One delegate disputed the idea that "treaties made under this Constitution are to be the supreme law . . . paramount to the Constitution itself and the laws of Congress. It is as clear as that two and two make four that the treaties made are to be binding on the States only"[56]—implying that Congress and the president could always override an improper treaty. Madison, calling this construction "rational," invoked broader principles:

> I do not conceive that power is given to the President and Senate to dismember the empire or alienate any great essential right. . . . I do not think the whole Legislative authority [of the federal government] have this power. The exercise of power must be consistent with the object of the delegation. . . . The object of treaties is the regulation of intercourse with foreign nations and is external.

Madison then offered an additional argument. In Britain, royal authority was restrained by Parliament in domestic affairs. But the king was allowed broad authority to negotiate treaties, on the assumption that, in dealings with foreign nations, his own self-interest would coincide with British national interests. The same reasoning should apply to an American government: "It is to be presumed, that in transactions with foreign countries, those who regulate them, will feel the whole force of national attachment to their own country. The contrast being between their own nations and a foreign nation, is it not presumable they will, as far as possible, advance the interest of their own country?"[57]

But Antifederalists were not satisfied with such assurances. They urged that if such a broad power had to be given to the federal government, it ought to be carefully guarded. George Mason proposed a requirement that treaties receive three-quarters approval from both the House and the Senate. Several state conventions urged that the Constitution be amended to impose similar safeguards on the treaty power.[58] What they got instead was a federal Bill of Rights.

But does the Bill of Rights and the rest of the Constitution take precedence over the treaty power? Early commentators certainly thought so. Alexander Hamilton, for example, acknowledged, as a necessary "exception to the power of making treaties," that a treaty "shall not change the Constitution; which results from this fundamental maxim, that a delegated authority cannot alter the constituting act. . . . An agent cannot new model his own commission."[59] Supreme Court Justice Joseph Story, in his *Commentaries on the Constitution*, elaborated the implications of this argument: "A treaty to change the organization of the government, to annihilate its sovereignty, to change its republican form, or to deprive it of its constitutional powers, would be void."[60]

American commentators on the law of nations also insisted that such conflicts—between the government's obligations under international law and its limitations under the U.S. Constitution—were most unlikely to arise. James Kent's *Commentaries on American Law*, among the foremost reference works of American lawyers down to the end of the nineteenth century, began with an extended discussion of the law of nations, emphasizing just this point. Paraphrasing Vattel (and the Declaration of Independence), Kent's account draws out the implications of the "natural" equality of nations:

> Nations are equal in respect to each other. . . . This perfect equality, and entire independence of all distinct states, is a fundamental principle of public [international] law. It is a necessary consequence of this equality, that each nation has a right to govern itself as it may think proper and no one nation is entitled to dictate a form of government, or religion, or a course of internal policy, to another. No state is entitled to take cognizance or notice of the domestic administration of another state or what passes within it as between the government and its own subjects.[61]

Kent drew most of his exposition from European treatises, summarizing accepted practices among European states. But he warned that it would be "improper to separate this law entirely from natural jurisprudence and not consider it as deriving much of its force and dignity from the . . . law of nature"[62]—including the background principle, establishing each nation's right to exclude outside interference in its "internal policy."

Henry Wheaton's *Elements of International Law* (1836) was the first full-length American treatise on the subject and it managed to achieve wide recognition even in Europe. Wheaton emphasized that "one or two treaties varying from the general usage and custom of nations cannot alter the international law," which he defined as "rules of conduct . . . consonant to justice" and consistent with "the nature of the society existing among independent nations."[63] On the eve of the Civil War, W. H. Halleck's treatise drew the moral most explicitly: Could a treaty "stipulation make it lawful" for an outside power to undertake "inteference" in the domestic affairs of another state? "We think not; for the reason that a contract against public morals has no binding force and there is more merit in its breach than in its fulfillment."[64]

THE LAW OF NATIONS AS A LIBERAL PROJECT

For all their cautions, the founding generation of American statesmen—and their successors in the following generations—remained quite respectful toward the "law of nations." Part of the reason is obvious.

Americans were launching a new nation, which was still vulnerable to encroachments from great powers in Europe. Naturally, they embraced a scheme that seemed to recognize the equal claim of every sovereign state to govern itself by its own lights.

But the attraction had deeper roots, too. At the time of the American founding and for generations thereafter, the law of nations was conceived as a special application of natural law principles. Vattel and his early American followers depict independent nations as co-existing in a state of nature, claiming the natural rights of individuals in that condition. As Jefferson put it, "The moral duties which exist between individual and individual in a state of nature, accompany them into a state of society and the aggregrate of the duties of all the individuals composing the society constitute the duties of that society toward any other."[65]

It was not merely a familiar metaphor but a useful one for a country committed to a liberal scheme of constitutional politics at home. John Locke's *Second Treatise of Government* had cited the relations of sovereign states as a continuing model for the state of nature.[66] Locke invokes this model to make credible his claim that individuals have rights "by nature," even where there is no larger framework of social obligation. The argument seeks to demonstrate that more extensive obligations cannot be imposed in the name of nature but must rest on consent. So, for followers of Locke's doctrine, the disconnectedness of nations stands as a continuing reminder that constitutional authority at home is a distinctive authority.

On the other hand, constitutional authority at home is a limited authority. It is limited in its claims regarding divine worship or religion. It is limited in its claims regarding private property. Locke insists that there is private property and a medium of exchange even in the state of nature, so the establishment of civil authority can be seen as a safeguard for rights that already exist and must, to some extent, continue to remain a matter of private control.

If government has limited claims, citizens can retain interests or concerns distinct from those of the government. A citizen has important ties with fellow citizens, as they all share the benefits and obligations of the same government. But each citizen may have other concerns and interests, connecting him with citizens of other states. Adherents of a particular faith may feel ties to those of the same faith in other countries. Merchants may have ties to merchants in other countries. Indeed, through such commerce, a whole range of producers and consumers may be linked across national boundaries.

The law of nations, as early American statesmen knew it, was quite accommodating to these implications of limited government. It abstracted from religion, so that a state's rights and obligations had no connection, in principle, with the predominant faith of its citizens (or even the faith formally established, within its domain, by its own government). The law of nations also sought to protect private property. The law of war was centrally concerned with limiting interference with ocean commerce and with private property in land wars. It aimed to ensure that war did not degenerate into total war, so that private life could continue despite conflicts among governments.

The classical scheme did not imagine an end to war. On the contrary, it relied on war as the ultimate means by which a nation would enforce its rights. But this meant that, ultimately, rights were settled in trial by combat—not a very reliable arbiter of legal disputes. One could hope that a clear-cut aggression would provoke other states to rally to the side of the victim. But all commentators, from Grotius onwards, were agreed that no third party was obligated to assist a victim state.

Under the circumstances, weaker states were bound to seek protectors and protectors would not always be bound to treat their dependents with scrupulous respect. Indeed, a larger power might offer special "protection" with the threat of something more menacing if a weaker neighbor did not accept the offered "assistance." A formerly independent territory could end up as a "protectorate." Special treaties could then, as the American Founders recognized, establish special exceptions from the general rules.

What the general law of nations offered was a set of baseline standards, against which particular disputes might be judged. In effect, it set out conditions for acceptable exchange in peace and mutually acceptable restraint in war, with the implicit threat that violations would trigger responses in kind. If the general doctrine abstracted from important aspects of life, much the same could be said about a domestic scheme of rights in which the rich and poor, the skilled and the uneducated, the new immigrant and the heir of old stock, were thought to stand on an equal footing with formal guarantees of equal rights before the law.

Stephen Krasner, a scholar of international relations, has recently called attention to the many exceptions to the legalist understanding of sovereignty that found their way into international treaties in the nineteenth century and the early twentieth century. European powers insisted on inserting treaty clauses obligating the Ottomans to respect the rights of their Christian subjects, as later, they required newly independent states in eastern Europe to protect the civic rights of their own ethnic or religious minorities—with western powers claiming some protective rights in the background over these subjects or citizens of other states.[67] But the fact is that, as Krasner's own account indicates, western powers had little disposition to enforce such protections for citizens of other nations and local governments found them easy to shake off.

The general doctrine of the law of nations, with its emphasis on the sovereignty and equality of states, appealed especially to liberal states, interested in fostering trade and not at all sympathetic to great schemes of transnational ordering. As late as the mid-nineteenth century, a survey of international law scholarship found that almost all the leading texts were written by Protestants in trading states.[68] It is only a slight exaggeration to say that the main development was by Anglophone or Anglophile writers.

The resistance or hesitation of others is not hard to understand. Napoleon Bonaparte, who styled himself emperor of the French but dreamed of becoming a new emperor of the west, sought to establish dependent and kindred regimes throughout Europe. In the wake of his defeat, the old dynastic empires, in Austria, Russia, and Prussia, sought for a time to make dynastic legitimacy a touchstone of international respectability (and conversely, to authorize international intervention to resist or reverse liberal revolutions). Britain preferred to trade with all and not to let itself become entangled in such schemes. It was the British view that generally prevailed in the diplomatic practice of the nineteenth century. And the British view was also the American view. Notions of a "Concert of Europe," by which great powers could commit even the smaller states, lingered in diplomatic practice at international conferences, but not in the doctrines of treatise writers—and certainly not in American understandings.

For all its limitations, nineteeth century diplomacy was remarkably effective in what it set out to do. Goods could be shipped almost anywhere. Letters could be delivered with stamps paid at the point of origin, telegrams sent in the same way. Merchants, scholars, even tourists could travel freely and with considerable security throughout Europe and through much of the rest of the world. This network of open trade and communication rested to a large extent on treaties, built on the system of mutual concessions and equality of states and on the underlying premise that conflicts among states need not hinder communication among private citizens. The British navy even succeeded in suppressing the centuries-old slave trade—though, characteristically, through treaties which focused on international shipping and rights of seizure on the high seas.[69]

This network of treaties and shared understandings still assumed, however, that states remained the ultimate source of rights and duties. A foreign citizen, mistreated by a host state, was obliged to appeal—as a matter of international law—to his home state, because only another state could assert "rights" under international law. Krasner's exceptions remained exceptional and largely ineffective, because outside states were rarely concerned enough to insist on respect for individuals who were not their own nationals. At the same time, states found ways (as they always found reasons) to try to evade outside interference in their dealings with their own citizens.

For people mistreated by their own government, outside protection may seem appealing. Where government rests on a genuine scheme of constitutional limitations and electoral accountability, however, most citizens are much less likely to favor interventions by outside powers in their internal system of government. For this reason, as for other reasons, the classical conception of the law of nations—as a law built on the rights of sovereign states—remained especially congenial to liberal states in the nineteenth century. For Americans, the attractions of a strong notion of sovereignty were hardly diminished in the course of the twentieth century, as the next chapter will show.

CHAPTER FIVE

DIPLOMACY OF INDEPENDENCE

IN THE ERA of global governance, the United States has frequently seemed to be the odd man out. It takes part in negotiations for great new projects—an international criminal court, global controls on carbon use, global protections for women and for children and for endangered species of plants and animals. And then the United States declines to sign or ratify the resulting international convention. To the fury of many Europeans, the United States seems to treat international negotiations as an a la carte menu, from which it can take the tasty bits and leave the rest to spoil.

Critics often attribute this conduct to the arrogance of a superpower. A superpower surely does find it easier to insist on its own preferences. But the United States insisted on an independent posture in world affairs even when it was a young nation, with little military strength.

The United States asserted its independence in 1776, relying on a certain doctrine of international law, which presupposed a certain vision of international affairs. It was a vision of international law and international affairs compatible with American notions of constitutional government at home.[1] Down to the present day, this vision has exerted great force on American policy.

In the twentieth century, there were important changes, but they were generally viewed by Americans as exceptional responses to exceptional circumstances. During the "long twilight struggle" of the Cold War era, so many seeming exceptions accumulated that analysts of foreign policy assumed the United States had irrevocably abandoned its historic postures. But the older tradition is anchored in the American Constitution and in American constitutional culture. It was never entirely buried and has now reemerged.

American inclinations in today's world are much easier to understand when seen against a longer view of American foreign policy. American policy was never "isolationist," if that term means fearful of contact with the outside world. The United States was always eager to pursue trade with outside nations and quite ready to assert its interests in the wider world. Nor was the United States contemptuous of international law. It was eager to advance a certain view of international law and a corresponding pattern of international relations. Europeans and some Americans tend to forget how much of contemporary policy—derided by critics as "unilateralist"—follows in a tradition of American policy that goes back to the Founding.

Commentators on American foreign policy often emphasize disagreements among competing "schools" or policy dispositions in the history of American policy. Much analysis of this kind simply projects disputes over the League of Nations back into earlier times—or forward into later eras. So "Wilsonian internationalism" always seems to be contending against "isolationist" impulses, generous-hearted "idealists" always struggling against hard-nosed or unimaginative "realists." On large questions of international law and practice, however, it is the underlying continuity that ought to receive more notice.

If Wilsonian idealism means subordination to international authority, the United States has never pursued a Wilsonian policy. Woodrow Wilson's League of Nations, denounced at the time as a challenge to American traditions, was, after all, rejected by the Senate. The United States has pursued more active or aggressive policies at some times and more cautious or restrained policies at other times. But no American administration has ever imagined that American policy could be divorced from particular American interests. Nor has any administration ever imagined that American interests could be defined or imposed by outside powers or outside circumstances, without regard for what kind of country America aspired to be at home.

What the American Constitution requires America to be at home has greatly shaped not only particular responses to particular international challenges, but the larger American vision of how the world ought to be. American policy has always looked for a version of international law or international relations which would allow the United States to live as it wished to live at home.

Constitutionally Constrained, Diplomatically Disentangled

The United States achieved its independence in a revolutionary struggle against the greatest empire of the era. To win that struggle, the infant United States turned for assistance to the second greatest power of the age. American leaders had few illusions about the corrupt, absolutist monarchy of Louis XVI. Still, they did not hesitate to sign a military alliance with France, when they recognized that they could not win a war of independence without French help. But neither did the first American diplomats feel any great sense of loyalty to America's first ally.

The treaty of alliance between France and the United States pledged that neither side would negotiate a separate peace with Britain. France supplied invaluable military and financial assistance and the naval support that made possible the great victory over British forces at Yorktown. Benjamin Franklin, the chief American diplomat in Paris, promptly opened secret negotiations with Britain without informing the French government. American diplomats then pursued a common position with the British in opposing new French acquisitions in North America.

By its own terms, the wartime alliance with France would not automatically lapse with the coming of peace. But having gained independence, American leaders did not want to remain dependent on French protection. A central argument for the new Constitution was that, without a strong central government, the states of the American Confederation would not be able to resist the pressures or intrigues of European powers. None of these arguments, of course, excluded the French from the category of potential predators or intriguers against American independence. And as subsequent experience proved, concerns about French meddling were not misplaced.[2]

So the new Constitution envisioned a national government with the power to maintain a standing army, to build a fleet, to raise revenue by its own taxation to sustain these forces. By building up its own independent power, *The Federalist* promised, the United States would soon "be able to incline the balance of European competitions in this part of the world as our interest may dictate." Instead of relying on European assistance, the United States would be the object of European entreaties: "A price would be set not only upon our friendship but upon our neutrality."[3]

The Framers of the Constitution might warm to the prospect of a government powerful enough to set its own "price" on the American policy toward other nations. But the Framers were not prepared to endow the national government with unchecked power, even in the field of foreign affairs. What they established was a scheme in which the conduct of foreign affairs remains subject to a number of the same checks and balances that constrain federal governing authority at home.

The president may have special powers as "Commander-in-Chief of the Army and Navy." Still, funds for the army and navy must be appropriated by Congress and appropriations must be renewed every second year. Congress is given the power to "declare war" and its power of the purse seems to give it ultimate control of military actions, even where war has not been formally declared.[4] The president has the power to "make treaties" but treaties take effect only when the Senate gives its consent. The Constitution specifies that the president has the power to "receive ambassadors," which implies special responsibility for the conduct of diplomacy. Yet the Congress can withhold funding for American envoys and the Senate may refuse to confirm a particular nominee for a diplomatic post.

In all of these provisions, the Framers were not simply borrowing British practice. The Framers created a quite new structure of checks and balances, because they were not willing to invest the executive authority with the full range of powers formally associated with royal prerogative in Britain. In practice, the king's ministers in Britain had to worry about parliamentary support for their policies, even in foreign affairs, as the American Founders were well aware. The constitutional scheme of the American Constitution remains quite different. The president has no power to discipline a balky Congress by ordering new elections ahead of schedule, nor has the Congress any means of replacing a president in mid term. The president is expressly denied the power to secure congressional acquiescence by appointing congressional leaders to posts in his administration (Art. 1, Sec. 6). The American scheme almost invites political conflict, even in the conduct of foreign affairs.

The provisions for treaty ratification are particularly revealing. Under the Articles of Confederation, treaties required the concurrence of nine states out of the thirteen. Substantially the same high hurdle is preserved by the constitutional requirement for ratification of treaties by a two-thirds majority in the Senate. The delegates at the Constitutional Convention were perfectly aware that this high hurdle might prove an obstacle to the approval of new treaties. In the ensuing debates over ratification of the Constitution, critics urged that an even higher majority of senators should be required, at least for certain kinds of treaties.[5]

One of the central concerns was that treaties would advance the interests of some regions in the country at the expense of others. A residue of this concern survives in the provision of Art. IV, Sec. 3, prohibiting any federal action that might "prejudice" the territorial claims of any one state. And the concerns were not at all hypothetical.

President Washington sent Chief Justice John Jay to London in 1793 to resolve a series of issues left over from the Revolution, such as the continued presence of British troops in lands claimed by the United States in unsettled territories in the "northwest" (now the Midwest). The resulting Jay Treaty proved immensely controversial, with critics protesting that the interests of western settlers had been sacrificed for the benefit of New England merchants. The treaty also provoked new constitutional controversy when the House of Representatives demanded a role in the debate over ratification, on the grounds that the House would be required to appropriate funds to implement the treaty.

Divisions over foreign policies, however, could be ideological as well as sectional. Differing responses to the French Revolution provoked intense disputes in the 1790s which helped inspire a "Republican" opposition to the Washington administration. These disputes quickly became entangled in disputes about constitutional powers. In 1794, President Washington issued a Proclamation of Neutrality in the war that had broken out between Britain and revolutionary France. Republican critics protested that the president had no authority to proclaim neutrality on his own, since the Constitution gave the president no authority to declare war on his own. The dispute provoked a minor pamphlet war in which Madison and Hamilton, collaborators in the *The Federalist Papers*, emerged on opposite sides with quite different theories about presidential powers in foreign affairs.[6]

It was quite as true in the 1790s as in every subsequent era that partisans seized on favorable constitutional theories to advance more immediate policy aims or to gain some partisan advantage in a wider political struggle. In the 1790s, critics protested the financial policies of Treasury Secretary Alexander Hamilton on many grounds. Then they charged that the Washington administration was pursuing pro-British policy abroad in order to encourage British monarchical practices at home. Federalists, in turn, accused the "Republican" opposition of dangerous sympathies for the radical aims of the revolutionary government in France. Disputes about the constitutional powers of the presidency (or of the House of Representatives) were simply one set of rhetorical volleys in a much larger debate.

Yet the structure of the Constitution did invite such debates. The system of checks and balances presumed that policy might often provoke controversy. Particular constraints were, in effect, an assurance that particular voices of protest, or particular interests, would have an opportunity to press their claims. One could say that a particularly stubborn faction was jeopardizing the broader interests of the nation. But critics could insist that, in demanding compliance with the Constitution, they were performing a public service, whatever their other motives. As Madison put it, a "trespass on the constitutional provisions" in any area should be "felt with the same keenness that resents an invasion of the dearest rights."[7]

Debate over foreign policy particularly worried the Founders, however. It was not just that the stakes might be far higher than in any debate about domestic legislation. There was also the worry that in foreign policy debates, particular factions would be tempted to seek support from foreign patrons—since outside powers were bound to have a special interest in American foreign policies. *The Federalist* famously argued that in a large republic, the great range and diversity of factions would encourage moderation, as rival interests resisted each other's claims. But what if particular factions drew special strength from foreign support? *The Federalist* warned that republics were particularly vulnerable to "foreign corruption," because temporary office holders in a republic would be more susceptible to foreign bribes or blandishments than a hereditary monarch.[8] The United States therefore needed to be particularly cautious about international commitments.

A decade later, the argument was no longer hypothetical, as factional debate over the American response to the wars of revolutionary France seemed to prove that such dangers were quite real. Washington's Farewell Address harped on the dangers of "passionate attachment" to particular foreign nations.[9] Such an attachment "gives to ambitious, corrupted or deluded citizens . . . facility to betray or sacrifice the interests of their own country without odium, sometimes even with popularity":

> Against the insidious wiles of foreign influence (I conjure you to believe me, fellow-citizens) the jealousy of a free people ought to be *constantly* awake [original emphasis], since history and experience prove that foreign influence is one of the most baneful foes of republican government. . . . The great rule of conduct for us in regard to foreign nations is, in extending our commercial relations to have with them as little *political* connection [original emphasis] as possible . . . there can be no greater error that to expect or calculate upon real favors from nation to nation. It is an illusion which experience must cure, which a just pride ought to discard.

In the circumstances of the late 1790s, Washington's admonitions sounded a particular caution against advocates of closer alignment with revolutionary France. Washington had to demand the removal of the French diplomatic envoy, Jean Genet, for intriguing with American opposition groups. In the new administration of John Adams, American warships had to fight off French attacks on American shipping in the Atlantic. Criticism from the "Republican" opposition mounted to new levels of partisan fury. Madison, as leader of the opposition in the House, insisted that it was not the French Republic but Britain which was the greater threat: "The truth is, Great Britain, as a monarchy . . . must view with a malignant eye the United States, as the real source of the present revolutionary state of the world, and as an example of republicanism more likely than any other . . . to convey contagion."[10] Federalists in Congress were so outraged by opposition rhetoric that they enacted the Sedition Act, making it a crime to publish defamatory claims about the federal government. That legislation, of course, provoked a new burst of constitutional debate about the proper limits of federal power.

Yet when Jefferson, the leader of the opposition, gained the presidency in 1801, he tried to calm partisan dissension. In his inaugural address, he promised a domestic policy of "equal and exact justice to all men of whatever . . . persuasion, religious or political." His foreign policy would be similar: "peace, commerce and honest friendship with all nations, entangling alliances with none." To those "honest men" who "fear that a republican government cannot be strong," Jefferson insisted that America had "the strongest Government on earth" because "the only one where every man . . . would meet invasions of the public order as his own personal concern."[11] The government did not need to invoke noble impulses or enthusiasm for universal creeds or worldwide causes: citizens would be loyal from "personal concern."

Federalists accused Jefferson of sentimental attachment to France, where he had served as American ambassador in the first, heady months of the French Revolution. Federalist concerns were exacerbated when Jefferson chose his Anglophobic friend, James Madison, to serve as secretary of state. Yet the Jefferson administration strove to maintain Washington's policy of neutrality in the war that continued to rage between Britain and France. When France gained control of the Louisiana territory, threatening American access to the Mississippi, Madison (with Jefferson's approval) instructed American diplomats to attempt to purchase Louisiana from France—and if they could not do so, to open negotiations for an alliance with Britain as a guarantor of American security.[12] Napoleon's decision to sell Louisiana allowed the Jefferson administration to revert to neutrality.

But neutrality did not mean the United States was passive or hesitant about asserting its interests. It meant precisely that American policy would pursue interests which could be conceived as immediate *American* interests. President Jefferson was quite prepared to act unilaterally in doing so. He launched a naval attack on the Barbary pirates to secure protection for American shipping in the Mediterranean without paying tribute to the pirate princes of Algiers and Tunis. Jefferson did not hesitate to take unilateral action, when Britain and France, preoccupied with larger strategic concerns, decided they would continue to pay the tribute. The American settlements with local rulers then made no provision for the protection of non-American shipping.

In the ongoing war in Europe, Britain and France tried to shut down the other's trade and the United States demanded respect for its own shipping rights as a neutral. The Jefferson administration resorted to a trade embargo on both Britain and France, professing its readiness to drop restrictions on whichever side would first give way to American claims. The failure of this tactic and the intensification of British attacks on American shipping finally led Madison, after attaining the White House as Jefferson's successor, to a declaration of war against Britain. Yet even when resorting to war against the world's greatest naval power, the Madison administration disdained to align itself with France. As it turned out, the United States was so badly prepared for war with Britain that it suffered the humiliation of a British raid on Washington, in which the White House and the Capitol were torched by contemptuous British troops.[13] The United States was prepared to undertake considerable risk to avoid "entangling alliances" with another European power.

The United States ended up settling for a treaty of peace in 1815, under which Britain made no concessions to American claims about shipping rights on the high seas. Fortunately, the final defeat of Napoleon, only a few months later, allowed Britain to renounce its restrictions on neutral shipping, anyway. But the defeat of Napoleon produced a new threat, as the restored Bourbon monarchy in France joined in a so-called "Holy Alliance" with monarchies in Prussia, Austria, and Russia, with the avowed intention of repressing any reversion to republican or liberal institutions in Europe. The Alliance did, in fact, sponsor a French invasion of Spain in 1822, to suppress a liberal revolution. Soon there was talk of organizing expeditions to suppress rebellions against Spanish colonial rule in South America.

The ultimate American response was the Monroe Doctrine, proclaimed by President Monroe in a Message to Congress in 1823. It was entirely characteristic of the thinking of the Founding generation. And it remained, well into the twentieth century, a cornerstone of American policy—both as a guide to strategy and as a symbol of a distinct American role in the world.

The famous "doctrine" was stated in one part of a long sentence: "we should consider any attempt [by European powers] to extend their system to any portion of this hemisphere as dangerous to our peace and safety."[14] Given the small size of the American navy at the time, the United States could not, by itself, hope to deter new European ventures in the western hemisphere. Monroe had been emboldened to issue this warning, only after the British government had offered to make a joint statement of opposition to recolonization efforts in South America (which Britain opposed for its own commercial reasons). Characteristically, the Monroe Administration decided to issue a unilateral statement of American policy, freeing that policy from any future dependence on British concurrence in the future.[15]

Just as Monroe's formulation avoided any appearance of an alliance with Britain, so it also avoided any general commitment to defend liberal revolutions. Monroe did call attention to the intervention of the Holy Alliance in Spain, as an illustration of its dangerous pretensions and its disdain for the principle of sovereignty. But Monroe acknowledged that American policy "nevertheless remains . . . not to interfere in the internal concerns of any" European power. Monroe expressed sympathy for the struggle of the Greeks, trying to regain their "separate and equal station" in the world—but disclaimed any intention to take sides in the Greek war against Turkish domination. Even in the Americas, Monroe acknowledged that the United States would respect existing colonial possessions and not take sides in wars of independence that had not yet been settled.

The Monroe Doctrine might be read as a warning that the United States now felt strong enough to resist European expansion in its own region. It might be read, that is, as announcing that the United States was prepared to play power politics in its hemisphere, as great powers had always done in Europe. But in staking this claim on American opposition to the European "system," Monroe connected the American interest with American ideals. The United States looked with a wary eye not only on absolutist monarchy, but on a concert of monarchs, puffing themselves with religious pretensions. The United States would not interfere with such pretensions in Europe but was prepared to resist the extension of this very old political "system" into the New World.

Monroe and his successors certainly held to the self-denying part of the doctrine. The United States remained aloof from the whole succession of conferences in which European powers subsequently agreed upon terms for the recognition of Greek independence, Belgian independence, independence for new nations in the Balkans. Diplomats could speak of a "Concert of Europe," guided by understandings among the dominant powers. The United States made no official acknowledgment of any such thing. It dealt individually with individual European states.

Americans might believe—as many American statesmen insisted—that the success of free government in the United States offered hope to oppressed people in other nations. That did not make the United States ready to risk its own peace and prosperity by intervening, even diplomatically, on behalf of liberal causes in Europe. As it had stood apart from the conflicts generated by the revolution in France in the 1790s, the United States remained detached from the convulsions provoked in Europe by liberal revolutions in 1848.

The prevailing American view was that, in standing up for itself, the United States was doing enough to stand up for liberal principles. Secretary of State Daniel Webster made the point in a staunch reply to the Austrian foreign minister, when the latter complained about President Tyler's expression of sympathy for the Hungarian revolution against Austrian rule, suppressed by Russian troops in 1849:

> True, indeed, it is, that the prevalence on the other continent [i.e., Europe] of sentiments favorable to republican liberty is the result of the reaction of America upon Europe. . . . The position thus belonging to the United States is a fact as inseparable from their history, their constitutional organization and their character, as the opposite position of the powers composing the European alliance is from the history and

constitutional organization of the Government of those powers. The sovereigns who form that alliance have not unfrequently felt it their right to interfere with the political movements of foreign states; and have, in their manifestoes and declarations, denounced the popular ideas of the age in terms so comprehensive as of necessity to include the United States, and their forms of government . . . if the United States wish success to countries contending for popular constitutions and national independence, it is only because they regard such constitutions and such national independence, not as imaginary, but as real blessings. They claim no right, however, to promote these ends. It is only in defense of his own Government, and its principles and character, that the undersigned has now expressed himself on this subject.[16]

A decade after Monroe's famous Message to Congress, a Message from President Jackson hammered home the implication. France had agreed to arbitration of claims arising from French attacks on American shipping decades earlier. France had then stalled in making payments on the sums it was held to owe. President Jackson warned that the United States was prepared to seize French property to satisfy this debt:

> Collision with France is the more to be regretted on account of the position she occupies in Europe in relation to liberal institutions, but in maintaining our national rights and honor all governments are alike to us. If by a collision with France in a case where she is clearly in the wrong the march of liberal principles shall be impeded, the responsibility for that result as well as every other will rest on her own head.[17]

Europeans might see no distinction between American self-assertion and the power claims of any other power. While disclaiming any connection with the European "system," the United States managed to acquire vast new territories for itself in North America. Yet even the course of American territorial expansion illustrated the special constitutional position under which the United States saw itself as operating.

TERRITORIAL EXPANSION WITHIN CONSTITUTIONAL LIMITS

The United States was born with an urge to expand. One of the complaints against Britain, in the Declaration of Independence, was that British authorities had tried to restrict Americans from settling in lands on the far side of the Allegheny mountains. In the peace negotiations, American diplomats were prepared to risk the continuation of war rather than relinquish American claims to the largely unsettled territory between the eastern mountains and the Mississippi.

One of the arguments for the new Constitution was that it would help to assure the loyalty of territories in the west, not yet sufficiently settled to be organized as new states of the union. Securing their loyalty meant, among other things, ensuring their unimpeded access to the mouth of the Mississippi river.

This access seemed imperiled, during the Napoleonic wars, when Spanish authorities agreed to transfer their control over the Louisiana territory to France. President Jefferson contemplated military action to seize New Orleans from the French. He contemplated an alliance with Britain to secure this conquest from French retaliation. He should have been delighted when, in response to American inquiries, Napoleon offered to sell not only New Orleans but the whole Louisiana territory.

But Jefferson had serious qualms about the constitutional propriety of this transaction. Where in the Constitution was the federal government authorized to purchase territory—and on a scale which might transform the whole nature of the Union? His concerns were not simply quibbles of a "strict constructionist." Writing to one of his followers, he acknowledged that the Constitution authorized Congress to "admit new states" but dismissed the relevance of this provision:

> But when I consider the limits of the U S are precisely fixed by the treaty of 1783, that the Constitution expressly declares itself to be made for the U S, I cannot help believing the intention was to permit Congress to admit into the Union new States, which would be formed out of the territory for which, & under whose authority alone, they were then acting. I do not believe it was meant that they might receive England, Ireland, Holland, &c. into it, which would be the case on your construction. When an instrument admits two constructions, the one safe, the other dangerous, the one precise, the other indefinite, I prefer that which is safe & precise. I had rather ask an enlargement of power from the nation, where it is found necessary, than to assume it by a construction which would make our powers boundless. Our peculiar security is in possession of a written Constitution. Let us not make it a blank paper by construction. I say the same as to the opinion of those who consider the grant of the treaty making power as boundless. If it is, then we have no Constitution.[18]

Jefferson was soon persuaded that Napoleon's offer could not be put on hold while the United States undertook the elaborate process of a constitutional amendment. So a constitutional amendment, actually proposed in the Senate by John Quincy Adams, was quickly abandoned. The treaty with France stipulated that residents of Louisiana would be treated as American citizens and the territories would become eligible for entry into the Union. The Jefferson administration took some trouble to ensure that Louisiana would be governed as an English-speaking territory.[19] The precedent thus established was followed without any controversy when Florida and west Florida (now southern Alabama and Mississippi) were acquired from Spain in the administrations of Madison and Monroe. The abstract power to acquire new territory for the United States has never been questioned since.

But that did not mean that territorial expansion had ceased to trigger major constitutional disputes. The first was faced in Texas. American settlers in this Mexican province mounted a successful rebellion in 1835, when the Mexican government tried to rescind previous promises of self-government within the province. Initially organizing themselves as an independent republic, Texans readily agreed to a treaty of annexation into the United States a few years later.

The treaty was defeated in the Senate, however, amidst northern concerns over the political implications of adding a new slave state to the Union. To evade this opposition, annexation was accomplished by a joint resolution of Congress (requiring only simple majorities in both houses) rather than a formal treaty. Shortly thereafter, a dispute with Britain over the U.S.-Canada border in the Pacific northwest—the so-called "Oregon Question"—was compromised, after much bluster on both sides, and this treaty received unanimous support in the Senate.

Then, as critics of Texas annexation had warned, a lingering dispute about the Texas-Mexico border triggered a war between the United States and Mexico. The success of American arms in that war forced Mexico to agree to the sale of further territory—what later became New Mexico, Arizona, Nevada, and California. This vast acquisition provoked a new round of disputes about the status of slavery in the new territories. In general, northerners favored federal legislation to prohibit slavery in the new territories or in all the territory north of a certain line, while southerners resisted such measures as intolerable interference with the rights of slave holders. The compromise patched together in Congress in 1850 then seemed to be entirely demolished by the Supreme Court's 1857 ruling in *Dred Scott v. Sandford*, holding that Congress lacked constitutional authority to prohibit slavery in federal territories.

For all its pro-slavery distortions, the Dred Scott decision raised a question which was already implicit in Jefferson's qualms about the Louisiana purchase and a problem not at all limited to slavery. An annexed territory, Chief Justice Taney insisted, was "acquired to become a State and not to be held as a colony and governed by Congress with absolute authority." If Congress had unlimited control over territories, it could start by prohibiting slavery and end by establishing an official religion or indeed a complete despotism within the new territories.[20]

The immediate question, regarding slavery, was settled by the Civil War.

Following the Union victory, the Thirteenth Amendment was adopted, prohibiting slavery everywhere in the United States. A few years later the Fourteenth Amendment was adopted, providing that anyone born in the United States, regardless of race or previous servitude, would be a full citizen of the United States. But what was "the United States"?

The Senate was prepared to endorse American annexation of unsettled Alaska, in a treaty of purchase from Russia, in 1867. Only a few years later, the Senate balked at the annexation of Santo Domingo, in a treaty negotiated by the Grant administration. Unlike Alaska, Santo Domingo was not at all empty or unsettled and it was not certain that the existing population wanted to become Americans.

On similar grounds, a treaty to annex the Hawaiian islands, negotiated by the outgoing Harrison administration after a successful revolution by American planters on the islands, was shelved by the new Cleveland administration in 1893. Amidst war with Spain in 1898, the McKinley administration succeeded in annexing Hawaii by joint resolution. It then acquired Puerto Rico in the Caribbean along with Guam and the Philippines in the Pacific in the peace treaty with Spain. What was to be the status of these new territories? Were they potential states in waiting? Or could they be ruled under any terms Congress chose to impose?

Debate about territorial acquisitions became a central issue in the elections of 1900, because the situation posed by this expansion seemed new and disturbing. Advocates of the new acquisitions spoke boldly of America's "civilizing mission" and "imperial responsibilities" in terms that would make later generations cringe. But "anti-imperialists" were even more emphatic in their denunciations of "amalgamation with inferior races" as a threat to constitutional government and republican principles.[21]

Following the success of the "imperialists" in the 1900 elections, the Supreme Court advanced an awkward compromise in a series of rulings known, quite fittingly, as "the Insular Cases"—designed for self-contained islands "out there." Some territories could be organized as something different from potential states. Constitutional restrictions would not necessarily apply to federally controlled government in such territories. On the other hand, basic principles of "Anglo-Saxon justice" would still be guarded by federal courts.[22] So the imperialists would get constitutional flexibility and the anti-imperialists would get assurances of the "Anglo-Saxon" legal heritage.

In practice, the compromise could not remain stable and it did not. Courts and Congress extended more and more constitutional protections to these territories, encouraging migration and economic integration, until Alaska and Hawaii could be admitted to the Union as fully equal states, with no special accommodations. By the 1950s, the Supreme

Court had ruled that the United States government was bound by procedural provisions in the Bill of Rights, whenever it imposed a judicial proceeding, even in overseas territories.[23]

In the Philippines, a period of brutal repression in the early 1900s was followed by reconstruction on American lines. Congress quickly grew tired of imperial responsibilities. In 1934, it committed the United States to the eventual granting of independence. The commitment was duly redeemed in 1946, after the United States had liberated the islands from wartime conquest by Japan. Guam and Puerto Rico, with non-English-speaking cultures, have substantial self-government under local institutions, still subject to federal law but with nearly full protections of the federal Constitution, as well. They would almost certainly be granted independence if they sought it (referenda have gone the other way). But they might not be admitted to statehood, given doubts about common nationality with such distinctly "insular" subgroups. So they remain in an odd constitutional limbo, mementos of another era.

The more telling fact is that these anomalous "possessions" have remained isolated because there have not been further acquisitions, apart from a handful of much smaller islands in the Caribbean and the Pacific. The American vocation for "empire"—as distinct from adding new states to the American republic—was very quickly sated. Having been among the last great powers to seek overseas colonies, the United States initiated the post–Second World War trend toward voluntary decolonization.

Still more telling is that the United States never considered an intermediate or alternative arrangement to link itself with semi-independent territories. When the Philippines were granted independence in 1946, the United States made no effort to incorporate them into a "commonwealth" of former American territories. There was no precedent for such an arrangement. And nobody seemed interested in improvising such a new approach. In the nineteenth century, the United States had helped to found a settlement in West Africa for emancipated American slaves. The United States never agreed to take any responsibility for Liberia and never developed any formal connection with this African offshoot.[24] So in the twentieth century there would be no American counterpart to the British Commonwealth or the Communauté Française.

In general, American policy made sharp distinctions between "inside" and "outside." The Jefferson administration wanted to *possess* New Orleans and the lands assuring access to the Mississippi: treaty assurances from other powers were not regarded as a reliable substitute. The annexation of Texas was prompted in part by fears that Texas would otherwise seek British protection. Nobody seems to have considered an agreement with Britain—sharing influence and protection over Texas—as a satisfactory alternative.[25]

When President Theodore Roosevelt embarked on the construction of a canal in Panama, he demanded direct and full American control of a "zone" on either side of the Canal—and sponsored a revolution in Colombia (then in control of Panama) to get it. Mere treaty rights would not do. Similarly, when the the United States began to maintain serious embassies in foreign capitals—something it had disdained to do until the twentieth century—it made great efforts to secure full title to the land on which American embassies would be situated.[26]

Some of this may be seen as the action of a power which feels strong enough to insist on its own terms. But the underlying pattern goes beyond that. The United States has been wary of treaty commitments setting up structures that might seem to compete with the authority of the United States government at home. And this pattern goes back to times when the United States was not very strong. If anything, the caution was stronger when the United States was weaker.

So, when Simón Bolívar called a conference of newly independent states in South America in 1821, the United States agreed to attend. But Secretary of State Henry Clay instructed the American delegates that the United States could not even consider participation in a permanent structure with anything resembling legislative powers.[27] The states of the United States were already grouped in a federation of their own and could not allow that federation to commit itself to some larger federation. Congress remained so wary that it delayed funding for the American delegation. By the time the U.S. delegates arrived, the other delegates had already dispersed.[28]

In the last decades of the nineteenth century, American diplomats did encourage new conferences on "Pan-American" affairs. There were a number of treaties promising cooperation. The cooperation was supposed to be enhanced by the establishment of a permanent forum for hemispheric discussions. But the Senate refused to consider proposals giving any sort of governing or regulatory authority to the "Pan-American Union."[29]

Yes to International Law—but with Limits

Steering clear of "entangling alliances," focusing on immediate national interests closer to home, American diplomacy might seem to have no concern with international law. In fact, the United States was an early, eager, and persistent champion of international law—but on terms that would have been entirely intelligible to the American Founders and the classic treatises on the law of nations.

To start with, the historic American policy of neutrality was more than a mere policy. It was understood as a status defined and secured by the law of nations. Neutrals were obligated to refrain from providing military assistance to either side. In return, they were entitled to assert rights to trade (in non-military goods) with both sides.

During his service as President Washington's secretary of state, Jefferson worked out detailed guidelines on American policy toward naval ships of the belligerents in the Anglo-French wars, which he sought to reconcile with principles of international law. He seems to have done reasonably well in this. A century later, scholars of international law recognized Jefferson's policy as a remarkably precise anticipation of the practices that became generally accepted law among trading states in the nineteenth century.[30] When Jefferson assumed the presidency, James Madison became secretary of state and struggled with the same issues, as the Napoleonic Wars provoked more and more extensive threats and demands from both sides against neutral shipping.

In 1806, Madison thought it worthwhile to publish a 200-page pamphlet outlining the case against a particular British doctrine restricting neutral shipping. Like *The Federalist*, and like Madison's subsequent "papers" on Washington's Neutrality Proclamation, this pamphlet was published anonymously, so that the intellectual force of the argument could stand on its own merits. The pamphlet argued its case with great erudition and scholarly care, starting with a summary of relevant passages in Grotius, Pufendorf, and Vattel, proceeding to a survey of treaties and prize court decisions, concluding with a digest of pertinent rulings by British admiralty courts.[31]

The argument did not persuade the British government to revise its policies. But it remains revealing that a man of Madison's political acumen thought it worthwhile to attempt to change British practice with an anonymous pamphlet. The premise—that the British government would be persuaded by argument based on legal precedent—was not utopian.[32] The British government itself provided special courts to determine when captured ships could be treated as "lawful prize of war" and when the ships or the cargoes must be returned to their original owners (or at least, when the owners must be compensated for losses). The logic of the practice was that every nation had some stake in the continuation of ocean commerce, so even countries using naval forces as weapons of war had some incentives to observe limits on the practice.[33]

During the American Civil War, it was the United States which sought to enforce blockade measures on neutral shipping. The United States accordingly administered its own prize courts and American government lawyers outdid their British predecessors in advancing ambitious arguments to justify naval seizures on the high seas. But no one claimed that the United States could simply establish its own rules on its own authority. American prize courts accordingly struggled to reconcile international precedents with American practice. In the Spanish-American war, another American blockade produced a new round of prize court rulings, including a ruling by the Supreme Court affirming that international practice in this area (which it canvassed in precedents stretching back to the fifteenth century) had now been embraced by American law.[34]

With the outbreak of war in Europe in 1914, the shoe was back on the other foot. British courts imposed a blockade and answered American objections on the severity of its terms (in regard to neutral shipping rights) by citing American precedents from the Civil War. As it became more and more concerned about German submarine attacks on American shipping, the United States did not press its objections to British practice. But it did not endorse the whole range of British legal claims.

There seemed to be an obvious answer to disputes over self-serving interpretations of international law. Why not assure the impartiality of tribunals by establishing them on a genuinely international basis? In fact, the United States was quite receptive to this approach. It was, indeed, one of the principal champions of international arbitration.

The first international claims commissions were established by the 1795 treaty between the United States and Great Britain, negotiated by Chief Justice John Jay. Claims of British subjects against American expropriations of their property would be submitted to a multinational panel of jurists in Philadelphia, while a parallel commission in London would assess claims of American merchants against improper British seizures on the high seas—with each government then providing special funds to cover the resulting monetary awards. A similar arbitration scheme was established in the 1830s to resolve disputes with France over injuries to American shipping during the undeclared naval war of the 1790s.[35]

Following the American Civil War, a more ambitious claims commission was established between the United States and Britain. It assessed conflicting claims arising out of American interference with British shipping during the blockade, on the one side, and British betrayal of neutral obligations, on the other. In particular, it addressed American claims regarding the sale of a raiding ship (the "Alabama") to Confederate forces, which then imposed much loss on American shipping. Besides these arbitrations of private claims against other governments (and against the United States government), the United States also submitted boundary disputes to arbitration, in regard to its own boundaries (in Maine). The United States then encouraged such arbitrations to settle boundary disputes in South America, most notably in a dispute between Venezuela and British Guyana in 1895.[36]

But there were limits to American support for international arbitration.

Some of the hesitations reflected domestic constitutional concerns. When the Cleveland administration negotiated a treaty with Britain, authorizing arbitration for a broad range of disputes that might arise between the two countries, the Senate raised strong objections. It was quite willing to authorize arbitrations of individual disputes or individual categories of disputes, according to a formula agreed in advance and submitted to the Senate in advance. The Senate was not willing to authorize arbitrations on whatever terms the president might negotiate in the future. Even with reservations to allay these concerns, the treaty died.

More than a decade later, President Taft negotiated a new arbitration treaty with Britain and proposed similar treaties with other great powers. To allay Senate concerns, the scheme would limit arbitration only to those questions suitable for judicial resolution, as determined by a special joint commission, with jurists from both countries. The Senate still balked, claiming that its own responsibility to determine the suitability of arbitration could not be delegated to an international commission.[37]

President Taft was equally unsuccessful in efforts to negotiate an international prize court, to rule on the legality of naval seizures in war time. Congressional critics protested the constitutional impropriety of allowing appeals from U.S. prize courts—that is, organs of the United States government—to an international body. The project died when European powers declined to accommodate American compromise proposals to avoid this constitutional problem.[38]

Given these constitutional scruples, the United States was naturally opposed to any notion of compulsory arbitration of international disputes. It was sympathetic to the practice of international arbitration but insistent on limits to the practice. When the Czar of Russia called an international conference to discuss conventions to preserve peace in 1898, the United States maintained that it could not take part in European conventions on arms control.[39] The U.S. delegation even maintained that it could not endorse a ban on privateering, which had been proscribed by international treaty in 1856. The United States had never ratified that treaty. American delegates now explained that the U.S. Constitution required Congress to retain the power to grant "letters of marque"—though the Congress had not, in fact, exercised that power since 1814.[40]

The American delegates were quite ready to use this forum to lobby for the establishment of a permanent court of international arbitration, however. Largely in response to American efforts, the conference produced a plan for establishing a permanent list of arbitrators available for arbitrations—which is all that this "court" entailed. To reassure the Senate, the American delegation did insist on a special "reservation," acknowledging the particular limits on American participation, as the Monroe Doctrine was still thought to require:

Nothing contained in this Convention shall be so construed as to require the United States of America to depart from its traditional policy
of not intruding upon, interfering with, or entangling itself in the political questions or policy or internal administration of any foreign
state; nor shall anything contained in the said Convention be construed
to imply a relinquishment by the United States of America of its traditional attitude toward purely American questions.

A second peace conference in 1907 expanded the matters on which arbitration was recommended. Arbitration remained a voluntary option,
however. With this assurance, the American Senate went along without
protest.

Some "peace activists" of the day argued that arbitration should be
made compulsory. The argument against such an approach was cogently
put by the head of the American delegation at the first Peace Conference
in 1899, Andrew Dickson White, a former diplomat and historian (who
was the founding president of Cornell University):

Obligatory arbitration between states is indeed possible in various petty
matters, but in many great matters absolutely impossible. While a few
nations were willing to accept it in regard to these minor matters—as
for example, postal or monetary difficulties and the like—not a single
power was willing to bind itself by a hard-and-fast rule to submit all
questions to it—and least of all the United States. The reason is very
simple: to do so would be to increase the chances of war and to enlarge
the standing armies throughout the world. Obligatory arbitration on
all questions would enable any power, at any moment, to bring before
the tribunal any other power against which it has, or thinks it has, a
grievance. Greece might thus summon Turkey; France might summon
Germany; the Papacy, Italy; England, Russia; China, Japan; Spain, the
United States, regarding matters in which the deepest human feelings—
questions of religion, questions of race, questions even of national
existence—are concerned. To enforce the decisions of the tribunal in
such cases would require armies compared to which those of the present day are a mere bagatelle, and plunge the world into a sea of troubles compared to which those now existing are as nothing.[41]

Arbitration looked plausible, so long as it did not claim to be an ultimate arbiter of national claims and restricted its reach to "petty matters." But where to draw the line? For Latin American countries, decisions about the scale of obligation to foreign creditors were not a "minor
matter" at all. They refused to subscribe to the Hague convention of
1907 providing for arbitration of such claims.

It tells much about the limited confidence in arbitration that when

Woodrow Wilson crafted a plan for a permanent international body to mediate disputes, he made no provision in the League of Nations for a court. That was added only after the League was established. Even the site of the League, left by the terms of the treaty to the choosing of the American president, was revealing: Wilson chose Geneva, home of the International Red Cross, rather than the Hague, site of the Permanent Court of Arbitration established by the prewar peace conferences. The grand vision of the League was not to be associated with the modest efforts of the international arbitration movement.[42] Of course, this did not make the League any easier to sell to Americans.

QUALMS ABOUT INTERNATIONAL ORGANIZATION

The Covenant of the League of Nations was, to a large extent, the special project of the American president, but it was finally rejected by the United States Senate. The Senate's rejection of the League provoked a great deal of recrimination, not least among American scholars in the interwar era. Was the League doomed by the relentless obstructionism of small-minded "isolationists"? Or by the partisanship of moderate Republicans who were prepared to endorse a League but only with extensive reservations? Or was it doomed by the inflexible refusal of President Wilson to compromise with moderate Republicans?[43]

It is very doubtful that all the hand-wringing mattered. The League failed to do anything at all to stop the rise of aggressive dictatorships. There is no good reason to think it would have been more effective with American membership. The League had no way of forcing its members to undertake any particular military action. President Wilson tried to obscure this central weakness with evasive rhetoric about moral obligations under the Covenant—which only heightened the suspicions of Republican critics at the time. Within a few years, however, the League, itself, formally acknowledged that it could not bind members to undertake any particular action.[44]

Britain and France, though they did join the League, never made any serious effort to enlist the League in mobilizing opposition to German or Japanese aggression. Instead, they placed their hopes in their own schemes of appeasement, pursued through diplomatic initiatives outside the League. It is highly improbable that adding the vote of a disarmed America would have provided any weight to the League's occasional, futile condemnations against aggression in the early 1930s.

What might have made a difference was a firm American guarantee to France, that the United States would immediately come to its defense in case of renewed German attack. The French wanted such a treaty much more than they wanted an international debating society. To win French support for the League, President Wilson indeed negotiated such a treaty, as a separate instrument, apart from the Covenant of the League. Henry Cabot Lodge, chairman of the Senate Foreign Relations Committee, indicated a willingness to support such a treaty. But Wilson gave priority to the universal peace which was supposed to be assured by the League.[45]

Republican administrations did nothing to revive the separate French treaty during the 1920s. When France proposed, as an alternative, that the United States sign a bilateral non-aggression pact—assuring, at least that the United States would not resist French attacks on Germany—the American State Department responded with a proposal for a universal non-aggression pact, what became the Kellogg-Briand Pact.[46] The Senate ratified this "international kiss" (understood as meaningless at the time), but still took care to add the "understanding" that it would not affect American commitments under the Monroe Doctrine.[47] Even after the experience of the World War, American thinking remained wedded to the spirit of Monroe: The United States was still seeking to avoid entanglement in European quarrels.

When the Senate wrestled with the League of Nations treaty in 1919, critics often indulged in a querulous suspicion of European intrigue. Republicans demanded, for example, that the United States be given six votes in the assembly of the League, to assure equality with the voting strength which (they assumed) Britain had secured through the separate League membership of nations in the British Commonwealth.[48] Yet the critics raised serious questions, too. The most serious questions would reverberate through all subsequent debates about American obligations to international organizations.

The largest issue went to the very heart of the League's purpose. By promising to guarantee the territorial integrity of every member state, the League threatened to entangle all its members in the quarrels of any one of its members. Senator Lodge protested that, by joining the League, the United States would give the king of the Hedjaz the right "to demand the sending of American troops to Arabia in order to preserve his independence against the assaults of the Wahabis" even though "most people have not the slightest idea where or what a King of the Hedjaz is."[49] Decades later—long after the Wahabis had succeeded in overturning the original dynasty and establishing their own rule under Prince Saud—Americans still wondered whether it was wise to commit the United States to the defense of the country that had come to be known as Saudi Arabia.

What if a people now trapped within the borders of an empire were prepared to risk war to establish their independence? Was the United States bound to defend the empire, just because it belonged to the

League? Senator Borah protested that, by promising to guarantee the territorial integrity of every member state, the League was committed to enforce "the standard of tyrants and despots, the protection of real estate regardless of how it is obtained. . . . It would exchange the doctrine of George Washington for the doctrine of Frederick the Great translated into mendacious phrases of peace."[50] Was it sensible to pretend that the League—or the "international community"—could be the final arbiter of which peoples could establish their independence and which could not?

Doubts on this score were by no means confined to "isolationists." The British legal scholar Lasa Oppenheim, one of the foremost commentators on international law in the decades before the First World War, shared these doubts. Writing in 1918, shortly before his death, Oppenheim endorsed the idea of a League of Nations but cautioned that "when we speak of a League of Nations, we do not really mean a League of Nations but a League of States." He dismissed as absurd the idea that the League could develop an international military force of its own or the constitutional machinery of a "world state":

> This international army and navy would be the most powerful instrument of force which the world has ever seen, because every attempt to resist it would be futile. . . . Who would keep in order those who are to keep the world in order? A League of Nations which can only be kept together by a powerful international army and navy is a contradiction in itself; for the independence and equality of the member states of the League would soon disappear. It is a fact—I make this statement although I am sure it will be violently contradicted—that just as hitherto, so within a League of Nations, some kind of Balance of Power only can guarantee the independence and equality of the smaller states.[51]

So Oppenheim proposed a League which would require states to submit to arbitration those questions which could be settled by "judicial process." But he acknowledged that the largest questions could not be settled by legal rulings. Where arbitration was inappropriate, he proposed that the League require submission of disputes to "conciliation . . . before resort to arms." He disavowed the notion that the League could prevent all armed conflict or determine its outcome.[52]

Of course, even this scheme looked more promising if one assumed a world of relatively like-minded states. But Oppenheim did not imagine that a peace league could ensure liberal or democratic government in the member states.[53] The actual Covenant of the League did not say anything directly about the internal government of states, either. It contained only vague references to a role for the League in sponsoring international cooperation on social and economic issues of common concern.

These provisions, modest as they might seem, provoked the second serious concern of Senate critics: How far should international commitments be allowed to intrude on American domestic policy? Senator Lodge pounced on the ambiguity, noting that even questions of immigration policy might be referred to the League, if the United States denied entry to citizens from a member state in the League:

> There should be no possibility of other nations deciding who shall come into the United States or under what conditions they shall enter. . . . If a nation cannot say without appeal who shall come within its gates and become a part of its citizenship it has ceased to be a sovereign nation . . . and it makes no difference whether it is subject to a league or to a conqueror.

Lodge persuaded the Senate Foreign Relations Committee to endorse the League only with reservations. One of these "Lodge Reservations" stipulated:

> The United States reserves to itself exclusively the right to decide what questions are within its domestic jurisdiction and declares that all domestic and political questions relating to its affairs . . . are not under this treaty submitted in any way . . . to the consideration . . . of the league of nations or to the decision or recommendation of any other power.[54]

From what is actually in the Covenant, one might regard these concerns as wildly exaggerated. But they may have been a legitimate reaction to the spirit of Wilson's vision. In 1914, a few months after the outbreak of war in Europe, Wilson had offered an extremely ambitious plan for assuring peace and stability to governments in the western hemisphere: His plan proposed that every western hemisphere state would sign a treaty by which they would guarantee to each other not only their territorial integrity but also a "republican form of government."[55] Latin American countries were not at all keen for such a guarantee, so the proposal went nowhere.

Wilson then pursued a unilateral policy of half-hearted American interventions to assure a "democratic" outcome among contending factions in Mexico. The United States would never have accepted such interventions from a particular outside power. American opinion would always be equally resistant to allowing any international organization to determine whether American governing arrangements were adequately "republican."

In fact, the United States displayed great resistance to any form of international monitoring of its domestic policy. At the same time that the Covenant of the League was under debate in the Senate, delegates from prospective members of the League gathered in Washington to draw up plans for an International Labour Organization (ILO), which was supposed to help coordinate common standards for the protection of workers. Samuel Gompers of the American Federation of Labor, speaking for the American delegation, insisted that the United States could not participate in a standard-setting organization of this kind if its standards were determined by simple majority vote of the members. Each standard proposed by the ILO must be formulated as a separate convention, which member states could then ratify or reject by domestic procedures, on a case by case basis. The American approach was accepted by other delegates— and the United States then declined to join the ILO, anyway.[56]

That such qualms were not simply inspired by partisan bitterness against Wilson is shown by the sequel. In the 1920s, Republican administrations, while continuing to steer clear of involvement in the League, itself, thought it might be useful to participate in the new Permanent Court of International Justice, organized by the League, essentially as a more formal alternative to the Hague arbitration court. The Senate became tangled in wrangling over necessary reservations. American critics were not content with retaining the right to refuse to participate in any particular international arbitration if the Court were still empowered to offer advisory opinions on issues which might affect the United States. No agreement could be reached between the League and the United States on how to prevent the Court from addressing issues which might incidentally affect American claims under international law.[57] So the United States remained aloof.

Another attempt was made in the mid-1930s, when a new Democratic president was quite adept at mobilizing support for his policies in a Senate which by then had an overwhelming Democratic majority. The proposal to affiliate with the Permanent Court of International Justice was still voted down. More Democrats than Republicans voted against the Court.[58] President Roosevelt was able to secure Senate approval for American membership in the International Labour Organization—but not for any actual standards proposed by the ILO.

Even after the outset of hostilities in Europe, even after the fall of France and the bombing of London, American opinion remained quite divided on whether or how much to aid Britain in its war with Nazi Germany. Among voices calling for neutrality were not only Republican conservatives but well-known progressives, like the historian Charles Beard, who warned about the consequences for domestic institutions if America plunged into another world war. The *American Journal of International Law* opened its pages to legal scholars protesting that Roosevelt's policy of providing military aid to Britain (while declining to enter the war as an active belligerent) was in violation of all accepted principles of neutrality. The argument certainly rested on a fair reading of past precedent and practice, but fidelity to past practice was not enough of an argument in such extraordinary circumstances.[59]

For most Americans, the Japanese attack on Pearl Harbor ended any lingering doubts. The United States would not merely seek respect for its own national rights, but justice for all victims of Axis aggression. Little over a year after America's entry into the war, President Roosevelt proclaimed that the United States would fight on, until it secured the "unconditional surrender" of the Axis aggressors.

President Wilson had primly characterized the United States as an "Associate" of the "Allied Powers" in the First World War. Wilson had refused to embrace specific war aims of the Allies, insisting that the United States must remain free to negotiate on its own with Germany. To the chagrin of French and British governments, Wilson did, in fact, pursue separate negotiations with Germany in October 1918, prior to the general armistice. President Roosevelt, having committed the United States to fight to the finish, quickly began to speak of American allies in the Second World War as "the forces of the United Nations." The phrase implied that, once the Axis powers had been utterly defeated, the forces of the United Nations would remain entirely unchallenged in the world.

Politicians of all stripes endorsed American participation in a postwar organization to keep the peace. In the 1944 presidential election, the idea was strongly endorsed in the Republican platform and supported by the Republican candidate, Thomas Dewey. But Roosevelt remained cautious.

State Department planners assumed, at first, that a successor to Wilson's League would need to be organized on a much stronger foundation than its ill-fated predecessor. They proposed that the charter of the new organization impose a requirement for compulsory arbitration of international disputes before an expanded International Court. They proposed that an executive council be authorized to make decisions by simple or qualified majority, rather than by unanimous agreement (as in the League). They proposed that any power on the executive council be disqualified from voting on a matter in which it was directly involved.

All of these proposals dropped out of the American plan, even before the meeting at Dunbarton Oaks in Washington, where the penultimate draft of the UN Charter was hammered out among the major wartime allies.[60] Probably none of the earlier proposals would have been acceptable to the Soviet Union. Roosevelt was also aware that they would not be acceptable to two-thirds of the U.S. Senate.

So the UN Charter was, in some respects, actually more constrained than its predecessor. Where the League had established a parity between its Assembly (of all members) and its Council (of great powers), the UN Charter restricted all binding authority to the Security Council. The Charter did make provision for decision by majority vote (as opposed to the requirement for unanimous agreement under the Covenant). But actions of the Security Council would be subject to veto by any one of the five permanent members (the four wartime allies, plus a now rehabilitated France). A provision for regional defense arrangements (none of which existed at the time) was inserted to mollify concerns about possible interference with the Monroe Doctrine.[61]

As further reassurance, the Charter stipulated, right at the outset, that "nothing" in its provisions "shall authorize the United Nations to intervene in matters which are essentially within the domestic jurisdiction of any state or shall require the Members to submit such matters to settlement under the present Charter" (Art. 2, Par. 7)—language tracking very closely with the reservations voted by the Senate in 1919 on the Covenant of the League.[62]

The Charter was then swept through the Senate after very little debate.[63] But only a few months later, the old concerns showed their enduring power in the Senate. The Charter reestablished the League's International Court of Justice (with minor changes) and left it to individual members to decide whether they wanted to be subject to "compulsory jurisdiction" (rather than consenting, case by case, to particular suits).

The Foreign Relations Committee recommended that the Senate accept compulsory jurisdiction, but with a reservation exempting "matters which are essentially within the jurisdiction of the United States." On the Senate floor, Senator Tom Connally of Texas, Chairman of the Committee, proposed to add the phrase, "as determined by the United States"— so that the United States, rather than the International Court, would always have the last word on the Court's jurisdiction. Though this amounted to a repudiation of consent to compulsory jurisdiction, Connally was adamant: "I do not want to surrender the sovereignty or the prestige of the United States on any question which may be merely domestic in character and contained within the boundaries of this Republic."[64] The Senate agreed to the change by fifty-one to twelve.

The Constitution Reemerges

Whatever hopes Americans may have held for the United Nations as a guarantor of peace, such hopes were quickly dashed. Wartime cooperation between the United States and the Soviet Union did not survive beyond the first year of the postwar era. The ensuing Cold War brought a much more important change in American policy. For the first time in its history, the United States became willing to take responsibility for the defense of other nations around the world. In 1947, the United States entered into the Rio Pact, a mutual defense agreement with the nations of

Latin America, formalized in the Organization of American States in 1948. The traditional impulse toward hemispheric defense was again the first instinct of the United States in the new era.[65] But no longer the main one.

The following year, defense commitments to Canada and western Europe were formalized in the North Atlantic Treaty Organization (NATO). A series of other defense commitments followed in various parts of the world. By 1950, the United States found itself in a major war in Korea, ostensibly on behalf of a world coalition of anti-communist states. Neutrality was no longer seen as a virtue or even as an option.

But the changes were less complete than they seemed at the time. By the late 1960s, a failing war in Vietnam prompted much rethinking. Protests against American "arrogance" were associated with the left by then. But they echoed arguments advanced by conservative critics against the League of Nations in 1919 and against FDR's "drift to war" in the 1930s. In 1950, President Truman had claimed that a UN Security Council resolution, authorizing armed response to communist aggression in Korea, made it unnecessary to seek direct congressional approval. By the 1960s, critics of the Vietnam war raised the question of presidential war powers with renewed urgency. Congress adopted the War Powers Act in 1974, purporting to limit presidential power to make war without explicit congressional endorsement. The measure expressly disavowed the notion that authorization from the United Nations or any other international organization could replace formal consent to war measures by the U.S. Congress.[66]

Leading scholars endorsed this view as a constitutional necessity. No mere treaty structure, they argued, could authorize the commitment of American fighting forces without separate authorization from Congress.[67] By 1990, when the Bush administration was preparing for a war against Iraq, it was not content to secure an authorizing resolution from the UN Security Council. It sought and won a separate authorization from Congress, even though the Democrats were still the majority in Congress and most Democrats were hostile to the venture. The appeal to Congress carried real risk of rebuff, but it was thought by then to be a risk that needed to be taken. Old constitutional arguments about the necessary powers of Congress had returned.

So did the treaty power of the Senate. During the Second World War, advocates of a postwar international organization worried about a repeat of the Senate rejection of the League. Prominent legal scholars accordingly argued that the federal government could make international commitments by joint legislative-executive resolution as an alternative to treaties. The same legal effect could then be secured by simple majorities in both houses even if a two-thirds majority were not available in the

Senate. This doctrine, based on scattered earlier precedents, became conventional wisdom among legal commentators.[68]

For a time, the Senate, itself, seemed to acquiesce. Perhaps it feared that resistance to this doctrine would provoke a clamor for a formal constitutional amendment to eliminate the original treaty ratification process altogether.[69] Such an amendment was endorsed by the House of Representatives in 1945. Perhaps the Senate felt pressure on this score (as well as others, reflecting the postwar mood) when it endorsed the UN Charter in 1945 and the major security treaties in the years thereafter. Trade legislation ultimately authorized approval of international trade agreements by simple majorities.

But the Senate did not agree to let all major commitments come before it as legislative-executive agreements. President Carter's Strategic Arms Limitation Treaty (SALT II) was withdrawn in the late 1970s, when a head count showed it could not secure support from two-thirds of the Senate. The Senate's rejection of the Comprehensive Test Ban Treaty, after it was submitted by President Clinton in 1999, was the first formal rejection of a treaty since the defeat of the League in 1919. Yet quite a few treaties in between were never put to a vote when it became clear that the Senate would not ratify them. Major environmental and human rights treaties languished for years without action by the Senate. Presidents did not dare to attempt an end-run around the Senate by recasting these treaties as measures which did not need ratification by the constitutionally prescribed two-thirds majority.

Indeed the Senate had a counterattack of its own. In the early 1950s, the Senate gave extensive attention to a proposed constitutional amendment by Senator John Bricker (R-Ohio) which would have required that no international agreement could take effect without separate congressional action. It also stipulated that no treaty could be implemented by Congress unless Congress already had the authority, within the existing allocation of constitutional powers, to enact such legislation. An aide to the Democratic leader, Senator Lyndon Johnson, recalled that the Bricker amendment aroused more "emotion" than "any other single legislative issue. . . . No one could vote against the Bricker amendment with impunity and very few could vote against it and survive at all—at least, they thought so."[70]

Among the chief targets of this amendment were human rights treaties.[71] Could Congress implement them on its own, even if they concerned matters ordinarily left to the states? Defenders of segregation in the South were keenly interested in this question but so were prominent and respectable legal scholars, including editors of the *American Journal of International Law*. The Eisenhower administration, concerned about possible limitations on presidential authority, was eager to bury the

Bricker amendment. It expressed great sympathy for the underlying concerns of the amendment and promised to respect them. Secretary of State Dulles promised not to seek American participation in any human rights treaty.[72] Such assurances, along with skillful maneuvering by Lyndon Johnson, left the Bricker amendment one vote shy of the necessary two-thirds majority in the Senate.

For decades thereafter, the policy announced by Dulles remained an unchallenged settlement. Presidents would not submit human rights treaties to the Senate. When President Carter insisted on signing and submitting a basket of such treaties, the Senate refused to consider ratifying any of them. The Senate was finally persuaded to ratify the UN Convention on the Punishment of Genocide when the Reagan administration urged it to do so in the late 1980s. But even that convention was adopted with reservations which essentially deprived the "ratification" of all force. Three other human rights conventions adopted under the Bush administrations in the early 1990s were saddled with the same reservations.[73] The United States has remained, at least in legal form, aloof from all other major human rights conventions.

In 1975, Congress authorized presidential negotiation of trade agreements, promising to accept or reject the results in a single package, without attempting any amendments or reservations (and allowing "ratification" by simple majorities in both houses). At the time, trade agreements were thought to be helpful to Cold War allies in Europe and East Asia. By the 1990s, when President Clinton indicated his intention to negotiate trade agreements specifying internal standards of conduct on labor relations and the environment, Congress balked. It refused to renew its approval for trade negotiations on these deferential terms, even as European countries pressed forward with new trade agreements, including agreements with Latin American nations in America's backyard. Some members of Congress were concerned about the effects of international competition on American industry. Many others remained eager to promote American exports but were not ready to do so if it meant surrendering too much authority over American internal policy.

It took a year-and-a-half for President Bush to regain this special "trade promotion authority" (as "fast track" was renamed). When the Republican-controlled House of Representatives agreed to authorize new trade negotiations on this basis in the summer of 2002, the margin of support was paper thin. Some of the support, at least, seems to have been secured by informal assurances that the administration would be quite cautious about entangling domestic regulatory issues in trade agreements.[74]

If one seeks to explain this pattern of caution, one might give some weight to the self-confidence of a superpower. But presidents, who ought to be commanding figures in a superpower, have signed many treaties and then found that they could not be ratified. The Senate continues to exercise a blocking power—and pays no price for doing so, because its position is not, for the voting public, very controversial.

A better explanation might be that the United States still lives with an eighteenth-century Constitution and an eighteenth- or nineteenth-century outlook on the meaning of national sovereignty. Certainly, the United States looks old-fashioned in many ways. It is the only major western country where politicians—as well as courts—routinely cite eighteenth- and nineteenth-century authorities in their constitutional arguments, on the assumption that the current Constitution can and should operate in accord with the expectations of its Framers or with the ideals of Lincoln.[75]

Americans may forget how remarkable this is. French politicians may secretly envy the grandeur of Louis XIV but do not, in their public appeals, invoke the sayings of royal advisors from the eighteenth century. German politicians and judges do not dwell on the sayings of Friedrich der Grosse or any subsequent Prussian or German ruler from Germany's forgotten past. The events of the twentieth century were not, for the United States, so traumatic that it needed to flee from its own history or repudiate its own political heritage.

To be sure, American constitutional pieties are not always what they seem. Even where the Supreme Court has elaborated constitutional standards in great detail, it has been known to change its mind from one era to the next. In the realm of foreign affairs, the Court has been notably cautious about laying down restrictive doctrines. Judges are not the only ones to show flexibility. Senators and other advocates who harp on constitutional scruples in one setting can be quite ready to bury them in a different setting. In war time, everyone seems ready to accept measures that would seem constitutionally intolerable in peace time. It is easy to view many international agreements in the light of exigencies only slightly removed from war.

Still, the fact is that constitutional arguments and objections raised with particular political motives in one era may be revived with quite different motives in the next. In the course of the twentieth century, fear of excessive presidential power was the cry of advocates on the political right during the 1930s and 1940s, then of advocates on the left in the 1960s and 1970s. Old warnings then reappeared on the right in the 1990s—and again the left in the first years of the new century. Protests against presidential war powers have been taken up from different sides in successive eras. The flexibility of the Constitution cuts both ways. Potential objections, long dormant, can be revived by new advocates in new contexts.

And, after all, something serious is at stake beyond temporary partisan advantage. Long before it was a great power, the United States took pride in having a democratic and constitutional government. Americans took pride in governing themselves by their own rules. In extreme emergencies, local preferences and even accepted practices may have to be sacrificed to desperate exigencies of the moment. It is not surprising that Americans—or at least sizable constituencies in America—keep coming back to the idea that we ought to be able to govern ourselves under our own rules.

But a great power has great responsibilities, because its choices have much more impact. Such responsibilities can be burdensome and the hope of escaping them can take different forms. Woodrow Wilson's vision—of perpetual peace through international organization—may have been a mirror image of the older American policy of neutrality. By embracing all nations, the League might also promise escape from "entangling alliances" with any particular nation.

The League could not have been a serious substitute for American foreign policy. The previous policy of non-entanglement in European affairs had always allowed for the possibility that the United States might come into conflict with a particular European power, that it might have to assert its own interests by force or the threat of force—as it did on several occasions in the nineteenth century. The Wilsonian vision offered the pleasing notion that the United States would never again have interests to protect or assert, except perhaps against outlaw nations condemned by all others. So the United States would no longer have to think very seriously about its own policy. Conflicts could be settled by accepted international norms—even as disputes at home might be settled by independent regulatory commissions.

In this sense, there was a strong Wilsonian element in the foreign policy of the Clinton administration: meaning well to all, it did not have to make hard commitments to any place in particular. The Clinton administration wished well to the United Nations and was vaguely sympathetic to universal ideals and global projects. And it was also not quite serious. Like Woodrow Wilson, President Clinton promised American support for great international projects, such as an international criminal court and a treaty to stop global warming. Unlike Woodrow Wilson, President Clinton did not even try to mobilize support for these controversial initiatives in the Senate. In the 1990s, the United States was not even serious about unserious projects.

A serious policy requires choices. Choices are difficult, all the more so for a superpower which seems to have so many options. The United States provokes great resentment whether it uses its power or holds it in reserve. The obvious alternative is to disguise this power or make it seem more consensual, by presenting American initiatives as the joint project of many nations. The Bush administration accordingly went to considerable lengths to associate other nations with the American war against Saddam Hussein in 2003. Critics warned that American power, for all its predominance, was not great enough to sustain unilateral action. And many of the same critics then sneered at small contributions of personnel recruited to postwar Iraq from Poland, Italy, Spain, Denmark, El Salvador, and other states—as if they were in a position to offer vast troop deployments.

For the most severe critics, the only assurance of acceptable American action would be submission to the legal authority of the United Nations. It is not easy to understand why the world would achieve lawful order by submitting American policy to the veto of China and Russia, which are not very strongly committed to rule by law at home. It is not even easy to understand why American action would be assured of legitimacy if submitted to the approval of France, a nation not famed for its selfless devotion to humanity.

What is certain, at any rate, is that the United States, if it submitted itself to the discipline of such international authorities, could no longer regard its own constitution as its "supreme law." Perhaps that would seem an acceptable sacrifice to people who imagine that the world would be assured complete harmony under the guidance of international institutions. But if we believed that harmony were so easily achieved, we would not have needed any sort of constitutional structure for our own government in the first place.

The UN as a guarantor of global harmony? The idea might seem preposterous to most Americans. It does have considerable momentum in today's world, however. It appeals to all who seek escape from life's challenges and choices and imagine that if government can take care of all personal challenges, then a world government—or at least a world constitution—can take care of all the world's problems. It has some appeal for Americans who hate competition—especially electoral competition which delivers the wrong result. But even losers in a particular round of elections may have a different view when their electoral fortunes improve. What gives force to this vision in today's world is that it is, in fact, the guiding inspiration of contemporary Europe.

CHAPTER SIX

A WORLD SAFE FOR EUROGOVERNANCE

SEVERAL FACTORS ENCOURAGED enthusiasts to place unprecedented hopes in an expanded version of international law during the 1990s. It would be not just a series of accommodations between states, at the margins of policy, but a system of standards and controls reaching inside every state. Germany's foreign minister, Joschka Fischer, called it "global domestic law."[1] Among the factors that made it seem plausible to many people was that within Europe itself, national sovereignty seemed to have been merged into a supranational framework. The European experience seemed to prove that this was possible. As many Europeans saw it, European experience was more than a model. It was also a cause. The success of the European project seemed to Europeans to require its global extension. What Germany had given up, everyone must give up.

The price of the project is that, along with national sovereignty, Europeans have also yielded up democratic constitutions. National constitutions can now be overridden by bureaucratic directives, resting on nothing more than the say-so of officials in Brussels. This unique scheme of government was devised long before European states began to consider a separate constitution for supranational Europe. The institutions of supranational Europe continue to function under a system of decision making removed from the disciplines of parliamentary democracy, under which national governments must still operate at home in the EU's member states. In giving more and more scope to international standards, European policy has increasingly undermined constitutional democracy within European nations. Rather than promoting a new, federal constitutional state across Europe, the trajectory of European integration has encouraged Europeans to embrace, or entangle, the rest of the world in their amorphous constructions. For many Europeans, Eurogovernance holds out a path to world peace—and a world arranged to European tastes.

SUPRANATIONAL SUPREMACY

The historic problem of international organization was already well-recognized in debates at the American Founding, as in the works of seventeenth- and eighteenth-century European thinkers. If international law rests on the consent of sovereign states, then it cannot exert much control when different states disagree on what that law means or how it applies to a particular dispute. If international law could be enforced on dissenters, in the manner of domestic law, then the dissenting states would no longer be sovereign. Not many states (or their peoples) would consent to yield up their independence in this way to outside powers.

European integration seemed to have solved this problem.[2] A European Coal and Steel Community, organized among six states in 1953, broadened into a European Economic Community ("Common Market") under the 1957 Treaty of Rome. The structure gradually came to embrace more states and acquire more powers until it emerged in 1992 as a European Union of twelve states, which expanded to fifteen states in 1995. By then, negotiations were already under way to embrace up to a dozen new states in the following decade. But the EU still has no army of its own, no police force, no criminal courts, not even an administrative field service to monitor compliance with EU policy in the member states. The EU policy is formulated by a permanent bureaucracy in Brussels, the European Commission, which acts under the general direction of ministers from the member states. European Union regulations are then implemented by the national governments of the member states.

Yet the member states do seem to follow EU regulations and directives, at least as faithfully as they follow their own law—because EU regulations are regarded as part of the internal law of the member states. The whole structure thus seems to be a triumph for the international rule of law. By some conventional criteria, it does remain a genuinely international structure. Along with their own armies and police, member states retain independent status in the world at large, exchanging ambassadors and negotiating treaties with other states, participating in international conferences and UN meetings, each with its own ambassador and its own vote. Within Europe, the authority exercised by EU institutions rests on a series of treaties among the member states. Each expansion of the structure—whether in admitting new states or granting new powers to EU organs—has required the individual consent of each member, in the same way as revisions in an ordinary international treaty.

Anyone who wants to see this structure as a triumph for international law must also recognize, however, that it has developed as a very special sort of international law. The central organ of the EU legal system is the European Court of Justice. The jurisprudence of that court has aimed at transforming the structure into something like a domestic legal system. Almost from the outset of the Common Market, the ECJ took an extremely activist approach to the Treaty of Rome, interpreting it as a proto-constitution. The ECJ's jurisprudence has been described as "teleological"—aiming not just at favored results in particular cases but at an ultimate vision of the European structure.[3] In effect, the ECJ approached an international treaty as if it were a national constitution.[4]

The first step was to read the treaty as conferring rights on individuals. The Treaty of Rome did provide that national courts could "refer" a dispute to the ECJ, when questions arose about the application of the treaty. The drafters of the treaty recognized that if impositions by national governments were challenged in national courts, national courts would not automatically approve a disputed measure simply because the European Commission had directed it. A national court was bound to ask whether the Commission had been properly authorized to direct the national government to undertake a particular measure. National courts might give different answers to such questions. The European Court could provide a common answer. It could hold the European Commission to a common standard of constraint under the treaty, rather than leaving the Commission exposed to a half dozen different standards of constraint, when it came to interpreting the powers conferred by the treaty.

Only five years into its institutional life, the ECJ began turning this provision inside out. In its 1963 decision in the van Gend case (dealing with a Dutch tax on imports), the Court held that citizens could not only challenge their government for improperly following the Commission, but also for failing to follow the Rome treaty, itself. The "objective" of the Rome treaty "implies" that it "is more than an agreement which . . . creates mutual obligations between the contracting states." Instead, the ECJ insisted, the treaty had created a "new order of international law" which, for citizens of the member states must "confer upon them rights which become part of their legal heritage." So the rights of citizens could now, for the first time in history, be directly settled by a supranational court.[5]

In the van Geld case, the Court had directed Dutch tax officials to ignore an earlier treaty. A year later, in *Costa v. ENEL,*[6] the Court held that even a subsequent parliamentary enactment (this time involving an Italian law nationalizing electric power generation) must be rendered void, if it conflicted with rights conferred in the Treaty of Rome. Otherwise, the Court warned, "the legal basis of the Community itself [would be] called into question."

In these early cases, the Court was laying down ambitious doctrines, but generally allowed national courts to tailor the precise applications to the circumstances in the national legal system. By the late 1970s, the ECJ felt strong enough to pursue much more aggressive applications of its doctrine. In its 1978 ruling in the Cassis de Dijon case,[7] the Court ruled, on the basis of general language regarding "free circulation of goods," that a product satisfying regulatory standards in one member state must be allowed entry into every state of the Common Market, even if the product did not satisfy existing regulatory standards in other states. At a stroke, the Court established limitations on the regulatory power of member states which were more severe than anything pronounced by the U.S. Supreme Court in its rulings on state interference with interstate commerce.[8]

The ECJ's doctrine certainly helped to undermine many questionable regulatory constraints in particular states. It also promoted a dramatic increase in Europe-wide regulation by the European Commission, as an alternative to every state's having to accept the standards set by the least restrictive state. By the 1980s, the Commission was laying down Europe-wide regulations on everything from the proper recipe for sausages and beer to the accent marks on keyboards, establishing itself as the central standard-setter (and allocator of regulatory advantage) for competing producers throughout Europe. The ECJ gave a further push to this regulatory expansion in its holdings, developed over the course of the 1980s, that even where the Commission had merely directed national governments to implement new policies (rather than imposing a precise EU regulation), national courts should read such policies into existing national law or hold governments financially accountable to private litigants for failing to do so.[9]

Meanwhile, the ECJ drove its supremacy doctrine to its logical conclusion. The Constitutional Court of Germany held that certain Commission regulations (restricting an owner's right to cultivate land) could not be enforced, because they conflicted with rights guarantees in the German constitution (the Basic Law). In its 1970 ruling in *Internationale Handelsgesellschaft*, the ECJ insisted that European law must take precedence even over national constitutions.[10] As the ECJ saw it, by agreeing to the Treaty of Rome, Germany had bound itself to a legal authority of higher standing than its own constitution—and bound itself to accept the ECJ's interpretation of the scope and limits of this highest legal authority.

None of these decisions has any counterpart in American law. American courts still regard treaties as subordinate to statutes, certainly to subsequent statutes, so it would be unthinkable for an American court to invalidate an act of Congress because it conflicted with a treaty. It would be altogether mind-boggling for an American court to hold a mere treaty superior to the Constitution. But before the European Court of Justice embarked on its activist course, European courts had no precedent for such doctrines, either.

It is true, of course, that federal courts in the United States routinely overturn state laws and state supreme court rulings based on state constitutions. Federal courts feel free to act in this way, because the federal Constitution clearly stipulates that federal law will be "supreme law of the land," binding on "the judges in every state . . . any Thing in the Constitution or Laws of any State to the Contrary notwithstanding" (Article VI).

There was no such supremacy clause in the Treaty of Rome and, indeed, nothing which stipulated that it was more than a treaty. Even so, European states generally complied with rulings of the European Court of Justice. As a recent study by Leslie Goldstein demonstrates, American states defied federal judicial authority in the decades before the Civil War far more often than European governments have defied the European Court of Justice.

Professor Goldstein speculates that the legal supremacy of the ECJ has been so readily established because modern Europeans have more respect for "the rule of law" than did early Americans.[11] Public opinion surveys, however, suggest that there is actually quite a bit of public skepticism toward the European Court of Justice among Europeans and no great reservoir of trust in its decisions.[12]

But in any case, the thesis begs the question of what "the rule of law" actually requires. American courts have always held that the rule of law requires that the Constitution take precedence over a mere treaty. It is not obvious why the contrary proposition is more in keeping with the rule of law—simply because a collection of foreign judges have so decreed.

As it happens, the judges of the European Court of Justice, for all their doctrinal boldness, have not been willing to express themselves with the openness to differing viewpoints that is characteristic of American courts— or for that matter, most other courts. The ECJ does not publish individually signed opinions, nor does it allow dissenting or concurring opinions. The judges, once appointed by each member state, speak in a single collective voice, with all differences of individual conviction about the law (or anything else) carefully hidden from view. This arrangement protects individual judges from political pressure. It makes it harder for governments in the member states to affect the Court's jurisprudence through strategic appointments.[13]

Perhaps the arrangement even gives the Court greater moral authority. But if so, it is more akin to the mystical authority of a synod of bishops, proclaiming the magisterium, than that of a normal court wrestling with legal questions on which reasonable minds might reasonably disagree.[14]

And still the question remains: Why is it consistent with the rule of law for a national government, otherwise bound by its own constitution, to authorize a supranational authority to override that constitution? Contemporary Europeans have been satisfied with very ambiguous or evasive answers to this question.

POST-MODERN POLITY

The jurisprudence of the ECJ might make sense if one viewed the European Community (or the original European Economic Community) as the embryo of a federal state. From this view, the ECJ would simply be relying on "teleological jurisprudence" to speed European governance on its predestined path. In some ways, that is a plausible account of what happened. Successive treaty revisions, agreed by the member states, expanded the powers of governance at the Community level. Still more power was then conferred on the Community's successor, the European Union. More and more law within European states came to be determined at the European level. By 2003, a survey of government officials in the member states found that they attributed more than half the legal standards they enforced to European-level requirements.[15]

Yet the European Union has remained a strange hybrid, a mix of state functions embedded in a framework that remains, in crucial ways, an international organization. The EU exercises very extensive legislative powers, but the outlines of new regulatory initiatives have continued to require approval from councils of ministers representing the national governments of the member states. Initiative for new regulatory ventures may come from the European Commission or the Court of Justice, but both the commissioners and the judges are appointed by national governments, in consultation with other national governments, according to formulas which allocate offices on the basis of nationality.

Meanwhile, some of the most basic attributes of statehood remain with the member states. The member states do not only maintain their own armies and their own embassies abroad. General taxing power has also remained an exclusive prerogative of national governments, with the Union (like the Community before it) living off revenue from tariff collections. In per capita terms, the Union remains a fiscal pigmy compared to the budgetary resources of member states (with the EU claiming little more than 1 percent of the aggregate GDP of the member states). Basic social welfare provision, like retirement pensions and unemployment payments, are financed and administered by national governments, in accord with national policies and priorities.

A "parliamentary assembly," a mere consultative body in the original scheme of the Rome Treaty (composed of delegates from national parliaments), evolved through successive treaty revisions into a directly elected European Parliament (EP). The EP was eventually given veto rights over the Union budget and over major "directives" from the Council of Ministers. But the European Parliament was denied any power to initiate legislation or expenditures. It was denied any say in the composition of the Council of Ministers, which is composed of relevant cabinet ministers of member states, chosen by the national political process in each state. The Parliament was denied any real control over the composition of the European Commission, whose commissioners are appointed by member states, according to agreed formulas reserving at least one place on the commission for each member state to fill. The Community (and later, the European Union) insisted that only bona fide democratic governments could join. The governing arrangements of the European Union, itself, would not satisfy the standards of democratic legitimacy it demanded of national governments seeking to join the Union.

To speak of a "democratic deficit," as many observers did in the 1990s, rather misses the point, however. Nations joined into a common market or an economic community did not think of themselves as a single European nation. Even if the European Union aspired to be something more than a manager of trade, fifteen countries speaking a dozen different languages did not form a unified political community. Turnouts for European Parliament elections have always been lower than for national elections. Candidates for the European Parliament framed their campaigns around salient issues in domestic politics in each state, rather than trying to associate themselves with European themes. Surveys in the late 1990s found that most voters had little interest in the EU Parliament and even less knowledge of EU governmental institutions.[16] It was, for most voters, either boring or baffling.

At any rate, national governments, which were accountable to voters, were not eager to share power with Europe-wide electorates. National governments negotiated the treaty revisions and council directives that formed the backbone of EU policy. On the other hand, the national governments were prepared to bind themselves to common regulatory schemes and, in an increasing number of fields, to let themselves be bound by voting formulas in the Council of Ministers that allowed "qualified majorities" or supermajorities to bind dissenting governments.

Rather than view the resulting structure as an inadequate democracy or an undeveloped federal state, a number of scholars in the 1990s argued that the EU must be understood as a unique entity—a "postmodern polity" that does not conform to any recognized pattern.[17] Other scholars have argued that, for all its delegations to common institutions, the Union remains fundamentally a structure in which national governments are in charge.[18] Or perhaps, as others argue, a structure in which the most powerful states are in charge.[19]

So France, one of the wealthiest states, has remained the smallest net contributor to EU spending (if French contributions to tariff receipts are compared with the flow of agricultural subsidies and other payments returning to France).[20] So, too, while Germany has some of the most ambitious environmental and social regulatory standards, EU policy has tended to emulate German standards rather than aiming at an average.[21] In effect, the central bargain has been that member states gain unimpeded access to French and German markets, in return for embracing German production standards and French agricultural protection schemes. A number of accounts of thinking within the Commission—a rather secretive bureaucracy—have stressed the influence, direct or indirect, of French and German priorities.[22] France and Germany feel free to defy agreed rules limiting the permissible size of national budget deficits in 2003, even after the Commission had enforced these limits against smaller members.

But it was surely easier for the two largest states to dominate policy in an Economic Community of six members in the 1960s. Such influence seems to have become progressively more diluted as the Community expanded to nine in the 1970s (embracing Britain, Ireland, and Denmark), then to twelve in the 1980s (with the addition of Spain, Portugal, and Greece) and then to fifteen in the Union of the 1990s (with Sweden, Finland, and Austria). The intergovernmental character of the Union faced its most serious challenge when the fifteen prepared to accept another ten states (stretching as far east as Estonia and Latvia and as far south as Malta and Cyprus) in the first decade of the new century. On the other hand, a community extending from Portugal to Finland (or now to Estonia), from Ireland to Greece (or now to Cyprus) is even harder to conceive as a single democratic polity.

Representatives of both the existing and prospective member states were convened in 2002 to propose a new framework for the EU. After decades of expansion and adjustment through new treaties, the EU would now have a formal "constitution." What was actually proposed, however, was simply a new treaty, which would take effect, like all previous treaty revisions, only when ratified by all the member states. And in its main provisions, the proposed constitutional treaty largely confirmed the strange hybrid quality and post-modern flavor of the European "construction."[23]

On the one hand, the text stipulated that the "Union shall respect the national identities of the Member States, inherent in their fundamental structures, political and constitutional . . ." (art. 5). On the other hand, it confirmed that the law of the Union "shall have primacy over the law of the Member States" (art. 10)—which, as the ECJ has established, means that bureaucratic directives of the Commission take precedence over national constitutional restrictions. The text stipulated that the Union "shall respect" the "essential State functions" of the member states (art. 5.1) but then assigned "competences" to the Union which would allow it to get into almost everything still handled by national governments (art. 12–16). The member states were only guaranteed some continued authority in relation to "research, technological development and space" and in "development cooperation and humanitarian aid" (that is, to outside nations)—and even in these areas the states were not assured exclusive jurisdiction (art. 13.3, 13.4).

The text said nothing about specific taxing powers but might have implied taxing powers for the Union in vague allusions to securing adequate "resources" (art. 53.3). The text said nothing about a common army but something of the sort might be implied in vague allusions to providing "a common Union defence policy" with "an operational capacity drawing on assets civilian and military" (art. 40.1). Instead of constituting new powers for the Union, in relation to these core state functions, the constitutional treaty simply suggested that the Union might exercise power in these fields, too, if all the member states agreed. The member states could always have expanded EU powers, as they had in the past, but in the past, major expansions had required formal treaty revisions. The constitutional treaty now seemed to authorize national governments to expand the Union's powers, without the bother of a new round of treaty ratifications—and without the awkwardness of involving national parliaments or national electorates. So the constitutional treaty, in the most fundamental ways, proposed to do the opposite of what a constitution normally does—that is, confer definite powers within demarcated limits. The constitutional treaty characteristically sought to evade the awkward implications of the term "power" by speaking instead of "competences."

For all its evasions, the constitutional treaty turned out to be too ambitious. Where previous treaty revisions had established complex voting schemes, reserving veto rights for smaller states, the constitutional treaty proposed that almost all governing decisions by the Council of Ministers could now be reached by a lower qualified majority. Initiatives in most areas could now be launched with a mere 60 percent of votes in the Council (art. 24.1). But votes would be allocated according to a formula giving Germany (with nearly a third more population) no more votes than France and giving France no more votes than Britain or Italy ("Protocol on Representation . . . and Weighting of Votes," art. 2). Poland and Spain, medium-sized states whose voting strength was devalued in the new formulas, opposed the new scheme and a conference of the heads of state had to abandon the proposed constitution in December 2003.

Even the failed compromises in this proposal are revealing, however. The text made explicit, for the first time, that dissatisfied states could leave the Union—though only on terms agreed by other members (art. 59). Simultaneously, it provided, again for the first time, a procedure by which states found to be violating their obligations could have their membership suspended by the other states (art. 58). Either provision would be regarded as unthinkable for a state government in the United States. But the United States aspires to be a single nation in ways that the EU does not.

Americans, with all their internal diversity, would find it very hard to imagine admitting nations of Latin America or East Asia as states of the Union—especially if these new states insisted on retaining their own armies, their own legal systems, their own differing systems of internal government. The EU has found it impossible to set limits to its own expansion, because it conceives itself to be founded on "values" which are or might as well be universal.[24]

But not all member states actually agree, even on projects for Europe—as the fate of the constitutional treaty in 2003 shows. For advocates of major new initiatives, it was frustrating to have initiatives blocked by states that refused to go along. Major treaty revisions always required unanimous consent, however, as revisions in any international treaty require the consent of all the parties. The European treaties were, after all, treaties.

One way of handling the problem was to allow dissenting states to opt out of new initiatives. So when most member states wanted to adopt a common currency, Britain's agreement was secured by allowing Britain to endorse the project for others, while preserving its own right to retain the pound. An agreement to suspend border controls on travel within Europe was secured, again, by allowing recalcitrant states to exempt themselves. The same technique secured agreement on a "social charter," setting out rights to social protection for labor and other constituencies—agreed by all EU states on condition that the charter would actually apply only to states willing to embrace it. The proposed constitutional treaty, for all its ambitions to formalize EU procedure, made explicit provision for continuing such special ventures in "enhanced cooperation" among subsets of the EU's overall membership (art. 43).

If one regards European treaty adjustments as the equivalent of constitutional amendments, such provisions for selective opt-outs are very odd. In the United States, an Equal Rights Amendment (ERA), supposed to guarantee broad-ranging equality between the sexes, was repeatedly endorsed by Congress but failed to secure the required assent from three-quarters of the states. Adopting the European technique, sponsors of the ERA might have cajoled recalcitrant states into ratifying the amendment, by cutting a deal which promised to exempt those states from any obligation to comply with the amendment—so long as they supported its imposition on other states. Of course, no one thought to propose such an expedient in the United States, because it so obviously undermines the whole logic of a national constitution.

The 2003 constitutional treaty proposal provided that states which decided to remain aloof from "enhanced cooperation" measures would not be allowed to vote on their conduct in the Council of Ministers (art. 43.3). It was not an unreasonable compromise from the point of view of the participating states. But it implied ongoing division between "core states" and member states with more doubts about European integration. Europe could then be a constitutional entity—but a unique one in which more ambitious states (or more recalcitrant ones) escape a common constitutional discipline. The collapse of the constitutional treaty in 2003 suggested the EU could not yet agree even to be a constitutional entity in these post-modern terms.

DEVICES OF SUPRANATIONALISM

The European Union grew out of a common market. It might be seen—and often has been seen—as little more than a device to assure economic integration. But economic integration has no clear meaning to economists. The term itself was popularized by the U.S. administrator of Marshall Plan aid in the late 1940s.[25] Whatever it was, "integration" could not simply be reduced to opening markets because most member states, with large socialist parties and traditions of state control, were not very comfortable with free markets. Even under the Coal and Steel Community, the dismantling of barriers to cross-border trade was balanced with efforts to protect particular mines and plants.[26] Under the more ambitious terms of the European Economic Community (and its various successors), the European Commission balanced opening of markets with protections for workers, for consumers, for the environment. The results were not dictated by economic logic but by political priorities of the member states—except that the member states did not quite cohere into a common political community.

Some commentators dismissed the complications and incongruities with an appeal to performance. If the post-modern logic of the EU was hard to follow, the crucial point was that it worked. Except it did not obviously work. During the 1990s, when the United States experienced sustained economic boom, Germany and France experienced continuing stagnation with high levels of unemployment. Their performance did not improve when the United States experienced its own economic recession in the first years of the new century—nor when the United States emerged from the recession in 2003. Some critics warned that European controls, if not preventing necessary reforms of labor policy and tax policy, encouraged governments to think that such reforms could be indefinitely postponed.

Nor were proponents of greater "integration" content to sell the policy in merely economic terms. In the early decades, integration was hailed as a solvent of national jealousies, as a way to assure that European states would never again resort to catastrophic wars. But there were already very high levels of trade and cross-border investment between major European states before 1914. On the other hand, for all the many new controls established by the Treaty of Rome, European states remained unwilling to entrust European-level authorities with the military capacity to enforce terms of peace. It was never clear why regulations, insisting on common definitions for sausage and chocolate, should be an ultimate guarantor of peace.

In the 1980s, the European Community embraced Spain, Portugal, and Greece, nations which had only recently emerged from dictatorships or military governments. Membership in the European Community, it was hoped, would help to stabilize democracy in these troubled nations. The same argument was made for extending the EU into post-communist nations of central and eastern Europe. Perhaps there were reasons to hope that EU controls would promote "stability." But it was a bit awkward to claim that democracy would be strengthened by submitting national governments to the tutelage of a structure which was not itself very democratic.

A normal constitutional state must retain the loyalty of citizens even amidst hard times. Europe remained a remote abstraction for most citizens of the EU. The European Quarter of Brussels, where most EU institutions are based, does not have monuments to common European heroes or common European struggles—as actual heroes or struggles pitted European states against each other in the past. Its modern glass buildings and abstract lawn sculptures have the look of a university campus or an industrial park. The common European currency features engravings of generic palaces, which might be anywhere and happen to be nowhere.

Why shouldn't states simply assert their own interests? European institutions gained strength by appealing to particular constituencies. Business firms with an interest in cross-border trade were drawn to the ECJ. The Commission would offer compensating benefits to those seeking regulatory protection. National judges were systematically wooed by judges of the European Court at conferences and professional gatherings. And national judges learned to appreciate the extra power and status they would gain as enforcers of European law against their own governments. Through the Council of Ministers—where votes are never recorded—national governments could press for European initiatives that would be too controversial with their own parliaments at home.

Still, there is always the threat that disaffected constituencies will try to rally nationalist sentiment to resist European policy. That governments remain quite fearful of this possibility was illustrated by their extraordinary response to the entry of a populist party into the Austrian cabinet in early 2000. Jorg Haidar, leader of the Freedom Party, had made tasteless remarks about Austria's Nazi past but generated more concern by protesting against the influx of foreign workers into Austria. All other governments demanded that Haidar's party be excluded from the governing coalition. Nothing in any EU treaty authorized the EU to determine who could hold national offices. So the national governments of the member states—acting on behalf of Europe, if not exactly as the European Union—declared a diplomatic embargo on Austria. The embargo did not have its intended effect and was finally abandoned when Austria threatened diplomatic countermeasures to disrupt EU meetings. But the episode demonstrated the great uneasiness of national governments about allowing opposition currents to develop within member states.[27]

Haidar's issue was a particular sore spot because most EU states have sizable populations of immigrants which they have not done well at assimilating. Until the end of the 1990s, German law made it particularly difficult for people of non-German ancestry to acquire German citizenship, so the children and grandchildren of "guest workers" from Turkey remained non-citizens, even though born and raised in Germany. Less restrictive citizenship laws in other states did not lessen social barriers between natives and immigrants, particularly immigrants from Muslim countries, nurturing a sense of separation and grievance against former colonial powers. Rather than working to assimilate growing populations of outsiders, most European states were happy to off-load this problem onto the European Union.

Citizenship in the European Union is determined by citizenship in member states, so the EU could not force national states to adopt new citizens. But it could spin a network of protections for non-citizens so their status was not simply that of outsiders. As one analyst has described it, the EU has promoted a post-modern solution to its post-modern political framework—"post-national citizenship."

In other ways, the EU has worked actively to undermine the allegiance of national citizens to national states. It has become a great sponsor of regional government—which often means, subnational ethnic identities. The EU has provided financial assistance for designated regions and also provided a parallel form of representation for the regions in a consultative assembly of regions. The scheme buys sympathy and support for Europe from Scots and Basques and other national minorities—and extends European protection to regions outside Germany in which ethnic Germans still live or might like to return.

The oldest and most prominent scheme for competing with national governments, however, has been the promotion of a Europe-wide system for protection of human rights. Formally, the European Convention on Human Rights is a creature of the Council of Europe. The Council is a loose grouping of European states formed in 1949 by western European states, affirming, amidst Cold War divisions, their common devotion to democracy. The Convention, drafted in 1949, was framed as a treaty among the states which remained something external to their own law. A European Court of Human Rights was authorized to hear complaints about violations of the convention, but only with approval of a council representing member state governments. For some decades, the whole institution remained rather peripheral.

The European human rights convention began to assume much more importance when it was embraced—or at least, invoked—by the European Court of Justice in the 1970s. The ECJ could reach into domestic legal systems. And it needed an answer to the complaint that, by superseding national constitutions, it risked endangering the fundamental rights of citizens. The ECJ announced that it would integrate into its decisions the rights protections of the member states and also those of international human treaties, such as the European Convention.

Whether inspired by the ECJ's implicit invitation or merely by its example, the Court of Human Rights began to take a much more activist approach to its charge. Britain was chastised for anti-terrorist measures in northern Ireland and told that it must rescind or amend its criminal prohibitions on homosexual relations. Ireland was told that it must reform its law on abortion.[28]

The European Court of Justice never held that it was bound by every provision of the human rights convention, however, much less by every ruling of the human rights court in Strasbourg. The Council of Europe, always a more encompassing entity than the European Economic Community (and its successors) expanded much more rapidly and extensively after the collapse of the Iron Curtain, eventually embracing forty-three countries including Albania, Ukraine, and Russia. And all of these states were entitled to send judges (one from each state) to participate in the human rights court.

A particularly striking fact about the subsequent evolution of the European Union is that the EU has been unwilling or unable to disentangle itself from this broader structure. The Maastricht Treaty, which launched the EU, gave a sympathetic nod to the human rights convention, without quite committing the EU to abide by all its provisions. The EU then developed its own charter of fundamental rights—supposed to be binding only on member states of the Union rather than on all members of the Council. The proposed new constitution provides an expanded version of this charter—and at the same time provides that the EU will commit itself to join the European human rights convention. So the European

Union will protect basic rights, as presumably the member states will, too. But none can be trusted to do so completely without assistance from such human rights exemplars as Ukraine and Albania.

The arrangement may seem rather odd. But it testifies to the Union's commitment to its "values" of "diversity, tolerance, pluralism"—even in governing, even in something so basic as defining and protecting rights. The Union can not trust member states to do this. And it can not bring itself to demand that member states trust the Union to do so. Fortunately, Ukraine is ready to help out.

ECONOMIC COMMUNITY EMBRACING THE GLOBAL ENVIRONMENT

The European Union emerged from what was, in essence, a trade organization with special powers. It might seem that a trade organization would attract the interest of economic constituencies, focused on marginal advantage. Why go beyond that? It might add to the prestige and moral authority of the "Economic Community" to associate it with idealistic causes like human rights. But what sort of idealism could attach to the numbing details of trade policy?

In fact, a new cause, inspiring great fervor, helped attach a whole new constituency to "Europe" in the 1980s. It was the cause of environmentalism. And it turned out to have everything to do with economic policy because environmental regulations have differing effects on different industries and on countries in differing circumstances.

The policy conflicts were more complicated than rich versus poor. Environmental concerns were particularly prominent in northern Protestant countries while commanding much less public sympathy in Catholic and Mediterranean countries.[29] Whatever the complex historical and cultural reasons for such divergences, they had to be smoothed over. And so they were.

In 1987, the then European Community embarked on an ambitious new scheme to eliminate all barriers to cross-border trade among the member states, the "Single Europe Act." The European Commission set out to establish "harmonizing" standards on a wide range of domestic regulations. Environmental standards were among those most often targeted for harmonizing. The staff of the Commission directorate, responsible for environmental affairs, jumped from fifty-five in 1986 to 450 in 1992. The number of environmental directives issued in the period 1989–91 exceeded all those issued in the preceding twenty years. Though the Commission might have invoked treaty provisions allowing for minimum standards, it tended to impose mandatory standards.[30]

Environmental advocacy groups played an important role in "selling" these new policies. The Commission was happy to encourage them. The European Environmental Bureau, representing a network of advocacy groups in Brussels, received half of its funding from direct EU grants. Five of the six independent environmental advocacy groups operating in Brussels by the end of the 1980s depended on Commission grants for sizable portions of their budgets.[31] Like their counterparts in human rights advocacy, environmentalists saw many reasons to extend their concerns into the wider world. And for their own reasons, so did the managers of European economic policy.

So, for example, in response to the demands of Green activists, Germany invested heavily in trash recycling facilities during the 1980s. To make these facilities economical, Germany successfully pressured Brussels to impose general recycling requirements across Europe—guaranteeing business for recycling facilities by blocking any cheaper method of waste disposal in neighboring countries. There was no reason to limit such maneuvering to Europe and some danger to the scheme if it could be circumvented by waste disposal abroad.

In 1989, European leaders took the lead in negotiating an international treaty against international trade in hazardous waste. Conveniently, the supposed dangers of "hazardous waste dumping" in Africa had already been dramatized by Greenpeace, an activist environmental advocacy group. Greenpeace happened to derive the bulk of its funding in northern Europe and particularly in Germany.[32]

The resulting Basel Convention established an "A" list of exporters, who pledged not to deliver anything from an expanding list of "hazards" to any country not on the list. And the "A" list was tightly guarded: Monaco and Israel, hardly backward countries, were refused admission to the list.[33] In effect, the Basel Convention established a reprocessing cartel, by which European facilities could monopolize the reprocessing business. The United States, which is not overly fond of international cartels, did not join.[34]

As agricultural protection is a major EU policy, the EU has launched other international initiatives to limit agricultural competition. The very vague and open-ended 1992 Biodiversity Convention—by which signatories pledged to cooperate in protecting endangered species—was taken up, within a few years, as the platform for a "Biosafety Protocol," aimed at limiting trade in genetically modified foods. Advocacy groups again helped to mobilize public opinion with alarmist warnings about the possibility that genetically altered species would get out of control and run amok like some vegetable Frankenstein: "Frankenfoods" would terrorize the peasantry.

To take seriously the European claim that such products are a hazard to human health, one would have to believe that American safety standards were far more lax than European, since genetically altered strains have already achieved a large place in American agriculture (as among farmers in Canada, Australia, Argentina, and other agricultural exporting countries). One would then have to believe that agricultural safety crises had broken out in Europe in the 1990s rather than in the Americas out of sheer bad luck.

Meanwhile, in parts of the world where human nutrition is more of a concern than agricultural esthetics, genetically modified crops provide hope of more abundant and pest-resistant harvests. The UN Development Program accordingly issued a strong endorsement of the new technologies in 2001.[35] After years of alarmist rhetoric from Europe, however, African countries announced in the summer of 2002 that they would reject famine relief supplies from the United States because they contained genetically modified corn.[36]

By far the most ambitious environmental venture backed by the EU, however, was the 1997 Kyoto Protocol on Climate Change. It was indeed the most staggeringly ambitious treaty venture ever proposed for the world to implement at one time. At the 1992 UN summit on "Environment and Development," almost all nations had agreed to a Framework Convention on Climate Change, promising in vague terms to limit the growth in emissions of so-called "greenhouse gases," thought by many scientists to be promoting a climatic warming trend. As the principal "greenhouse gas" is carbon dioxide, limiting such emissions seemed to require limiting consumption of fossil fuels (oil, coal, natural gas)—the lifeblood of economic development. In fact, almost all nations continued to use more fuel during the economic expansion of the 1990s and almost all, accordingly, continued to emit more carbon dioxide. Developing countries refused to make any commitments to reducing their own fuel consumption, so the Kyoto Protocol committed some two dozen affluent nations to specified reductions in carbon emissions over the next fifteen years.

The European Union successfully pressed for commitments based on the base-year of 1990. That meant that the closing of coal-burning installations in the former East Germany (GDR)—which would have happened in any case, as western investment and western pollution controls were extended to the GDR's antiquated industrial plant—could now be portrayed as a contribution to reducing global warming. Britain, which was shifting from coal to natural gas under the Thatcher government, got the same bonus. The EU then won the right to make EU-wide commitments, so that some member states could make smaller commitments on emission reductions (or none at all) and the EU would still be credited for overall reductions—and demand the same of other nations. In subsequent negotiations over implementing rules for Kyoto, European negotiators successfully resisted proposals to allow other signatories the same latitude as European states would have within the EU, for achieving aggregate emission reductions by "trading" emission rights with other countries.

The resulting regulatory scheme would have put the United States at a staggering disadvantage. According to the calculations of William Nordhaus, an economist sympathetic to environmental regulation, full implementation of Kyoto would have cost the United States $2.2 trillion, while EU states would have borne implementation costs less than one quarter of that amount (about $0.5 trillion).[37]

Meanwhile, however, the scheme had no chance of actually reducing the build-up of carbon dioxide in the atmosphere without parallel commitments from developing countries. In 1997, China alone was already emitting two-thirds as much carbon each year as the United States. Even if the United States achieved its emission reduction targets under Kyoto, the net effect on global emissions would be more than off-set by continuing increases in Chinese fuel consumption. Even if all the reduction in American emission were allocated to China as permissible growth, moreover, Chinese emission levels, calculated on a per capita basis, would still be less than 20 percent of those in the United States.[38]

Within the EU, Kyoto allowed for "catch-up" development. Greece was authorized to increase its carbon emissions, for example, in recognition of its lagging development. On a per capita basis, however, Greek consumption of electricity at the time of the Kyoto negotiations was already some 70 percent of that in Britain and Germany. India's electricity consumption, on a per capita basis, was 7 percent of that in Britain and Germany.[39] Kyoto could make no impact on reducing carbon build-up in the atmosphere unless it was considered as the first step in a scheme eventually freezing development in poor countries at vastly lower standards of living. Otherwise, it made sense only as a means of crippling the U.S. economy, which, to the chagrin of European planners, was consistently outperforming core EU states in the 1990s.

The Clinton administration did sign the Kyoto Protocol but made no effort to fight the overwhelming hostility to it in the Senate. When the Bush administration subsequently announced its opposition to the treaty, Europeans expressed great indignation about American "selfishness." The chorus of condemnation did not prevent Australia and Japan from embracing the American position and subsequently Russia. Much of the "independent" advocacy on behalf of Kyoto, by ostensibly "nongovernmental" organizations, was funded by European governments.[40]

Successive reports of the European Commission insisted that the EU would set an example by implementing Kyoto commitments on its own. In fact, national governments in Europe largely ignored Kyoto and fossil fuel use continued to rise. If European action depended on parallel action in other countries, there was no obvious means of inducing others to cooperate except by threatening trade sanctions. That idea appealed to important advocates in Europe. Friends of the Earth petitioned the European Commission to impose trade penalties on the United States for failing to implement Kyoto.[41]

For obvious reasons, trade penalties are fiercely opposed by developing countries but they have been repeatedly urged, since the early 1990s, by the European Parliament.[42] Advocates insist that without such trade measures, states with inadequate environmental policies (or in some versions, inadequate protection for workers) would secure an unfair competitive advantage against the nations (or the supranational entities) which do impose suitable regulation on their own industry. The reasoning has obvious logic: Europe itself imposes such standards on low-wage countries like Portugal and Greece, so why not on the world at large?

Of course, the European Union also provides sizable cash compensations to its less affluent member states and cannot afford anything remotely comparable for India or China. But the EU can promote the idea that international trade is linked to wider schemes of "developmental" assistance. Europe does more of this than the United States. Europe is more committed to the idea that "the world" is drawing closer together.

Meanwhile, talk about global governance provides a vehicle for Europe to act in the world—even when it can not agree on deployment of armed forces or on shared strategic commitments on serious matters. Saving "the environment" has great appeal for advocates of collectivist policies, among European socialists (or Christian Democrats, keen to catch up with them) as among left-leaning activists in America. After all, the environment is all around us, it affects us all, so we all have a stake in common policies. The fact that we do not all agree about these policies—even in the different parts of Europe—is an awkward fact that is easy to brush aside.

PEACE THROUGH PIETY

As far back as the early 1970s, sympathetic commentators had described the European Economic Community as "Kantian."[43] It would subsume national rivalries in a common structure of peace. But different states had different ideas about how to advance peace or how to organize ultimate structures of peace. German Chancellor Adenauer had embraced the Coal and Steel Community with enthusiasm in the 1950s, as a structure in which German revival could be made to seem unthreatening to Germany's neighbors. Charles de Gaulle muttered warnings against the hidden German agenda of the German High Commissioner for the Coal and Steel Community and demanded that further steps toward European integration acknowledge French primacy in Europe.

When President de Gaulle withdrew France from NATO in the late 1960s, other European states clung to the American alliance. Other Europeans did not rally to the French vision, which implied that France could do as well as the United States in ensuring that a rearmed Germany would pose no dangers to its neighbors. Perhaps other nations in the region had noticed that this French conceit did not accord with past experience.

When the collapse of communism in eastern Europe suddenly made German unification a real possibility, West Germany pursued its own vision in direct negotiations with Moscow and Washington. "Europe," as a common entity, played almost no role in shaping the ensuing grand settlement. Not all of Germany's partners were happy with the result. But German Chancellor Kohl assured his European partners that Germany would remain firmly anchored in European institutions, building "a European Germany" rather than "a German Europe"—at least so long as other European nations embraced the German vision for Europe. The 1991 Maastricht Treaty, projecting a common European currency and a "common foreign and security policy" in a firmly united Europe, provided a new name (European Union) and a new structure to secure this hopeful vision.

The hope was not universally shared, however, even at the outset. Margaret Thatcher, shortly after retiring as British prime minister, warned that "Germany's preponderance within the Community is such that no major decision can really be taken against German wishes. In these circumstances, the Community augments German power rather than containing it." Accordingly, she urged that European institutions focus on promoting trade while allowing "individual nation states [to] retain their freedom of action" on larger questions. Otherwise, "a serious dispute between EC member states locked into a common foreign policy would precipitate a crisis affecting everything covered by the Community."[44]

The warning certainly seemed borne out by the rancor that accompanied the collapse of any "common" European policy toward Iraq in 2002. The German government, without consulting its European partners and without waiting for any decision from NATO or the United Nations, announced that it would in no circumstances participate in an international military action against Iraq: Vital questions affecting Germans would be decided, Chancellor Schroeder insisted, "in Berlin," according to the "German way." France embraced the German policy of opposition to war. French diplomats then sought to mobilize international opposition to any military action against Saddam Hussein, even as France's EU partner, Britain, joined the United States in urging the Security Council to

authorize a military strike. Early in 2003, the Spanish government—
without consulting France or Germany—took the initiative of organizing
a majority of other EU governments in signing a public declaration of
support for the Anglo-American policy. Candidates for EU membership
in eastern Europe also organized a public statement of support for Anglo-
American war aims.

Such demonstrations of independent thinking provoked fury in Paris
and Berlin. French President Chirac chided the candidate states for
"missing an opportunity to keep silent." Jürgen Habermas, Germany's
most prominent philosopher, denounced the joint statement of other EU
governments as an "oath of loyalty to Bush, to which the Spanish Prime
Minister had invited European governments willing to go to war behind
the backs of their other European Union colleagues." In Paris, Jacques
Derrida, his French counterpart, demanded that Europe organize itself to
assume "a new European responsibility" to secure "an effective transformation of international law" which would constrain American military
power—though in a way which "goes beyond every form of Eurocen-
trism."[45] The majority of other EU governments ignored such calls and
ended up sending units from their national armed forces to assist in the
Anglo-American occupation of Iraq in 2003. Even France and Germany
eventually gave grudging support to a Security Council resolution acknowledging the validity of the occupation force, though they pointedly
refused to contribute either financing or personnel to the reconstruction
effort in Iraq.

Whatever the ultimate course of events in Iraq, the conditions which
led to this crisis for the EU will continue to trouble the EU—and the
wider world. The proposed new constitution for Europe perfectly encap-
sulates all the old tensions. Governments would be obliged to support
the agreed foreign policy of the EU, which could now be articulated by a
European minister for foreign affairs with a definite term of office. But
the constitutional treaty did not propose to establish a European army
nor prevent EU member states from deploying their own forces at their
own direction, if European organs did not disapprove. The member
states would continue to be responsible for traditional security obligations, yet still, somehow, subordinate to a European structure. The European structure would constrain and direct member states, which were
still lacking the capacity to replace state policies on national security.

If they pooled their resources in this area, the member states of the European Union could certainly afford to finance a common military force
rivaling that of the United States. Most member states, however, still
seem quite disinclined to entrust any sort of serious military power to the
precarious structures of the European Union. Only a handful of EU states
responded favorably to the call of France and Germany in the spring of

2003 to organize a common European "reaction force." Not even the French and German governments, in fact, seem prepared to invest significant resources in such a project. So the EU seems destined, at least for some considerable time to come, to operate without any serious military capacity of its own.

Under the circumstances, the foreign policy of the EU is bound to lean toward the pleasing notion that all disputes can be compromised and resolved through international negotiations and international institutions. In these fields, the EU has a good deal of experience and can conceive itself as having a special vocation. Member states, retaining the capacity to undermine European policy with their own national diplomacy, will have to be cajoled to remain within the bounds of a common EU policy. To maintain such discipline, the EU will have further incentives to cast its policies in the rhetoric of moralism and legalism pitched at high levels of abstraction. In the background, there remains the problem of Germany, too large to be simply another member state but eager to reassure its partners—and perhaps itself—that it can never be a threat to harmony as in the awkward past. For this reason, too, a united Europe must express a foreign policy cast as a universal commitment to universal ideals, a complete break from the discredited past in which nations felt free to pursue their own selfish interests.

The strains were already evident in maneuvering over the International Criminal Court. When NGOs tried to mobilize support for such an institution, in the mid-1990s, both France and Britain responded quite cautiously. They were initially drawn to the American position that any international court should be firmly under the control of the Security Council—where Britain and France, as well as the United States, retained powers of veto. Germany embraced a vision of the court as a free-standing entity. At the UN-sponsored conference in Rome in 1998, where the plans for the court were hammered out, Britain and France came around to the German view.

It was a vision that appealed to human rights advocacy groups, insisting that international justice must be disentangled from the interests of any particular nation. German officials, rebuffed in their efforts to secure a permanent seat on the Security Council (with separate veto power) some years before, undoubtedly saw the advantage of establishing an independent institution, not subordinate to the power realities of 1945, when the design for the Security Council had been settled. Since the new Court would have the authority to pronounce which wars were legal and which were not, it would effectively supersede the authority of the Security Council. The German government announced that it would provide the largest single contribution (some 20 percent) to the Court's budget and expected to name a proportional share of the Court's personnel.[46]

The Court would, in convenient contrast to the Security Council, be financed by voluntary contributions, as well as assessments agreed among the participating states (art. 116). Both the European Commission and the Council of Europe soon announced that gaining international support for the Court would be a high priority.[47]

The United States sought to limit the threat which the Court posed to American interests. The United States did not want to be judged in an international forum in which it had no veto power. In the summer of 2002, the United States urged the Security Council to exempt UN peacekeeping forces from the court's jurisdiction. France would not hear of it. The Court was now a European project. Awkward compromises were negotiated by which UN peacekeepers would be immunized only for a year at a time—as the ICC Statute already authorized (art. 16). Safeguarding the prestige of the new International Court was now given priority, in European diplomacy, over respecting the authority of Security Council. The UN Charter had asserted priority for its own institutions over any subsequent treaty.[48] The Charter expressed the world view of 1945, however. Much had changed in European thinking since then.

So the United States sought to negotiate bilateral agreements with other nations, promising that neither would extradite nationals of the other to the ICC. The ICC Statute even seemed to sanction such agreements—at least if a rather opaque clause in the Statute (art. 98) were interpreted as the United States chose to interpret it. When Romania became the first country to embrace such an agreement with the United States, EU officials warned that this action might well jeopardize Romania's chances of joining the EU in the future. Then Britain announced that it would sign such an agreement with the United States and one by one, a majority of other EU states did the same. France and Germany were among the holdouts. Just as they were in the debate over Iraq. It was hardly a coincidence.

The strains among EU states—and the resulting moralism of the EU—were most apparent in efforts to establish a common EU policy toward the Middle East. In 1967, President de Gaulle tried to revive French prestige in the Arab world by cutting off French assistance to Israel and voicing mildly anti-Semitic remarks about the "self-assurance" of Jews. Postwar Germany remained eager to position itself as a special friend of Israel. In the Yom Kippur war of 1973, a successful surprise attack by Egypt and Syria, with Soviet military assistance, imposed nearly ruinous losses on Israel. The United States organized an airlift of desperately needed military supplies to Israel. Germany and the Netherlands agreed to provide refueling bases. Other EC states insisted on displaying their "dissociation" from American policy by refusing even to allow American transport planes to use their airspace.

By November, with the Organization of the Petroleum Exporting Countries (OPEC) cartel threatening to embargo oil shipments to Europe, "panic replaced analysis" among EC leaders, as Henry Kissinger complained.[49] A summit of EC heads of state urged that Israel immediately withdraw from all territories captured in the 1967 war. The position was reaffirmed in a more formal EC statement in 1980, urging Israel to cede the captured territories to an independent Palestinian state, under the Palestine Liberation Organization (PLO). At the time, the Palestinian Liberation Organization was still organizing terrorist attacks on civilians with the professed aim of destroying the Jewish state.[50]

It was not until a decade later, after the collapse of the Soviet Union and the repulse of Saddam Hussein's attempted annexation of Kuwait, that such negotiations came to seem at all plausible. The new European Union eagerly claimed a special role as a cosponsor of negotiations that culminated in the Oslo Agreements of 1994, in which Israel agreed, in principle, to the establishment of a Palestinian state in the territories and the PLO agreed to renounce its claims to the whole of Israel.

During the 1990s, Israeli forces did withdraw, in stages, from all centers of Palestinian population. A Palestinian Authority (PA) assumed control over Gaza and the West Bank. The EU poured a billion dollars in aid into the new Palestinian entity, becoming the largest single contributor to Palestinian development and making the new Palestinian Authority the largest single recipient of EU financial assistance.[51] The EU also stepped up its diplomatic assistance. EU officials demanded that Israel dismantle Jewish settlements in "Palestinian territory"—on the premise that international law prohibited any occupying power from "transporting" its citizens to "occupied territory."

This view assumed that Jordan, which had annexed the West Bank in 1948 (without international sanction), had acted reasonably in expelling thousands of Jews from that territory, so any return, even to neighborhoods in Jerusalem, was now intolerable. It was understandable that Arab states, which had expelled hundreds of thousands of Jews from their own countries after 1948 (and almost all the rest after 1967), embraced this interpretation of international law. Europeans might have been expected to shrink from endorsing the notion that some territories must be entirely cleansed of Jews—or rendered, in an older European expression, *Judenrein*.

In fact, the EU was so comfortable with this approach to international law that it threw itself into organizing an international conference in 1997 to focus exclusively on Israeli violations of the Geneva Convention on treatment of persons in occupied territory. It would have been the first and only conference of its kind ever summoned since the Geneva Convention had been adopted in 1949. The Swiss government, supposed to host the conference, warned that the parties to the convention had no agreement on how such a conference should proceed or what it could accomplish. But the proposal was immensely popular with Arab countries and the EU was determined to assert "leadership." In effect, the EU had replaced the Soviet Union as the most important international sponsor of Arab nationalist rhetoric.

The issue was a matter of international law, however, so universal principles were now at stake. On the other hand, policy considerations might also enter into the matter. Palestinian Authority Chairman Arafat asked that the conference be postponed, when elections in Israel brought a new government, under Ehud Barak, which had promised rapid progress in peace negotiations. The EU obligingly agreed that the conference should be adjourned after a meeting of less than one hour in Geneva.[52]

Meanwhile, European delegations at the Rome conference supported a provision for the ICC Statute which defined Jewish residence in the Old City of Jerusalem as a "war crime."[53] Only a few years later, the EU provoked considerable controversy when it insisted that Poland and the Czech Republic must rescind their 1945 decrees, expelling Germans from their territory. Germans, like other Europeans, must be free to buy land and "settle" anywhere in any part of the EU, since the EU embraced universal values.[54] But the claims of Germans in Europe were now in an entirely different category from the claims of Jews in Hebron or Jerusalem. Again, much had changed in European ideals since 1945.

Israel drew the conclusion that the EU should be kept away from serious negotiations. No EU representatives were invited to attend the negotiations between Israel and the Palestinians hosted by President Clinton at Camp David in the summer of 2000. In September, PA Chairman Yasser Arafat rejected Israeli proposals for final borders and reverted to a campaign of terror bombings. Six hundred Israeli civilians were murdered in terror attacks over the next three years—a death toll which, in proportion to the country's small population, was ten times greater than the toll of Americans on September 11. Even when an Israeli interception showed that Arafat was importing heavy weapons from Iran, the EU continued to pour assistance into the PA—as if a cessation of violence could be purchased by EU financial contributions to those sponsoring the violence.

After a particularly devastating terror attack in March of 2002, Israeli troops entered towns on the West Bank to root out terrorist organizers. Many buildings were destroyed and several dozen Palestinians were killed, when terrorists chose to stage firefights in civilian population centers. European Union officials reacted with fury. The European Parliament, ringing with cries of "massacre," voted to suspend Israel's trading privileges with the EU. The European Parliament gave no consideration to suspending aid to Palestinians. A German newspaper then documented Israeli claims that EU funding had been diverted to finance suicide bombings of civilians in Israeli cities. European Union External Affairs Commissioner Chris Patten brushed aside challenges with the explanation that the EU could not be responsible for monitoring how all its assistance was actually expended.[55]

One might have expected European governments to feel some queasiness about funding the murder of Jews. In fact, some EU states endorsed terrorist attacks on civilians in Israeli cities. In April of 2002, France, Belgium, Austria, and Portugal voted for a resolution at the UN Human Rights Commission endorsing the Palestinian struggle by "all means of armed struggle"—at a time when the preferred means of those engaged in the armed struggle was a continuation of suicide terror attacks. Britain and Germany voted against the resolution.[56] The disagreement was hastily smoothed over. European Union officials, claiming to speak for all member states, continued to denounce Israel for "extra-judicial murders" of terrorist leaders—that is, for the same tactics which the United States had begun to employ in striking at Al Qaeda. The EU also denounced Israel for building a fence to make terrorist infiltration difficult.

Even creative diplomacy was rejected. When the United States expressed support for a Palestinian state in the spring of 2002, conditioned on the establishment of a democratic Palestinian government, Arafat was persuaded to name a prime minister, who called for an end to violence in a formal meeting with President Bush and Israeli Prime Minister Sharon in June 2002. The United States tried to enhance the status of the new prime minister by refusing to deal with Arafat. European Union officials and ministers insisted that they must continue meeting with Arafat and proceeded to do so. Arafat soon maneuvered Prime Minister Abas into resigning. The EU was left to pursue its discussions with Arafat, while Israel refused to meet with the EU special representative to the Mideast.[57]

The EU was for peace. As it had for decades, the EU urged Israel to withdraw from all territories seized in the 1967 war as the way to assure peace. What if Israel withdrew its forces from all Palestinian territory and then found itself subject to more intense terror attacks? That had been Israel's experience after it agreed to place Arafat's Palestinian Authority in charge of all towns in the West Bank and Gaza during the 1990s. A poll conducted in the fall of 2003 indicated that a majority of Palestinians favored continued terror attacks on Israel, even if all territory in the West Bank and Gaza were organized as an independent Palestinian state.[58] The EU offered the assurances of international law. Many Europeans expressed indignation at Israel's refusal to trust in the protective shield of international law.

Most national governments in the EU remained disinclined to back up the admonitions expressed by the European Union, however. National governments were unwilling to impose trade sanctions on Israel, despite urging from the European Parliament. Even within the EU, Javier Solana, High Representative for the Common Foreign and Security Policy, representing the national governments in the council of ministers, spoke in more conciliatory terms than External Affairs Commissioner Chris Patten, who represented the European Commission and its aid policies.[59] Patten was reasonably described by a European newspaper as "viscerally anti-Israel."[60] Within the European Parliament, the most fiercely hostile members of the EP (MEPs) were those who identified most insistently with European integration, while Euro-skeptics expressed far more understanding of Israel's plight.[61]

The same pattern emerged, of course, in debate over the Anglo-American war in Iraq. Governments which joined the coalition, like Britain and Poland and conservative governments in Spain and the Netherlands, were not only more pro-American but more cautious about supplanting the NATO alliance with a "common European foreign policy." These governments acknowledged, by their actions, that conflicts could not always be dissolved with words.

France, clinging tightly to Germany, insisted that resort to war must be authorized by the United Nations and the Anglo-American war against Iraq was accordingly unlawful and illegitimate. The war, in the official French view, was not undertaken to disarm a dangerous and evil tyrant but to further the conspiratorial aims of a distinct group. The French foreign minister blamed a "Zionist lobby" in Washington. Crowds in Paris were less subtle, protesting the war with the chant, "Vive Chirac! Stop the Jews!"[62]

While most national governments in Europe endorsed the Anglo-American coalition, the French view was widely embraced by European public opinion. A poll conducted by the European Commission, in the fall of 2003, after new revelations of Saddam's atrocities, found that a sizable majority of Europeans still regarded the war to overthrow Saddam as "illegitimate." The same poll found that Europeans believed that the greatest threat to world peace was posed by Israel—followed by the United States.[63]

It was not an expression of European nationalism, at least in any ordinary sense. European opinion reacted with complete indifference when efforts to secure agreement on a European constitution collapsed in December 2003. Spain and Poland suffered no recrimination for successfully opposing the proposed new constitution. European opinion was not insistent on constitutional agreement but simply on harmony—or on peace. Europeans had learned to live in peace, even without a common constitution. Why could not Israel learn to live with Arafat or the United

States with Saddam Hussein? Those who insisted on facing threats were themselves the greatest threats.

One might think of this outlook as a predictable outcome of European efforts at "integration" over the preceding decades. The success of the EU seemed to prove that international law was not different, in principle, from domestic law. International agreements could control sovereign states, just as the law declared and enforced by sovereign states at home controlled private citizens. If European disputes could be settled by a European Court of Justice, Europeans readily concluded that even the most intractible international conflicts could be settled by legalistic formulas.

Or one might think that this approach to international conflicts reflected much deeper and older patterns of thought, which postwar projects had done little to alter.[64] At an earlier time, too, Europeans had rallied to the call for peace and harmony—and to the argument that selfish intriguers were destroying Europe's hopes for peace. In the early 1940s, the elected government of France decided that peace would be best secured by deporting French Jews to be gassed. Local police in the Netherlands and Belgium also cooperated in genocide as the price for peace. At the time, Europeans feared the consequences of a prolonged conflict between Germany and the Anglo-American alliance.[65]

The current view is, of course, entirely different. Advanced opinion in Europe insists that peace can be secured by replacing the state of Israel with an international protectorate—but this proposal, its advocates insist, is meant for the good of Jews as well as Arabs.[66] In the 1940s, French government officials insisted in postwar trials that their collaboration with Nazi projects was also for the good of those affected—but that was in another time. Europe now embraces the ideals of humanity. If Americans see things differently, they must be manipulated by those who hold themselves aloof from humanity.

So the United States is frightening. Not for the reasons that it frightened Europeans in 1942. Among other things, the United States looks frightening because it does not fully endorse the new European creed, an entirely different creed than Europeans embraced in the past. Under the new creed, it is wrong to make war on tyrants. European opinion is sure of this conclusion, as the European Commission survey shows. But Europeans now think this for entirely different reasons, of course, than they did in the past. Europeans now believe it is wrong to make war on tyrants because that will undermine the world's commitment to human rights.

CHAPTER SEVEN

THE HUMAN RIGHTS CRUSADE

INTERNATIONAL PROTECTION FOR human rights is the central pillar of current ambitions toward global governance. It is the ultimate moral trump card in debates about the proper reach of international law. Sovereignty? "It can't be absolute in today's world," say believers in global governance. "That would mean governments are free to abuse the human rights of their own people!" For the sake of human rights, we must have a law that guarantees the rights of individuals and not just the rights of sovereign states.

Then again, if international law can guarantee the human rights of individuals, why should it not guarantee them an adequate diet, proper housing, basic education? Why should international law not guarantee a clean and safe physical environment and a sustainable use of resources? Should not these claims, after all, be considered "human rights," too?

So, in the spring of 2002, a UN committee labored over a plan to provide "enforcement" for a universal right to "adequate housing."[1] It was, according to some interpretations, a way of ensuring that tenants who fell behind in their rent would not be evicted from their homes—anywhere in the world. Was this trivializing the original idea of international human rights protection?

As a matter of fact, such projects are quite in keeping with the underlying logic and the historic spirit of international human rights programs. If rights protection is too important to be left to sovereign states, then anything which is important may also be characterized as a right and so removed from the exclusive responsibility of sovereign states. There is no clear line today marking the boundary of matters that can properly be deemed "rights." The idea of international rights protection began by smudging any possible line. Certainly, international human rights can not be limited to the right to independence, the right to be left alone—otherwise, sovereign states might claim that right for themselves, undermining the whole premise of the enterprise!

PROSPECTS IN RETROSPECT

There has been so much earnest talk about "international human rights law" in recent decades, it is easy to forget that the underlying concept remains quite disorienting. At the least it is very hard to reconcile with normal thinking about government. For the UN or the international community actually to guarantee rights to individuals, international authority would require the power to override rights-denying policies of actual governments. International authority would have to function as a higher authority, as an ultimate authority, as something like a world government above national states. Yet this is not a description of the world that many people would recognize as current reality.

Textbooks on international human rights nonetheless insist that there already is a well-established body of international law on this subject, developing a long and widely accepted tradition. To make such claims credible, contemporary discussions of human rights are depicted as extrapolations from the doctrines of seventeenth-century natural rights theorists like John Locke or from eighteenth-century documents like the American Declaration of Independence and the French Declaration of the Rights of Man.[2]

To anyone who actually reads the old books, such derivations look like rhetorical sleight of hand. It is the game of the medieval juggler, intoning "hocus pocus" to play on the superstitious credulity of an audience which still heard the cognate phrase in the Latin mass ("hoc est corpus"). Perhaps that is an overly harsh judgment. Many advocates of international human rights protection may actually believe that their project simply extends the traditions of liberal, constitutional government. But performers at medieval fairs may also have been naive enough to believe that their incantations were actually Latin and actually had some magical power on that account.

The American Declaration of Independence does affirm that men are "endowed by their Creator with certain unalienable rights." But it immediately goes on to say that "to secure these rights, governments are instituted among men, deriving their just powers from the consent of the governed." Individual rights may derive moral impetus from a prior or higher claim—the "Law of Nature and Nature's God," perhaps. But the Declaration is quite clear that rights are not "secure" without an actual government to enforce them. Most of the complaints against the British government, in the body of the Declaration, protest interference with colonial legislatures and courts—they protest, in other words, not direct constraints on individuals but constraints on colonial *governments*. The argument of the Declaration presumes that individuals can only be secure in their rights when their government is secure in its powers.

At the same time, the American Declaration takes for granted that different governments may have somewhat different ways of interpreting or enforcing rights. Even just governments or governments exercising "just powers" may have different approaches to rights protection. That is why the "just powers" of government rest ultimately on "the consent of the governed": Consent is necessary because it is not always clear what should be done to make rights secure. People who are governed by different governments may well consent to different arrangements.

International human rights law now seems to stand in place of natural law (or the "law of nature and nature's God") as a sort of ultimate appeal. But the ultimate appeal envisaged by the Declaration of Independence is a popular revolution—that is what the Declaration was written to justify, after all. International human rights law, on the other hand, presents itself as law in a more ordinary sense: It is not an appeal for popular revolution but for an orderly legal process. And it therefore has tried to spell out "human rights" in considerable detail. The American Declaration invokes "self-evident truths," which might, in principle, be understood by anyone. International human rights law offers, somewhat like a domestic legal code, an extensive list of requirements—culminating in that right to housing. No sane person could claim these to be "necessary" deductions from self-evident truths. But then, no one in the eighteenth century—or until quite recently—actually imagined such a thing as "international human rights law."

Well into the twentieth century, states were assumed to have legitimate claims to protect their own nationals and to act on their behalf when they were threatened by foreign states. The idea that any state could claim to act on behalf of humanity at large was rejected, after the seventeenth century, as an outrageous presumption. Even the Covenant of the League of Nations made no provision for universal human rights protection. The peace treaties negotiated at the same time did include some provisions designed to protect the rights of minorities in particular states. The victorious powers felt entitled to impose minority rights guarantees on small, new states, much as they imposed new borders. They did not think to embrace such international obligations for themselves. Nor did the victors in the First World War prove any more committed to enforcing such rights guarantees for minorities than they were to defending the borders of the new states from brutal aggression from other states.

The notion of universal human rights standards made its first appearance in 1945, in the United Nations Charter. Even then, it was barely more than an appearance. The outlines of the Charter had been negotiated among the leading Allied powers while they were still battling their enemies in the Second World War. References to human rights were inserted only at the last minute, at the San Francisco conference in June 1945, in response to lobbying from humanitarian advocacy organizations. Honestly viewed, these human rights references did not amount to very much.

So the Preamble to the UN Charter pledges the organization, among other things, to "promote respect for human rights." The Charter's substantive provisions, however, setting out the powers and responsibilities of actual UN organs, speak only of "recommendations" regarding human rights. Even these provisions are offset by the proviso that the organization will not interfere in "matters essentially within the domestic jurisdiction of member states." The Charter's human rights provisions seemed so innocuous in 1945 that they aroused no serious objections in the U.S. Senate, which was otherwise quite wary of international interference in American domestic affairs. Everyone was glad to endorse unspecified concerns for "human rights" along with a generalized commitment to "peace."

But peace remained the priority. Hopes for a peaceful postwar world depended on cooperation between the victorious powers—above all, between the Soviet Union and the United States and Britain. Optimists could hope that a revived China and a revived France would also cooperate in keeping the peace. These great powers might be able to agree on countering future threats of aggression, as they had come to agree (more or less) in the war just past. With the Soviet Union still ruled by a monstrous tyrant, there was no reason to expect agreement on schemes for guaranteeing human rights to people in all countries.

So the UN Charter emphasized the safeguarding of international peace. The only organ of the new organization which was empowered to issue binding directives—even to states which did not consent to them—was the Security Council, charged with "preservation of peace." But even then, the Charter came with a catch: The five great Allied powers were given permanent seats on the Security Council and the Council could act only with the approval (or at least, acquiescence) of all five.

As it turned out, the great powers were rarely in agreement and the Security Council was not able to command peace. When regional wars broke out, the great powers were rarely able to agree on which side was the aggressor, deserving international condemnation, and which side was the victim, deserving international support in its defensive efforts. In most conflicts, during the long decades of the Cold War, the United States and the Soviet Union consulted their opposing strategic priorities and ended up backing different sides. For the most part, the Security Council remained on the sidelines. The veto was there to ensure that the UN would remain on the sidelines when the great powers disagreed. If the great powers could not agree on common approaches to the suppression of war, with all its menace and destruction, how could they be expected to agree on schemes for global enforcement of human rights?

In the last analysis, however, these were not competing concerns but different aspects of the same problem. If the United Nations could promulgate a genuine law of human rights, then it would need some means of enforcing this law. An actual government can, as a last resort, send troops to enforce rights claims, as President Eisenhower sent airborne troops to Little Rock, Arkansas in 1957 to enforce the Supreme Court's ruling on school desegregation against defiant local officials. Would the UN be empowered to send troops in this way to ensure that a recalcitrant government complied with a UN determination on human rights? If not, would a UN ruling really be any different from a mere moral exhortation? Would it simply be sermonizing rather than actually adjudicating rights?

Even citizens groaning under the most oppressive regimes might not welcome a world in which international authorities claimed the right to make war on their own government. Would the international authority make fair and honest decisions or simply respond to the promptings of other powers, consulting their own selfish concerns? Those who experienced tyrannical government at first hand might be the last to take for granted that higher authority would operate fairly and honestly. And even if international authority acted from sound motives, could it be trusted to make sound tactical decisions? Would it be worth a new world war, for example, to liberate the peoples of eastern Europe from communist tyranny?

For citizens living under reasonably free governments, the prospect of international "protection" would seem even more questionable. If their own constitution already placed limits on their government, they could hope to safeguard their rights through ordinary constitutional process. If they had lived under this constitution for some time, they could appeal to common political traditions and rally their fellow citizens against current governmental abuses. Why would citizens in such a fortunate country expect that their rights could be made more secure through international intervention? Why would they imagine that an international authority would be a better guardian of their rights than their own constitutional scheme?

If an international authority actually tried to enforce its own standards against their government, why would citizens of a free country side with the international authority rather than their own constitutional government? Would the international authority then try to enforce its judgments by force—even if that meant making war on a democratic, constitutional state? And would an international authority equipped to take such measures actually make people feel that their rights would be more secure in the end?

If all this sounds fantastical, it is only because such reasoning takes at face value the notion that international human rights protections could constitute an actual law—and like actual law, could be reliably enforced. In fact, some visionaries did look forward to such a development. Philip Jessup, a professor of international law at Columbia and subsequently a justice on the International Court of Justice, held out this vision in his 1947 book: "in the early stages of the international development of protection of human rights, enforcement [would be] left to the national state, subject to review by an international authority" but "gradually" the scheme could evolve toward "a situation analogous to that in the federal system of the United States, where constitutional rights may be first considered by state courts and ultimately reviewed by federal courts."[3]

Jessup's speculations did not include discussion of whether "international authority" would have command of troops to enforce its judgments. But he did concede, in passing, that for international rights guarantees to be made fully effective "not merely international law and the international system, but also human nature . . . must be revolutionized"—projects which he seemed to think would simply take a bit more time.[4]

In the meanwhile, advocates of international human rights protection insisted that they were not challenging the sovereignty of existing states. International programs would "promote" and "recommend"—or inspire and admonish—but not actually enforce human rights claims. Who could object to that?

The problem with this answer remains what it always was: it looks to a realm of "governance" which is very hard to sustain in the modern world. It did not work well, even in the pre-modern world—which is why modern thinkers began by orienting political thought around the concept of sovereignty. If we could all agree on a universal church, we might want to establish the bishops of that church as authoritative monitors on our governments. But we do not all agree. Most of us may agree, in broad terms, on many moral and religious premises. But we do not agree on all the details nor on the conclusions that should follow from these premises in particular circumstances. These disagreements can sometimes matter a great deal. Do we have more agreement on human rights? If we are all agreed, when it comes to human rights, why would we need international human rights monitors? Or if it is only a matter of dealing with a small number of recalcitrants, why do we not actually entrust these international monitors with full powers of enforcement?

The obvious danger is that a merely moral authority will be disregarded. Then to win itself more regard, this moral authority will seek political alliances with interests or powers having quite different motives but more effective force. The history of medieval Europe offers many illustrations of the danger. Alternately, if this merely moral authority is so dutifully attended that its word is as good as law, is it not, after all, exercising the very power it purports to disclaim? Is that not also dangerous? Medieval history offers many examples of that danger, as well.

Human rights law also presents a danger that is perhaps characteristically modern. What is presented as merely admonitory is entered into without much care. After all, it is not "real law." Certainly, it is not the carefully considered doctrine of the medieval Church, working within a centuries-old tradition. Contemporary human rights law has instead developed with the logrolling abandon of a modern legislature—only more so, as it is freed from any constitutional framework or any concern about the reactions of voters when actual policies are actually enforced. It is, after all, mostly talk. Then the apparent success of talkfests encourages the very misplaced belief that there is a genuine consensus when there is not. And this misplaced belief encourages ventures that go wildly beyond what the actual international community is actually able to sustain, igniting or exacerbating very serious conflicts.

All these dangers might well have been foreseen. But for many decades, the whole enterprise was so peripheral to actual international politics that only technical experts paid much attention. The experts were priests in the new faith and not given to doubts. By the 1990s, the dangers had become obvious to anyone willing to look. Surprisingly few were willing.

The idea that the world could be reformed by human rights crusaders—properly anointed by international human rights authorities—was too inspiring, too comforting, to question in public. European governments no longer anchored in traditional religion were very ready to embrace new pieties. Rights talk escaped from the confines of settled constitutional orders, first into the neverland of international conferences, then on to the real world of deadly conflict. But it would all turn out well if only people believed in the magic words "human rights." Hocus pocus!

STANDARDS

It started with the establishment of a Commission on Human Rights at the opening session of the UN General Assembly in 1945. Eleanor Roosevelt, widow of the American war leader, was chosen to chair the new commission. The new commission embarked, as its first order of business, on the drafting of a systematic statement on human rights. The UN would not just "promote" and "recommend," after all, but also give detailed instruction in this field. After much debate, a Universal Declaration of Human Rights was approved by the General Assembly in December of 1948. Its preamble quoted words from President Roosevelt, now certified as having "proclaimed the highest aspiration of the common people"—apparently all of them, everywhere.

The text of the Universal Declaration was indeed crafted to express a consensus on fundamental principles. At that time, consensus meant that English-speaking democracies, along with the recently restored (and often still shaky) democracies of western Europe, would find common ground with Stalin's government in Moscow and with communist puppet governments of eastern Europe. Of course, there could also be suggestions from intermittently constitutional governments in Latin America and from war-torn China—and from assorted Muslim countries which made scarcely any pretense to democracy or constitutional government.

Under the circumstances, the drafters of the Declaration did not do that badly. At least, one can say there is nothing in the Universal Declaration that is inherently offensive to democratic or constitutional principles, as traditionally conceived by Americans. But if one takes the Declaration at face value as a statement of fundamental principles for domestic governance, it is certainly no improvement on the founding texts of the American constitutional tradition. It retains many marks of its origins, as a consensus document, designed to paper over divisions between socialist tyrannies and western democracies.

The provisions regarding democratic accountability, for example, stipulate that no one may be denied access to voting but they say nothing about the right of opposition parties or candidates to compete in these elections (art. 21). For all that appears, the election rituals of one-party communist dictatorships—which often required everyone to take part in elections—would entirely satisfy the standards of the Universal Declaration. Another provision stipulates that no one "shall be arbitrarily deprived of his property" without saying a word about compensation for takings of property nor about limits on general expropriations (art. 17). Communist states might, again, seem to be in perfect compliance since their expropriations were not "arbitrary" but entirely systematic. Meanwhile, provisions dealing with fundamental rights, such as freedom of religion or freedom of speech, are jumbled together with debatable policy prescriptions, such as government guarantees of "periodic holidays with pay" (art. 24). Nothing is indicated as more fundamental than anything else. They are all "universal" claims.

And they are all, it seems, to be backed by nothing more than moral force. The Declaration was adopted by unanimous vote of the General Assembly on the understanding that it was not legally binding. As if to compensate for this weakness, the Preamble proclaims the Declaration's moral authority in bombastic terms. The Preamble characterizes the ensuing document as "a common standard . . . for all peoples and all nations" which "every individual and every organ of society, keeping this Declaration constantly in mind, shall strive by teaching and education to promote respect for." As such, "all peoples and nations" must "strive" by "progressive measures, national and international, to secure . . . universal and effective recognition and observance [for provisions of the Declaration]." This is not the language of a treaty or even of a national constitution. It is the language of a sermon—though perhaps from a clergyman with more earnest devotion than literary skill.

The language is particularly odd in what purports to be an affirmation of individual rights. What if individuals prefer to keep "constantly in mind" the Sermon on the Mount rather than the nostrums of the General Assembly? What if churches—which seem to have as much claim to be "organs of society" as any other social group—prefer to "strive by teaching and education" to "promote respect for" the Ten Commandments? The framers of the U.S. Bill of Rights did not presume to admonish "every individual" to be "keeping" its legal formulas "constantly in mind." But the American Founders were working with long-established English legal practices. They were founding a new governmental structure, not a new religion.

For enthusiasts of the new faith in human rights, the Universal Declaration did indeed take on the status of a sacred text. It could be seen, as one distinguished human rights advocate subsequently described it, as "the essential document, the touchstone, the creed of humanity that sums up all other creeds directing human behavior."[5] The hope of those who sponsored the Universal Declaration was that, through this new "creed," they could mobilize the allegiance of citizens in all countries, against their own governments if necessary.

Governments, it turned out, were not in any hurry to turn these abstract affirmations into formal treaties. It took almost two decades for the UN to agree on precise implementing language for the formal treaties. Another decade was then required to achieve sufficient ratifications by national governments for these treaties to take effect among those states which did ratify them. These first implementing treaties were dubbed "covenants." It was quite unclear who was bound to whom in these covenants. Certainly God was not mentioned. But an atmosphere of surrogate piety was still regarded as essential to the enterprise. The texts of the documents suggest that no one was much concerned about the details.

To sooth debates about priorities, the consensus jumble in the Universal Declaration was divided into a "Covenant on Civil and Political Rights" and a separate "Covenant on Economic, Social and Cultural Rights." But professional human rights advocates have loudly insisted ever since that these covenants are of equal priority, so the point of the division remains obscure. The Covenant on Economic Rights—a catalog of welfare benefits which states must provide—was actually ratified somewhat ahead of the Covenant on Political Rights, in what was doubtless an accurate reflection of priorities among UN member states.

The Covenant on Political Rights largely duplicates language in the Universal Declaration, repeating, for example, with no further clarification, the call for "genuine elections" without any reference to competing parties or a choice of candidates (art. 25). The Covenant does take the trouble, however, to restrict the Universal Declaration's call for "freedom of opinion and expression" with the admonition that "propaganda for war shall be prohibited by law" along with "advocacy of national, racial or religious hatred" (art. 20)—broad demands for censorship in no way confined or explained within the documents.

The Covenant on Economic Rights affirms the obligation of governments to ensure "the right of everyone to . . . a decent living" (art. 7.a.ii) and "the right of everyone to an adequate standard of living" (art. 11.1) and "the right of everyone to continuous improvement of living conditions" (art. 11.1) and "the right of everyone to the enjoyment of the highest attainable standard of physical and mental health" (art. 12.1) and the "right of everyone to education . . . directed to the full development of the human personality" (art. 13.1). Any state which thought it could press for lower living standards would now be set straight.

Amidst all its other verbiage, the Covenant on Economic Rights finds no place to mention a right to property or a right to enforce contracts or a right to engage in private commerce. The Covenant offers no hint that an entirely government-directed economy might not work very well in producing wealth and alleviating poverty. But neither does the Covenant on Political Rights offer any hint that an entirely government-controlled economy might be a bit of a burden on individual freedom. These were meant to be consensus documents.

At least, the Covenants do not demand that "everyone" go about "teaching" their provisions to everyone else. The Covenants are supposed to be legally binding and therefore not dependent on moral exhortation. But what it means for them to be legally binding is quite obscure. The Covenant on Civil and Political Rights makes provision for a Human Rights Committee to receive reports on compliance from ratifying states and review complaints by one state about the compliance of another (art. 28–45). But no sanctions are provided for defying this Committee. It is not even specified that any state is bound by the Committee's advice or even by its interpretation of the language in the Covenant. What is provided in other words, is a forum for further discussions.

The Covenant on Economic Rights provides, even more vaguely, that "international action for the achievement" of its provisions "includes such methods as the conclusion of conventions, the adoption of recommendations, the furnishing of technical assistance and the holding of . . . technical meetings for the purpose of consultation and study" (art. 23)—in other words, more talk. So a new protocol is now proposed to give a special monitoring committee the power to hear individualized complaints. It requires a special sort of faith to believe it will do much good.

It is true that central enforcement mechanisms are quite rare in international treaties. But these are not conventional treaties. Under a conventional treaty, a state that feels another state has reneged on its treaty commitments can try to enforce compliance by withholding its own implementation. But human rights treaties are not commitments which one state makes to other states. They are commitments which each state makes to its own citizens. If Burma, for example, does not honor this commitment, Canada can hardly compel Burma's compliance by taking back rights from Canadians. The Burmese government is likely to care even less about the rights of Canadians than it does about the rights of Burmese—and Canadian citizens might object to having their rights withheld in order to impress rulers in Rangoon. Without some element of central enforcement, the scheme makes little sense.

But the UN simply went forward with new declarations and new conventions, as if the Covenants were a well-proven model. Most notably, the UN produced conventions prohibiting race discrimination and sex discrimination in the 1970s, followed by conventions for the suppression of torture and for the protection of children's rights in the 1980s. All were arranged in the same way—laundry lists of broad affirmations, with no provision for enforcement. They are less like contracts between states than like religious revival meetings, where one person may be inspired to come forward and renounce sin by the example of others doing the same and all may be strengthened in their resolve to sin no more by taking a pledge to do so in common.

The new conventions offered somewhat more detail, though not much. And the new detail was usually coupled with new ambitions. The Convention on the Elimination of All Forms of Discrimination Against Women (CEDAW) admonished, for example, that states must "modify the social and cultural patterns of conduct . . . which are based on . . . stereotyped roles for men and women" (art. 5.a). It nowhere acknowledges that individual liberties—or the freedom of religious institutions—might require limits on this state-imposed project of remaking cultures and "modifying" behavior. CEDAW also directs governments to assure that women receive "equal remuneration" for jobs of "comparable value" (art. 11.d). The provision simply takes it for granted that governments can determine the "value" of every individual worker's individual contribution and then impose this determination on employers throughout the economy.

The Convention on the Rights of the Child directs government to assure day-care facilities so that children do not suffer from their mothers' employment outside the home (art. 18.3). The same convention stipulates that children must be assured "freedom to seek, receive and impart information and ideas of all kinds . . . either orally, in writing or in print, in the form of art, or through any other media of the child's choice" (art. 13.1). The provision authorizes "restrictions" on this freedom for the sake of "public health or morals" and similar concerns—but says nothing about parental control and makes no distinction between younger and older children. These provisions were not likely to find favor among adherents of traditional cultures in developing countries. But, after all, these new rights were not going to be enforced any more seriously than the Covenant on Political Rights.

In the absence of other sanctions, the one thing the UN might have done was to focus international disapprobation. But the system was designed to avoid this. An optional protocol to the Covenant on Civil and Political Rights authorized the Human Rights Committee to hear complaints—or rather "communications"—from individual citizens, alleging mistreatment by their own governments. In response, the Committee is authorized to make inquiries of the government and then offer its "views"—but not authorized to make them public. The procedure is so ineffective, even today, that a leading human rights scholar has urged that it be abandoned as a waste of valuable Committee time and resources.[6] Naturally, the UN simply went forward with similar optional protocols under other conventions.

But it is not clear what better service the Human Rights Committee or parallel monitoring committees under later conventions could offer. The main business is the review of reports by each party. Many states which have ratified the conventions submit only cursory, unrevealing reports and quite a few simply fail to submit anything. There is no means of enforcing compliance even with the reporting requirements.[7]

And certainly there is no means of focusing on the worst offenders or even identifying the worst offenders. The human rights treaties are so encompassing and so broadly worded that there are bound to be deficiencies—or what are plausibly regarded as such—in every country's level of compliance. And there is no set of priorities, so no clear means, if one goes by the treaties, to distinguish what we might call misdemeanor deficiencies from felony offenses. So the committees tend to operate in the spirit of a progressive kindergarten, where there is no such thing as a passing or failing grade but simply a kindly, persistent admonition that everyone has room for improvement. Or rather, the committees operate in the spirit of a church, where all must confess that they are, in some way, sinners.

There is an important difference, however. An actual church can excommunicate or shun or exclude those who make a total mockery of its faith. The human rights faith remains open to all—without precondition and without any subsequent conditions. Asking to join is all that is necessary for admission. No one is ever expelled for betraying international standards. So the Soviet Union, under Leonid Brezhnev, felt free to claim that it was committed to the Covenant on Civil and Political Rights. So did Saddam Hussein's Iraq and the Islamic Republic of Iran and a long string of repressive states.

Egypt and Libya and most other Muslim countries also claimed to be committed to the Convention on the Elimination of All Forms of Discrimination Against Women—except, as they specified in broadly worded reservations, if the demands of Sharia law required otherwise. The traditional rule for treaties was that a party which ratified with reservations was not a party, unless other parties accepted the reservations. The rule was generally insisted upon because it rested on a very clear logic: without it, a state could claim all the benefits of concessions from others, while withholding its own concessions in unilateral reservations.

But the International Court of Justice held, in an advisory opinion in 1951, that a different approach should be taken to human rights conventions, in recognition of the fact that the intended beneficiaries were not other states but private individuals within all states. It should be enough that reservations would not "substantially impair the purpose of the treaty"—an approach so vague that, as four dissenting judges protested at the time, it threatens to make nonsense of treaty ratifications.[8]

By the 1980s, only a few European states bothered to pursue challenges to the Sharia reservations and no one thought to return the issue to the International Court of Justice.[9] In practice, any state can be a party to a human rights convention if it claims to be. It is then bound only by its own unilateral understanding of the convention. Other states are simply witnesses to its pledge, under no obligation to question the pledging state's good faith and not really in any position to do so. No state has ever pursued a complaint against another's human rights conduct to the International Court of Justice.

So in 2002, Saudi Arabia was criticized for practicing bodily mutilation as a routine form of punishment for thievery and other crimes, in clear violation of the Convention Against Torture, which the Saudi government had duly ratified. Saudi Arabia rejected the complaint out of hand, on the grounds that it fell within its Sharia reservation. The monitoring committee for the torture convention moved on to the next case.[10] At least Saudi Arabia had been induced to ratify the convention in some form. Wasn't that a contribution to the building of international consensus on the wrongfulness of torture?

In fact, it was not. A careful study of ratification patterns, published in the *Yale Law Journal* in 2002, found that actual compliance with human rights standards commonly went down after states ratified human rights conventions.[11] The seeming paradox was easy to explain. In the wonderland of international human rights, states subject to criticism for abuses of human rights could demonstrate their commitment to reform—simply by ratifying another toothless human rights convention. Ratifying conventions has been a reliable technique for states to deflect criticism of their actual conduct.

Most states are not, in fact, inclined to criticize the human rights failings of other states. The United States repeatedly pressed the UN Human Rights Commission in the late 1990s to launch inquiries into human rights failings in China. China threatened to cancel contracts with European states which voted for such inquiries and every European state on the Commission compliantly joined the majority rejecting the American proposals. Europeans finally put an end to the embarrassment by voting the United States off of the Commission in 2001—in favor of Austria, then under diplomatic sanctions by EU states for including a somewhat xenophobic party in the governing coalition in Vienna.

Other states followed their own calculations of advantage in human rights forums. Latin American states, even when pledging support for democracy at home, decided that their region would be best represented on the Human Rights Commission by the communist tyranny in Cuba. Other regions decided that China, Pakistan, Syria, and Libya would make worthy spokesmen for the cause of human rights on the Commission. Libya was elected to chair that body in 2001.

Signing human rights conventions made some of the world's most brutal regimes eligible to participate in human rights committees at the UN. So, far from stigmatizing the worst offenders, in practice, the UN system helped to exonerate them, indeed to elevate them. It was, in a way, an entirely logical outcome of a system that aspired, above all, to universality. Human rights, as the UN had proclaimed at the outset, was a slogan which could be embraced by all governments in the world.

CONSTITUENCIES

The twin "covenants" on human rights were supposed to make the ideals in the Universal Declaration legally binding. The covenants were declared in effect (for ratifying states) in 1976. There was, by then, very little reason for optimism about the project.

The framers of the Universal Declaration had hoped to ensure that horrors perpetrated in the Second World War would never be repeated. By 1976, the United Nations had elected and reelected a Nazi war criminal to serve as UN secretary general. True, diplomats did not know the details of Kurt Waldheim's war record. No one troubled to inquire at the time—though the relevant facts were, as it turned out, available in war crimes records in the UN's own archives.

Yet, however improbably, from the mid-1970s onwards, human rights rhetoric did begin to gain increasing momentum in international politics. Actual trends in the world might offer no obvious basis for optimism. But there was more and more talk on the theme of human rights. The talk appealed to three distinct but overlapping constituencies.

At the United Nations, it appealed, most obviously, to the organization's new governing majority. By the 1970s, European states had granted independence to almost all their former colonies in Africa and Asia. The new states joined with Latin America and communist China in what was called the "Third World" or the "Non-Aligned Movement." For practical purposes, they were generally aligned with the Soviet Union and its communist satellites, since they were all eager to blame their troubles on "imperialism" which they associated with western states or on "capitalist exploitation" which they naturally associated with non-communist states. Communist and Third World states made common cause and began to insist that the UN was not just a body to adjust disputes between existing states but a vehicle for transforming the world—at the direction of the new majority in the world organization.

South Africa was the first target. In their eagerness to condemn the apartheid system of racial exclusion, newly independent African states agreed to make exceptions to the original, self-denying rule of the Human Rights Commission against criticizing particular states. Racism was so intolerable that the provision in the UN Charter, restricting the organization from interfering in "matters essentially within the domestic jurisdiction" of a member state, was waived aside.

Nearly a hundred thousand Hutus were slaughtered by the Tutsi-controlled government of Burundi in 1972. This slaughter was never discussed at the UN, presumably because tribal violence was not "racism." Soon after, Idi Amin, the demented tyrant of Uganda, summarily expelled a hundred thousand people of Asian descent, after expropriating their property. That episode also passed without comment at the United Nations. South Africa received an unending series of condemnations, culminating in a 1976 resolution proclaiming a full decade of struggle against apartheid—which was followed, of course, by more struggle.

Communist regimes were infuriated in 1973 when a military coup deposed the Marxist regime of Salvador Allende in Chile. The UN resounded over the next decade with relentless condemnations of Chile's right-wing military government. Equally repressive military governments, even in Latin America, escaped without censure by proclaiming themselves to be left-wing.

Arab rejection of a Jewish state in the Middle East also brought relentless condemnation of Israel, culminating in the 1975 resolution which pronounced Zionism, the founding doctrine of the state, to be "a form of racism." The resolution received enthusiastic backing in the General Assembly, even from non-Muslim states which had once had friendly relations with Israel.

Two years before, the OPEC oil cartel had demonstrated the power of Arab states to inflict severe economic pain on Europe and North America. The doubling of oil prices inflicted even more pain on most Third World countries but the example was inspiring. The General Assembly voted a series of resolutions demanding the creation of a New International Economic Order, by which international trade would be organized around cartels for other raw materials. Eventually, the General Assembly proclaimed a "fundamental right to development"—a right whose implementation was supposed to be, in some way, the responsibility of the already developed.

Western states hardly bothered to resist most of these resolutions. They were easy to shrug off, after all, because the UN had no means of enforcing General Assembly resolutions. Why would rich countries in Europe and North America want to acknowledge the authority of such resolutions? Yet there turned out to be growing support for the abstract proposition that the UN was, in some sense, a governing council for the world—because the world needed world law.

"World peace through world law"—the idea had been around for decades. In the 1970s, earnest professors dusted off the idea and linked it to the cause of human rights. A leading international law scholar at the Harvard Law School expounded the doctrine that, since the UN Charter took priority over every other treaty, it must also be understood as taking priority over national legislation. And the Universal Declaration of Human Rights, as an authoritative guide to the human rights commitments in the Charter, had become supreme law for all nations.[12] In 1980, distinguished professors at the Yale Law School published a 900-page tome, *Human Rights and World Public Order*, which depicted the "activities of the General Assembly" as providing "what is in effect a new modality of law making" and "a closer approximation to parliamentary enactment."[13] With great earnestness, the authors amassed citations from UN resolutions to demonstrate that "world law" already addressed all "basic human needs," such as "respect" and "sustenance" and "values."

Such ramblings were heard with more sympathy by the end of the 1970s. In 1973, the United States had limped away from a decade of brutal conflict in Southeast Asia. Denounced as "imperialist" by communist and Third World states, the war had become deeply unpopular in western Europe and finally, in its last years, unpopular with most Americans. The fall of South Vietnam to a communist army in 1975 provoked only a sigh of resignation. Tens of thousands of desperate refugees risked their lives seeking to escape from Vietnam in small, fragile boats. They were treated as a nuisance. A million people were slaughtered by the new Marxist government of Cambodia. Again there was little reaction.

Even Amnesty International (A1), the most prominent human rights advocacy organization in the mid-1970s, remained silent. It had started in London a decade earlier, with a campaign to rescue "political prisoners." The idea was to uphold a minimal standard of decency, which might transcend ideological quarrels. In its eagerness to stand apart from other quarrels, Amnesty found it more prudent to keep silent while a million people were slaughtered in Cambodia. The organization did not want to give retroactive sanction to the American war in the region. In the following decade, it averted its gaze from Soviet repression and devoted itself to mobilizing support for an international convention against torture.[14]

It was a well-worn path by then. *Human Rights and World Public Order*, amidst all its learned citations, offered no direct mention of mass slaughter in Cambodia. The authors were content to note, in a discussion of "claims for freedom from discrimination because of nonconforming political opinions," that in many countries only "precarious deference and defense . . . have been given to opinions that contravene the doctrines, formulas and folklore of an established order." An accompanying footnote guided readers to U.S. congressional hearings on human rights abuses in seventeen different countries in Asia and Latin America, including a set of hearings on Cambodia.[15] The professorial authors did not think it necessary to unsettle their readers by explaining that such deplorable lack of "deference" might, in some cases, mean the murder of a million people—which might have put the whole learned discussion of world standards on freedom for "nonconforming opinion" in a somewhat different perspective.

Neither the lapses of humanitarian organizations nor the professional vanity of legal scholars would have mattered, in themselves, except that they fed a much wider and deeper impulse. The idea that the world already had a framework for humane order was immensely appealing to a generation that was weary of the Cold War, weary of conflict, weary of complexity. It offered an outlet for high moral sentiment without the burden of serious policy. Even in the United States, it appealed for a time to the highest policy makers.

President Jimmy Carter insisted, at the outset of his administration, that human rights must become the centerpiece of American foreign policy. He proceeded to sign almost every extant human rights treaty. The Senate declined to ratify a single one of them. Carter's secretary of state then proclaimed "fundamental agreement" between the American president and the dictator of the Soviet Union, Leonid Brezhnev.

The Carter administration criticized the Shah of Iran for human rights abuses. The United States then stood aloof as the Shah was over-thrown and replaced by a far more tyrannical—and far more anti-western—Islamic Republic. The Carter administration criticized the petty tyranny of the Nicaraguan dictator, Anastasio Somoza, and then found itself facing a more tyrannical, Cuban-backed Marxist regime of the Sandinistas. In 1980, the Soviet Union marched an army into Afghanistan and began to develop a submarine base in Cuba. It was re-assuring, amidst these challenges, to think that the world, after all, was governed by international law, so nothing that happened could be very threatening.

The Reagan administration came to office with a determination to ad-dress what it saw as genuine threats to American security. The new ad-ministration commenced a substantial increase in defense spending. It also pursued a more confrontational stance toward communist regimes. The Reagan administration was quite willing to deploy the rhetoric of human rights against communist tyranny. But human rights rhetoric now appealed even more to critics of the new policy.

Europeans warned that confrontation would undermine international cooperation—in such fields as human rights. Meanwhile, Reagan policies in Central America, backing anti-Marxist governments against Marxist insurgencies, and anti-Marxist insurgencies against Marxist governments, provoked intense controversy. Much of the ensuing criticism was framed in terms of human rights and their violation by American-backed forces. As in the 1970s, human rights rhetoric often appealed to sympathizers with Third World "liberation movements" who hoped that denouncing American policy in human rights terms would help to inhibit that policy. Human rights rhetoric appealed also to those who simply wanted to be-lieve that American force was unnecessary, because conflicts could be re-solved through international standards.

Yet a third constituency emerged by the end of the 1970s—people who conceived international law and international human rights law in partic-ular as a source of leverage in their own countries. In some way, this was always the hope—that domestic constituencies would use international standards to press for reform at home. The idea that this would operate even in western countries was always affirmed in principle but for some decades generated little interest. By the 1970s, the idea began to gather momentum in western Europe, where the European Court of Human Rights was feeling its way toward more ambitious rulings.

American advocacy groups took up the idea in turn. Through the 1960s and early 1970s, American advocacy groups had experienced great success in pressing their reform agendas through litigation based on the U.S. Constitution and federal statutes. The success of civil rights ad-vocates in dismantling racial segregation had become an inspiring legend.

New vistas opened to legal advocates when they thought about invoking international standards in American courts.

A great breakthrough seemed to be achieved in the 1980 ruling of the U.S. Court of Appeals for the Second Circuit in *Filartiga v. Pena-Irala*.[16] A Yale Law School professor would later call it the *"Brown v. Board . . . [of] transnational public law litigation."*[17] The plaintiff was a Paraguayan, whose son had been tortured and murdered by a Paraguayan official in Paraguay. The trial court could find no basis for taking jurisdiction in the plaintiff's claim for damages. Briefs submitted by distinguished legal scholars persuaded the appeals court that a federal statute, the Alien Tort Claims Act, enacted in 1789, should apply to the case because it authorized federal courts to hear tort claims for "offenses against the law of nations." In 1789, the first Congress had been thinking about injuries to foreign ambassadors, but legal scholars insisted that "the law of nations" had in the meanwhile come to embrace fundamental human rights standards—quite apart from whether the U.S. Senate had ratified a relevant treaty (which it had not) or whether the home country of the defendant had done so (which it had not).

By the mid-1980s, a new edition of the *Restatement of Foreign Relations Law*, a distinguished scholarly commentary on American obligations under international law, included an entire chapter on the "customary international law of human rights."[18] International law could be determined, according to this commentary, by UN resolutions and other diplomatic pronouncements, rather than by the actual practices of states in their mutual interactions. So many human rights standards had become binding on the United States, even without ratification of treaties by the Senate. An earlier edition of this commentary, published in the mid-1960s, had said nothing about this new body of law. Now it had, somehow, become binding law for the United States—and was "still evolving."

To make sure the lesson was not lost, Professor Louis Henkin, chief reporter for the new *Restatement*, organized seminars with federal judges to spread the word. The American Civil Liberties Union (ACLU) published pamphlets attacking human rights deficiencies in the policies of American state and local (and federal) governments: now the ACLU cited international conventions to advance its views, not merely American constitution precedents. Amnesty International threw itself into a campaign against capital punishment in the U.S., invoking various international treaties to show that executions in the United States were contrary to international law. It was not abandoning the stance of neutrality that had led it to withhold comment about mass murder in Cambodia. It was following the same principle—demonstrating its neutrality by criticizing the United States.

And after all, many Americans had similar criticisms and were glad to learn that international law was on their side. Along with opponents of capital punishment, AI appealed to other such constituencies. Later in the 1990s it helped organize a campaign to secure U.S. ratification of the Convention on the Elimination of All Forms of Sex Discrimination.[19] CEDAW's call for subsidized day-care provisions and the elimination of sex stereotyping could now be conceived as universal aspirations of humanity, transcending political differences.

Feminist ideologues found their way onto monitoring committees for CEDAW and other human rights conventions. So when UN monitors looked at Belarus, one of the post-communist states where government repression remained most heavy-handed, they took aim at the state's reintroduction of Mother's Day as a holiday and its general failure to combat "sex-role stereotypes" and its inadequate implementation of "gender education aimed at countering such stereotyping."[20]

Another UN committee denounced the federal government of Australia for allowing the conservative government in Tasmania to maintain a traditional law against sodomy—now found to violate the equality guarantees in the 1966 Covenant on Civil and Political Rights.[21] With a Labor government in power in Canberra, the federal Parliament promptly invoked international treaty obligations as its rationale for superseding state jurisdiction over public morals and nullifying Tasmanian law in this area.

At other UN forums, activists urged that abortion must be recognized as a right guaranteed by international human rights law.[22] When Vatican representatives tried to organize opposition to such claims, NGOs organized a campaign to exclude the Vatican from representation at international forums. The Vatican remained eager to participate, however, in the great project of laying down laws for humanity.

Delegations from Muslim states were more emphatic in rejecting the sexual agenda of western NGOs. Surveys demonstrated that public opinion among Muslims was overwhelmingly opposed to the NGO agenda in this area.[23] Would it help to build support for liberalizing trends in Islamic countries by associating human rights with the sexual standards of western Europe? Building local support for liberal institutions was not the priority of international human rights advocates.

Besides, NGOs could find other ways to conciliate Islamic opinion. By the beginning of the next century, even Amnesty International and the U.S.-based Human Rights Watch had endorsed the most extreme Palestinian claims for a "right of return" to the pre-1967 borders of Israel, while remaining silent in the face of suicide bombings for two years after the unleashing of this terror tactic in the fall of 2000.[24] United Nations forums declined to condemn this terror tactic. As a German writer on the "power" of human rights advocacy remarked, groups like Amnesty "*define* what constitutes a human rights violation" [original emphasis].[25] By the summer of 2001, NGOs organized a parallel conference to accompany the official UN conference on racism in Durban, South Africa which indulged in such extreme and explicit anti-Semitic tirades—among other things, reviving classic incitements to genocide like the Protocols of Zion—that even the UN's Commissioner for Human Rights, Mary Robinson, expressed concerns.[26] But by then it was well accepted that NGOs spoke for "humanity."

UNCHECKED BY REALITY

It must be said for NGO enthusiasts in the 1990s that world events did, for some time, seem to confirm their optimistic visions. One by one, nations in Latin America had made peaceful transitions from military dictatorship to restored democracies. Following the collapse of the Soviet empire, new democracies emerged in central and eastern Europe. Efforts at building democratic systems got underway even in successor states of the Soviet Union. After decades of struggle, apartheid was abandoned in South Africa and replaced with a multiracial democracy.

Human rights advocacy may have helped to encourage these wondrous developments. American conservatives might think pressures generated by the Reagan administration deserved much of the credit. Some of the credit surely belonged to the steadfast stands of a Polish pope in Rome. No one could say that the United Nations had contributed anything.[27] United Nations standards seem to have had no effect on any government. If it was unreasonable to think that Washington or the Vatican should become the world's moral monitor in the 1990s, it was even more fanciful to think the UN had earned the right to lead the world to universal human rights protection.

Nonetheless, the UN sought in the 1990s to mobilize the hopes of the post–Cold War era. Its first great venture in the new era focused on global environmental issues. The Rio "Earth Summit" tried to connect the environmental enthusiasms of western advocacy groups with the rather different priorities of less developed countries. It was officially the Conference on Environment and Development. It drew over 1,400 nongovernmental organizations to a parallel NGO conference ("Global Power") which lobbied for inserting a wide variety of concerns under the rubric of "sustainable development"—from technology transfers to protection for indigenous peoples and respect for herbal medicine.[28]

The following year, the UN followed the same formula for a World Conference on Human Rights in Vienna, where another vast throng of NGO advocates tried to attach their own priorities to the common rubric of "human rights," now conceived to encompass not only a "right to development" but a right to environmental protection. A series of conferences on such topics as "population" and "women's rights" and "human habitat" drew nearly comparable crowds of NGO observers and lobbyists to Cairo, Beijing, Copenhagen, and other sites over the next several years. Non-governmental organization involvement was sustained in follow-on conferences to monitor progress in implementing past conference resolutions and add precision to previous platitudes. "Human rights" and "gender equality" and "sustainable development" came to look, at least to many advocates, as mutually supporting causes in a single great movement, which advocates called "global civil society."

Non-governmental organizations responded to the new opportunities. In 1948, only forty-one NGOs had been accredited to attend UN conferences, by 1986 there were already over 700. By 1999, there were over 1,500, more than 1,100 of which claimed a special interest in environmental and/or human rights issues.[29] United Nations officials were only too happy to play hosts and partners to "global civil society." Secretary General Boutros-Ghali explained that a new "world system" had undermined "the exclusive claims of the state to jurisdiction over the lives of its citizens" but international institutions could not take up necessary new responsibilities on their own: "NGOs also carry out an essential representational role, an essential part of the legitimacy without which no international activity can be meaningful."[30] Kofi Annan, who succeeded Boutros-Ghali as secretary general in the mid-1990s, enthused about a "global society" held together by "common values" and a new common language: "The language of global society is international law."[31]

The enthusiasms of western advocacy groups would provide the infrastructure of world law. The vision was so captivating that it remained almost unaffected by awful reminders that not everyone saw the world in quite the same way as international human rights activists. For a time, terrible episodes simply added momentum to human rights enthusiasm.

In the Balkans, the breakup of Yugoslavia led to murderous conflict, as rival Croatian and Serb militias tried to carve ethnic enclaves out of hapless Bosnia. The UN imposed an arms embargo, which left Muslims in Bosnia more helpless, since Croatian and Serb militias continued to receive arms from their ethnic sponsors, now organized as independent states on the borders of Bosnia. The UN authorized peacekeepers. European states volunteered troops for these missions but then turned out to be quite reluctant to expose these troops to the hazards of actual fighting. In effect, peacekeepers became hostages to warring parties, deterring more decisive action for fear that outside troops would be threatened.

In the most terrible episode, the Security Council proclaimed that the town of Srebrenica would be a safe haven for civilians, guarded by UN forces. In July 1995, Serb militias entered the town and slaughtered some 8,000 civilians. Dutch peacekeepers made no resistance. They did not even notify the UN military command of what was happening, because the Serbs had taken the precaution of holding some of the Dutch troops as hostages. Rather than endanger their own comrades, the other Dutch soldiers had thought it more prudent to remain silent.[32]

It should not have been very surprising. In 1940, the Dutch relied on international law for their protection and were overrun by Germany in a matter of hours. A Dutch resistance movement did not develop for several years—well after the Dutch allowed their Jewish fellow citizens to be rounded up for extermination.[33] Were the Dutch now going to take risks for people on the other side of Europe?

Meanwhile, Africa witnessed slaughter on a scale which far exceeded anything in the Balkans. In Rwanda, in 1994, a Hutu government resolved on a final solution to longstanding conflicts with the Tutsi minority. The government embarked on a literal program of genocide, which proceeded in quite methodical fashion over several months. Nearly a million people were killed, from infants to grandmothers, most of them hacked to death by primitive weapons.

There were, in fact, UN peacekeepers already on the ground. They did not intervene. To the contrary, peacekeepers from Belgium—the former colonial guardian of Rwanda, which might have been expected to show some concern for the country—actually devoted their energies to protecting the small number of white people in the country. White aid workers were in no sense targets of the genocide, but it was not mere racism that accounted for the priority they received. The death of Europeans might have triggered demands for more international intervention and western states were determined to avoid getting entangled in Rwanda.

The Clinton administration was as guilty as any government—perhaps more so. Still reeling from attacks on American troops in Somalia, where they had been sent on an ill-prepared humanitarian mission in the early 1990s, the Clinton administration urged the Security Council to withdraw the peacekeepers. But the sad truth is that no other government resisted this policy. Nor did the UN official responsible for peacekeeping. Kofi Annan proved so amenable to the priorities of western governments that he was subsequently chosen to be UN secretary general.

Instead of deploying force, the UN Security Council consoled itself by sending lawyers to these tormented places. In 1993, the Council created an International Criminal Tribunal for the Former Yugoslavia (ICTY). The following year it created a second international tribunal for Rwanda. To call these gestures belated justice is too charitable. The tribunals were not so much belated action as a substitute for action. Yet both tribunals stirred considerable excitement among human rights advocates. The enthusiasm of NGOs made these tribunals ready partners to the indifference of western governments.

The ICTY was not in control of the territory for which it was supposed to be delivering justice. It was, in fact, the first tribunal in modern history to face this problem. Whatever else might be said about the war crimes tribunals established after the Second World War, they at least had the defendants in custody: The Allied nations which organized these tribunals had already conquered Germany and Japan and imposed their own military governments on their territory.

In the Balkans, UN peacekeepers were not prepared to assume direct control, even when European forces were bolstered by small contingents of American troops in the mid-1990s. So the new tribunal, based in the Hague, proceeded to issue indictments. NATO forces on the ground in Bosnia more or less ignored them. NATO commanders did not want to endanger their own troops by mounting arrest raids in hostile terrain. Those responsible for the massacre at Srebrenica were never apprehended.[34]

For some observers, the ICTY subsequently redeemed itself by organizing a trial of Serb dictator Slobodan Milosevic. After NATO nations had negotiated directly with Milosevic to secure a fragile "settlement" in Bosnia during the mid-1990s, the ICTY indicted him for war crimes in the late spring of 1999, just at the time NATO was conducting a bombing campaign against Serbia in a dispute over Kosovo. NATO leaders spoke of a hundred thousand murdered civilians in Kosovo and Milosevic was duly indicted for "genocide." He was forced to abandon office in the fall of 2000, after a coalition of opposition forces prevailed in a new presidential election and Milsovevic was subsequently arrested by the new government. Under intense pressure from the NATO nations, the new government handed Milosevic to the custody of the ICTY—over the strenuous opposition of Serbia's elected president and its own supreme court.[35] When the ICTY was only able to confirm 3,000 civilian deaths in Kosovo (mostly of young men), the charges were quietly changed at the Hague to hold Milosevic responsible for Serb militia units in Bosnia in the mid-1990s.[36]

Back in Serbia, the prime minister who had ordered Milosevic's extradition was subsequently assassinated, apparently by Milosevic loyalists seeking to forestall further extraditions. After a year of public trial proceedings in the Hague, supposed to demonstrate the evils of his rule, Milosevic himself was subsequently elected to the Serb Parliament with his party winning the largest share of the vote in December 2003—even while Milosevic remained in custody in the Hague. If the point of the ICTY prosecution was to reinforce stable democracy in Serbia, the proceedings can not be judged very successful. But that does not seem to have been the real point.

In Rwanda, the situation was better in some respects—and the UN policy even more unpardonable. Mass slaughter had been halted, after an army of Tutsi rebels, supported by neighboring states, managed to seize control of Rwanda from the genocidal Hutu government. By indifference or intention—the French and Belgian governments had extensive political ties with the genocidal government—the UN's postwar intervention essentially operated to shield perpetrators of genocide. The UN tribunal claimed priority over the new Rwandan government. The new Tutsi government, it was said, could not deliver adequate justice. The UN tribunal, by its charter, excluded death sentences from its arsenal of penalties. European opinion by the 1990s regarded capital punishment as barbaric—even for perpetrators of genocide (who had been so barbarously hanged by Americans after 1945).

The international tribunal then organized such intricate proceedings that over the next eight years, only ten officials were actually brought to trial.[37] The defendants must have competent counsel. Rates for defense attorneys proved so attractive—and organizers of the tribunal so indifferent—that attorneys were allowed to recruit clients among the defendants by promising to kick back some of the UN-paid fees to these mass killers.[38]

Prosecutors had other priorities. While perpetrators of mass killing remained untried, prosecutors strove to develop precedents to show that humiliation of women could be a war crime, even if it did not involve direct physical contact. The precedents were celebrated by human rights advocates in western countries.[39] Whether any of this was doing any good for Rwanda was not the point. The UN tribunals were building universal law.

By 1998, enthusiasm had gathered so much momentum that the UN could call an international conference in Rome to lay plans for a permanent international criminal tribunal. The idea had been floated by scholars from the earliest years of the United Nations. Almost no one imagined that it had any prospect of implementation once the Cold War became the central focus of international politics. By the 1990s, the idea seemed not only feasible but to many advocates altogether inevitable—indeed unstoppable. At the Rome conference, the United States repeatedly urged political constraints on the court, most notably by making the court's actions conditional on the approval of the Security Council (where the United States has a veto).

European delegations were swept along by the enthusiasm of human rights advocacy groups, who swarmed around conference proceedings urging more ambitious approaches. Some governments had their own incentives to promote the authority of the new court. Germany, still rankled about the failure of its bid for a permanent seat on the Security Council, gave particularly strong support to the vision of a freestanding court, operating apart from the Council. It was assumed the United States would have to accept the plan eventually.

The Rome Statute produced a plan for an independent prosecutor, accountable solely to the judges of the court, itself. The prosecutor would not only be empowered to intervene against states which ratified, but also against states which failed to ratify, if they were accused by a state which sought an ICC prosecution, even if that state were unwilling to subject its own activities to ICC scrutiny and declined to ratify, itself.[40]

The rules were largely taken from a Geneva Conference in 1976, which amended the standards agreed among victors in the Second World War in 1949. The "Additional Protocol" to the earlier conventions was drawn up by the first conference on the laws of war at which Third World states formed the majority. They sought, with considerable success, to even the playing field between Third World and First World states by extending protection to guerrilla fighters, even when the latter would not conform to the traditional rules of war, and then restricting the use of air power by countries which could deploy it. An Egyptian participant in the negotiations acknowledged soon afterwards that for "the Third World" the precise rules in the Protocol were "considered as nonsense."[41] None of these rules, of course, were observed in the appalling conflicts in central Africa in the 1990s or anywhere else in the developing world.

But symbolism remained. Apartheid became a special war crime, while "mercenaries" (employed by South Africa in the 1970s against Cuban forces in Angola) were denied protections extended to all other combatants. The "transfer of population to occupied territory" was also singled out as a "grave breach" of the laws of war—a provision aimed at the effrontery of the state of Israel in allowing Jews to return, after the 1967 victory, to places (like the Old City of Jerusalem) from which all Jews had been forcibly expelled in 1948.

Most NATO members declined to commit themselves to laws of war which would so constrain their own war-fighting capacity and provide so much new protection for lawless guerrilla forces. With the end of the Cold War, even most NATO nations found it easier to embrace such rules, as they came to seem increasingly theoretical—or, as Third World advocates had said, "symbolic." In the end, even Britain and France signed on, though the United States continued to reject a formal commitment to these new rules.

The ICC Statute formalized this division among western countries. Its definitions of "crimes against humanity" and "war crimes" were taken straight from the 1976 Additional Protocol. Years after the end of white minority rule in South Africa, the ICC Statute still listed "apartheid" as a "crime against humanity," perhaps for its nostalgia value. Stigmatization of Israel remained as relevant as ever and a provision aimed at Israeli settlements was sharpened to make clear that any presence of Jews in forbidden territory would constitute a "war crime."

The Preamble to the ICC Statute gestured toward a wider system of international criminal justice, "Recalling that it is the duty of every state to exercise its criminal jurisdiction over those responsible for international crimes."[42] The ink was barely dry on the text before European states rose to the challenge.

Augusto Pinochet, who had come to power in Chile in 1973 in a bloody military coup, had agreed to relinquish power to an elected government in 1990. The democratic opposition in Chile had, in turn, agreed to respect the terms of a general amnesty for human rights abuses which the military government had earlier proclaimed (for the government as well as for terrorist attacks by its opponents). Pinochet had been admitted to Britain on a Chilean arms purchasing expedition in 1998 and stayed on to undergo back surgery in a London hospital. From his hospital recovery room, Pinochet was taken into custody by British police in September 1998, because a Spanish magistrate had meanwhile sought Pinochet's extradition to stand trial for "genocide" of Marxist opponents. Ensuing legal proceedings in London lasted for many months and aroused much attention.

The Pinochet case brought together all the constituencies of the human rights movement. Prominent human rights advocacy organizations trumpeted the case as establishing the principle that perpetrators of extreme human rights abuses could be held to account by the "international community"—that is, by any state which wanted to mount a prosecution. When the democratic government of Chile protested, both the British and Spanish governments insisted that they had no authority to intervene in a judicial process: it was not, after all, a dispute between different governments, with different policies, but a matter of international law to be settled by courts, removed from political or diplomatic pressures.

For left-wing opinion, the prosecution seemed to vindicate decades of special fury against Pinochet for overthrowing a Marxist government, embraced by Fidel Castro—and then making Chile a model of free-market economic development and constitutional stability. The European Parliament endorsed the prosecution and several European governments offered to undertake their own prosecutions, if Spain changed its mind.

In the end, Britain's highest court (by a divided vote) affirmed a universal jurisdiction to prosecute violators of the 1987 Convention Against Torture.[43] The British government promptly let Pinochet return to Chile, ostensibly because he was too sick to stand trial. Even the precedent, though much celebrated by human rights advocates, turned out to be difficult to apply. One of the British judges who endorsed the extradition subsequently cautioned that universal jurisdiction should not be applied to Muslim terrorists, since Islamic states might retaliate on the prosecuting states with terror attacks.[44] But even governments opposed to terrorism turned out to have means of retaliating.

When Belgian courts took up the principle of universal jurisdiction for human rights offenses, prosecutors quickly turned to pressing charges against Israeli Prime Minister Ariel Sharon—for having failed to stop Christian militias who committed a massacre in Lebanon in 1982. The proceeding sparked predictable enthusiasm in Europe, where international justice was thought to take priority over negotiating with a head of state supposed to be engaged in a peace process with European backing. In 2003, Belgian prosecutors announced their readiness to pursue justice for supposed violations of the laws of war in the 1991 Gulf War, with then president George Bush (the father of the current U.S. president) and then defense secretary (now vice president) Richard Cheney included among the targets for prosecution.

American officials quietly explained that the United States would have difficulty in participating in NATO deliberations, if NATO continued to have its headquarters in Brussels and Belgium continued to set itself up as vindicator of international criminal charges directed at U.S. officials. In short order, the Belgian Parliament was persuaded to rescind its legislation, which had authorized its prosecutors to act against international crimes.[45]

Some advocates continued to endorse the notion that national prosecutions, asserting universal jurisdiction to punish internationally agreed offenses, would still provide useful supplements to the authority of the new International Criminal Court. Anyone who believed that nasty politics would not enter into such national prosecutions might well believe that the ICC, too, would be accepted as the voice of humanity.

RECKONINGS

European conceit reached a moment of reckoning in the spring of 2003. In a lightning campaign, with very few casualties, American and British forces overthrew one of the world's worst tyrants. No one could regret Saddam's removal from power. Saddam was known to be an admirer of Hitler and Stalin and emulated their methods, so far as he could with his more limited resources. He had launched wars of aggression in which more than two million people had died. He had slaughtered hundreds of thousands of civilians in his own country, terrorized its people through torture and totalitarian control.

Anyone who took human rights rhetoric at face value might have expected universal rejoicing over the toppling of Saddam's evil regime. That was not the world's response. Arab governments and many Third World states expressed great concern. More strikingly, the governments of France and Germany, having strenuously opposed resort to war beforehand, remained critical of the war in the months that followed. European public opinion in general remained quite hostile.

There were certainly reasonable arguments about the wisdom of the war. The United States emphasized the threat posed by weapons of mass destruction and naturally faced much skepticism when the invading armies failed to uncover such weapons (even if they found considerable evidence of programs to revive their production in the future). One could argue, as some critics did, that the war would inflame Muslim opinion and provoke more terrorism in the future. One could argue, as even more critics did, that the war set a dangerous precedent, since Saddam's government had not posed an imminent threat.

But if peace were the priority, might it not, after all, have been a bit threatening to license national courts to indict leaders of other nations for their violations of international human rights standards? Might it not have been a bit provocative to establish an international tribunal, empowered to prosecute even officials of nations which did not consent to its jurisdiction? If the concern were peace, why not pursue peace by withholding criticism?

Even when it came to military interventions, European governments had not always been so concerned about legality and precedents, as they professed themselves to be in the spring of 2003. European governments had supported a NATO bombing campaign against Serbia in the spring of 1999, ostensibly to stop Serb atrocities in the province of Kosovo. That war had not been authorized by the Security Council, either, but European governments insisted in that case that humanitarian concerns must take priority over legal niceties. Distinguished legal commentators endorsed this claim. As some commentators noted, the embrace of "humanitarian intervention" in the Balkans seemed to coincide with larger arguments regarding necessary limits on sovereignty.[46] Kofi Annan, the UN secretary general, commented after the Kosovo war that it showed that sovereignty had to be understood as a claim that would give way to the higher claims of human rights—an argument that evoked much protest among developing countries but that seemed to gain wide approval in Europe.[47]

Yet the target of the Kosovo war, the Serb dictator, Slobodan Milosevic, was guilty of minor thuggery compared with the mass murder perpetrated by Saddam Hussein. Prominent critics insisted that the Kosovo bombing campaign was different, because it had been undertaken by NATO. Nothing in the NATO treaty or in existing international law, however, provided any special authority for NATO to use force against a non-member state, if the latter had not attacked a NATO member. The NATO alliance now embraces some two dozen states but nearly twice that number ultimately joined the Anglo-American coalition against Iraq in 2003, many sending military units to assist in the postwar occupation. The French view seemed to be that humanitarian war would be proper, if endorsed by France—and otherwise not. It was not a doctrine that was well-calculated to attract support outside of France.

Yet much European opinion seemed to find a profound moral distinction between the Kosovo war and the war against Iraq four years later. Whatever the differences between its founding purposes and its subsequent venture, NATO had not been organized on the eve of the Kosovo war. It was not merely an instrument of the latest American policy priority. And NATO leaders had emphasized their humanitarian objectives in making war on Serbia, whereas the Bush administration had emphasized American security concerns in its arguments for war against Iraq.

Governments in France and Germany may have had less high-minded reasons for their stance. They may have wanted to thwart American policy for larger strategic reasons. They may have wanted to build political support in Islamic countries or to retain a valuable business client in Saddam Hussein. But much European opinion—and some currents of opinion even in the United States—remained convinced that there were high moral distinctions at stake.

The issue, for many critics, including prominent human rights advocates, was one of motive. Amnesty International protested that the Blair government in Britain was not entitled to invoke Saddam's record of atrocities to build support for the Iraq war, because the British government had not consistently protested Saddam's brutalities in the past.[48] Samantha Powers, Carr Professor of Human Rights at Harvard, had attracted considerable notice a year earlier, with a book castigating American policy for indifference to mass slaughter in Africa and Asia. She too condemned the war in Iraq, because it had not really been undertaken with human rights concerns in mind.[49] So did President Clinton's assistant secretary of state for human rights, who had urged humanitarian interventions elsewhere in the 1990s (usually without success).[50] Actual consequences were not the issue for such critics, nor even technical questions of legality. The issue seemed to be whether governments embraced the proper faith.

For some, the question of faith was quite literal. The Archbishop of Canterbury, religious leader of the Church of England, protested that Britain and America, by resorting to war without international approval, had acted as "private citizens" and law could not be enforced by private citizens.[51] The metaphor presumed, of course, that the world already had a reliable law, already in place, which could have saved Iraqis and their neighbors without Anglo-American force. The UN's record in dealing with Saddam over the previous twelve years did not provide much evidence for this complacent view. But one might take it on faith—especially if faith were the point.

And as a matter of fact, faith in universal institutions had been running at high tide in the 1990s. When the Security Council established a criminal tribunal for Yugoslavia, it gave the institution jurisdiction over all forces operating in the region, so NATO forces, too, remained under its scrutiny. Following the air war in Kosovo, human rights advocates pressed the prosecutor to investigate charges that NATO bombing had been excessive or improperly targeted. The subsequent exoneration of NATO commanders was probably inevitable for a court which, for practical purposes, had been created by the NATO powers and remained dependent on NATO cooperation. Naturally, the decision was criticized by human rights activists. Shortly after the end of the war in Iraq, activists demanded that the new ICC undertake an investigation of British actions in that war.

One might think that human rights activists and humanitarian advocates are really arguing for restraints on war, because they regard peace as the highest moral claim and peaceful compromise a better result than any possible war. Whatever the merits or limits of this pacifist outlook, however, it is not the doctrine on which institutions of international justice have been constructed. International criminal law is not, in fact, well-equipped to nurture compromise and does not see the safeguarding of peaceful compromise as its mission.

The problem may be most obvious in relation to internal conflicts. Civil wars often end with general amnesties. That was the policy adopted by the United States government in 1865, at the end of the American Civil War. Even successful rebellions or insurgencies often try to secure support for the new government with broad amnesties. Every new democracy in eastern Europe followed that policy, after the collapse of communist governments in the early 1990s. Every new democracy in Latin America followed that policy in the 1980s and early 1990s. Even the African National Congress followed that policy in the course of establishing the new multiracial democracy in South Africa.

New democracies might well have been too generous with former oppressors. Perhaps some were too eager to smooth their path to power by agreeing to honor amnesties proclaimed by the outgoing regime. That is what many critics said of the bargain struck by democratic parties in 1990 with General Pinochet in Chile, whose regime was responsible for the deaths of some 3,000 Marxist opponents. For some reason, human rights activists were more patient with Boris Yeltsin's government in post-communist Russia, which sought no justice for the tens of millions of civilians murdered, tortured or "resettled" by the Soviet government. The question is the same: Who ought to decide?

The premise of the Pinochet prosecution was that national courts anywhere in the world could decide when and whether the amnesty adopted in another country should be honored. The premise of the International Criminal Court was that international civil servants in the Hague should decide. Is this approach well-calculated to secure fragile peace settlements? That does not seem to be a priority for the framers of the ICC or for advocates of international criminal law doctrine, since they make no provision for peace settlements.

One can argue that a "peace settlement" which is attained by letting a tyrant "forgive" his own crimes is not the sort of peace settlement that deserves to endure. But what if it is a democratic government which makes or endorses such a settlement? In fact, advocates for international justice do not even claim to be supporting democratic decision making. They claim to be advancing universal standards. They claim to be asserting a standard which binds even democratic governments. To defer to a government because it is democratic would seem to be favoring democracy. International justice is universal and does not take sides.

So, the ICC Statute makes no distinction between actions of democratic governments and actions of tyrannies. It invites all governments, tyrannies as well as democracies, to subscribe to the Statute and help elect the prosecutor and judges who will operate it. European governments pressed former colonies in Africa to subscribe and the majority of ratifying states, as of 2003, were, in fact, states cited by the U.S. State Department for serious human rights failings.[52]

The project may not look very promising for settling international conflicts, either. Suppose that Israel and the Palestinians are finally able to negotiate some framework for peace. Will it be helpful for the ICC prosecutor to insist that perpetrators of "war crimes" must still be tried and punished in the Hague? Suppose there is no peace for some time. Will it be helpful for the prosecutor to insist that Israeli officials must be tried for allowing Jews to return to places, like the Old City of Jerusalem or the holy city of Hebron, from which they were expelled in 1948? Certainly, Israel cannot expect any sympathy as a democracy. The main hope for international justice—since under the best of circumstances, it cannot expect to mount more than a few trials each year—is to play on public opinion. That means international prosecutions will have most leverage in playing on opinion in democratic countries which have some respect for notions of law.

Even a democracy at war cannot expect the ICC to take account of what it may need to do to defend itself. The ICC Statute, like the

Additional Protocol to the Geneva Convention on which it draws so heavily, insists that restraints in war are binding—whatever the opposing side may do. So it is a crime to interfere with ambulances—even if the other side uses ambulances to smuggle guns and fighters. It is a crime to attack churches and mosques—even if the other side uses them to shield its fighters. It is a crime to attack civilian installations—even if the other side uses them to shield its weapons and fighters. It goes without saying that Israel will find itself in violation.

Indeed, if the ICC had the courage to enforce its own standards, it might well have prosecuted British commanders for pursuing Iraqi troops who used human shields of various sorts to defend themselves. That is, in fact, what a succession of legal advocates urged the ICC to do in the aftermath of the Iraq war.[53]

The only way of making sense of this project is to assume that upholding a higher law must take precedence over actual consequences on the ground. But that, again, is the underlying point: Whether the actual ICC does more harm than good is less important to its proponents than what it symbolizes. It is a monument not merely to good intentions. It is a monument to a faith in world law.

The vision is often described as the fulfillment of principles established by the Nuremberg trials at the end of the Second World War. It is almost the opposite. To start with, appealing to Nuremberg as the precedent is to abstract from the war which preceded Nuremberg. During that war, the Allies used almost any technique they thought would help them prevail. Some war measures, like the firebombing of German and Japanese cities, might well raise moral questions. That did not mean the Allies were prepared to let these questions be resolved by neutral umpires.

During the Battle of Britain, Prime Minister Winston Churchill dismissed out of hand the offer of the International Red Cross to monitor the effects of bombing on both sides. He feared that the Red Cross would favor the Germans (given Swiss concerns to stay on good terms with powerful neighbors). He did not, in any case, want war tactics to be determined by neutrals.[54] After the war, the Nuremberg tribunal—like its counterpart in Tokyo—limited its jurisdiction to offenses by the former enemy. Allied practices were excluded from questioning. The judges and prosecutors were recruited exclusively from Allied states.[55]

The Germans protested at the time that Nuremberg was mere "victors' justice" and in many ways this was so. But it is hard to understand why neutral justice is any improvement when it comes to the most serious international disputes. Why believe that a state which does not care enough to fight evil is the best judge of what should or should not be done in that fight? Neutrality might make sense in some conflicts, where the moral claims on each side are more closely balanced. But even then, why would a country which is prepared to make the sacrifices of war agree to be judged by outsiders who risk nothing and can never care as much about that country's fate as its own government?

Rejecting neutral monitoring was entirely logical from the traditional American perspective. The first American treatise on international law, published in the 1830s, asserted, as a well-established doctrine, that a nation must give priority to its own security needs:

> Of the absolute rights of States, one of the most essential and important, and that which lies at the foundation of all the rest, is the right of self-preservation. It is not only a right with respect to other States, but a duty with respect to its own members and the most solemn and important which a State owes to them. This right necessarily involves all incidental rights which are essential as means to give effect to the principal end.[56]

From this perspective, it would would seem absurd to let some ostensibly impartial international authority determine such questions as resort to war or strategy and tactics in war. A nation does not want an impartial judge. It wants a friend. Of course, treaties to end conflicts and even treaties embracing certain constraints in the conduct of war might be sensible policies—and Wheaton's treatise, like all its counterparts in the nineteenth century (and for that matter, in the eighteenth and seventeenth centuries) devoted many pages to such practices. But when other states failed to comply with agreed restrictions, a state had to decide for itself what it could do to defend itself. Still more, it reserved to itself the authority to determine what compromises should be made to preserve domestic peace at home—or retain support for an established constitutional scheme of government at home.

The alternate view, that international authority can determine what is just, has obvious appeal for international authorities. The International Red Cross, which insists that states in war must take extra risks to ensure that they do not violate the ICRC's idea of proper tactics, simply fled from postwar Iraq when its inspectors were attacked by terrorist forces.[57] The ICRC can afford to tell others what risks to take, as it need take no risks of its own. It is above every fight—as it was above the fight during the Second World War.

This alternate vision has obvious appeal for many Europeans. If the world can agree on standards for fighting wars, then the world must already have very broad consensus. A world with such broad consensus can not include real dangers—so the fact that Brussels cannot be trusted with military or police forces capable of defending Europeans is no obstacle to entrusting Brussels with power to veto the security policies of EU member states. A world with such broad consensus does not need constitutional constraints, either, so it is no disadvantage that European governments delegate broad legislative powers to a European entity with no reliable constitutional structure. There is no problem projecting an international prosecuting authority onto the world at large, even if the world at large has even less constitutional structure. Goodwill can cover the gaps. And world law is strengthening goodwill.

It is not even surprising that this vision appeals to many Americans who imagine that they know better than their fellow citizens (or those elected by them) what would improve life in the United States or make the United States more secure in the world. For people who know better, it is heady to imagine a whole world—or at least a whole Europe—which is already in agreement with them. Why should this international consensus not override the contrary inclinations of misguided American leaders or the misguided American voters who elect them?

The only mystery is why anyone imagined this vision could be sold to the American people as a reliable substitute for the scheme bequeathed by the Framers of the United States Constitution.

CHAPTER EIGHT

IS SOVEREIGNTY TRADED IN TRADE AGREEMENTS?

CALLS FOR IMPROVING global governance were a stock theme of political discussion in the 1990s—as if governing the world were a quite straightforward project. The project looks vastly more difficult today. For many advocates, that is all the more reason to redouble efforts to strengthen international institutions and international norms.

Even in the more carefree world of the 1990s, however, global governance meant very different things to different enthusiasts. For some, it was a call to high ideals, a demand for international reinforcement of universal ideals, disdaining political boundaries as selfish. For many others, the slogan implied a readiness to manage global problems on a global scale. For such pragmatists, the problem with political boundaries was not so much that they were selfish as unrealistic or impractical: global responses to global challenges would be in everyone's interest.

The world has responded differently to these differing visions. International human rights law, building on good intentions and pious hopes, has received broad endorsement—in the abstract. But advocates have had to link the cause with more immediate interests to provide it with any traction. They drew political support by tapping into the enthusiasms of diverse constituencies—the anger of western feminists at traditional sex roles, the resentment of Europeans at the success of the United States, the hatred of Arabs toward the state of Israel.

Paying lip service to ideological nostrums is one thing, however. In the real world, no government is prepared to subordinate its interests to the universal ambitions of human rights advocates. For now, international human rights law has culminated in a series of international forums without serious powers of enforcement—even if some of these forums are given impressive names, like the International Criminal Court. A criminal court without police is the logical culmination for a law without force.

Meanwhile, the 1990s saw the birth of a quite different kind of international institution in the World Trade Organization (WTO). Unlike other international institutions, the WTO can condemn an American statute and get the United States government to change it. It is not just a power claimed in principle by legal analysts, but a proven capacity, proven more than once, in fact. The power of the WTO provokes anger—and envy and a great deal of thought about how that power might be harnessed and redirected toward other agendas than mere trade. Human rights advocates struggle to engage the interest of other constituencies amidst general indifference. The WTO must struggle to hold off or safely accommodate a clamor of very interested interest groups and advocates. Governments must be reminded to take an interest in human rights. No one has to remind governments to take an interest in the WTO.

It is an old story. The Council of Europe, founded in 1949 to defend democratic ideals, launched a European Convention on Human Rights and a European Court of Human Rights in its first decade. All these institutions labored in relative obscurity for two generations. After the collapse of the Iron Curtain, Russia and Ukraine and other former communist states joined the Council and endorsed the Human Rights Convention. Few people imagine that Russia is now firmly tied to western Europe or that human rights are securely protected in that vast land, merely because Russia has committed itself, on paper, to follow European human rights norms.

By contrast, no one doubts that states joining the European Union—an entirely different thing from the Council of Europe—are committing themselves to very intrusive and constraining governing structures. There is still much controversy about the EU in states like Poland and the Czech Republic, which have recently committed to joining. There is no comparable controversy in Russia or Ukraine about their membership in the Council of Europe, though they have participated in its human rights programs for over a decade. The European Union has evolved from a structure that was originally known as the "Common Market."

European experience suggests this obvious lesson: Talk about human rights may not lead very far but arrangements to regulate trade can end up reaching very far indeed. The European experience suggests why this is so. The power to regulate trade attracts the attention of powerful constituencies whose support lends more power to regulators. That power attracts all sorts of constituencies whose interests or agendas may be quite removed from trade. Regulators may then extend their reach by conciliating or embracing these new constituencies. So the European Commission, which began by focusing on tariffs and border controls eventually developed an ambitious agenda for standardizing products and then for laying down standards for environmental protection, for protection of workers and women and cultural minorities.

In its formative decade, when it focused on the removal of trade barriers, European integration was regarded as a vaguely conservative project, threatening to the ideals of the left. When a Conservative government negotiated Britain's entry into the Common Market in the early 1970s, it faced strenuous opposition from the Labour Party. By the 1990s, the European Union had become the pet project of governments of the left, often viewed with skepticism by parties of the right. In Britain, there was a nearly complete reversal of party attitudes, as the Tories became the party of "Eurosceptics" and Labour the champion of "European ideals."

In the wider world, international trade agreements remained, in the 1990s, at the earlier stage of European integration. The Reagan administration and the immediately succeeding Bush administration negotiated the framework for what became the North American Free Trade Agreement (NAFTA) and the set of agreements establishing the World Trade Organization. These agreements were approved by Congress only because Republicans gave them full support. The majority of Democrats had come to distrust trade agreements, viewing them as gift offerings to corporate investors, which might have troubling implications for labor unions, for environmental policies, for a range of other social regulatory programs.

By 1999 a meeting of the trade ministers from WTO member states drew large crowds of protesters. The protesters were so passionate that they finally turned to mob violence—in, of all places, the latte capital of America: prosperous, progressive Seattle. Meetings in European capitals provoked similar large crowds with varying degrees of rowdiness.

Opponents of the WTO and other sponsors of international trade rallied to the banner of "anti-globalization"—by which they meant, opposition to global trade. Anti-globalization protests did not oppose global undertakings of other kinds. Quite to the contrary, anti-globalization forces often demanded a strengthening of other international institutions, which they conceived as helpful to poor countries or to the environment. As Kofi Annan noted, they envisioned "a global grassroots uprising against globalization—however paradoxical that may seem."[1] Sometimes the claim was even put in terms of defending the sovereignty of poor countries—or not so poor countries—from the assaults of global commerce.

In the trade context, sovereignty could be the cause of the left as well as the right, just as international institutions could be seen as special vehicles for business or for other constituencies. President Clinton, characteristically, tried to have it both ways by urging the WTO to embrace expanded trade along with expanded protections for labor and the environment in what he called "a global economy with a human face."[2] The proposal was rejected by ministers of developing countries at the Seattle summit. But it drew considerable support from labor unions and environmental advocates in western Europe and in the United States. And it has remained an alluring vision for advocates of global governance.

Business could still reap the advantages of expanding global commerce, but only if the concerns of other constituencies were properly accommodated. Transnational markets could then be supplemented with transnational regulation to prevent the ill effects of market pressures. No one would then need to rally against globalization. Properly regulated, by properly restructured global institutions, global commerce could satisfy high ideals and still tend to practical problems. Once global institutions had been properly restructured, anti-globalists could be reconciled and slogans about sovereignty safely discarded.

But what if different nations have different ideals or different problems? Who decides what the global policy should be? What if nations are prepared to trade, but not prepared to embrace the same regulatory agenda? Must trade deals await agreement on larger political agendas? Perhaps something is lost, after all, in dismissing sovereignty—or pretending that it does not matter how it is defined.

Sovereignty and Economy

At a very high level of abstraction, sovereignty might seem to have no connection with economic policy. States of many different economic systems might all claim to be sovereign in relation to other states. That was indeed the doctrine proclaimed by the UN General Assembly in 1974, in its grandly titled Charter of Economic Rights and Duties of States: "Every State has the sovereign and inalienable right to choose its economic system as well as its political, social and cultural systems . . . without outside interference, coercion or threat in any form whatsoever" (art. 1).

The Charter of Economic Rights was endorsed by the General Assembly over the opposition of the United States and a number of other affluent trading nations. It reflects the priorities of the broad coalition of communist and Third World nations which dominated the General Assembly in the 1970s. Among other things, the Charter worried western states with its belligerent association of sovereign authority with total (or potentially total) economic control: "Every State has and shall freely exercise full permanent sovereignty, including possession, use and disposal, over all its wealth, natural resources and economic activities" (art. 2).

Yet even the General Assembly of that era still acknowledged, in such formulations, that economic resources are not, in general, to be regarded as "the common heritage of mankind" (as the Charter itself describes the seabed beneath the high seas, outside the jurisdiction of any particular state, art. 29). It would not matter who owned resources if they were not widely prized (as inaccessible mineral deposits on the ocean floor had not previously been prized). It is normally the owner who determines how resources will be used, if only by deciding to sell a particular resource to a prospective user. For all its insistence on ultimate state control of resources, the Charter of Economic Rights recognized the value of exchange—and indeed insisted upon it: "Every State has the right to engage in international trade . . . irrespective of any differences in political, economic and social systems. No State shall be subjected to discrimination of any kind based solely on such differences" (art. 4).

Amidst all its Third World bombast, the Charter of Economic Rights noticed the underlying connection between sovereignty and trade. States would not need to insist on their sovereign rights if they were not interacting with other states, any more than owners of resources would need to assert property rights if others did not seek to claim the same resources. Sovereign authority is, among other things, a mechanism for settling the property rights which make it possible to have regular exchange among owners of property.

The Charter assumed that free exchange, at least at the international level, would benefit both parties. It assumed that, even if an entirely controlled economy would best serve the people of a particular territory, exchange between that economy and outside economic actors—whether investors, consumers, or producers—could generally be left to free bargaining on both sides, without political direction from the international community. Other provisions gestured, in vague terms, toward a duty of developed states to assist less developed states in increasing or improving their export trade. But in its opening provisions and its most emphatic provisions, the Charter of Economic Rights sought to separate politics from economics, at least at the international level. Its most insistent political doctrine was a demand for political non-discrimination in economic exchange.

If the Charter of Economic Rights displays a residual liberalism, for all its preoccupation with sovereignty, the fact is that sovereignty was originally a liberal doctrine. If it is mutually advantageous to separate politics and economics at the international level, it can be even more advantageous to separate political authority from economic exchange within a nation, since it is within nations that most economic exchange takes place. Sovereignty, in its origins, was a device for separating political from economic claims.

Sovereignty was an alternative to feudal arrangements, where the lord of each piece of land was lord over those who worked that land but only by virtue of personal or political fealty to some higher lord. Sovereignty began as a claim about political supremacy which held out the prospect of distinguishing or limiting political authority from the sort of control exercised by an owner. A secure sovereignty would make it possible for people to cooperate in economic activity, without swearing personal loyalty and obedience to those for whom or with whom they worked.

Jean Bodin, the first great theorist of sovereignty, held that the overriding purpose of sovereign authority was the protection of private property under a reliable, common law. From this perspective, it might not seem to matter to the sovereign authority whether private citizens used their property to trade with locals or with foreigners, any more than it need matter whether citizens, in their private life, adhered to the prevailing religious faith among other citizens or to a faith more prevalent in other states. Bodin, as we saw in chapter 3, was, in fact, a proponent of both free trade among states and religious freedom within the state.

But sovereignty was never quite reducible to liberal policies, much less to adherence by every state to the same liberal policies. Even Bodin acknowledged that circumstances might require different policies at different times and places. In the seventeenth century, states that were eager to claim sovereignty were not at all eager to embrace religious toleration—not when Protestant and Catholic monarchs claimed to be champions of their coreligionists in other states, so adherence to a different faith might well imply political attachments to a foreign sovereign. Well into the eighteenth century, as we have seen, Blackstone's *Commentaries* still defended disabilities on English Catholics as necessary to the security of the English Constitution, though he looked forward to a day when they could be discarded as no longer necessary.

So, too, a sovereign might see no reason, in principle, to stop merchants from acquiring foreign goods for domestic consumption or finding external markets for domestic products. But what if such trade enriched a rival state even more than one's own? What if such trade helped a rival state to prepare for war against one's own state? What if a stream of imports imposed hardships on domestic producers, thus risking dangerous discontent at home? Just as most sovereign rulers in the seventeenth century insisted on their authority to limit religious freedom, they insisted on a residual authority to limit trade.

It was more than a matter of accommodating exceptions to the general rule. As a doctrine, sovereignty was always somewhat skeptical toward international rules. In the sixteenth century, Spanish theologians taught that exchange and "communication" were natural goods. Every people, by natural law, thus had a moral obligation to extend hospitality to foreigner travelers. Seventeenth-century theorists, at least in Protestant countries, emphasized the duty of sovereigns to deliver security to their own people.

As Samuel Pufendorf put it, "this 'natural communication' cannot prevent a property-holder from having the final decision on the question, whether he wishes to share with others the use of his property . . . it is crude indeed to try to give others so definite a right to journey and live among us, with no thought of the numbers in which they come, their purpose in coming . . . whether . . . they propose to stay a short time or to settle among us permanently, as if upon some right of theirs."[3] Such theorists disparaged any broad natural law duty of hospitality and openness to exchange—which, as they noticed, had been invoked to justify Spanish conquests in the New World.[4]

Sovereignty was, in its original formulations, favorable to trade—but was not indifferent to the political implications of trade. Sovereignty was a doctrine that sought to limit political claims but did not aspire to eliminate political authority. The point of sovereignty was, in fact, to ground political authority more securely. It was a doctrine that sought to narrow differences among governments but not to transcend or suppress all differences. All governments could be seen as versions of the same kind of thing—a sovereign state. That very thing, however, was conceived as something distinct and exclusive. Sovereignty was still a political doctrine, respectful of differences.

Vattel's treatise struck a characteristic compromise. According to the "necessary law of nations," the law concerned with moral principles, sovereign states should open their ports to all other nations. According to the "conventional law," that is, the law grounded in actual practice, each state must decide for itself how far to open its ports and borders to outsiders—and each state remained quite free to play favorites.[5] But states could also commit themselves to more open policies through formal treaties with other states.[6]

In fact, trade agreements were an important element of international negotiation in the eighteenth century and customary law reflected widely shared concerns to protect commerce. Treaties of "friendship, navigation and commerce" opened ports and promised protections for merchants. The law of war on land was understood to prohibit wanton seizures of private property—so that war would not work general economic calamity. War at sea was thought to encompass seizure of enemy ships as "prize of war" but protections were accorded to neutral ships and neutral cargoes. The British government went so far as to allow British insurance companies to underwrite foreign ships and then pay for losses inflicted by the Royal Navy.[7] It was useful for the British insurance companies, even if it somewhat limited the coercive effects of naval war. In a way it was characteristic—a liberal state sought to promote its commerce as well as its war aims. Adam Smith noticed the connection in his *Wealth of Nations* (1776): by removing barriers to trade, a government would assure more adequate financing for "the first duty of the sovereign . . . that of defending the society from the violence and injustice of other independent societies."[8]

Following the defeat of Napoleon, British supremacy on the seas was unchallenged. New industries poured out a broadening stream of manufactured goods, which could be sold around the world, in exchange for raw materials and agricultural supplies. The commerce moved in British ships, financed and insured by British investors, protected by the Royal Navy. By the 1840s, a conservative government had repealed remaining tariff barriers on food imports and Britain committed itself to a policy of free trade. Free trade would bring still greater wealth and greater wealth would ensure continued naval supremacy for the protection of trade.

British success inspired jealousy—but still more, emulation. Encouragement to commerce seemed to be the secret of British wealth and British power. Governments across Europe coveted both. They sought to provide more reliable legal guarantees for investors, including foreign investors, while reducing barriers to exchange. In the 1860s, France committed itself to a major reduction of tariff barriers in a treaty with Britain and the example was widely emulated. By the last decades of the nineteenth century, governments in Germany and Austria had started to move in the opposite direction, trying to protect domestic producers from world competition with higher tariffs. Advocates of protection insisted that free trade worked for Britain because it was the most advanced industrial producer but others would do better to protect their own industry in order to catch up. National rivalries were exacerbated by conflicts over colonial acquisitions and struggles to obtain special trade concessions in territories outside Europe, notably in the Ottoman domains and in China.

Still, the era before the First World War was a great age of trade and international investment. Britain remained committed to free trade. The resource-rich dominions of the British Empire, including India and other colonies in Asia, remained open to the trade of all other nations. Dutch and Belgian colonies remained open to trade with all the world, along with investment.[9] Czarist Russia eagerly sought foreign investment to build its railways and develop its mines and new industries. Foreign investment helped to develop oil fields in Persia and in the Ottoman Empire and agricultural production in Latin America. It was a true era of economic globalization. As a percentage of GNP, foreign investment and foreign trade loomed larger for leading countries (and many smaller ones), on the eve of the First World War, than they would ever be again in the twentieth century.

And all of this was accomplished with no international organization. Bilateral treaties encouraged the lowering of tariffs and dismantling of trade barriers between particular states but the general trend did not depend on particular treaties. Customary practice (and what treatise writers were already recording as customary international law) recognized that host states had certain obligations to foreign investors and foreign merchants. A government might refuse to deal with foreign businessmen. It could not welcome their loans, their investments or their products, however, and then refuse to pay, or confiscate their property, or physically threaten their representatives. Strong European states felt justified in deploying military expeditions to enforce financial obligations on weaker states in Latin America or in Asia. The threat to do so was often enough to secure agreement to arbitration of differences by foreign jurists, chosen by mutual agreement of the contending governments. The striking fact is that such practices were rarely required within Europe itself, because respect for the perquisites of trade and investment were so widely accepted and respected.

On the eve of the First World War, the world's most developed economies were closely linked in many ways without any international authority to monitor or enforce these linkages. Governments could maintain political differences without allowing them to intrude—or intrude overly much—into economic relations. Political authority had been separated, to a very great extent, from economic relations. On the eve of the First World War, the two great leaders of the opposing coalitions in that war, Britain and Germany, were each other's largest trade partners. Steel plants in France, Germany, and Belgium drew on iron and coal deposits in the different countries, with little regard to their origin. Germany's great arms manufacturer, Krupp, operated joint ventures with British, French, and Russian firms.[10]

In most ways, the United States was an eager participant in this first age of globalization. In some ways, it was the earliest and most persistent champion of the liberal ideals which guided it.

American Stances

British colonial policy in the eighteenth century was still dominated by the notion that colonies should be administered for the special benefit of British trade. Trade restrictions on colonial trade with other nations were extensive and much resented by the American colonists. This resentment was one of the factors that helped to set off the American Revolution.

At the very outset of the Revolution, then, American diplomats were sent to negotiate trade treaties with European powers. The first such treaty—in fact, the first treaty of any kind signed by the United States—was negotiated with France in 1778, shortly before the French committed to a military alliance.

The contents of this first commercial treaty are quite instructive. Each signatory acknowledged that the other was "at liberty to make . . . those interior regulations which it shall find most convenient to itself." But each promised "the most perfect equality and reciprocity" in accepting imports from the other, "founding the advantage of commerce solely on reciprocal utility and the just rules of free intercourse" (preamble). Each was assured the same trading privileges and benefits as that of the other's "most favored" trading partner, while each still retained "the liberty of admitting, at its pleasure, other nations to a participation of the same advantages" (preamble). If either one of the signatories sought to impose trade sanctions on an enemy in war time, the other would remain free to trade with that enemy and transport commercial goods of that enemy in its own ships (Art. XXIII). If the signatories were at war with each other, they pledged to give six months notice to merchants of the other residing in their territory, so that merchants could sell off their holdings before returning home (Art. XX). Even war, it was hoped, could be constrained to respect the reasonable claims of commerce.

Almost fifty years later, Secretary of State John Quincy Adams affirmed that this treaty had "laid the corner stone for all our subsequent transactions of intercourse with foreign nations." Its outlines, as Adams noted, followed instructions to American diplomats approved by the same Congress that proclaimed the Declaration of Independence. John Quincy Adams was well acquainted with the record of that Congress, in which his father had played such a prominent role. He looked back on these two famous achievements as "parts of one and the same system": the French treaty was "to the foundation of our commercial intercourse with the rest of mankind, what the Declaration of Independence was to that of our internal Government."[11] The Articles of Confederation, the other great document produced by this Congress, expressly stipulated that the newly independent American states must do nothing to violate the terms of the French trade treaty. American diplomacy aimed at severing—or at least, greatly loosening—links between the free flow of private commerce and the strategic calculations of governments: the leaders of the American revolution "dreamed of free trade throughout the world."[12]

The leaders of the Revolution soon discovered that few other nations were prepared to follow the French example. Part of the argument for the new Constitution was that it would help the United States to secure better trade terms with foreign powers. Even then, the United States found many foreign ports closed to American commerce. But the hopes of the 1770s were still echoed two decades later in President Washington's Farewell Address: "The great rule of conduct for us in regard to foreign nations is, in extending our commercial relations to have with them as little *political* connection as possible" (original emphasis).

For decades thereafter, the overwhelming majority of American treaties were, in fact, agreements for the mutual exchange of trading rights.

Among other things, the United States negotiated treaties to allow access to foreign ports and to permit American consuls (to look after the interests of American merchants) to operate in European cities, with counterparts from Europe in American cities. Treaties also assured reciprocal rights to buy and inherit land, which could be enforced, on the American side, in federal courts, despite any contrary provisions in the law of a U.S. state.

Among the more notable early American treaties was the 1794 Jay Treaty, promising compensation to British landowners, whose property had been confiscated during the American Revolution. In return, Britain promised compensation to American merchants for improper seizures by the British navy. The precise amounts would be determined by arbitration panels in Philadelphia and in London, composed of jurists designated by the two governments.

American diplomacy did not place so much emphasis on trade agreements because trade was regarded as a safely peripheral concern. Trade was thought to be extremely important. Amidst the Napoleonic wars, President Jefferson tried to force Britain and France to modify their wartime restrictions on American shipping by prohibiting American trade with both sides. Jefferson's embargo assumed that European powers would relent, rather than lose the benefits of American commerce.

The tactic failed to impress European governments but proved to have nearly ruinous effects in the United States. New England merchants became so embittered that they organized a political campaign to take northern states out of the federal union in order to escape Jefferson's trade constraints. This political reaction came to nothing, only because both the Anglo-American conflict and the larger Anglo-French wars came to an end, just as the political campaign in New England was reaching its climax. Less than twenty years later, South Carolina provoked a new constitutional crisis when it sought to "nullify" a federal tariff law that southerners regarded as a threat to their own commercial interests.

Following the crisis over South Carolina's attempted "nullification" of the tariff of 1828, Congress came to accept the principle, as an implicit constitutional requirement, that tariffs could only be imposed for revenue purposes and not to protect particular American industries from foreign competition.[13] But there continued to be active political maneuvering in Congress to see that revenue was raised through duties on politically disfavored imports.[14]

With the outbreak of the Civil War, revenue demands were vastly increased. A Congress now dominated by northern interests pushed up tariff rates accordingly. The new policy continued for many decades, as protected interests fought to retain or improve their protection against foreign competition and Republicans came to accept such protection as, after all, a valid aim of federal policy. In an age when the federal government did not attempt much economic regulation, the tariff was a principal tool for helping favored interests. By 1908, when Arthur Bentley launched a new approach to political science as the study of "pressure groups," he offered a detailed study of tariff politics as the best illustration of his theme.[15]

Yet even as Congress embraced and extended protective tariffs in many areas, the United States did not retreat into economic isolation. American policy continued to welcome most imports with no duty. American producers continued to seek foreign markets and welcome foreign investors. By the last decades of the nineteenth century, as other countries began to retreat from the earlier trend toward free trade, American policy devoted more attention to retaining open markets abroad.

To start with, American policy became more assertive in denouncing discriminatory trade measures in other countries. American diplomats, for example, demanded an "Open Door" in China, in place of efforts by European nations to carve special, national trading privileges in different parts of China. At the same time—not always consistently—the United States sought to lower tariffs with particular countries by mutual agreement. Such reciprocity treaties were, as a State Department legal analyst noted at the time, "a policy recommended by free-traders as an escape from protection, and by protectionists as an escape from free trade."[16] In pursuit of such agreements, the United States was prepared to brandish sticks as well as offer carrots. As early as the McKinley Tariff of 1890, Congress authorized the president to impose special, additional tariffs on countries that would not provide assured access for American exports. The Supreme Court promptly endorsed this arrangement, rejecting claims that it improperly delegated legislative power to the executive. As the Court saw it, the president would only be exercising a degree of administrative discretion well contained within statutory guidelines.[17]

Even where tariffs were established unilaterally by Congress—as remained true for the bulk of the tariff schedule—Congress had great difficulty determining how much protection was appropriate. Or rather, Congress had great difficulty disappointing lobbyists clamoring for new or extended protections. Amidst widespread denunciations of corrupt dealings, Congress established a U.S. Tariff Commission in 1916 to provide technical assessments of suitable tariff rates for different products. In 1922, the Tariff Commission was granted "quasi-legislative" powers to adjust tariff rates on particular products in response to actions by other countries. The United States was already moving toward a tariff policy based on coordination with other countries.[18]

But the United States did not feel the need to move very far in this direction. International trade continued to expand in the decades before the First World War. Despite rising tariffs, American trade moved upward with the world trend.[19] In 1913, American imports and exports, as a percentage of GNP, reached heights they would not reach again until the late 1980s. Railroads and steam ships had brought dramatic declines in shipping costs, making American agricultural exports more competitive. American manufacturing, boosted by adaptations of new technologies, began to compete with European producers for export markets, despite higher wage rates in the United States. Even as it maintained a tariff wall against overseas manufacturing by "cheap foreign labor," the United States opened its own doors to immigration from Europe, which helped to reduce the gap between European and American wage rates and made American exports more competitive.[20]

Even after the devastations and economic dislocations brought by the World War in Europe, the United States felt no great pressure to alter its prewar trade policy. During the 1920s, the Harding and Coolidge administrations sought to revive international trade by encouraging American banks to make new loans to the war-ravaged economies of Europe. Congress did not venture to reduce American tariffs to help European nations revive their export trade.

In defiance of economic logic, Congress actually raised American tariff rates still higher in the 1930 Smoot-Hawley tariff, setting off a reactive wave of protective measures in other countries. Trade spiraled downward, along with general economic activity in almost every western country. European governments stopped making payments on their American bank loans. The collapse of international payments, following on the collapse of the U.S. stock market, drove many American banks and brokerage houses into insolvency.

For decades, prior to the collapse of trade in the 1930s, the United States had benefited from liberal trade policies in other countries without doing very much, on its own, to encourage liberalization. After the Second World War, American policy makers took a far more active role in encouraging trade liberalization in other countries. But the most important elements of the American response in the postwar decades had already been pioneered in the 1930s.

THE POST-WAR SYSTEM

The administration of Franklin Roosevelt, coming into office at the depths of the Depression in 1933, did not start with any great enthusiasm for organized international programs for reviving trade. It sent an American delegation to the World Economic Conference, which was convened in London in June 1933. The American delegation then refused to make any commitments regarding the stabilization of international exchange rates, following the Roosevelt administration's decision to take the dollar off the gold standard. All delegations deplored tariff increases and restrictions on monetary exchange. And no governments would commit themselves to vague proposals for different policies.[21]

A year later, however, the Roosevelt administration persuaded Congress to endorse a unilateral American initiative to revive international trade. The Reciprocal Trade Agreements Act of 1934 authorized the president to negotiate agreements with particular countries and then lower American tariffs accordingly. It was more ambitious than previous ventures in trying to open foreign markets through reciprocal trade agreements. This time the president was authorized to include "unconditional most favored nation" clauses in these agreements, so that other countries could claim the benefits of their lower tariff rates, without having to agree (as in the past "conditional MFN" policy) to exactly the same set of concessions to the United States. Even this "unconditional" policy, however, still required would-be beneficiaries to assure nondiscriminatory treatment of American exports.

Over twenty agreements under this scheme were negotiated during the 1930s. They did have some effect. Exports to agreement countries revived much more sharply than overall exports. But international trade remained quite depressed. Even the tariff reduction agreements that were concluded were rather modest. The main priority of New Deal policy at home was to boost American prices by limiting production. Opening American markets to foreign imports ran against the main thrust of this policy. There was constant friction between the trade negotiators at the State Department and planning officials of the National Industrial Recovery Administration (NIRA). The Roosevelt administration was also sensitive to protests in Congress from representatives of agricultural interests, who were supposed to be served by the New Deal scheme for boosting prices by limiting production. Republican policy, before the 1930s, had favored tariffs as a way of protecting particular economic interests. The New Dealers, championing more direct schemes of regulatory assistance, still had to accept tariffs to protect their regulatory programs.[22]

Larger trends in the world also worked to thwart the revival of trade, which rebounded more slowly than overall economic output on both sides of the Atlantic. Many countries tried to correct trade imbalances with currency controls, which choked off the purchase of imports. Many countries adopted more direct methods, too, by imposing "quantitative restrictions" on the volume of imports in what were regarded as vulnerable economic sectors. More ominously, dictatorships in Germany, Italy, and Japan pursued openly autarchic economic policies, seeking to shield themselves from larger economic trends in the world—ultimately by conquest of resources in neighboring countries. Even before the end of the Second World War, American policy makers looked back on the collapse of trade in the 1930s as a major cause of political instability in Europe and Asia and a major contributor to the world's descent into the World War.

The United States would now take the lead in trying to ensure a revival of trade in the postwar world. In 1944, even while war was still raging in Europe and Asia, the United States hosted a meeting of finance ministers from Allied states convened at Bretton Woods, New Hampshire. Plans agreed to at this conference led to the postwar creation of the International Monetary Fund (IMF), as a device for stabilizing currency exchange rates. It was supposed to facilitate the phasing out of special, national currency controls and it did so over the next decade for the minority of countries that agreed to participate in the IMF at the time. A separate institution, the World Bank, was supposed to encourage foreign investment and economic development by providing subsidized loans to governments for major infrastructure projects. The United States committed itself to provide the largest share of the funding for both institutions.

Plans for a new trading system culminated in a conference in Havana in 1948, where delegates drew up the charter of the International Trade Organization (ITO). The ITO then ran into intense criticism in the U.S. Congress. Critics protested that the ITO charter failed to secure an immediate prohibition on currency controls and on "quantitative restrictions" on imports. American business groups warned the ITO would thus embrace the idea of "centralized national governmental planning of foreign trade."[23] The ITO Charter was also faulted for allowing British Commonwealth countries to retain the tariff "preference" system among themselves, which had been established in the early 1930s, to the detriment of American exporters. The ITO Charter looked likely to face the fate of the League of Nations Covenant in the Senate.[24]

American negotiators fell back on a different approach. In preparing for the Havana conference, trade ministers had patched together a provisional or interim program, the General Agreement on Tariffs and Trade (GATT). The Truman administration had negotiated American adherence to the GATT under the 1945 congressional reauthorization of the Reciprocal Trade Agreements Act (RTAA). No separate ratification by the Senate was required to implement its commitments.

For the most part, the GATT followed the pattern set by RTAA agreements of the 1930s. It pledged reciprocal tariff reductions on specified items of trade, with assurances of most-favored nation status for GATT participants, so that subsequent tariff reductions would reinforce or complement these initial concessions. With certain exceptions, the GATT proscribed quantitative restrictions on imports and other regulatory controls, so that tariffs would remain the principal government lever on trade—and tariff levels could then be subject to reduction agreements on a non-discriminatory basis.

The big difference between the GATT and the RTAA agreements was that under the GATT, negotiations on tariff reduction could be pursued simultaneously rather than bilaterally or seriatim. The GATT aimed at a single, overall agreement on common tariff reductions. The hope was that bargaining over a common agreement would induce larger concessions, as state X waived concerns about exports from state Y in order to induce larger concessions from states A, B, and C. Common or simultaneous negotiations would allow participating states to see the whole range of concessions that might be on offer in return for their own concessions.

The difficulty in this approach was that, if unanimous consent were required, particular states could block any agreement among any of the participants until their own terms were met. The GATT negotiations met this problem by not requiring unanimous consent. States that found the GATT too restrictive were allowed to drop out of the bargaining or to reject the final agreement. The negotiations for the International Trade Organization tried to secure as wide a membership as possible to ensure that the new organization had broad international authority. Negotiations on the GATT were "meant to serve the particular interests of the major commercial powers who wanted a prompt reduction of tariffs among themselves."[25] Accordingly, of the fifty-five countries that endorsed the ITO Charter in Havana, only twenty-three remained with the GATT.

What began as an interim improvisation, then turned out to have remarkable staying power. The initial round of tariff reductions among the first two dozen participants were followed by new rounds of negotiations, producing deeper tariff reductions on a wider range of products. Tariffs started a steady and ultimately quite steep path of decline and world trade rebounded sharply. The GATT gained more and more participants even as it reached for more and more ambitious agreements. And it ended up enduring for nearly half a century.

Special circumstances might account for the momentum of GATT negotiations in its first decades. New Deal planning ambitions had been left behind after the war, especially when Republicans gained control of Congress in the 1946 elections. The war had brought such devastation to Europe that even traditional supporters of protectionism in the United States did not see much threat from European exports. Instead, American exporters saw new opportunities.

By 1948, the United States was providing massive financial assistance to revive economic activity in western Europe under the Marshall Plan. Economic revival in Europe meant expanded markets for American exports.

Administrators of Marshall Plan funding prodded European states to pursue trade liberalization as an element of revival. With American tariffs still set by statute at Smoot-Hawley levels (where they remained, in principle, until a statutory reform in 1974), Europeans had their own reasons to reach agreements on downward adjustments while American policy was still oriented toward tariff reduction.

As GATT negotiations showed their potential for achieving new rounds of reduction, the participants developed new ways of ensuring that agreements would be implemented. In the first decade of GATT, meetings of trade officials from the participating states reviewed complaints of noncompliance in general sessions. To save time and allow the disputes to be framed in more focused terms, trade ministers agreed thereafter to refer particular disputes about compliance to panels of trade experts, recruited on an ad hoc basis for each separate dispute. The experts heard presentations from affected countries, digested the details of the dispute and then recommended a specific settlement of the dispute. The authority of these panel reports was not very clearly defined. In form, they were reports to a conference of representatives from all those states which had embraced the latest GATT round. Reports could be "approved" by unanimous vote of these states—which meant that a single state, including one of the parties to the dispute in question, could prevent the report from being "approved." There was a good deal of diplomatic pressure to go along with the reports. But the whole undertaking depended on negotiation and diplomacy, because the GATT had no independent means of enforcing its own standards.

The GATT was not an organization claiming independent powers in the manner of the UN Security Council. The GATT provided no mechanism for organizing general economic sanctions on a violator of its standards. The ultimate sanction had to be supplied by the complaining state, if its complaint could not be settled by negotiation. Even the ITO Charter had assumed that the ultimate sanction for noncompliance would be just what it was under the RTAA agreement—a "withdrawal of concessions" by an injured state toward any state which did not make good on its own commitments. At the ITO drafting conference in 1948, one of the American delegates described the logic of the system with admirable bluntness:

There are many commitments in the [ITO] Charter. . . . But if any of these commitments are violated, there is only one sanction that can be applied. And that, in its crudest terms, is [economic] retaliation by another state. Now this sanction was not invented by the framers of the Charter. It has existed from time immemorial. It exists today. It will exist tomorrow, even though the Organization that we have conceived is never brought to life. What then have we done [in the Charter]? We have asked the nations of the world to confer upon an international organization the right to limit their power to retaliate. We have sought to tame retaliation, to discipline it, to keep it within bounds.[26]

The GATT, with even less trappings of a formal organization, offered even less assurance of compliance. But the very fragility of the framework may have encouraged patience and forbearance. Actual retaliatory sanctions were almost never applied. Rather than wreck the general negotiating framework for future tariff reductions, most states accepted compromises or worked out special arrangements to accommodate particular challenges (such as temporary restrictions on imports), even if not authorized under the agreement.

The original GATT of 1947 allowed for certain large exceptions to its general policy of nondiscrimination. Special treatment was authorized for members of special trade organizations. In the early decades of GATT, this provision accommodated special preferences for members of the British Commonwealth. It was subsequently invoked to authorize special tariff rules within the European Economic Community. In the 1960s, special preferences were authorized for former colonies and other less developed nations. Known as the General System of Preferences, it was, in fact, an accommodation to special preferences, allowing some trade partners to receive more favor than the "most favored nation" rule would otherwise allow.

The concessions were not as generous as poor countries might have liked. A United Nations Conference on Trade and Development (UNCTAD) was organized in 1964 to air the concerns of developing countries. It was converted into a permanent fixture of UN operations. By the mid-1970s, Third World nations tried to use their majority in the General Assembly to demand international support for cartel arrangements to boost prices for exports of raw materials.[27] There was no system available for states to impose new economic obligations on other states without their consent. Any one state could try to induce concessions from another state, by threatening to withhold concessions of its own to the target state. But a poor country was not in a very good position to wield such tactics.

Here again, one of the American delegates at the drafting conference for the ITO had put the point "bluntly": "If we are to arm the nations of the world with this [economic] 'weapon' and send them into economic battle, the advantages will not be with the smaller and the weaker adversaries [but] with the big and the strong."[28] More and more states decided it would be to their advantage to join the GATT.

Meanwhile, however, the United States, itself, was forced to adopt a new negotiating process to keep other countries committed to the GATT framework. In the Kennedy Round of the 1960s, GATT negotiations sought to impose limits on nontariff barriers, such as subsidies which some nations reserved for their own producers (thereby imposing discriminatory burdens on competing imports). The actual tariff reductions agreed to in this round could still be implemented by direct executive action, under repeatedly renewed authorizations dating back to the 1930s. But Congress balked at implementing promised reductions in subsidy programs. When other trading states expressed reluctance to enter a further round of bargaining with the United States—if it could not guarantee its own implementation of the ultimate agreements—a new American negotiating framework was established in the Trade Act of 1974.[29]

Under the new scheme, the president would be authorized to negotiate agreements within broad limits and Congress would commit itself to vote on the entire package (that is, vote up or down without making separate amendments) within a relatively tight schedule for action. The new approach restored sufficient trust to secure the successful completion of the Tokyo Round of tariff and subsidy reductions in the 1970s. A new round was started in the 1980s, called the Uruguay Round, after the site of the conference at which the negotiations were launched. The Reagan administration had the same negotiating authority but negotiations for the Uruguay Round turned out to be much more difficult.

In Europe, trade negotiations had become the common project of the European Community and European negotiators were quite resistant to American proposals for reducing subsidies on agricultural products. The Reagan administration responded by showing that the United States could develop its own regional alternatives to the GATT. It used its negotiating authority to develop a North American alternative to the European Community.

NAFTA: Reciprocity and Recourse

The U.S. venture in regional trade agreements began with a special trade pact with Canada, completed in 1989. It was quickly followed by negotiations to include Mexico in the agreement, which resulted in the North American Free Trade Agreement in 1993. For the most part, NAFTA simply expanded the basic architecture of the earlier U.S.-Canada Free Trade Agreement.

Both these agreements were negotiated under the same fast-track negotiating authority utilized for previous GATT rounds. Both agreements, in fact, followed the general pattern of GATT agreements. Certainly these regional trade pacts bear far more resemblance to the GATT than to the institutional architecture of the European Economic Community. Negotiations for the ambitious "Single Europe Act," which took effect in 1987, were well under way when the United States and Canada began their negotiations in the mid-1980s. American and Canadian trade negotiators were certainly familiar, in general terms, with the ongoing development of European institutions for managing trade relations among members of the European Community. The North American agreements rejected this model.

Even the term "free trade" was a somewhat misleading name for these agreements, though it was more apt than "community" or "common market." The North American agreements did not eliminate all tariff barriers, let alone all border controls. They did not establish a common tariff policy toward the outside world. What they did was to reduce tariffs on a wide range of products below levels required under the previous round of the GATT. Like the GATT rounds, these agreements stipulated particular reductions for particular items of trade, with different products subject to somewhat different standards, as agreed among the negotiators on a category-by-category basis. The ultimate agreements run to many hundreds of pages.[30]

The resulting agreements were not conceived as a new body of supranational law. They are binding on the "parties" (as they are called) in the same manner as previous trade agreements. There are various provisions for ongoing consultation among trade ministers. But the ministers were not empowered to make new agreements outside the existing framework for trade diplomacy with all other states. There is no provision for filling out details by issuing new directives, as the European Commission may do, under the direction of the EU Council of Ministers. The North American agreements accept the existing framework for making trade law within each country and add no new machinery for extending or revising national law. The U.S. Congress delegated no more authority to NAFTA officials (nor even to U.S. officials) than it had already delegated to U.S. officials under existing trade law.

Where disputes cannot be resolved by diplomatic discussion, the agreements make provision for submission of binational disputes to arbitration. The arbitration system is modeled on what had already been developed under the GATT. Canadian negotiators had suggested that the agreement ought to establish a permanent body for adjudicating disputes. United States negotiators insisted on retaining the GATT model, where each dispute would be submitted to a new ad hoc panel, chosen from a list of approved arbitrators to hear only the specific complaints in this specific dispute. The panel's "recommendation" would not change U.S. law (or Canadian law) but merely point out the best path for resolving the dispute, in the view of the binational panel of arbitrators.

There was one innovation in the original U.S.-Canada Free Trade Agreement, however, that did raise some constitutional concerns in the United States. American negotiators refused to give up the provision in American trade law allowing retaliatory tariffs against foreign products "dumped" into the American market below their true cost. Under U.S. law, private parties could file complaints with a commission in the U.S. Commerce Department demanding the imposition of such "countervailing duties." The commission tended to respond quite sympathetically. Even though the commission's decisions could be appealed to a federal court (by the affected foreign firm or by U.S. importers), Canadian negotiators wanted further protection against this practice. A special provision in the FTA accordingly authorized parties to such disputes to appeal from the ruling of the U.S. trade commission (or in protests against Canadian policies, from rulings of its northern counterpart) to a binational panel of arbitrators. The provision then stipulated that the ruling of the panel could not be reviewed by further appeals in the national courts of either country. The same arrangement was retained in the NAFTA scheme.

In this one area, then, the United States has agreed to allow an international arbitration panel to determine internal American law, in such a way as to bind U.S. courts from imposing their own independent interpretation of what U.S. law requires. It is a very small exception to the general pattern, a very small step toward the European model of supranational law. It affects only a very small area of policy and a very small category of private complainants. It does not make a new body of supranational law superior to U.S. domestic law but simply allows the interpretation of one area of existing U.S. law to be withheld from federal judicial review and handed to a binational panel for definitive interpretation.

Nonetheless, critics have argued that this arrangement does violate the U.S. Constitution by subjecting U.S. law to the final interpretation of a judicial authority which is not appointed by the president (since some of the specialists on the panel would be Canadian or Mexican appointees).[31] On the other hand, this arrangement does not affect constitutionally protected rights, since no one has a constitutional right to any particular level of tariff protection. Congress could eliminate all tariff protections without affording any direct compensation, just as it could eliminate other sorts of regulatory protections or subsidies without affecting constitutionally protected property rights. If it wanted to do so, Congress could eliminate any appeal at all from decisions of the Commerce Department's trade commission. Arguably, therefore, it can limit appeals to the special procedure set down in the FTA. Despite several efforts to challenge this provision in U.S. courts, the question has not yet been squarely faced by a federal court.[32]

The precedent might be extended in ways that would be more worrisome.

It was not further extended, however, when the FTA was expanded to embrace Mexico. NAFTA incorporates almost all the same provisions as the FTA, including the same provision for challenging U.S. countervailing duties. The principal innovation in NAFTA was a provision protecting investors from policies amounting to confiscation of their investment. Here again, private complainants can pursue a remedy on their own initiative and the challenged government is obligated to submit the dispute to arbitration. But the provision is only innovative in relation to the immediate terms of the Canada-U.S. FTA. It is not, in principle, a significant innovation in American international practice.

The United States has always claimed the right—indeed the obligation—to protect American investors from outright confiscation by foreign governments. At times, in the early twentieth century, it was prepared (in conformity with existing international practice) to threaten or even to exercise military force to secure compensation for such seizures. The usual practice, however, is to submit such disputes to international arbitration. The United States could not usually gain another country's agreement for arbitration without agreeing that its claims against the United States would also be submitted to the arbitrators. That was the approach taken in the 1794 Jay Treaty. In principle, there is nothing novel about agreeing to allow arbitration of such claims.

Some advocates have claimed in recent years that this provision in NAFTA will become an engine for stifling social regulation in the name of neoliberal orthodoxy. Certainly, if arbitrators did take an extremely activist approach to such claims, there might be some danger of constraining national regulatory prerogatives. But there is not much sign of this tendency in arbitrations that have already been conducted. There are good reasons, moreover, to doubt that it is at all likely to develop in the future.

In the first place, arbitrators are not authorized to invalidate any national law but merely to assess claims for compensation, even if they do find a measure to have confiscatory effect. Moreover, arbitrators cannot order any sanctions to enforce payment of compensation. That remains the prerogative of governments. Governments have always had the capacity to impose economic penalties on other governments for withholding what an aggrieved government regards as its due. NAFTA provides no new sanction in this regard.

There is another safeguard against overreaching claims here. NAFTA negotiators assigned the task of arbitrating such claims to an arbitration service administered by the World Bank, entirely apart from NAFTA. The arbitrators chosen to hear these claims have much incentive to avoid developing overly ambitious doctrines, since they are likely to be thinking about claims that could actually be maintained against countries whose policies are not already embedded in the NAFTA framework.[33]

In the early 1990s, champions of social regulation had quite different concerns about NAFTA. Labor unions feared that free trade would make it easier for American manufacturers to relocate production to low-wage and nonunionized factories in Mexico, from where they could then readily ship their products back into the United States. Environmentalists warned, among other things, that manufacturers would relocate to Mexico to avoid the cost of compliance with American environmental regulations. Advocates warned that such trends would put pressure on American legislators to relax existing regulatory standards in order to retain jobs and investment within the United States.

To reassure such critics, the Clinton administration negotiated new "side accords" on labor and the environment, which it submitted to Congress together with the original agreement in 1993. With these side-accords, NAFTA did mark a new departure in American trade policy. No previous U.S. trade agreement had linked trading rights with measures not themselves subject to international exchange.

The point was not to protect foreign workers in the U.S. or U.S. workers in Mexico and Canada. NAFTA made no provision to change immigration laws in the three countries to facilitate the opening of labor markets. The point was not to correct cross-border pollution, where again NAFTA made no provisions for a common policy. The point was to shield the economy of each "party" from the indirect trade consequences of changes in the labor policies and environmental policies of the other—that is, to restrain any impulse to seek competitive advantage by lowering domestic regulatory standards. In this sense, the side accords were a step toward the European model in which the ultimate object of regulation is not cross-border trade but a common market among trading states.

Even here, however, this step was, as a practical matter, not much more than gesture. If it was a step toward the European model, it was at most a baby step. The side accords did not envision uniform standards among the three parties. The side accords did not attempt to set a common floor for policy in regard to labor or the environment. The side accords did not even prohibit relaxation of existing standards in these fields. What they did, instead, was to insist that each country must enforce its labor and environmental standards—whatever they happened to be.

The accords did not purport to limit the sovereign prerogatives of legislatures to set national policy but merely imposed limits on the administrative discretion of enforcement agencies. Even then, these limits apply only to the extent that enforcement policy is motivated by the desire for trade-related competitive advantage. Each accord established an elaborate dispute settlement process for resolving claims of this kind. If these procedures put "teeth" into the accords, they are no more than baby teeth.[34]

The procedure is quite cumbersome. If attempts at finding a negotiated compromise fail, if the recommendations of an arbitration panel are not satisfactorily implemented, if further efforts at conciliation fail, a complaining party may impose additional tariffs against the offending party. But the proceeds from these tariff collections must be consigned to a fund to finance more effective future enforcement of the offending state's own standards by its own enforcement agencies. The threat of "sanctions" comes down to this: Enforce your own laws—or another NAFTA state may collect money to finance your enforcement programs in the future! Even then, the accords place severe limits on how much money can be collected for this purpose.

These provisions are quite a long way from the regulatory power of the European Commission. They may well be regarded as merely cosmetic gestures. Certainly there is no mechanism here to coerce national legislatures into enacting new standards, let alone a mechanism to render national legislation invalid, on the say-so of a supranational body. A decade's worth of experience does not suggest that the side accords have done much of anything to change labor or environmental policy in any of the NAFTA countries. In fact, no complaint under the side accords has yet been raised by any of the three governments, which confirms, according to some commentators, that the governments are not very serious about coordinating labor or environmental regulation.

Private parties are also authorized to raise complaints about non-enforcement and have done so with some regularity. As of 2001, some two dozen complaints about environmental deficiencies had been sent to the North American Commission on Environmental Cooperation by various advocacy groups. In practice, groups have complained about their own countries, showing that the link to trade (the premise that regulatory coordination is required for the sake of eliminating trade disadvantages) is not very serious. In practice, NAFTA commissions on labor rights and the environment have simply provided alternative forums for protesting policy—alternatives, that is, to the existing constitutional system in each country. But these alternative forums have not proved to be very credible alternatives to the normal, constitutional channels for policy debate in each country. No changes in American law have yet been made as a result of complaints pursued to NAFTA commissions.[35]

Nonetheless, there has remained serious debate. It is not only a North American debate but a debate in the wider world. In the early 1990s the United States initiated talks for a regional trade understanding among nations on the Pacific rim—what eventually emerged as the Asia-Pacific Economic Cooperation (APEC) forum. In deference to Asian practices, APEC offered less formal machinery even than the GATT. It offered even less acknowledgment than the NAFTA side accords for the indirect trade effects of domestic labor or environmental policies.

But much of the debate was internal to the United States. President Clinton's negotiating authority expired in 1994 and Congress refused to re-extend it while Clinton remained in office. Democrats in Congress, responding to protests of American labor leaders and environmental advocates, insisted that further agreements must include more serious provisions on labor and the environment. Republicans, now in the majority, refused to authorize trade negotiations with such matters on the agenda.

There had been talk in the early 1990s of extending NAFTA to all or almost all nations in the western hemisphere in a Free Trade Agreement for the Americas. Without presidential negotiating authority, the vision floundered. Chile, the most free-trade-oriented nation in Latin America, sought to join an expanded NAFTA. It ended up concluding separate agreements with Canada and with Mexico, while the United States remained unable to join the bargaining.

In 2002, a Republican-controlled Congress finally did grant the new Bush administration trade-negotiating authority, with permission to link trade with environmental and labor concerns—and the expectation that it would not do so very seriously. A free trade agreement was promptly concluded with Chile, then another with Jordan, following an earlier agreement with Israel. Each followed the NAFTA model of cosmetic concessions on labor rights and the environment, without any serious provision for enforcement. Negotiations for an expanded Free Trade Agreement of the Americas reached agreement on an outline for such a project at a conference in Miami in November of 2003, embracing thirty-four countries. But the proposal would allow participating states to opt out of particular features of this expanded NAFTA, so it might prove, in practice, to be a framework for not much more than a network of separate bilateral trade deals.

In the meantime, however, the completion of NAFTA and APEC negotiations had helped to secure the completion of the Uruguay round and a relaunching of GATT as the World Trade Organization. Whether the NAFTA precedents would amount to much more—and whether that would matter—seemed to depend, in the end, on what happened with the World Trade Organization.

A Constitution for World Trade

The agreements which established the WTO worked several changes in the GATT. To start with, the trade forum was given legal personality: What had been an "agreement" with "parties" for almost fifty years now became an "organization" with "members." It was, in itself, a formality. But it had consequences.

As a single organization, the WTO could now embrace a number of separate agreements within the same structure. The Uruguay Round completed an agreement on trade in services (General Understanding on Trade in Services, GUTS). It had also completed a new agreement on intellectual property, tying longstanding treaties on the subject into a new instrument, authorizing trade sanctions for enforcing its standards (the Trade Related Intellectual Property Rights agreement, TRIPS). These might have been cast as separate agreements, which individual states could accept or reject without affecting their adherence to other trade agreements, as had been done since the 1970s on a number of GATT-related agreements. Now it was all or nothing: A nation could not be a "member" of the WTO without binding itself to the whole package of agreements.

Of course, a holdout could still try to negotiate separate agreements with WTO members. Nothing in the WTO agreements prevented members from offering the same terms to nonmembers—or the same terms, minus those standards which a nonmember might reject. But now the WTO was more than a negotiating forum. At least in form, it was a body which could impose new rules on its members, which meant that membership conferred voting rights on the formulation of new rules rather than simply providing a forum for bargaining.

In principle, the new structure allowed a majority of members to amend the last agreement and impose the result even on members who did not accept the result. In principle, this would seem to be exactly the sort of delegation to an international authority that American negotiators had rejected in the past—and that traditional commentators had regarded as unconstitutional. In fact, American trade negotiators had given some attention to this problem.

Under WTO rules, an amendment to an existing agreement can only be adopted if supported by three-quarters of WTO members. To impose the new rule on members who reject it requires a majority of seven-eighths of the members. Controversial measures are quite unlikely to be adopted. A measure opposed by the United States is even more unlikely to be imposed on it by other members. No amendment of any kind has yet been adopted by this "legislative process."

The most distinctive innovation in the new organization, however, turned out to provide an alternate route for modifying the rules. Under the GATT, recommendations of panels could be adopted only by unanimous vote of the participating states, which meant that any state which rejected a recommendation could readily block it. Under the WTO, panel agreements can be appealed to an appellate panel of three "judges," drawn from a standing Appellate Body (AB) of seven judges. Rulings of the AB would then be "final." American negotiators had favored this institutional innovation as a way of assuring more prompt and reliable adherence to agreed rules. The procedures for dispute resolution were accompanied by fixed and relatively tight deadlines for each stage of arbitration. The new procedure also eliminated the possibility of blocking the result in a meeting of member states.

There was an immediate upsurge in the filing of formal complaints under the new procedure. More disputes were submitted to arbitration panels in the WTO's first five years than in the previous forty years under GATT. Partly the acceleration in legal filings reflected the greatly enlarged membership of the new organization, which had 140 members by the mid-1990s and was still gaining new members. Partly the upsurge reflected the extension of agreements into new and knottier policies than mere disputes over tariff levels. But the increase also reflected a fundamental change in the character of the forum. The GATT had provided a diplomatic bargaining forum in which formal dispute proceedings played an auxiliary role. The WTO now looked like a governing authority for trade, in which an independent court could play the foremost role.

The AB, itself, was quick to make the most of its position. In its very first ruling, it insisted that WTO agreements were now part of the general body of public international law and must be interpreted with reference to "general principles of international law."[36] Among other things, the AB invoked the Vienna Convention on the Law of Treaties, a 1969 codification of customary practices concerning the interpretation of treaty commitments—which had not, in fact, ever been ratified by the U.S. Senate. The rhetoric of the AB treated the trade agreements assembled under the WTO not as a special set of agreements but as simply one among many provisions in a vast corpus of international law. The AB seemed ready to assume the responsibility of harmonizing the various strands in the larger scheme of public international law.

This approach might seem entirely logical for an international court. If the WTO agreements are regarded as international law, there must be some way, after all, in which the obligations entailed in this body of law can be reconciled with other treaties, which pose other claims under public international law. But the AB's approach was not a mere extension of past practice in international arbitration. In fact, it promised a dramatic transformation in the traditional pattern of international adjudication.

Governments often make treaty commitments to other states, even when domestic statutes make contrary commitments at home. One might call all these commitments "law," but effecting a reconciliation of these divergent commitments is usually left to diplomatic bargaining—both with treaty partners and with domestic legislators. In the same way, governments often promise some things to a particular set of treaty partners while promising other things to a different set of partners. Often a government promises seemingly contrary things to the same foreign states, under treaties negotiated in different policy fields or in different political contexts. It is one thing to say that a government has an obligation, in principle, to reconcile its various commitments. It is something else again to say that the proper terms of reconciliation—or the proper priority among competing commitments, in the event of irreconcilable commitments—can be established by a single international court.

International arbitration panels had been convened to settle particular disputes between particular nations since the mid–nineteenth century. Legal commentators analyzed and compared the resulting reports, trying to distill the most widely accepted principles, on the assumption that a coherent body of principles might be assembled from these various fragments. But the speculations of commentators were not, in themselves, binding on governments. Commentators on international law (as on so many other subjects) often disagreed about the right way to read the underlying principles in so many scattered decisions.

Governments retained great leeway in addressing their responsibilities under international law, because arbitrations only occurred where governments were willing to submit to them. Every arbitration was preceded by careful negotiation over which issues would be submitted and which would not. Well into the twentieth century, distinguished scholars of international law acknowledged that some issues could never be settled by arbitration, so international law would always remain, in some areas, a matter of ongoing dispute or diplomacy.[37]

Optimists might hope that the establishment of a permanent international court under the League of Nations (the ironically named "Permanent Court of International Justice") would gradually reduce competing strands of treaty law to a harmonious system. Those determined to be optimistic could still nourish such hopes for the International Court of Justice, established under the United Nations in 1945. But these institutions were not much more than nineteenth-century arbitration panels with a permanent roster of judges.

Neither "court" could compel a state to submit to its authority, even when another state was eager for judicial resolution of its claims against that state. Barely two cases a year were decided by these courts. The terms on which states agreed to submit disputes were carefully negotiated between the affected states themselves, before any particular dispute was submitted to the international court in the Hague. Where governments wished to insist on their own interpretations of their obligations, they had no difficulty excluding certain issues from international adjudication.

The dispute resolution scheme in the WTO offered something quite new. When a member raised a complaint against the trade policy of another member, the accused state was obligated to address the complaint within a specified time period or face a formal adjudication of the complaint. Members could not escape from the judicial process of the WTO. Disputes which might otherwise have been left to the time-honored arts of diplomacy—including obfuscation and procrastination—could now be pressed forward for definitive decision, as in domestic litigation.

In form, these were still disputes between governments. But the opportunity for definitive rulings generated great pressure to pursue any claim which had, as a matter of purely legal analysis, a good chance of prevailing with WTO judges. A whole new legal practice developed in the 1990s, as specialists in international trade law offered to prepare formal briefs for business clients, showing why another country's trade policies violated WTO standards. In effect, the briefs demanded that a foreign government respect the "rights" of the client, under international trade rules.

For the home government, it was often the path of least resistance to forget about wider political or diplomatic considerations and simply pass along the brief (or the substance of the brief) as the government's own complaint against the particular foreign nation involved. Some commentators indeed urged that WTO rules should be amended to allow private interests to pursue their own claims directly, since WTO members were already obligated to provide all benefits incorporated into the agreements.[38]

In a system where disputes could be so readily pressed for formal adjudication, potential conflicts between trade law and other international standards could no longer be readily evaded. And there were some obvious conflicts. At the very meeting in Marakesh, Morocco in 1994, where the WTO agreements were formally signed, President Mitterand of France and the U.S. vice-president, Albert Gore, emphasized the need for the new organization to sort out potential conflicts between environmental agreements and trade standards. Some environmental treaties negotiated in the 1990s had specifically envisioned limits on trade in hazardous materials or atmospheric pollutants (like chlorofluorocarbons, used in refrigerants but thought to trigger reactions depleting the ozone layer). Yet the WTO agreements did not explicitly authorize trade limits for the sake of compliance with environmental treaties, even when treaties seem to require certain restrictions on trade.

Apart from provisions of specific treaties, there was a more general problem. Imposing trade sanctions was a time-honored way of protesting another state's policy. If the WTO enforced a strict obligation not to interfere with trade, it might be much harder to impose sanctions against violators of important treaties on such matters as environmental protection.

The WTO organized a Committee on Trade and Environment, composed of trade officials from a sampling of member states, to propose formulas for resolving the problem. It labored for years without reaching any agreement on an acceptable compromise. Less developed countries, by now a majority of WTO members, were fiercely opposed to any rule which would allow affluent countries to enforce environmental standards with trade sanctions. Poor countries, often still struggling with food shortages and epidemic diseases, understandably insisted that their own economic development must take priority over the environmental concerns of affluent countries. Poor countries also feared that affluent countries would use environmental concerns as a pretext to suppress competition from low-wage producers in the developing world.[39] Labor advocates in affluent countries were already demanding that WTO rules should be amended to authorize trade sanctions to enforce the rights of workers in all countries participating in international trade. A formal proposal to this effect was pressed on the WTO in 1996 by the International Confederation of Trade Unions (ICTFU). It was fiercely resisted by trade ministers from developing countries.[40]

Kofi Annan, speaking for the poor nations, urged in 1999 that environmental and labor issues should be kept away from the WTO and addressed by strengthening separate UN programs, such as the International Labour Organization.[41] Renato Ruggiero, the first secretary general of the WTO, proposed that a Global Environmental Organization should be established and all environmental issues referred to this new entity for coordination and reconciliation.[42] These proposals did not stir any enthusiasm and soon faded into oblivion, much like the WTO's own Committee on Trade and Environment.

The Appellate Body might have tried to evade these issues by insisting that its authority was limited to interpreting the actual provisions of actual trade agreements, leaving the member governments to sort out other issues in other forums. Instead, it implied that it would manage the necessary adjustments in the name of a presumptively coherent body of international law of which trade agreements were merely one element.

The AB went a long step in this direction in addressing a dispute about an American law which excluded all shrimp from U.S. markets, unless the shrimp were harvested with special nets, preventing endangered sea turtles from inadvertent capture along with the shrimp.[43] The initial arbitration panel, following past precedent, had found the U.S. legislation in violation of basic GATT principles, since the shrimp posed no danger to American consumers, regardless of how they happened to be harvested in the country of origin. The AB agreed that the United States could not use a trade ban to impose its own preferred fishing policy on other countries. But the appellate judges suggested that such a ban might be compatible with WTO rules if imposed in pursuance of a multilateral environmental agreement.

The Clinton administration opened negotiations with a number of countries on proper techniques for protecting sea turtles. The AB subsequently held that such efforts would be sufficient to justify a U.S. restriction on shrimp imports—even for countries which did not subscribe to the U.S.-sponsored agreement and indeed, even before the agreement was formally concluded with any nation.[44]

If followed, this precedent might have very wide implications. Commentators insisted that, if properly interpreted, the existing trade agreements would also allow WTO members to exclude trade from nations which failed to respect conventions of the International Labour Organization.[45] Other scholars insisted that international human rights treaties must also be read into trade agreements, including the Covenant on Economic and Social Rights.[46] According to this view, states which did not provide internationally mandated social benefits to their own people could be coerced, by trade sanctions, to bring their policies into compliance with international law in this area. When the United States complained that the European Union had imposed arbitrary restrictions on the importation of genetically modified agricultural products, European trade officials pointed to international agreements on genetically modified products—which the United States and a number of other agricultural exporters had not endorsed. The Appellate Body would face a great many claims if it held to the doctrine that trade agreements must be interpreted in light of a wide range of other treaties on other subjects.

Meanwhile, in the shrimp-turtle dispute, itself, the AB launched another revealing change in the procedure for handling trade disputes. Environmental advocacy groups protested that a ruling on the U.S. law should not be treated as a mere conflict between trade ministers of the complaining states and the trade representative of the United States. The AB agreed, for the first time, that panels should consider "amicus" briefs by private advocacy groups concerned about the wider implications of a particular dispute. Advocacy groups were quick to embrace this new opportunity. Not only official government filings but amicus briefs from a wide variety of advocacy groups have now become a standard part of the WTO's dispute resolution process.

The new procedure was entirely logical, if one accepted the premise that the WTO's dispute resolution process would be responsible for harmonizing trade law with other concerns.[47] Not only importers and exporters but a wide array of affected interests and constituencies would then have a stake in WTO decisions. All affected interests might claim a hearing for their views in WTO proceedings, quite apart from what actual governments of actual member states might choose to present in their own filings.

Private beneficiaries of WTO decisions should have their say and also those interests which might be adversely affected by a WTO ruling. If the WTO rejected a state's resort to trade sanctions to enforce an environmental treaty or an ILO standard or a human rights convention, it would be making these elements of public international law more difficult to enforce. The converse was equally true—that permission to enforce these often vague and hortatory treaties with trade sanctions would provide these other treaties with the same bite as a trade agreement. Whether this should be allowed or to what extent and in what circumstances were questions which the Appellate Body would now resolve—with advice from affected interests and advocacy groups.

It made some sense if one regarded the WTO not as a forum for bargaining over a particular set of trade agreements but as an institution standing above the members, imposing international discipline on an unruly world. Some commentators spoke with enthusiasm of an emerging "constitution" for world trade.[48] If trade was now subject to something so formal as a constitution, then the Appellate Body was the supreme court, the ultimate arbiter of that constitution.

In fact, the Appellate Body might evolve into an international counterpart of the European Court of Justice. Like the European Court of Justice, it would address the concerns of business constituencies directly. But it would also address the competing concerns of advocates for environmental protection and the rights of labor and for a whole broad vision of human rights. Somehow, differences over these agendas—between rival interests, between rival political parties, between rival nations—would all be harmonized. That is what the European Union aims to do in its "internal" governance.

THE RETURN OF SOVEREIGNTY CONCERNS

The World Trade Organization is still a long way from wielding the governing capacities of the European Union. The WTO has no capacity to impose new regulations. There is no WTO administrative organ which can devise new regulations for member states in the manner of the European Commission. Unlike the European Court of Justice, the WTO's dispute resolution process is still, in form, limited to disputes between governments, with no direct right of appeal by private groups. Moreover, the rulings of the WTO's Appellate Body do not enter directly into domestic law. National courts in Europe treat rulings of the European Court of Justice as directly binding on their own determinations. The same case may move from national courts to the ECJ and back for final determination. No U.S. court has treated AB rulings as authority for interpreting—much less overruling—existing domestic law in the United States. No litigant in a U.S. court proceeding can appeal directly from a U.S. court to the AB, let alone insist that a U.S. court then adopt the AB's ruling.

All of these procedural differences speak to this underlying formal principle: What the United States government does, in regard to trade, is still determined, in the last resort, by the United States government. In formal terms, the WTO is not different from trade agreements and arbitration practices dating back to the era of the American Founding. One can see the whole thing as a mere elaboration of principles accepted in the original commercial treaty with France or in the Jay Treaty with Britain. As a matter of American law, the United States can refuse to comply with WTO obligations. In the last resort, it can simply repudiate all its commitments to the WTO and withdraw from the organization.

Much criticism of the WTO, as a threat to sovereignty, is not only exaggerated but misdirected. The United States may or may not be better off with higher tariffs. But just as the United States does not become less sovereign when it lowers its tariffs, it does not become less sovereign when it agrees to lower its tariffs in parallel with similar reductions by trading partners. Nor is it any more of a threat to sovereignty if the United States agrees, for the sake of improved trade relations, not to impose environmental sanctions—any more than it is a threat to sovereignty to agree not to impose tariffs for the protection of American industry. A sovereign state can choose what policy to pursue. It does not forfeit its sovereignty merely because it agrees to coordinate its policies with other sovereign states or to commit itself to such coordination under an international treaty.

Sovereignty is necessarily a somewhat formal or legalistic concept. It would never have made much sense if it were not. To claim sovereignty is to claim a status which other states are expected to recognize because it is a status claimed by others. At least since the seventeenth century, sovereignty has been associated with the claim that all sovereign states are equal. That claim could only make sense on a very abstract or formal understanding of sovereignty. Even if viewed as a claim about the power to make and enforce internal law, sovereignty is a claim which not all states are equally well situated to exercise. A rich and stable country, where the government retains the loyalty of its citizens, is much better situated to exercise sovereign authority, even at home, than a poor, turbulent state, where many nominal citizens might cheerfully lend their efforts to overthrowing the government or seceding from its control, if they found the opportunity or the necessary degree of outside assistance to do so. Both kinds of government may have, in formal terms, the same right to make their own laws and enforce them. They do not have the same capacity to exercise this prerogative of sovereign authority.

So, too, if states must respect each other's sovereign rights, then improper interference by one state justifies retaliation by the victim state. Acts of retaliation, up to and including naval blockade or outright invasion, have historically been considered proper prerogatives of sovereign states, at least in the right circumstances. A state threatened with blockade or invasion may be very much constrained in its choices. To say that it still has the sovereign right to decide how it will respond to such threats is not at all silly. To think in these terms, however, does require one to think of sovereign authority as a legal or formal claim rather than a functional capacity to make good on any policy which a state might prefer to wield.

If sovereignty is necessarily a formal or juridical concept, however, it is not a mystical or metaphysical essence, which can still be claimed in the face of an overwhelmingly contrary reality. At the least, few people have been prepared to think about sovereignty in such rarefied terms for very long. There was a time when a deposed monarch, like England's King James II (or his heir, the "Old Pretender"), could insist that he was the rightful sovereign of his country, even if a new, usurping dynasty were actually exercising his authority. After enough time had passed, even sympathizers with the claim no longer took it very seriously. Almost alone among major powers, the United States refused to recognize the Bolshevik regime in Russia (for sixteen years) and then refused to recognize the communist regime in China (for twenty-nine years). But even the United States did eventually acknowledge the new realities of sovereignty in these unfortunate nations.

Well into the twentieth century, meanwhile, British courts could insist that Indian rajahs, who had delegated almost all their governing authority to British civil servants, acting for the Empire, were still in some legal sense "sovereign."[49] Outsiders refused to take the claim very seriously. European legal theorists may claim, as some occasionally do, that member states of the European Union retain ultimate sovereignty because the whole structure of the EU rests on their consent. It is more reasonable to say, as most commentators do, that a structure which makes more law than the national governments has come to exercise the "pooled sovereignty" of the member states, no one of which is sovereign on its own.

The ultimate question is political: Will citizens comply when the sovereign power so directs? Perhaps that is not a question which can be settled for all time, even by a formal constitution. But the immediate question is whether, in a dispute between a disputably sovereign state and some purportedly higher authority, the state can make its own choice and assume that its own citizens, or its own political structure, will feel bound by this choice. National governments in the European Union have not been willing to put the matter to the test. The whole structure of the EU—along with the precise provisions of the proposed new constitution—presumes that the Union must prevail.

Viewed in these terms, it is not at all silly to worry about the sovereignty implications of the WTO. In the most immediate, formal terms, the WTO threatens to supersede the normal decision-making process set down in the U.S. Constitution, which is supposed to be the "supreme law of the land" for Americans, defining the sovereign authority of the United States government. If the agreements establishing the WTO take priority over the Constitution, in the event of conflict, then the Constitution is no longer supreme law. Both foreign governments and American citizens can then come to accept that the United States government may escape the constraints of its own Constitution by delegating American governing authority to an international body.

That result is threatened, in the most literal terms, by the provision which authorizes the WTO membership to impose new trade standards on nonconsenting members: it is, in effect, a delegation of treaty-making power from the president and the Senate to a body of foreign officials. In practice, it is unlikely that the United States will come out on the losing side of a seven-eighths majority—though even that outcome is not impossible. There is some dispute about whether the current procedure for committing to trade agreements (with simple majorities in both houses of Congress, rather than the two-third majority in the Senate, required for formal treaties) is consistent with traditional constitutional understandings.[50] It is indisputably a big leap beyond the traditional scheme to say that American treaty obligations can be fashioned by foreign governments, without the direct approval of any organ of the United States government.

The treaty power is far more likely to escape any American constitutional process, however, through the more indirect procedure which the WTO has already set in motion. The Appellate Body may "interpret" WTO agreements in such creative ways that they end up, as a practical matter, looking quite different from what Congress originally approved. The danger is particularly great if the AB approaches the whole body of international treaties, on non-trade issues, as potential qualifiers or restrictions on the actual terms of trade agreements. In effect, the United States would then be bound not by trade agreements actually endorsed by the U.S. government but by a synthesis of trade agreements and a range of other agreements—many of which may well have been explicitly rejected by the U.S. government or the U.S. Senate.

As a formal matter, American officials might still claim the right to resist the implementation of an AB ruling. Trade sanctions from another state might then be authorized. True, other states would have the power to impose trade sanctions, even if there had never been a WTO. But even as a formal matter, there is the difficulty that, in the absence of the WTO, the United States could retaliate in kind for another state's trade sanctions. Under the WTO agreements, the United States has promised not to do so, which may make it harder to deflect or contain coercive sanctions from others.

The United States might defy even its promise not to resort to unauthorized retaliation. As a formal matter, that would require the United States to disregard its own legal commitments. States have been known to do just that, of course, and even the United States has been accused of doing so many times before. But in the typical diplomatic dispute, each side may claim that the other was the first to infringe a prior agreement, thereby justifying its own departures from the agreement by way of retaliation or compensation. The WTO agreements require that such conflicting claims be submitted to formal arbitration, which may yield a judgment standing above the claims of either side.

Past decisions of the Appellate Body and a growing chorus of legal commentators insist that obligations under the WTO agreements are binding obligations of public international law, not mere contract commitments for which a delinquent may accept a proportional withdrawal of concessions from other parties as the penalty for breach. At least as the AB conceives it, the obligation to adhere to WTO rulings is an obligation which each member owes to the world at large.[51] A state which defies such duties must therefore be considered an international outlaw.

The distinctions at the bottom of such claims might be dismissed as semantic quibbling or legal pedantry. That is, mere words. But the fact is that the United States has been remarkably ready to comply with WTO rulings. It has changed environmental regulations to comply with a ruling on the treatment of imported gasoline. It has even agreed to change its tax law to comply with a highly controversial AB ruling against tax treatment of off-shore earnings by U.S. corporations, designed to avoid double-taxation by crediting foreign value-added tax (VAT) payments against U.S. income tax liabilities (in ways that European authorities do not do, because the U.S. does not impose value-added taxes on corporate activity in the United States).[52]

In the background is a quite serious question. In the last resort, the United States might walk away from the WTO. That is an ultimate safeguard of sovereignty, if it is a plausible threat. Remaining within the organization might then be seen as a genuine expression of consent. The threat to withdraw altogether may well be a plausible threat or a reasonable policy recourse, especially for the United States. The United States remains the world's largest trading state. Most countries will want to retain trade relationships with the United States whether they are embedded in an international organization or negotiated in separate treaties.

Still, the claim that the WTO can impose binding "law" rests on the hope that interests within each country will support the organization and its authority, even if they are disappointed in particular rulings. The hope is that the organization will retain the loyalty of major constituencies. These political constituencies will then mobilize, when necessary, to prevent their own governments from defying WTO rulings. The hope, then, is that the AB can reach over governments and form its own political ties with important constituencies in member states. The hope, in sum, is that the AB can duplicate the political strategy of the European Court of Justice.

For business, this arrangement offers the promise of assured trading access, protection for patents and other benefits, a relatively predictable international business environment. For other constituencies, it promises that business concerns will be balanced against the concerns of environmentalists, labor unions, human rights advocates, social welfare advocates, and many others. If the Appellate Body is able to sustain an ongoing project of harmonizing these various concerns in a single body of law, non-business constituencies can hope that treaties which gesture toward their concerns will now, for the first time, have the prospect of serious enforcement through WTO adjudication of such obligations, backed by the threat of trade sanctions for noncompliance.

It is an appealing vision for advocates of global governance. President Clinton spoke of New Deal reforms for global commerce. Such rhetoric is misleading. The American New Deal of the 1930s was the policy of an established government in its own territory. Realized through the WTO, this vision would actually imply something like an extension of European governance techniques to the world at large.

It is probably a vision that is too ambitious to succeed—at least in the immediate future. But the establishment of Europe-wide regulatory authority, claiming supremacy over national governments, took decades to achieve. In Europe, too, the need to maintain the supremacy of economic regulations was the premise—or pretext—for harmonizing market regulations with wider controls on behalf of the environment, human rights, and other concerns, lest supranational market controls otherwise seem to preempt national policies in other areas and national constitutional protections.

Whatever hope of success there is in the global counterpart depends, as the European project did, on blurring lines between the authority of national law, enacted by national legislatures, and the claims of supranational authority, binding on national governments because no national legislature can hope to resist it. In Europe, resistance has always been denounced as reopening the threat of war between European states—even as that threat becomes more and more fantastical in the actual circumstances of contemporary Europe. For the international version to succeed, it is only necessary to persuade people that the alternative to the WTO is a return to the nationalist trade wars of the 1930s, which may seem a far more plausible threat.

If withdrawal from the WTO is unthinkable, or nearly so, then the WTO must retain its authority to direct member states. And its decisions must be implemented. Domestic constituencies already have a stake in urging compliance with WTO rulings, rather than risk a general collapse of international trade rules. Advocates for European social standards in American policy already argue, too, that the United States will face trade sanctions down the road if it does not conform to "international standards." Acting on this theory, Friends of the Earth filed a petition with the European Commission in the summer of 2003, demanding European trade sanctions against the United States for failing to implement the Kyoto Protocol on Climate Change—a treaty never ratified by the U.S. Senate.

From the claim that the United States must accept sanctions for failing to comply with AB-approved international environmental norms, it is only a short step to the argument that the United States has, in some vague sense, a legal duty to embrace those environmental standards, itself. Then, of course, the United States must also embrace those labor standards or human rights standards which the AB may approve. The process might be extended, over time, to embrace more international standards on a wider range of issues.[53] There are already a vast number of international standards, purporting to determine how states should regulate their own citizens in their own territory. Legal scholars have published ingenious arguments to show that the existing WTO agreements already presuppose that states can—as they must—comply with these standards and protect themselves (with trade barriers) from states which do not.

Once it is accepted that trade may be conditioned on compliance with domestic environmental or social norms, there is no obvious limit to what can be imposed. Within the United States, the constitutional power of Congress to "regulate commerce among the states" was long regarded as a limited power, extending only to actual commercial exchange across state lines. To lend support to New Deal programs, the U.S. Supreme Court expanded the historic understanding of "commerce" in the 1940s and ended up giving approval to almost anything Congress might decide to regulate, even if very far removed from "commerce among the states." But Congress remains subject to other constitutional constraints and remains accountable to American voters. The process set in motion by the WTO would be quite another thing.[54]

The classical liberal view was that individuals could escape from the state of nature by establishing a common legislature and a common executive power to enforce its enactments, but each independent government would remain in a state of nature with every other. In the classical liberal view, the state of nature could sustain property rights and exchange, though not reliably. The thought of revolution, with its risk of a return to a state of nature, was sobering but not utterly terrifying—and certainly not always a more terrible prospect than submission to the abuses of an existing government.

Even today, some commentators speak of a world without a trade organization as an "economic state of nature." If such a world seems terrifying, then it might seem prudent to put up with almost anything to avoid a return to such a world. Defying or withdrawing from the WTO looks far less ominous, if one thinks that trade and exchange have a natural appeal, so that new agreements to facilitate trade would likely reappear in some form or another, even without a permanent international trade organization to promote and protect them. Some scholars argue that the major trading states were already stepping back from the extremes of protectionism in the 1930s and would have continued on a path toward liberalization even if the GATT system had not been organized.[55]

Perhaps that view is too optimistic. But it may be even more optimistic to think that a handful of judges on the WTO's Appellate Body can discipline states to maintain just the proper degree of openness. Some commentators, sympathetic to markets and open trade, have argued that a properly constructed World Trade Organization would actually reinforce national sovereignty in member states, by preventing special interests from distorting national trade policies away from lines that national majorities would actually approve, if fully informed.[56] To imagine that the AB will use its authority to restrain only the improper trade barriers— determined in abstraction from what national governments have actually agreed to—is highly optimistic. It is even more optimistic to imagine that the AB can determine precisely the right mix of trade and social regulation for the entire world. And if WTO judges err? How are these world monitors to be controlled, if even the world's largest trading state cannot seriously contemplate defying their rulings?

Hopes for the WTO as the grand harmonizer of world economic policy are the most realistic hopes for achieving global governance. That does not mean these hopes are reasonable. One may think the world needs a great deal of international regulation. It does not follow that the world is now organized to provide a constitutional framework for agreeing on the proper content and direction for such regulation.[57] The old view, relying on actual agreements among actual governments, undoubtedly constrained international regulation. A scheme of international law which relied on consent not only allowed many governments to withhold consent but made potential adherents to a new standard cautious, lest they put themselves at a disadvantage in ongoing competition with other states. But after all, restraining new impositions was also part of the point of constitutional government. A world which can impose new international standards, even on states which do not accept them, is a world in which sovereignty has less and less meaning. A world which has moved beyond sovereignty is a world which has moved beyond the premises of liberalism and beyond the premises of constitutional government, in any traditional understanding of that term.

The United States would have to sacrifice much of its own political tradition and much of its own constitutional culture to embrace such a world. Less powerful countries might be attracted to a structure that can constrain the United States, even in regard to its exercise of its economic strength. It is highly doubtful, however, that an international structure which is strong enough to discipline the United States will still be tender enough to safeguard the concerns of the weakest countries. As it is, developing countries are among the loudest critics of the notion that the World Trade Organization should embrace international environmental and labor standards. Why suppose that a structure which is powerful enough to harness the trade policies of the world's largest states, the U.S., the EU, and Japan, would place this power in the hands of the states that happen to form the "legislative" majority in the WTO? Why suppose that global governance would actually be democratic? And why suppose that even a majority of states would know how to the run the whole world in ways that would work to their own long-term benefit?

The differences between the richest and poorest states in Europe are dwarfed by the gaps between the richest and poorest states in the world at large. What has worked to some extent in Europe may not continue to work, as Europe expands to embrace a new tier of much less developed states. It is an enormous leap to imagine that European models can be applied to the world at large. Euro-governance may encourage the belief that all differences can be bridged by supranational legalisms. But Europe is not the world. That is a confusion which the American constitutional tradition does not encourage. In thinking about the difficulties of global governance even in this area, we might, after all, return to recognizing the appeal of sovereignty.

CHAPTER NINE

AMERICAN INDEPENDENCE AND THE OPINIONS OF MANKIND

AMERICAN INDEPENDENCE WAS launched with a Declaration. That Declaration began by acknowledging that Americans were obliged to justify their claim to independence: "a decent respect to the opinions of mankind requires that they should declare the causes that impel them to the separation."

But the very sentence that acknowledges this obligation also recognizes, by its phrasing, the inevitable limits on politics by persuasion. It is part of that "decent respect" to notice that "mankind" has more than one view. The "opinions of mankind" may, in fact, be quite diverse. So claims to independence from the rest of mankind should be expected, from time to time, "in the course of human events."

Subtle qualifications also appear in the famous second sentence: "We hold these truths to be self-evident." The phrase lays claim to truth, while acknowledging that there is more than one truth. The same phrase makes a rationalist apeal to undeniable logic—to truths that are "self-evident." Yet it combines this appeal with a confession of faith—in truths that "we" now "hold" as such.[1] So the boldness of the principal assertion remains somewhat qualified. It allows for the possibility that what "*we*" hold to be self-evident," others may see in a different light.

This famous phrase illuminates the principal claim in the opening sentence, that "the laws of nature and nature's God . . . entitle" the United States to reject any superior "among the powers of the earth." Other states may have an "equal" claim to their own "separate station." But the Declaration emphasizes the readiness of the United States to fight for American independence.

To many people in today's world, national independence no longer seems a "self-evident" claim. Many governments have endorsed plans for an international criminal court, to which individual nations will be subordinate. This project is only the most dramatic instance of a larger trend toward establishing a body of international law and a network of global institutions to which individual nations are subordinated. Given its own constitutional history and culture, the United States was bound to resist such measures. And so it has. But the American view has been subject to much disapprobation. It is appropriate, in this final chapter, to address some of the most common objections to the traditional American view, in the course of reviewing the historic arguments that have sustained it since the era of the American Founding.

WHOSE WORLD?

Perhaps the fundamental objection to the traditional American view is that independence invites dispute: A world of "separate" states is a world where states may be in conflict. Europeans are persuaded that supranational institutions have preserved peace in Europe. Now they argue for an international criminal court and a strengthened United Nations to preserve a wider peace throughout the world.

But outside of Europe, many nations have learned to live in peace without supranational institutions constraining or directing their own national governments. There has been no war between the nations of North America since the mid–nineteenth century. There has been no full-scale war between the nations of Latin America, either. Even in Europe, it is far too abstract to blame the horrifying conflicts of the twentieth century on the existence of independent nations in general.

The world wars did not arise, after all, because Belgians were constantly launching wars of aggression against the Netherlands or because Spaniards were constantly menacing France. The central problem was the unwillingness of Germany to live at peace with its neighbors. That problem was not solved, in the first instance, by "European integration" but by a temporary military alliance among entirely independent states.[2] Europeans have bet a great deal on the hope that this problem has now been solved for all time.

Viewing the question in more general terms, it is not obvious that supranational authority is a proven formula for achieving peace. If it were, the agonizing Mideast conflict could be readily solved by coaxing all the peoples of the region into a union of Levantine states. The conflict between India and Pakistan could be solved by coaxing both nations into a federation of the former British Raj. All the conflicts of Serbs and Croats and Bosnian Muslims could be solved by coaxing them back into a common federal entity. A name is already available for this entity: Yugoslavia. In the real world, allowing different peoples to go their separate ways is often the best hope for peace.

Of course, there is still conflict. Often conflict can only be settled by force of arms. When there is genuine conflict, as in the Mideast, it is not obvious why people who risk their lives should submit to the admonitions of people who sit on the sidelines, risking nothing. It is quite obvious, at any rate, that people prepared to fight do not pay much heed to name-calling by international authorities, which, after all, is only a pale echo of name-calling by opponents waging or preparing to wage war.

International authority would be more heeded if it had actual force with which to enforce its determinations. But the world has not been willing to entrust such force to international authority. Europeans have not even been willing to trust armed forces to the European Union which exercises so much governing authority in other ways. Why be more trustful of a global authority? Why suppose that a global authority, if possessed of overwhelming power, would deploy it justly or wisely? The United Nations General Assembly (where all states have an equal vote) is no strong argument for the wisdom and benevolence of the "international community."

Any state that is actually threatened wants an ally that is prepared to assist with more than words. Often in the twentieth century, the United States was that ally. Even when it is not committed to either side, American power has made it possible to mediate conflicts—as between India and Pakistan, for example, in the spring of 2002—while the UN has remained impotent. Of course, the United States may not, even in such cases, act in an entirely disinterested way. Still, it has an interest in the preservation of peace and the capacity to act for this interest with some decisiveness. International bodies like the UN (or the Organization of American States [OAS] or the EU) are more often paralyzed by conflicting interests among their member states. Yet they are not obviously more impartial or disinterested when they do take sides. It is not obvious why Americans should be willing to put their own forces at the disposal of an international authority which has higher authority than the United States.

If other states want an effective global authority to exist, they will have to supply the financing and forces to make it a reality. But they must then expect that this authority may often be in conflict with the United States and with other states that still value their independence. Even if this global authority succeeded in overcoming American resistance, it might very well find itself challenged by the defiance of other nations. Rather than exhaust itself in battling revolts, the would-be global authority might have to acknowledge the full sovereignty of independent entities elsewhere. That has, after all, been the history of empires.

Such visions are dismissed by contemporary advocates of expanded international law. They are not talking about force but only about the moral authority of law. The "international community" and the body of "international law" it prescribes will not so much command as "promote" and "coordinate." It will not establish a new sovereignty over states but will encourage states to "pool" their sovereignty in particular "governance" ventures. As these ventures expand and proliferate, they will gradually accustom people to accepting different and competing authorities, at different levels, all linked by a flexible scheme of law.

All very nice—but what happens when different people or their different governments disagree? Does the dissenting state get to walk out? How is it compelled to cooperate? The idea is that, though international authority may not be reliable in enforcing peace, it can seduce people into compliance with new international norms. And while it cannot be trusted with actual force, it can be trusted to exercise the moral authority of governments which actually are trusted to wield force. More than that, international law can somehow, in this vision, come to exercise a greater force than that of governments, because it can overawe mere governments in the name of international order.

The vision is often associated with the "idealistic" view of Immanuel Kant, who urged that "perpetual peace" could be secured by a federation of states. But Kant was "realistic" enough to insist that the peace federation must retain sufficient force of its own to enforce the terms of peace. And he acknowledged that states would only submit to such a federation if it were limited to the enforcement of peace and refrained from interfering at all in the domestic government of member states.

In some ways, advocates of global governance are less ambitious. They disclaim any immediate project for a global military force to enforce the obligations of international law on recalcitrant states. At the same time, they embrace a vision which is, in other ways, vastly more ambitious than Kant's project. Today's advocates assume that an unarmed power can penetrate into states and somehow coax whole peoples into complying with international standards, even if their governments might prefer to follow different policies.

The United States, founded in the era of Enlightenment, is, of all nations, among the most unlikely to embrace the post-modern vision of global governance without compulsion. There are many reasons for American resistance to this project. But it is worth emphasizing the largest reason why the United States is not inclined to take many risks on its behalf: the whole project necessarily undermines the notion of constitutional government at home.

THE VIEW FROM INSIDE

In a nation like the United States, with a stable constitution, most citizens will be loyal to the constituted government. Some people may strongly object to particular policies or laws of that government. If they cannot succeed in changing such policies through normal constitutional means, such people may welcome pressures from outside. But why should the majority of citizens want their own government to change its policies in response to demands from outside?

Even if these outside pressures are endorsed by some supranational authority, why assume that outside arbiters will have the good of one's own country at heart? Even if the outside arbiters claim to be interpreting or applying international law, why should outsiders be more trusted to interpret or apply that law than one's own government? On minor matters, involving a dispute between one's own state and another state, it may be convenient to accept international arbitration, in order to enlist the co-operation of other states. But in a dispute between different interests at home, why assume that the preferred policies of the internal minority will be accepted by the domestic majority, just because an international authority has identified the minority view with international law? Why believe there is such magic in the word "law"?

The United States was founded on the opposite belief: that law is not a magic answer but often the central problem, because we do not all agree on what the law is or should be. The Declaration of Independence, after all, does not start by proclaiming universal duties but, to the contrary, asserts a claim to individual rights—including a very open-ended right to "the pursuit of happiness." What happens when different individuals construe this right differently?

The answer to this problem is sovereignty—the doctrine that a particular policy becomes law because the sovereign authority has determined that it is law. It is not a sufficient answer to all questions about law and justice. But it is a sensible start. It acknowledges that the law may be one thing here and something else there, because different sovereigns may have different laws. And it acknowledges that authority to give law requires the power to enforce law, that authority to command presupposes the power to protect.

That was, at the outset, the argument for constituting a national government for the United States. The "common defense" requires fundamental powers of taxation and legislation. These powers must be "under the direction of the same councils which are appointed to preside over the common defense," as Hamilton remarks in *The Federalist*. The argument rests on "one of those truths which . . . carries its own evidence along with it" and "cannot be made plainer by argument or reasoning."[3] The truth of the argument is, in other words, as "self-evident" as the Declaration's claim that individuals are "endowed with unalienable rights" and that "to secure these rights, governments are instituted." For rights to be secure, there must be a power somewhere which is sufficient to protect rights—and it needs to be an adequate power.

The argument is not weakened by the assertion that individuals are "endowed by their Creator with certain unalienable rights." Quite the contrary. In the treatises on natural rights, which inspired the framers of the Declaration, natural rights were associated with the claims of individuals in the state of nature. In these treatises, the state of nature was said to have an enduring model in the relations between sovereign states.[4] Sovereigns, everyone knew, were more eager to assert their rights than to acknowledge their duties. They were constrained from exaggerating their own rights only by the willingness of other sovereigns to insist on their own competing rights.

Taking this pattern as the model of human nature implies that human affairs are prone to conflict, because the individual will insist on his due, whenever he can. So Grotius, the first writer to speak about natural rights, depicted sovereignty as a special sort of property—something the owner is entitled and expected to hold for his own use. Grotius argued that restraints, founded on the mutual consent of sovereigns, could lessen the frequency and ferocity of conflict. Still, he took for granted that conflict would continue.

To suppress violence within a state requires a strong power. And a strong power may prove abusive. Liberal philosophers sought to make sovereign power less prone to abuse by insisting that it must be conceived as a trust from the people—who could only be conceived as delegating power within constitutional limits. But precisely if sovereignty is viewed as a conditional grant, the idea that it can be redelegated at will seems deeply threatening. So John Locke, as we have seen (chapter 3), denounced the delegation of legislative powers to a foreign government as a just cause for popular rebellion.

To talk of social contracts in the state of nature is to engage, of course, in metaphor. Certainly "the course of human events" displays many more motivations than rational self-interest and a great many more human types than the calculating individual. Sympathy plays a great role in human affairs—along with jealousy and resentment. Generous faith can have great influence along with selfish calculation. But human events also show the force of vanity, power-lust, and cruelty. And the most generous impulses can sometimes generate cruel results or help to empower the most power-mad tyrannies.

A decent society requires a degree of mutual concern among its members. But a successful and adaptive society also needs to preserve room for individuals to disagree and to try new approaches. Society benefits greatly from allowing individuals to develop their different talents and to pursue their different capacities. Society cannot reap the full benefits of such individual differences unless it allows its strivers to retain a substantial portion of the reward they gain from exercising their different choices and their different levels of energy and skill. Socialism produced poverty and misery wherever it was pursued to its ultimate logic. Central authorities turned out to lack the requisite knowledge and the requisite moral discipline to allocate resources and direct individual efforts through the whole myriad of transactions that make up a modern economy.

Of course, there is more to life than getting and spending. A sturdy individual, even a minimally decent human being, must also retain some concern for his own soul—or, as post-modernists like to say, for "post-material values."[5] But efforts of governments to foster the spiritual well-being of their citizens have often generated conflict and cyncism more than saving faith or a genuine sense of religious community. Jean Bodin, the first great theorist of sovereignty, took pains to emphasize this fact. Even the medieval Church recognized, in its way, that different souls may have different spiritual needs. So the Church sponsored or sheltered a great variety of religious orders and a diverse range of outlets for religious devotion. Modern totalitarian states, seeking to enlist all citizens in the same robotic rituals of collective faith, have left vast spiritual wreckage in their wake. The passivity of citizens in post–Soviet Russia would probably have startled people in fourteenth-century France.

For a modern society to operate effectively, then, individuals must have reliable guarantees of their capacity to make separate decisions. That requires a government with the strength to enforce such guarantees and the restraint to respect them. There is no single, proven formula for achieving an optimal balance of individual rights and governmental powers. But liberal constitutions have certainly had more success in countries where there is a certain level of minimal trust among citizens, recognizing some minimal commonalities in their shared nationality.

Supranational organizations cannot readily inspire such background trust. So they are bound to betray the hopes invested in them. For the most part, they fail because they cannot compel compliance—and they cannot do so because they cannot inspire trust. But it does not do justice to the argument for sovereignty simply to contrast the "power" of sovereign states with the impotence of international organizations. A great part of the appeal of sovereignty is precisely that it limits the power of any particular state. A world of sovereign states is, after all, a world of multiple and competing powers. That is, in many ways, a good thing.

Within any one country, critics or innovators gain strength when they can point to the success of different approaches in other countries. International controls might suppress such opportunities for contrast and emulation. The Soviet Union might still exist if the whole world had been subjected to communist control. The free market initiatives of the Thatcher government in Britain would not have been emulated—or attempted in the first place—if international authorities had been able to lay down the basic requirements for each country's policy. After many centuries of opposing liberal government, the Roman Catholic Church endorsed liberty of conscience in the 1960s. And the change seems to have been inspired, at least in part, by the recognition that liberal government might be entirely compatible with continuing religious faith among citizens—as proven by two centuries of American experience.

Sovereignty is not just a fact of life. As a mechanism, but perhaps even as a metaphor, sovereign rights may be a crucial safeguard of human well-being.

THE POST-SOVEREIGN VISION

In the eyes of a global planner, claims to sovereignty may appear no more than a nuisance. To planners, the rights of individuals are always a nuisance when they interfere with the master plan. Individual states can be a particular nuisance because states are not quite so easily coerced as individuals. But if one thinks that sovereign states can and should be readily enrolled in international projects, one must be even more contemptuous of the claims of mere individual citizens. At the least, one must assume that citizens have no particular partiality to their own state. On that understanding, it is plausible to assume that citizens have no particular attachment to their own constitution, so no very strong attachment to their own rights, at least as legal claims secured by their own constitution.

This view—what might be called global managerialism—was already apparent in the UN human rights covenants, drafted in the 1950s and designed to express a worldwide consensus. "Everyone has a right to a rising standard of living"—but no one has a right to property or a right to have contracts enforced. This is not necessarily a call for socialism, let alone global socialism. But just as the rights of individual property owners are glossed over, the precise claims of individual states—what they may rightfully claim and from precisely which other states—is neatly evaded in that inclusive talk about "everyone."

Contemporary discussion of "global governance" has this same evasive character. A major international relations theorist defines "governance" as "a more encompassing phenomenon than government. It embraces governmental institutions, but it also subsumes informal, nongovernmental mechanisms whereby those persons and organizations within its purview move ahead, satisfy their needs and fulfill their wants."[6] So "governance" may be private and voluntary or it may be governmental and mandatory, but coordinating structures can be readily coordinated because, after all, individuals submit to so much coordinating, anyway. In this view, it should be easy to induce governments to submit to international coordination of their coordinating efforts, because some form of "governance" is everywhere.

It is a perspective that seems more compelling to students of European practice, where governments regularly coerce or cajole citizens, without any authorization from their own parliaments, on the grounds that a bureaucrat in Brussels has demanded adherence to a new standard. But one can see the same underlying logic at work in the writings of American scholars who embrace ambitious projects in global governance. Indeed, one could see the point decades ago.

The connection between disdain for sovereignty and disdain for individual rights was already quite evident in the Yale School of "international legal process," which gained prominence decades ago. By the 1960s, its leading lights, Myres McDougal and Harold Lasswell, were publishing articles that spoke complacently of "international legislation" and "international constitutional standards," as if these already existed.[7] It seemed not to matter that Americans had never actually consented to be governed by such "legislation" or such "constitutional standards."

In the early 1940s, at the end of the New Deal, the same writers exhorted American law schools to recognize that "legal education . . . must be conscious, efficient, and systematic *training for policy-making*"—training in "goal-thinking, trend-thinking, and scientific-thinking"—on the explicit premise that all law is a form of "policy-making" on "the distribution of values." Lasswell and McDougal did not overlook the insight of later theorists: "The power function . . . may be exercised not only by agencies called 'government' . . . but by private pressure organizations, business enterprises, churches and others. . . . [The] identity of the institutions that exert power can only be determined by proper investigation, and must not be taken for granted through verbal coincidence."[8] Lasswell and McDougal never speak of "rights." They regarded "rights" as mere legalism. Just as actual legal rights have no place in this vision, so sovereignty has no place in their later writings on the international policy process.

New Deal planning turned out not to be a good system for managing a diverse and complex modern economy, however. So, by the 1980s and early 1990s, a new generation of academic specialists—this time inspired by scholars at Harvard—emphasized the importance of individual incentives in reaching and securing agreements. But rights still get short-shrift. As progressive thinkers of an earlier generation dismissed "bourgeois rights" as empty abstractions, the Harvard School, led by Robert Keohane and Joseph Nye, distinguished "formal sovereignty"—a mere formality, of course—from "effective sovereignty," which means getting what you want.[9] Getting what you want (or should want) as a nation may turn out to require bypassing constitutional limitations in order to secure wider international agreement. But that is another sort of "formality" that is easily brushed aside in the rush to more policy-oriented or "operational" notions of sovereignty.

Even if one puts old-fashioned notions like sovereignty and constitutional loyalty to one side, however, analyzing international legal commitments in terms of interest and self-interest is not sufficient. It is not sufficient, at least, if one aspires to more ambitious ventures in governance. What about those who do not think it is in their interest to let their rights be determined by international policy managers? Advocates may emphasize the logic of enlightened self-interest, but hold-outs may not see the light.

Other scholars, less patient with interests and bargaining, thus try to reframe the whole issue. What is the claim of the individual rights-holder compared to the larger claims of humanity? If the skeptic asks how the interests of humanity are known or who gets to determine them, the answer is that progress requires many things to be taken on faith.

After decades of writing in the tradition of the international legal process school, Princeton Professor Richard Falk recently published a book urging that only "a religiously grounded transnational movement for a just world order . . . gives hope that humane global governance can become a reality . . . sometime early in the twenty-first century. . . . Without religious identity, prospects for global humane governance appear to lack a credible social or political foundation."[10]

Falk's call for "a form of reconstructive post modernism" with a "post-Westphalian" and "post-Enlightenment" perspective seems to invite a return to the medieval vision of Christendom, a spiritual community hovering above the claims of particular rulers. But in keeping with his global ambitions, Falk affirms that "religion cannot be reduced to any single religious tradition."[11] Falk's "religious identity" is not, it turns out, a religion of commandments and firm thou-shalt-nots. So far as an ordinary reader can tell, it is a religion of universal benevolence (combined with disgust at commerce)—with all the particular applications left to some undefined priesthood.

It is not what the founders of Massachusetts Bay Colony or the framers of the First Amendment would have recognized as "religion." Perhaps it is not what many Americans even today would recognize as "religion." But the underlying thought is hardly unique to Professor Falk. If we need to inspire loyalties stronger than those that people feel toward their national constitutions, we need to draw on very deep sources of motivation. Religion—or something that operates like religious inspiration—is the obvious alternative.

Michael Ignatieff, a professor of human rights at Harvard, warns that human rights advocates risk turning their cause into a secular religion—or rather, as he says, a form of "idolatry."[12] There is a comparable syndrome among environmental enthusiasts. Vice President Albert Gore, for example, admonished Americans to "make the rescue of the environment the central organizing principle for civilization." Far more was at stake than mere public policy: "the global environmental crisis," according to Gore, "is an outer manifestation of an inner crisis that is, for lack of a better word, spiritual" because it engages "the collection of values and assumptions that determine our basic understanding of how we fit into the universe."[13] Those who hold to somewhat more traditional faiths may not be quite so inspired by Gore's call for "a new generation of international agreements that will embody the regulatory frameworks, specific prohibitions, enforcement mechanisms, cooperative planning, sharing arrangements, incentives, penalties and mutual obligations" to "enable world civilization to . . . save the global environment."[14]

Confronted with such "spiritual" ambitions, adherents of older faiths might, after all, seek protection within the confines of sovereign states. Heinrich Rommen's treatise, *The State in Catholic Thought*, had already sensed the impulses inspiring such visions of global management—and firmly rejected them. Writing in the 1940s, amidst all the emotional pressures bound to be felt by a refugee from Germany, Rommen still endorsed a broadly traditional view of national sovereignty:

> If someone thinks the word "sovereignty" should be given up, this does not matter, as long as its content . . . is not lost: namely, that it is merely a term to define the state as a self-sufficient . . . order of law, peace, justice and security, and consequently with the competence to decide finally and authoritatively in conflicts arising within the order. . . . The necessity of a concrete decision in recurring conflicts among beings who are free, though compelled to live in unity, makes the dream of a civitas maximas [a universal society] in the strict sense unreal. . . . The state and all other forms of political life have no existence as forms without their matter, that is, the people as an historical entity and so a potential political body.[15]

Even religious thinkers who distrust extreme individualism, even those who favor greater curbs on commerce, still may recognize the benefits of a constitutional state—and recognize that it is, inevitably, a sovereign state. Compared with a fully Christian state or some other religious ideal, the modern constitutional state might appear as a mere second-best: the provisions of a civil constitution might be embraced, as a great Jesuit theologian put it, as "articles of peace, not articles of faith."[16] A constitutional state still might seem the safest or most reasonable of the currently practical alternatives.

In a constitutional state, at least, religious communities would not be at the mercy of international forums demanding the elimination of gender stereotyping. In a constitutional state, if the government did interfere with the internal authority of a church, religious leaders would know at least where to register their protest and where to lay the blame.[17]

WHY INTERNATIONAL LAW NOW TENDS TOWARD LAWLESSNESS

For those who chafe at the constraints of a constitutional state at home, a very loose and fuzzy notion of international law or international authority is quite congenial. It is also necessary. If you still want to speak of a "global constitution"—as many writers on international law now do— you must retreat to fuzziness. Especially on the question of sovereignty.

The law of nations already had a considerable history at the time of the American Founding. The Framers of the Constitution were quite prepared to endorse this law. In the eighteenth century it was largely a customary law of courtesies or mutually agreed limitations in the interactions of sovereign states. As the leading treatises of that era presented it, it was a law that recognized and to some extent entrenched the claims of sovereign states rather than a law overriding the claims of sovereignty.

From the Founding until the present day, American statesmen have also been quite ready to seek wider cooperation through treaties, as in treaties to extend trading rights. But the obligations imposed by such agreements were understood to derive from the consent of the states which concluded them—and the obligation remained conditional on the good faith compliance of the other parties. When one state failed to live up to its agreement, other states felt free to renounce the agreement or to curtail their own compliance. The parties to a treaty were also its enforcers, hence its final interpreters.

A sovereign state imposes law in a quite different way. It does not need anything like unanimous or general agreement—among its own citizens— before it proclaims its own law. And for most purposes, the state is the enforcer, not the citizens. That is the historic meaning of sovereignty, as Bodin made clear: A sovereign has the right to make and enforce law and the citizens are obliged to obey, even if they dislike the law and even if they do not approve the way the law is implemented or enforced against others.

A constitutional sovereign, however, promises that the law will, in general, be reliably and consistently enforced. That is, in itself, a very considerable constraint. Every serious notion of what is entailed in the rule of law looks to some ideal of consistency, which means that interpretations or applications of the law in the present case imply a readiness to hold to the same standard in the next case. Beyond that, there is a procedure for holding legislators accountable—by a constitutional scheme of elections to offices with formally delineated terms and powers. Within these constraints, however, a constitutional state can still impose its law on dissidents, even if they are a substantial minority, even if they are (measured by opinion polls) the current majority. That is what makes its authority "sovereign."

Perhaps the European Union has found a stable and constitutionally acceptable formula for imposing supranational law. There is, in fact, much reason to doubt that it will prove stable and it certainly does not conform to American ideas of constitutional government. But in any case, the European Union remains a very special sort of international institution. The international community at large has very little capacity to impose its will on individual states with the same reliability as the bureaucrats of Brussels.

Those who look for a wider and more ambitious development of international law must therefore blur the meaning of law. Agreements of a very abstract character may then be implemented or interpreted by specialized international bodies, presumed to be expressing the original agreement. Most international organizations still operate by unanimity, so there is no clear distinction between contractual commitment and constitutional imposition. There is more ambiguity, however, about organizations that have the capacity to bind the dissident members by majority vote. Can the minority repudiate such decisions without exiting the whole organization? Is there always freedom of exit? Does the same rule then come to be taken as "law" in another forum, even against dissenting states? Can the WTO, for example, apply an environmental "norm" even to states that have not accepted that "norm" but do want to retain their full trading rights in other respects?

Some of these questions still have reasonably clear answers (or at least probable answers) in specific contexts. The general trend, however, is to fuzz the answers so that contractual agreements begin to look something like public law, binding even on dissenting states. Just as this does not establish anything like a world-state, it does not, in any way, address the constitutional problems involved in formulating world law.

Certainly, no one seriously imagines that world law could be made by a democratically accountable legislature. What somewhat similar states in western Europe are unwilling to do—entrust genuine legislative power to a directly elected parliament—the world as a whole is even less willing to do. If seats in the world legislature were apportioned on a population basis, the very poor and very populous countries of the developing world could vote themselves vast transfers of resources from the less populous but far more affluent states of Europe and North America. If seats were apportioned on a one-state-one-vote basis (as in the UN's General

Assembly), the world parliament would still pose the same threat. Not even western Europeans want to see this sort of arrangement. So for global law making, any serious scheme of democratic accountability is out of the question.

But so is any other sort of constitutional discipline. Powerful states like China, recalcitrant states like Syria, failed states like Sierra Leone, can not be easily held to the same standards as other states. So "international standards," when they involve any serious obligation, always turn out to be "standards" in a very vague sense. The most idealistic standards, as for "international human rights," turn out to be the most undisciplined. In a world that cannot even agree, in real life, on the wrongness of outright terrorism, UN bodies are off dreaming about universal day-care provisions for working moms and protections for unconventional sexual lifestyles.

These are standards that have almost no application to most of the countries that claim to endorse them. With that understanding in the background, it is all the easier for international bodies to proclaim and endorse such "standards," just as their courtesy adherents claim to endorse them. Saudi Arabia becomes a recognized adherent to the convention against sex discrimination, just as China claims to be in full compliance with the Covenant on Civil and Political Rights. The international rule of law marches from one triumph to the next!

International lawyers have invented a new category of law to deal with this problem. It is called "soft law." Technically, it refers to nonbinding resolutions of bodies, like the UN General Assembly, or to hortatory language in declarations adopted by international conferences. What starts as "soft law" of this sort is often made legally binding by subsequent inclusion in formal treaties. But many scholars insist that "soft law" can attain binding force merely by continued acknowledgment in subsequent international conferences. So, for example, it is commonly asserted that the Universal Declaration of Human Rights, though originally non-binding, has now "hardened" into binding, customary law.

There is no agreed formula to determine when rhetoric has metamorphized into binding customary law. In the view of many scholars, however, nothing like formal consent is required. At home, of course, constitutional states have a quite formal process for marking the passage of opinions into law: it is called legislation. But then, constitutional states do not talk about "soft law" at home. The point of the category in international practice is to get around the absence of an international legislative authority—without having to fall back on actual treaties, binding only those states which actually agree to them.

But solving or alleviating the problem of missing legislatures still does not solve the problem of missing electorates. Advocates of global governance have a different answer for that: NGOs. Greenpeace and Amnesty International and a thousand smaller groups will speak for "global civil society" and so ensure that the "global polity" remains "democratic" and "accountable"—though these groups are not accountable themselves to any constitutional process.

If one gives serious weight to the representative character of self-appointed advocates, one can also believe that soft law is continually hardening into real law—because NGOs have endorsed it and relied on it and repeatedly invoked it. Or because diplomats, at conferences swarming with NGO prompters, have repeated the accepted formulas. Then it becomes plausible to conceive an "international community" with the power to discipline and direct national states in their domestic law. Then it becomes plausible to conclude that sovereignty does not matter or has no very definite meaning because "law" can be made without the consent of a sovereign state.

So the UN Committee on Human Rights insists that the United States is now legally obligated to change its criminal justice system even when it has not consented—and has specifically renounced—international standards bearing on the point. United Nations experts insist (and many American law professors affirm) that the absence of American consent is irrelevant, because the pertinent standards have simply become "binding" on all states, even those which disagree.[18] It does not matter, either, that these standards can not actually be enforced and are not actually observed in much of the world. These standards are binding because they have, in the view of their supporters, a higher moral authority and they have a higher moral authority because they are already endorsed by so many states and so many other organizations. Because they have a higher moral authority, they do not need to be endorsed by any particular state before they become binding on that state.

The domestic counterpart would be to claim that a bill passed by the House of Representatives should be treated as "law," even though rejected by the Senate, so long as it has also been endorsed by Ralph Nader's Public Citizen organization, by the University of Wisconsin Faculty Senate, by the Berkeley City Council, by the New England Chamber of Commerce, and by many other "voices." Normal Americans would scoff at such a "procedure" for making law. It would seem obvious that such an unconstrained law making procedure, by allowing end runs around our actual constitutional scheme, would jeopardize the rights of individuals.

But here that is the very point. The "individual" in the classical scheme of international law was the sovereign state. The new approach not only implies but insists that states do not actually have fixed rights.[19] Which means, of course, that a domestic constitution no longer has the force it was once supposed to have. Constitutional guarantees might be trumped by international agreement, as in schemes for an international court that evades the basic guarantees in the Bill of Rights. More generally, the losers in political contests, when played according to the constitutional rules of their own system, can now appeal to a higher level authority to reverse the constitutionally determined policy in their home state.

The game has obvious appeal, even for some policy makers in the United States. In June of 2002, the U.S. Supreme Court announced that capital punishment could not be imposed on murderers who scored too poorly on IQ tests. It had given the exact opposite answer to the same question in 1989. In the meantime, as the Court noted, a number of state legislatures had moved to exempt mentally retarded persons from capital punishment and execution of the retarded was now condemned by "the world community."[20] The latter fact was attested by a brief submitted to the Court by the European Union, where capital punishment is actually favored by majorities in a number of countries but condemned by the Council of Europe, on the grounds that it is "undemocratic" not to follow the accepted practice (abolishing capital punishment) among the majority of democratic states. The Court again invoked European practice as its authority, when it reversed its position on state sodomy laws in 2003.[21]

This political shell game has been honed to a fine art by supranational authorities in Europe and the various constituencies appealing across national borders to get their way back home. There are many reasons to doubt, however, that "international constitutional common law" (as it has aptly been called) has a bright future in the United States.[22] Or that it has a secure future in other countries that are not Eurocentric.

THE AMERICAN EXCEPTION—AND THE OTHERS

Whatever others may say, the abandonment of sovereignty will be a very hard sell in the United States. The United States has always been jealous of its own sovereignty. "We cannot barter away our independence or our sovereignty," President Coolidge admonished.[23] Decades later, when the United States had assumed leadership of a worldwide network of alliances, President Eisenhower felt compelled to reaffirm the old faith: "Sovereignty is never bartered among free men."[24] To reorient the United States toward schemes of global governance would require more than a change of policy at the top. It would require fundamental changes in American constitutional and political culture.

Is there a new spiritual force in the world, overriding the selfish claims of sovereign states, as Professor Falk contends? That new spiritual "force" will face great resistance in America. The United States is the one Christian country in the world where the majority of religious adherents belong to "dissenting sects" (or "nonconforming sects," as they used to be called). The dominant religious tradition is not merely Protestant but a version of Protestantism free from any association with an established church in Europe. The culture of the "dissenting sects" has informed the whole popular culture of America. Religious belief and religious practice is far more pervasive in America than in Europe, but the predominant religious tradition does not take well to official direction. And it is particularly prickly and suspicious toward governmental direction of religion.

The United States is also the only major country in the west where guns of all sorts are widely held. Nearly half of American families own guns. A sizable body of Americans insist on their constitutional right to do so. A major reason why gun ownership is so widespread and so widely supported is that many Americans view guns as necessary for self-defense. A high proportion of Americans take for granted that the world can be dangerous, so you must be able to defend yourself. Trust a global consensus? Half the people in America can barely bring themselves to trust the federal government at home!

So the United States is also one of the very few modern states that does not have a socialist party worth talking about. The same people who do not trust the government very much in other matters do not warm to the thought of a government exercising vast powers of control over the economy. The United States has a smaller public sector and a more limited welfare state than almost any other western country.

And, yes, the United States is also exceptional in continuing to endorse—and administer—capital punishment. Europeans may believe that the United States was acting in violation of sound ethical standards when it executed Nazi war criminals. It will be hard to persuade most Americans to embrace this opinion. Most Americans still hold to the old-fashioned belief that the most terrible crimes require the sternest punishment.

The American belief in personal accountability is, after all, the flip side of the American belief in individual rights. The Supreme Court may limit the availability of capital punishment. It would likely face a major political upheaval if it invoked European norms to read capital punishment out of the U.S. Constitution (where it is mentioned in five different places). As Justice Scalia remarked, dissenting from the Court's ruling in 2002, "the 'world community'" has "notions of justice [which] are (thankfully) not those of our people."[25]

Traditional American views may change over time. But Americans are likely to prove less malleable than the docile peoples of Europe, who are far more accustomed to seeing constitutions replaced or radically altered from one decade to the next. Strange as it may seem to Europeans, most Americans are rather content with their country as it is, though the Constitution is difficult to amend and rarely has been amended. Americans take pride in the continuity of their institutions.

National pride is controversial in Germany and seems to be discouraged elsewhere in Europe in order to make union with Germany work more smoothly. In America, waving the flag is an instinctive response to crisis, as in the aftermath of the September 11 attacks. Heroes and victories of the past—along with the admonitions of founding statesmen—are the standard props of contemporary political rhetoric in America. That is not only true among avowed conservatives. Advocates on the left rally to a website named for Tom Paine and punctuate their appeals with quotations from Thomas Jefferson.

It may seem incongruous that Americans are very touchy about their rights while very patriotic about their country. But in America, people have a certain possessiveness about their rights and a related possessiveness about the Constitution and the country that guarantees those rights. A European writer saw the connection pretty clearly in the 1830s. Alexis de Tocqueville's book is still widely admired as a depiction of American thinking—admired, at least, in America.[26]

Post-modern theorists may insist that "sovereignty" is a mere "social construction." It will not impress many Americans to learn that their political institutions are a "social construction." That is, after all, what the American Declaration of Independence asserts. Taken as a whole, American society is the most successful self-conscious construction in human history. Most Americans are descendants of people who came to America with the hope of making a new start. It should not be surprising that most Americans still resist the idea that their country—or their new country—must be governed in accord with standards approved by the governing elites in their old countries.

The American political system still makes it far easier for populist organizers to challenge or frustrate projects endorsed by elite opinion.[27] All of this history may have something to do with the reluctance of American judges to embrace the customary international law of human rights and impose it on elected officials in America.[28]

But is America so unique in wanting to govern itself? Given its power and prominence, its resistance to global regulation naturally provokes particular attention and resentment among enthusiasts of these projects. These projects cannot work without American support. But is that all that's lacking?

Start with China, the most populous country in the world. It is quite as firm as the United States in rejecting the International Criminal Court. China has also been more emphatic in rejecting any commitment to reducing its own emission of greenhouse gases. China has been even more averse than the United States to ratifying human rights conventions. It has ratified the Covenant on Civil and Political Rights but insists that it is only bound by its own interpretations of that treaty. Its own interpretations seem to be compatible with quite ruthless repression. China has joined the World Trade Organization and promised to live up to its obligations as a trading state. But it is strongly opposed to any mixing of trade rules with environmental or labor standards. Some scholars claim to see signs that China is gradually easing its insistence on protecting its own sovereignty. But the signs of this are certainly very modest and remain quite equivocal.[29]

What is true for China is also true for India, the world's second most populous state. India opposes the International Criminal Court. It opposes any commitment to reduce its own emissions of greenhouse gases. It is one of the loudest and most persistent critics of entangling WTO trading rules with internal standards for the protection of labor or the environment.

What goes for China and India also goes for many other developing countries. Poor countries share similar perspectives, based on similar interests. In international forums, smaller countries often follow the diplomatic lead of China and India, the great powers of the developing world. But it is not only among the poorest countries that resistance to supranational management remains very strong.

Most Latin American nations have a shared language, a common religious and cultural background, and a history of relative peace among themselves. Regional government along European lines might seem much more promising among these countries than among the states of the European Union. But periodic efforts at regional governance have continually faltered. An Inter-American Human Rights Convention has far less influence or authority than its European counterpart. Similar as they are, individual states in Latin America remain jealous of their own national independence.

Even among English-speaking countries, there has not been a clear trend toward supranational governance—apart from Britain's own relinquishment of sovereign powers to the European Union. Canada and Australia have drifted away from any serious notion of policy coordination within the British Commonwealth. They readily sign every new human rights convention and fall in with many other international projects. But in the summer of 2000, the prime minister of Australia openly rebuked the UN for its hypocrisy, after Australia had been the subject of several critical human rights reports. The following year, Prime Minister Howard defied reproaches and demands from the UN High Commissioner for Refugees over Australian asylum policies—and made the defense of Australian independence a major theme in his successful quest for an unprecedented third term in office.[30] Australian troops joined American and British troops in making war against Saddam Hussein in the spring of 2003, despite the absence of a Security Council resolution.

Canada typically voices more sympathy for international projects. Canada stood aloof from the war against Saddam in 2003—despite the participation of its Commonwealth partners. But even Canada was quite willing to ignore the criticism of a UN human rights panel in a dispute over Quebec's language laws.[31] And both Canada and Australia have taken leading roles in opposing international controls on bio-engineered crops.

The United States, then, has reason to expect continuing disputes with the European Union over new international standards and projects. But it also has much reason to think that, when it resists new projects of global governance, it will find other important states agreeing or at least secretly welcoming its resistance. It is European conceit to imagine that the United States faces a world largely in tune with European ambitions. It is a flattering view for Europeans and perhaps to those Americans who still look to Europe for moral affirmation. That does not make it an accurate view.

The Appeal of Sovereignty

Still, the influence of the United States will count for more, perhaps, than that of any other single country. Is it playing a mischievous role if it tries to constrain the reach of international organizations and international legal standards? The truth is that sovereignty has strong moral claims as the practical prerequisite of decent political arrangements. And those claims are likely to have enduring appeal.

"Governance" is indeed a more pervasive phenomenon than the authority of sovereign states. Through most of history, human life has been organized by tribal traditions, not easily changed by any one chieftan and not easily resisted by any one member. Different peoples could therefore preserve their distinctive ways while acknowledging the overriding authority of a common imperial power. In the ancient world, all empires were multinational—that is what made them empires. And as they were already quite diverse, they did not worry that further expansion would complicate their internal governing arrangements.

Empires generally ruled subject peoples with the aid of local chieftains or local priests, who retained authority with their own people. It was precisely the persistence, in subject territories, of tribal authority (or some other form of local authority), that made large empires feasible, when the cost of maintaining standing armies in vast territories would have been prohibitively expensive. In modern times, the British Empire ruled vast territories with minimal forces, by relying on local authorities—whose status (regarding claims to independence) often remained carefully ill-defined. So it was with the Soviet empire of modern times, where rulers in Moscow were not very attentive to the difference between a federated state in the Soviet Union, like Ukraine or Latvia, and nominal "allies" like Poland or East Germany.

The city-states of ancient Greece prided themselves on retaining a form of freedom, equally remote from the conformity of the tribe and the tyranny of the empire. The city-state resisted subordination to great empires but also allowed a body of citizens to question mere tribal traditions and deliberate among themselves on the laws they would live by. The freedom of the ancient city-states has continued to fascinate western political thinkers. The Greek word for the city-state—the "polis"—remains the root of the words for "politics" or "political" in all western languages. It is still hard for us to find alternate terminology to express the Greek sense of a sphere for debate and decision on common matters.

If the civil freedom of the city-state inspired admiration in later ages, however, the actual history of ancient republics also taught a cautionary lesson about politics. "It is impossible," *The Federalist* remarks, "to read the history of the petty republics of Greece and Italy without feeling sensations of horror and disgust at the distractions with which they were continually agitated and at [their] . . . perpetual vibration between the extremes of tyranny and anarchy." If "models of a more perfect structure" had not developed in the modern world, "enlightened friends to liberty would have been obliged to abandon the cause [of republican government] as indefensible."[32]

The appeal of sovereignty in the modern world is that it seems to offer escape from the constraints of the tribe or the empire, without inviting the political instability of the polis. Almost any modern nation encompasses more diverse ways of life than, say, the early Franks or Goths—or the contemporary Pashtoons. Partly, the heterogeneity or pluralism of modern nations reflects their more liberal or tolerant spirit. But a more tolerant spirit is in itself encouraged—as *The Federalist* famously argued—by the scale of a modern state. It is harder for any one group to conceive itself as embodying the interests or the proper aims of the whole community when the community is very large and therefore, almost inevitably, more diverse than a city-state, let alone a tribe. Sovereignty, as a political doctrine, was invented in the sixteenth century precisely to deal with the problem of diversity. Anyone who agreed to be bound by the same law, as Bodin argued, could be conceived as a citizen of the same state.

It is certainly possible to have sovereign states which are extremely intolerant and repressive, as any number of national tyrannies have proven. It is possible, on the other hand, to have a great empire which does, to a considerable degree, maintain the rule of law in a liberal spirit, as was often true of the British empire or the Habsburg Empire in its last decades. It is hard to sustain liberal rule, however, when the sovereign power remains altogether unaccountable. Most empires have not ruled in a liberal spirit. And it is hard to persuade people that their own interests—or their own self-respect—will be protected by an imperial power that remains altogether unaccountable.

To the extent that they disrupt tribal traditions, empires raise political questions among subjects which empires are not well equipped to answer. Empires have not been able to accommodate demands for broader accountability, without unleashing claims for independence that finally break the empire into pieces. This was the British experience in Ireland and India and even in the self-governing dominions that remained in the nominal sphere of the Commonwealth. It was also, of course, the experience of the Soviet empire in eastern Europe, which fell to pieces as soon as communist control began to relax, quickly triggering the disintegration of the Soviet Union, itself.

Empires, it turns out, do not inspire much loyalty. Nation-states have a far better record of endurance in the modern world, precisely because they have been able to draw on reserves of loyalty and devotion. National states of western Europe retain more or less the same boundaries today that they achieved in the sixteenth century. It was the collapse of empires that required repeated redrawing of boundaries in other parts of Europe.

Nationalist ideologies have often played a role in rallying opposition to imperial powers. But it requires no mystical doctrine of national destiny to persuade people they will be better off if they shake free of a larger empire. The strength of nation-states derives precisely from their claims on residual loyalty, their capacity to summon loyalties in ways that an empire cannot. Multi-ethnic federations in many parts of the world have gone the way of larger empires. States that have been able to sustain a notion of common nationality—in spite of remaining differences among citizens—have been able to endure through crises, because they can summon citizens to make compromises and sometimes great sacrifices to hold the nation together.

Because they can summon such loyalty, national states have been able to sustain constitutional democracy where empires could not. They have been able to draw on a willingness to compromise for the sake of maintaining common institutions and nurturing some shared sense of common allegiance. The formula not only worked in many parts of Europe, it has often worked in Latin America and even amidst the astonishing diversity of India: people have been prepared to restrain themselves to make a common constitution work, because a common constitution is seen as the guarantor of a peaceful common life—of a common nationality.

A national state makes it possible for people to live under common institutions without requiring so much commonality as the tribe—and without requiring the fatalism or passivity of a multinational empire. The nation-state is, in this way, a sort of compromise between the tribe and the empire in the demands it makes on identity. So also, a nation-state, to the extent that it can sustain representative institutions, seems to offer a compromise between the intensely politicized and unstable direct democracy of the city-state and the denial of all political accountability in the empire. Sovereignty is at the heart of all of these compromises, because it supplies the idea of a political authority which can accommodate differences—precisely because it is distinguished from private life—and yet still demand (and sustain) ultimate political allegiance.

Liberal democracy is not admired everywhere and compromise is not the highest political philosophy. There is no obvious reason why outsiders should care whether any particular people does organize itself under liberal institutions, if that people does not threaten others.[33] But history suggests that liberal states are much more inclined to live at peace with their neighbors. And it is only in sovereign states that liberal institutions have taken solid root. Whatever else might be said for various political alternatives in theory, no one should ignore the moral claims of sovereignty as a vehicle for moderate, limited government with staying power—able to inspire ongoing loyalty without summoning fanatacism and without requiring vast repression.

The European Union may now seem to present a unique alternative to the historic patterns. It seems to offer imperial control—in the literal sense of vast law-making powers—with a sufficiently democratic atmosphere (or sufficient mechanisms of indirect accountability) to satisfy democratic demands in the nations subject to its superintending control. Some observers argue that subordination to European control has actually strengthened liberal and democratic institutions in member states. This was part of the original hope for European integregation, that it would anchor West Germany in the liberal and democratic patterns of western Europe. In the 1980s, shaky new democracies in Spain, Portugal, and Greece may well have been stabilized by membership in the European Community. It is now argued that the promise of ultimate EU membership has, in similar ways, strengthened liberal and democratic institutions in prospective member states in eastern Europe since the mid-1990s.

But it is not at all clear that the European construction has escaped the historic dilemmas. European nations have not been willing to trust serious military or policing powers to European-level authorities. Nor have they been willing to trust extensive tax powers (or the broad social welfare responsibilities that require such tax powers) to European-level authorities. Efforts to establish a constitutional treaty collapsed at the end of 2003, when medium-sized states resisted voting formulas they feared would unacceptably diminish their own weight in EU councils. The empire still seems to be distrusted.

It may be that, over time, more and more powers will be delegated to European-level authorities and citizens will come to place their primary political loyalty in the European Union. In that case, it will become a larger and more diverse federal nation, rather than an exception to the historic alternatives.

This development does not seem likely, however. The European Union could afford to lavish generous "structural adjustment" payments on new members in the 1980s and 1990s. Demographic and economic realities will make it impossible to offer new member states in eastern Europe the same reward for compliance with Euro-level standards. Old tensions between the Franco-German core of Europe and other states have already become more pronounced. In 2003, France and Germany each asserted their right to defy European budgetary rules, previously enforced on other EU states. Without consulting other EU states, France and Germany launched highly public diplomatic campaigns to thwart Anglo-American policy on Iraq in 2002 and persisted in driving a wedge into the Atlantic alliance, even when a majority of national governments in the EU states rallied to the Anglo-American poisition. Where many EU governments want to retain strong ties with the United States, as a hedge against domination by France and Germany, the latter have pressed forward with plans for an independent European military force, which would undermine NATO.

These tensions are likely to be aggravated by the presence of new members in the east. Since all member states do have democratic institutions in their own territory, there will be opportunities for political opposition to mobilize. Why should not opponents play on nationalist resentment of foreign domination? How will the EU enforce discipline without further aggravating nationalist resentment?

The EU has tried to weaken national unity within each member state by sponsoring ethnic and regional identities and by offering business and special interest constituencies a special stake in the supremacy of EU policy. The beneficiaries of such policies may be strong enough to counter nationalist political insurgencies within each member state. But it does not follow that the EU will therefore retain the loyalty that citizens have elsewhere given to national governments and national constitutions. Europe may simply become a more resentful and chaotic region, where a

European constitution proves to have constituted nothing that is in any way politically solid or legally reliable.

Whatever the fate of Europe, there is no reason at all to think that this post-modern model can be extended to the wider world—even if European authorities are bound to think they have a new model for the world. The European Union was constructed on top of functioning nation-states, most of which (at least in the formative decades of European integregation) had a good deal of experience with constitutional and democratic institutions. It requires more than a leap of faith to think that the African Union will solve the murderous chaos that afflicts so many nations of post-colonial Africa. To think so requires not so much political faith as the sort of magical thinking associated with rites like the Cargo Cult of South Pacific islanders: build a wooden replica of a European construction and the blessings of wealth and stability will appear—as if by magic.

Failed states are a great challenge to the world's functioning states. States which cannot control their own territory not only expose their own people to murderous assaults by warlords and marauders but may provide havens to terrorist networks and forces seeking to evade controls on weapons of mass destruction. In the extreme case, as in Afghanistan, outside intervention may be required to restore some form of order. Many peoples might well be better off under colonial control—except that states which might have the resources to impose such control are not disposed to deploy it, not least because they cannot count on the long-term acquiescence of local people.

Former colonial powers do not have a very good record in guiding former colonies toward constitutional democracy or even toward stable government. French financial and military assistance in Africa worked to entrench murderous despots, some of whom, like the self-proclaimed Emperor Bokassa, turned out to be cannibals in the most literal sense. It is not obvious why international institutions—which pool the resources and potential leverage of many different states, relieving them all from paying any degree of close attention—are better situated to make the right choices for the people they try to guide. Some of the most terrible bloodlettings in Africa in the 1990s have been analyzed as struggles to see which warlord would be able to claim the right to cash checks from international funding sources.

Whatever improvisations are attempted to handle the problem of failed states, it makes no more sense to view these sad extremities as models for the world at large than it does to view the European Union as a typical venture. Even if some states cannot sustain sovereignty, it does not follow that all others should pretend that they are equally in need of international supervision. Domestic law recognizes that some people, due to mental incapacity, cannot be trusted to manage their own finances, so courts will appoint special guardians to do so on their behalf.

We do not pretend that because some people need this arrangement, it would be reasonable for everyone's property to be controlled by court-appointed guardians. That arrangement would not even be helpful to those whose property is held in trust for them, since guardians are bound to judge what should be done for an incapacitated person by looking at what capable people actually do with their property.

Of course, people in the poorest countries would like international assistance. But then they are often resentful of conditions attached to such assistance by international agencies or by national aid programs. People in poor countries may often have good reason to wonder whether these conditions reflect concern for their own priorities or the priorities of donors.[34] But they have no reason to believe (even if they have many incentives to dream) that international organizations will provide just the kind and amount of assistance they want, if only these organizations can be wrested from the control of the donor states. Organizations controlled by recipients are not going to be funded, any more than banks controlled by loan applicants are going to stay in business.

Sovereignty, as the base line marker of who gets to decide what, retains powerful appeal for the poor and weak, as it does for more affluent or more powerful states. Self-control remains the surest alternative to outside control. And most people, in most parts of the world, still seem to find outside control quite irksome.

Hard Cases that Aren't, Easy Answers that Aren't

But what happens when sovereign power is held by entirely unaccountable and vicious rulers? That is, for many people, the great objection to sovereignty. It is the moral trump card in demands for global justice—the warning that, left to its sovereignty, a state may embark on terrible crimes against its own people. Accounts of the human rights movement commonly portray it as a response of a horror-struck world to the discovery of Nazi atrocities at the end of the Second World War.[35] Without a deeper sense of international community, goes the argument, self-absorbed states will look the other way when evil states commit atrocities against their own people.

But the perpetrators of the original genocide—the one which provoked a refugee lawyer to coin the term in 1943—were not acting in the name of a nation-state. They acted in the name of a "movement" which championed a racial theory that disdained the borders of historic nations, disdained the formalities of a structured state and set out to conquer all

Europe. Mass murder on a comparable scale was committed by the Soviet tyranny, again in the name of a "movement" that disdained borders and disdained fixed state structures.

It is true that other states, including western democratic states, did not extend themselves as much as they might have done for the victims of these murderous regimes. But it is rather silly to pretend that this pattern reflects the structure of sovereignty or the distinctive priorities of nation-states. The Catholic Church declined to make much protest against the Nazi genocide. The International Committee of the Red Cross was almost entirely silent.[36] These transnational institutions also gave priority to their own concerns.

After the war, Eleanor Roosevelt and other forerunners of the "international human rights movement" began their enterprise by undertaking respectful bargaining with the murderous regime of Josef Stalin, as if Stalin could be a respectable partner in the project. Millions in the Gulag were passed over in silence. International human rights activists also had priorities of their own—as they still do.

Abolish sovereignty to put a stop to state crimes? One might as well call for the abolition of professional armies, since they are the prime instruments of aggression in the modern world. But pre-modern Crusaders were also quite capable of aggression and mass slaughter. So are Islamist terrorists today. As Burke observed, "Wickedness is a little more inventive."

Nor is there any magic solution in "outlawing" genocide or other extreme horrors under "international law." Perpetrators of such crimes are not motivated by ignorance or misunderstanding of proper international standards. A government that is monstrous enough to contemplate mass murder is monstrous enough to contemplate breaking international law. The only serious issue is what outsiders should do about such crimes.

In the extreme case, it is easy to sympathize with calls for outside intervention to put an end to a murderous regime. But the United States and its coalition partners were not widely applauded when they did exactly this in Iraq in the spring of 2003. Nor was the adverse reaction at all unusual. Outsiders are bound to question the motives of a state which makes war on another state when it has not, itself, been attacked. States do not embrace the risks of war for purely altruistic reasons. Outside interventions always have a mix of motives—as was acknowledged by the American-led coalition against Iraq in 2003.

Among other things, successful intervention brings a change of government in the territory that has been invaded. Those who force a change of government will want to establish a new government that is more to their liking—and not only because it governs more humanely. That naturally arouses much concern among other states. Vietnam was not widely praised for overthrowing the genocidal regime of Pol Pot in Cambodia, because Vietnam proceeded to install a successor regime over which it retained great control. Syria ended years of bloodshed in Lebanon by reducing the whole country to a Syrian protectorate.

There are perfectly good reasons why, in a world of sovereign states, there should be strong resistance to claims of humanitarian intervention. If sovereignty remains the organizing principle in international politics, humanitarian intervention must be suspect because it creates an exception to the underlying rule. An international commission, sponsored by the Canadian foreign ministry, proposed new standards to justify international intervention in proper cases—and found its proposals greeted with a mix of hostility and indifference. We may not be able to improve on the formula offered by international lawyers at the beginning of the twentieth century, that humanitarian intervention may be regarded as morally praiseworthy in special circumstances, but should not be recognized as a proper exception to the general rule.[37]

The underlying challenge is not answered by insisting that humanitarian intervention can only be justified when authorized by the UN. The United Nations, as now constituted, will rarely be prepared to authorize humanitarian intervention. The United Nations cannot even agree on when resort to force is necessary for self-defense against aggressors (or potential aggressors), which is why most states, for most of the UN's existence, have paid little attention to its admonitions when determining their own security policy. It is not easier to determine when humanitarian action is required.

Wars cannot be stopped—not at least without serious outside force— merely because outsiders think a particular war is overly destructive. And there is often legitimate disagreement about what is going on. NATO insisted that it had to bomb Serbia in 1999 to stop what was asserted to be "genocide" in Kosovo. After Serbia submitted to NATO's demands and allowed an international occupation to be established in Kosovo, international monitors acknowledged that there had been no genocide— though there had been vast suffering and dislocation as a result of the NATO air war and the Serb response.[38]

If there is any hope for pressuring the worst regimes to reform—or building broad support for intervention—it lies in isolating the most intolerable practices. The international campaign to suppress the slave trade in the mid–nineteenth century was extremely effective, not only because it was backed by the world's largest naval powers but because it focused on a precise evil, which few states were prepared to defend. But the fact is that, while everyone now condemns slavery, there is not much agreement on what other practices are so terrible that perpetrators should never be able to rally defenders.[39] Saddam's mass murders did not prevent him from rallying many defenders, even in western Europe. The EU welcomed the Ba'athist government of Syria into the ranks of EU "associates" in 2003, even while Syria remained on the U.S. list of terror-exporting states.

Since the world cannot agree on terms for authorizing actual resort to force, enthusiasts of global governance have focused instead on legal responses—that is, responses delivered by lawyers rather than soldiers. It is hardly necessary to emphasize that the threat of a subpoena is not the most devastating threat to a leader who can contemplate mass murder as a state policy. A world which is not organized to deploy force against a monster is not organized to enforce a subpoena. History's worst mass murderers—Hitler, Stalin, Mao, or even their latter-day imitators from Pol Pot to Saddam Hussein—were not given to globe-trotting excursions. Paranoid tryants do not like to deprive their home territories of their own watchful presence. Nor have other states been willing to take great risks to arrest terrorists or henchmen of terrorist governments. Even European governments, amidst pious pronouncements on human rights, have regularly allowed murderous thugs to slip away from custody, lest an arrest antagonize the sponsors of terror and provoke attacks on Europeans.[40]

The idea that lawyers can substitute for soldiers is particularly appealing to countries that do not want to take risks in confronting evil. But if they do not want to take risks, they may not be all that forceful even when it comes to lawyering. The actual trajectory of international law in recent decades proclaims its fundamental unseriousness. Rather than focus on defining the most intolerable practices, human rights standards have embraced feminist concerns regarding life-styles and the concerns of social welfare advocates for more extensive public services. Human rights advocacy naturally responds to the concerns of people in the most advanced countries—who are the people who actually fund most human rights advocacy. For donors to human rights organizations, slaughter in Africa or Asia is usually a much lower priority than issues at home.

But the priorities of human rights advocates also seem to reflect their eagerness to escape into a world in which evil is not a genuine challenge. If one imagines a world in which the policy lapses of western governments are merely on a continuum with mass murder perpetrated by the worst tyrants, then the special capacities of human rights advocates—legal arguments, moral appeals, adverse publicity—ought to work against the latter as against the former. Then there would be no need for the military capacities that remain beyond the reach of human rights organizations.

This outlook is very seductive to many Europeans for much the same reason. If the issue is military action, then Europeans have very little to contribute. But if the world can be fixed by moral and legal appeals,

Europeans can imagine that they have more skill with such tools than people anywhere else and certainly much more skill in this arena than government officials in the United States.

So, carried along by the enthusiasm of human rights advocates and European governments, the world has now established an International Criminal Court. It is not likely to impress terror chieftans. The Court's independent prosecutor will focus on—well, we do not know what he will focus on. But he is authorized to second-guess details of NATO or American military tactics, whenever these tactics have an effect on another country which wants international justice to be brought into play.

The ICC prosecutor will not have jurisdiction over tyrants who restrict their murderous policies to their own territory and take the precaution of declining to ratify the ICC Statute. But the ICC can hold a sword over democratic states, which may inhibit them from intervening where intervention might be helpful. Where civil wars or revolutions are ended by compromise involving amnesties for past abuses, the ICC prosecutor can blow apart the compromise by insisting on a new international prosecution in defiance of the local amnesty. Where insurgents or outside states are pressuring a particularly brutal ruler to leave power and go into exile, the ICC prosecutor can jeopardize this bargaining by pledging to pursue the former tyrant for later prosecution. Where nations at war are trying to negotiate a peace, and offer to drop criminal claims against each other for the sake of reaching an agreement, the ICC prosecutor can refuse to go along.

It is not just that the prosecutor is authorized to ignore political reality. The terms of the Statute require him to do so. The prosecutor is not authorized to grant any assurance against prosecution. Even if one prosecutor determines that it is more prudent to exercise discretion and steer clear of a particular political dispute, he cannot prevent his successor from re-opening the issue. There is no statute of limitations in the ICC Statute. Indeed, ICC rules allow outside activists to raise legal challenges to the prosecutor's decision not to pursue a particular case.[41]

It may be that in practice, the prosecutor and the Court will prove extremely sensitive to political considerations and intervene only where international prosecution would be helpful. It is not easy to understand why such confidence is placed in the wisdom and prudence of an international prosecutor when no democratic state places such uncontrolled discretion in the hands of a domestic prosecutor (by, for example, preventing higher authorities from overriding prosecutorial action with pardons or legislative revisions or even dismissal over policy differences). It is hard to understand why people think an international civil servant, looking out at a hundred foreign countries, can be more trusted than a domestic prosecutor looking solely at his own country.

Or rather, it is all too easy to understand. The premise of contemporary international law is that political conflicts will disappear if we just pretend they are not there. The ICC is a grand monument to this pretense. It is not a guarantor of basic rules in a world constitution. It is a monument to the belief that we do not need constitutional structures because we all agree, already, on fundamentals and governing is simply an extrapolation from fundamental principles. We may not have sufficient agreement to entrust the exercise of actual military force to a world authority. Nonetheless, we can still entrust international authority with the historic attribute of sovereign power—the authority to punish.

Prior to the 1990s, for many centuries past, criminal prosecution had been regarded as the exclusive prerogative of sovereign states. Bodin had described both the power to prosecute and the power to pardon as among the defining attributes of sovereignty. The sovereign power has responsibility for the common good of the territory over which its sovereignty extends. The idea that "justice" could be separated from wider responsibilities for governing would have struck earlier generations as absurd. Among other reasons, such a separation would imply that legal justice had no necessary connection with the common good of a particular political community.

By the end of the 1990s, many advocates had come to think that international justice—a power to punish, removed from any particular political community—was an idea whose time had come. The ICC was regarded as a project so inevitable, that opposition to the project by the world's most powerful state was a minor obstacle which would assuredly be overcome in time. Confidence in progress or a higher planetary providence made it unnecessary to think politically or strategically or even rationally.

CONSTITUTIONAL SUPREMACY

Under the traditional scheme of international law, it was axiomatic that courts in one nation could not judge the official acts taken by officials of another nation. A court empowered to judge officials of a different government would seem to exercise sovereign powers over that government. The traditional view was that courts in each nation had to respect the "sovereign" rights of other governments, because any other approach would provoke hostile retaliation from other states. Respecting sovereignty was the first premise of international law.[42]

The old rule began to break down in the 1990s, as European states claimed the right to exercise "universal jurisdiction" over acts of brutality committed by any government. In practice, that meant that European courts could set themselves up as judges of what General Pinochet had done in Chile or General Sharon had done in Lebanon in earlier decades. The new rules bumped up against the old rules when European prosecutors imagined they might prosecute American officials—or explained to themselves why they should not even imagine the possibility of prosecuting Russian or Chinese or (before 2003) Iraqi officials. One of the British judges who endorsed the application of "universal jurisdiction" to Chile admonished against taking this precedent too far, lest its application to terrorists from Muslim countries provoke terrorist retaliation.[43]

The new understanding presumed from the outset that only some states would forfeit the traditional rights—or the traditional immunities—of sovereignty. The new approach would have the prestige of international law with the flexibility of political accommodations built into it. International law could be more ambitious, because it was more politically minded. And over time, political accommodations might allow for more ambition.

Academic analysts had a new theory to explain and justify these accommodations. It was not that some states would still retain sovereignty while others were divested of sovereign attributes. It was rather that sovereignty itself was an inherently flexible concept. According to this understanding, sovereignty is actually a basket of attributes which can be redistributed to different governmental levels, according to convenience.[44] European experience seemed to prove it.

This view is much more plausible if one thinks that there is no essential connection among the attributes of sovereign authority. So, for example, the power to define the rights of citizens within a nation can be entirely separated from the power to protect citizens against foreign enemies. Questions of national security may then be determined by international authority. On the other hand, policies which have direct implications for national security can be insisted upon at levels of government with no responsibility for national security. There are, in this view, a vast range of mechanisms to cooordinate and cooperate, and these mechanisms can be arranged in almost any combination.

So European-level authorities can now instruct national governments on which foreigners they must admit, even when those foreigners are suspected of terrorist connections. But there is no need to join this power with powers that would permit European-level authorities to protect the European continent as a whole from terror threats. One can mix and match powers to taste or the political convenience of the moment.[45]

From this perspective, it does not matter if some citizens feel more loyalty to one level of government because, for example, they are more focused on trade regulations, while other citizens give more loyalty to another level of government because, for example, they are focused on concerns about terror attacks. Specific functions or powers can not only be allocated to separate hands in the same government. Those hands can now belong to different bodies. And it is not necessary to say which is supreme or which has ultimate claims on the loyalty of citizens. Governance can be infinitely varied in its patterns because no governmental "function" is more fundamental than any other.

It was, in a way, the theory behind the Confederate rebellion in 1861: The states, said southerners, had delegated broad powers to a supra-state authority but retained such fundamental governing claims at home that they did not lose their sovereign rights. The theory was defeated on the battlefield because, among other things, it did not make sense to most Americans at the time. It does not make more sense today.

The Constitution of the United States does not equivocate. The federal government has limited powers but within these powers it is not merely a partner, which might share its authority with other partners. Federal law is "supreme law of the land." It was not a random assortment of powers that the founding generation consented to assign to the federal government, but the fundamental attributes of sovereignty. The federal government retains exclusive powers to assure "the common defense." The federal government has the responsibility to "guarantee" each state a "republican form of government" and the responsibility to guarantee citizens of the states a range of fundamental rights, even against their own state governments. The states have no authority to guarantee anything in federal policy.

So the states are prohibited from making treaties or compacts with foreign nations or even among themselves without federal approval (Art. 1, Sec. 10). Proclaimed in the name of "We the People," the Constitution presumes that there is, in the words of the Declaration of Independence, already "one people" in the background. Perhaps it would be more correct to say, both legally and historically, that consent to the Constitution is what established a common nationality. In all their diversity, Americans must share this point of commonality, that they are prepared to be governed under the same Constitution. The Constitution constitutes a nation as well as a government. We do not have to impose wide conformity on fellow citizens, so long as we retain this fundamental bond of union.

The Constitution binds the government no less than the citizenry. It is precisely because it does bind the government that citizens can feel underlying "political bands" that "connect them" with each other (to borrow again, the language of the Declaration of Independence). Citizens who might prefer to join themselves with foreign nations can repudiate their American citizenship. Even if they remain American citizens, they can advocate foreign models of government for the United States. But they cannot expect to have foreign bodies grafted onto the American governmental structure in defiance of the existing constitutional scheme. That sort of innovation cannot be attempted so long as the American people remain attached to the U.S. Constitution, in the form it has had from the beginning.

If the United States can be subject to the will of outside powers, it cannot be governed by the scheme ordained in the Constitution. Foreigners might prefer to see the American people entangled in such schemes. The Constitution does not allow Americans to experiment with implant surgery on their common political body—not at least without first changing the Constitution.

The United States can certainly make treaties. But international commitments become binding on the United States because the United States government agrees to them. And the United States government, because it is constrained by the Constitution, cannot lawfully adhere to just anything that might be offered up in the outward form of a treaty. A treaty cannot supersede the Constitution and it cannot transform the Constitution by establishing a different scheme of law making or treaty making in place of the one established in the Constitution, itself. Under the Constitution, the federal government and the governments of the states make law for Americans. This power cannot, consistently with the Constitution, be delegated to international authorities, operating outside the Constitution.

All of these propositions were once taken for granted. Probably most constitutional scholars would still find them unexceptionable. There is reasonable debate about the precise constitutional limits on the treaty power. Not many scholars argue openly, however, that a treaty can constitutionally delegate broad governing powers to a supranational bureaucracy, as Europeans have done.[46] Fewer still argue that a treaty can constitutionally empower a supranational bureaucracy to override the Constitution, itself, or the interpretations of the Constitution pronounced by the U.S. Supreme Court. European governments have subjected themselves to such arrangements. But the United States remains a sovereign nation, loyal to its own law.

So long as it seeks to retain its constitutional independence, the United States must preserve its right to repudiate any treaty, as its ultimate means of enforcing its own understanding of what a treaty requires. A treaty is a contract with other states. It is not a new social contract, establishing a new sovereign to interpret and enforce its terms. Europeans may approach treaties in this light but the United States cannot do so. The Constitution does not permit the United States to establish a treaty that has higher authority than the Constitution, itself, or a treaty that has higher authority than the government established by the Constitution.

If the government persistently defied the terms and limits, set down in the Constitution, the American people would be justified, according to the theory of the Declaration, in defying the government. The Constitution was designed with checks and balances, however, to keep that possibility remote. It cannot be the point of any treaty to keep the international counterpart—a repudiation of the treaty and a consequent parting of ways among treaty partners—comparably remote.

The Constitution does not forbid the United States from proclaiming good intentions, in company with other states. Human rights treaties may be understood as constitutional, then, so long as they are conceived as registers of common opinion, having no legal effect on actual American practices. But such treaties cannot be constitutional if they are understood as establishing an authority above that of American governing institutions, empowered to direct the American government in its treatment of American citizens.[47]

There can be dispute about how far the United States can go in mutual concessions regarding the treatment of foreigners. The United States cannot go anywhere in admitting foreign bodies to a share of authority in determining how American citizens are treated in their own country, when there is no direct connection with anything that happens in a foreign country. A commitment of that kind would not be a legitimate excercise of the treaty power. It would instead invoke the form of a treaty to amend the Constitution. That has been the fundamental technique by which European states ceded their sovereignty to a post-modern construction in Brussels. It is not a technique that the United States can emulate, so long as the United States remains attached to its own Constitution.

If there are some things to which the United States government cannot formally consent, there must also be limits to what it can accept indirectly, by committing itself to a process that develops international law without American consent. The United States cannot be bound by evolving norms of international law to which it has not expressly consented through its own constitutional process. Otherwise, it has opened a back door to "governance" which entirely escapes the confines of the Constitution. But the Constitution requires American officials to swear allegiance to the Constitution, itself—not to some competing scheme of international justice, some higher law for humanity, some spiritual trust for the whole planet.

All this may sound rather formalistic or legalistic. Foreign policy must respond to outside circumstances and circumstances do not always permit what Americans might otherwise prefer. But the question is not whether the United States can always do what it wants to do. It is whether the United States government can ever do what the Constitution forbids it to do. One of those forbidden things is for the United States to let itself be bound by laws to which it has not properly consented, through the prescribed constitutional procedures.

Is that still too formalistic? Serious theorists of legal justice and individual rights—whether one looks at F. A. Hayek on the right or Ronald Dworkin on the left—have always gravitated toward formal notions of what law is. Without some element of formality—of following the rules just because they are the rules—"law" collapses into mere policy and the rights of the individual are continually hostage to the policy imperatives of the moment. What preserves the formalist or legalist element in law is the obligation to maintain consistency, which, at least in the historic American understanding, means the obligation to respect past precedent and practice. Without a sense that law follows from the national constitution and the past understandings of that constitution, "law" can be manipulated into anything a judge may like it to be and individual rights are as uncertain or ephemeral as this "law."

In the last analysis, liberty and property are largely dependent on legal forms. They do not ensure that the individual can actually secure anything he might desire. These rights simply impose legal limits on the direct coercion of individuals. Constitutional government as a whole depends on legal forms. We accept that measures adopted by the House and Senate and signed by the president are law, even if they acted from ignorance or cowardice or delusion. A valid law, under the formal rules of the American system, is not always a wise or equitable measure. By the same token, even a wise measure is not a legal rule for the United States, unless it has been adopted by the constitutional procedure for establishing law.

The United States might achieve more "effective sovereignty," as Professor Keohane suggests, by delegating broad powers to international authorities—presumably when the latter are wiser or more courageous or better informed. The United States might have more "effective" policies by going with the flow and letting international norms develop informally. The United States might have more "effective" government by allowing incremental adjustments to American laws, on the basis of what American judges or others determine to be the best international custom of the moment. All this might be more "effective" or might produce better results. But it would not be constitutional government in the American understanding and few Americans will want to give up the security provided by the actual Constitution for the alluring promises of global governance.

In the long run, however, it is hard for the United States to insist on its own sovereignty without respecting the sovereign rights of other states. That means the United States has a stake in promoting respect for sovereignty internationally. If the United States continually endorses supranational authorities that constrain the sovereignty of other states (as in human rights forums), it will be (as it now is) pressed to show its good faith by submitting to such authorities, itself.

Meanwhile, the United States can not prevent advocacy groups or other governments from saying what they will at international forums. The United States government can not prevent its own citizens from making demagogic speeches or publishing erudite articles claiming to discern new international norms on this or on that. By itself, the United States government cannot prevent others from generating a mood of expectation or acceptance. But it can insist that it will not be bound by a mood, it will not be bound by "norms" that simply reflect the atmosphere of international discussion.

"Norms" may well play a useful role in international affairs. Even in domestic affairs, in politics and business and social life, informal norms constrain what is said and done and often that is much to the good. But norms are not law. We have social norms to discourage many things which the law permits, including things which, under the Constitution, the law must permit. It remains a great safeguard of religious conscience, of free speech and of commercial innovation, that the dissident, if willing to brave social disapprobation, can still try a different approach, without fear of direct legal sanctions. So, at the international level, the United States may offer rhetorical support to useful norms—but it cannot transform a norm into a binding law.

There are many reasons to think that the world would be worse off if subject to an encompassing universal law. But it is enough to recognize that the United States would no longer be governed by its own Constitution. True, the actual choice in today's world is not between a world state and an American state. There is a quite serious choice, however, between a world which pretends that it can sustain ambitious ventures in global governance and one which acknowledges sharp limits on such ventures, because it acknowledges sovereign states as the sole source of legal authority.

The United States Constitution is not neutral on this choice. The most serious danger, from dabbling in schemes of global governance, is a continuous erosion of American constitutional culture, so that what can and can not be attempted by an American government becomes harder and harder for politicians to remember or for citizens to ascertain.

Human rights advocates often caricature resistance to their projects as the residue of a "realist" outlook on international relations, which they identify with belligerent postures of the Cold War era.[48] But the historic American view does not rest on the Hobbesian premise that nations are always in conflict. One need only turn the challenge around to see the logic in the historic American view.

What must one presume about the world to think that international bodies can protect human rights, everywhere in the world? To regard this as a plausible project, you must believe that governments readily cooperate with other governments on common projects, even when such cooperation promises no direct exchange of benefits to each side. In the end, you must believe that human beings cooperate easily and naturally without much constraint—without much actual enforcement, hence without much need for force.

To believe this, you must believe that almost all human beings are well-meaning, even to strangers. And you must believe that human beings have no very serious disagreements on fundamental matters. These are not the premises of historic liberal doctrine. Classical liberal thinkers took the opposite view—that property and religion should be private, because individuals do not readily agree on fundamental things and should not have to agree. So it is not, in the classical liberal view, a casual enterprise to establish an authority that is capable of protecting fundamental rights.

In the end, the debate comes down to the importance of boundaries. Setting boundaries to power is what a constitution does. It can not do that job without boundaries between nations. The American Founders insisted that independent nations were "entitled" to sovereign rights, against other nations, by "the law of Nature and Nature's God." They did not pretend that any individual nation derives its identity, much less its government, from God or Nature. They recognized that to create a free nation is a great human achievement—precisely because it requires that individuals cooperate in many matters while retaining their rights, as individuals, to differ in other things. To unite all humanity in a common construction would, surely, have struck them as a venture defying both divine precept and human nature.

It may be part of human nature to long for heavenly harmony, above all human divisions. The Constitution of the United States requires that individuals find their way to heaven on their own. The task of government is more modest—but should not be despised for that. What keeps the United States government within proper limits is the Constitution. What preserves the Constitution is American independence. They can not be reconciled with boundless schemes of global governance.

NOTES

CHAPTER ONE
INTRODUCTION: BY OUR OWN LIGHTS

1. Clyde Prestowitz, *Rogue Nation, American Unilateralism and the Failure of Good Intentions* (Basic Books, 2003), p. 284, written before the actual start of the war, is still a useful compendium of European complaints against American "unilateralism" on policy toward Iraq, toward global agreements, toward trade, and (in a whole separate chapter) on the Middle East, where Prestowitz faults U.S. policy for blindly supporting Israel in the face of international condemnation. Perhaps because the author's name does not sound Scottish, he takes the trouble to reassure readers that he is "an elder of the Presbyterian church."

2. Robert Kagan, *Of Paradise and Power, America and Europe in the New World Order* (Knopf, 2003), p. 3.

3. Samuel Huntington, *The Clash of Civilizations and the Remaking of World Order* (Simon and Schuster, 1996).

4. Mark Mazower, *Dark Continent, Europe's Twentieth Century* (Vintage Books, 2000), pp. 138–50, describes the initial impulse to embrace the "new order," which was reinforced in most western countries by the mood of disgust at parliamentary and constitutional government that had been gaining in the 1930s. Tony Judt offers a compelling account of the moral pressures and psychological evasions which, in the years after 1945, caused Europeans to forget this era of hopeful collaboration during the period of German occupation or (in the French case) of implicit alliance with Germany. "Myth and Memory in Postwar Europe," in István Deák, Jan Gross, and Tony Judt, eds., *The Politics of Retribution in Europe, World War II and its Aftermath* (Princeton University Press, 2000), pp. 293–305.

5. Robert O. Paxton, *Vichy France, Old Guard and New Order* (Knopf, 1972), p. 289. The prevailing view, among French government officials, was that "occupation might be bad, but liberation by force would be worse" (ibid.), p. 287.

6. Mazower, *Dark Continent*, p. 143, citing H. Trevor-Roper, ed., *Hitler's Table Talk, 1941–44* (Weidenfeld and Nicholson, 1973), p. 6 (entry for July 11, 1941). The parallels between later efforts at European integration and this earlier version, in the early 1940s, are extensively documented (along with reminders that some of the same figures who took a leading role in the postwar version were already attracted to the prior, German version) in John Laughlin, *The Tainted Source, The Undemocratic Origins of the European Idea* (Little, Brown, 1997).

7. Mark Gilbert, *Surpassing Realism, The Politics of European Integration since 1945* (Rowman & Littlefield, 2003), pp. 25–31, emphasizes the roots of the

European federalism movement in the late 1940s in a broader vision of a "harmonious society" within each nation. The Union of European Federalists (Union Européene des fédéralistes), founded in 1947, urged "the creation of a European federation which shall be a constitutive element of a world federation" and worked, in the meantime, for "the creation of a 'Third Force' that could act as a bridge between Soviet Communism and the Western European tradition of democratic socialism."

8. The 1957 Treaty of Rome launched the European Economic Community (EEC). Why Rome? Perhaps it was just chance. But it was a somewhat curious choice. Of the original six states which joined in the treaty, all but Italy shared extensive borders and historic trade patterns in the Rhine valley. Italy was not a central location for the treaty signing but the most peripheral location that could be chosen for the final ceremonies. Perhaps it was understood as a symbolic location. Governments in all six states were, at the time, dominated by Christian Democratic parties—that is, parties with roots in Catholic social teaching. For these political leaders, Rome symbolized a source of European unity far older and more respectable than more recent efforts at unity imposed from Berlin or from Paris.

9. Quoted in R.E.M. Irving, *The Christian Democratic Parties of Western Europe* (George Allen & Unwin, 1979), p. 237.

10. Herodotus, *Histories*, translation by Aubrey de Selincourt (Penguin Classics, 1954), book 7, section 139, p. 460; sec. 143, p. 462. After acknowledging uncertainty about what other Greeks did in secret negotiations with the Persians, Herodotus subsequently offers this observation: "One thing, however, I am very sure of: and that is, that if all mankind agreed to meet, and everyone brought his own faults along with him for the purpose of exchanging them for somebody else's, there is not a man who, after taking a good look at his neighbor's faults, would not be only too happy to return home with his own" book 7, sec. 152, p. 467.

11. Chaucer's "The Tale of the Malibee" illustrates part of the enduring appeal of the story in the western imagination, when "Prudence," the wife, speaks of "Judas Machabeus, which was goddes knight, when he sholde fighte agayn his adversarie that hadde a greet nombre, and a gretter multitude of folk and strenger than was his people of Machabee." Walter W. Skeade, ed., *The Complete Works of Geoffrey Chaucer* (Clarendon Press, Oxford, 1972, originally published 1894), vol. 4 ("The Canterbury Tales"), p. 231.

12. This precise phrase appears in a sermon by Ezra Stiles, "The United States Elevated to Glory and Honour" (1783), reprinted in Conrad Cherry, ed., *God's New Israel, Religious Interpretations of American Destiny* (University of North Carolina Press, 1998), p. 83. Stiles opened his sermon by remarking that, to hear the Law, Moses "assembled three millions of people, the number of the United States" [at the time of independence] (ibid.), p. 82. Rather than presenting the United States as a literal successor to Israel, Stiles immediately proceeded to affirm that, at some future time, "the words of Moses . . . will be literally fulfilled when . . . the posterity of Abraham shall be nationally collected . . . and they shall become 'a holy people unto the Lord' their God." But clergymen of that era were taken with the parallel: "It has often been remarked that the people of the United States come nearer to a parallel with Ancient Israel, than any other nation

upon the globe. Hence OUR AMERICAN ISRAEL is a term frequently used; and common consent allows it apt and proper." Abiel Abbot, "Thanksgiving Sermon," 1799 (ibid., frontispiece) Even lay political leaders—and some not known for piety—were taken with biblical analogies. When the Continental Congress assembled a committee to design an official seal for the United States, Benjamin Franklin proposed a portrayal of "Moses lifting his hand and the Red Sea dividing" while Thomas Jefferson proposed "a representation of the children of Israel in the wilderness, led by a cloud by day and a pillar of fire by night" (ibid.), p. 65. Jefferson returned to the theme in his Second Inaugural, appealing to "the favor of that Being in whose hands we are, who led our fathers, as Israel of old, from their native land and planted them in a country flowing with all the necessaries and comforts of life."

13. The more famous lines of the Gettysburg Address were already prefigured in Lincoln's speech to the New Jersey Senate of February 21, 1861, in which he describes the war for American independence as a struggle for "something even more than National Independence . . . something that held out a great promise to all the people of the world to all time to come" and affirms his willingness to serve as "an humble instrument in the hands of the Almighty, and of this, his almost chosen people, for perpetuating the object of that great struggle."

14. "Jews Attacked in French Anti-war Protests," *Sunday Telegraph* (UK), April 6, 2003.

15. A socialist member of the French National Assembly complained to foreign journalists that "the phrase 'Anglo-Americans' thrown around in the [French] media and in political circles to describe the coalition in Iraq—sometimes linked with 'supported by the Jews'—echoes the rhetoric of Vichy France." But he was described as "one of a handful in parliament as a whole" to protest the tone of official rhetoric. "France's Realists, Continued," *The Wall Street Journal*, April 9, 2003.

16. Jürgen Habermas, "Nach dem Krieg: Die Wiedergeburt Europas" (After the War: A Reborn Europe), *Frankfurter Allgemeine Zeitung*, (May 31, 2003). An English translation by Ludwig von Tranzivan was subsequently published on the website <http://www.Aldiborontiphoscophornio.blogspot.com> on its archive for the week of June 1, 2003. This philosophic outlook seems to have trickled down to the mass public. A study by the Allensbach Institute in Germany found that while a solid majority of Americans agreed with the claim that "there are absolute benchmarks of good and evil," fewer than a third of Germans agreed: "Most Germans find such unconditional morality incomprehensible." Thomas Petersen, "Issues Endanger Trans-Atlantic Friendship," *FAZ*, March 21, 2003.

17. General Eisenhower's speech is reprinted in David Eisenhower, *Eisenhower at War, 1943–45* (Vintage Books, 1987), pp. 256–57. President Roosevelt did not simply invoke divine assistance. Less than a month after the attack on Pearl Harbor, Roosevelt explained to Congress that "victory for us means victory for religion" because "Nazis have now announced their plan . . . by which the Holy Bible and the Cross of Mercy would be displaced by 'Mein Kampf' and the swastika and the naked sword." America and its allies, he concluded, "are inspired by a faith which goes back through all the years to the first chapter of the Book of Genesis" (Annual Message to Congress, January 6, 1942).

18. See, for example, the statement of 103 German professors and intellectuals, "Eine Welt der Gerrechtigkeit und des Friedens sieht anders aus," originally published in *Frankfurter Allgemeine Zeitung*, May 2, 2002, which condemns the U.S. war in Afghanistan with "the same rigorousness with which we condemn the mass murder of innocent bystanders by the terrorist attack" and then completes the moral identification by warning against "the growing influence of fundamentalism in the United States."

19. See, for example, Kurt Burch, *"Property" and the Making of the International System* (Lynne Rienner, 1998), pp. 159–60: "sovereignty is a social practice. . . . The same holds for the conceptual split between economics and politics and for the conceptual borders marking other allegedly distinct social realms: religion, culture, class, family, gender, public/private, home/work, home/homeless, and religion/school, for example. Each is staked and built from some sense of property and rights, just as sovereignty is . . . we as social members . . . may construct alternatives." Or, Laura Brace and John Hoffman, *Reclaiming Sovereignty* (Pinter, 1997), pp. 23–24: "In the same way that modernity makes postmodernity possible, so *liberal* statism enables us to look beyond the state. . . . Classical liberalism has already identified the 'sovereign' capacity of individuals to govern their own lives. This idea can only become historical, dynamic and relational by locating it within a changing world. . . . In making a case for detaching sovereignty from the state in the spirit of 'utopian' realism, we need to point to the way in which a post-statist concept of sovereignty is struggling to emerge from the contradictory logic of the liberal state."

20. Christine Sylvester, *Feminist Theory and International Relations in a Postmodern Era* (Cambridge University Press, 1994), pp. 213, 221, 220.

21. John Locke, *Essay Concerning Human Understanding (ECHU)* (J. M. Dent, 1961), pp. 39–40.

22. Most scholars who apply "constructivist" insights to international relations emphasize the way relationships structure (or "construct") the goals of states, so the better analogy might be, not with construction of a bridge, but with construction of expectations within a marriage or a family. Still, family practices often reflect purposive effort—which is why marital counseling is often effective and why marriage, as an institution, is structured along particular lines, on the assumption that "participants" will respond in characteristic ways over time. That is why most societies have "constructed" marriage in similar forms, though a vast range of alternatives is conceivable.

23. Stephen Krasner, *Sovereignty, Organized Hypocrisy* (Princeton University Press, 1999). The term "organized hypocrisy" might be better applied to international organization—that is, to the pretense that there is something above sovereign states. Krasner's book has the merit of highlighting the continuing centrality of states in international politics. He shows that, amidst many opportunities for self-dealing, states are not always consistent in the way they interpret sovereignty claims. And "sovereignty," as he shows, has been understood in quite different ways by different writers, particularly in recent times. But Krasner makes little effort to analyze which of these conceptions is more reasonable. Such a distinction would be an obvious place to start in making sense of the concept—if one started from the premise it might be more than a mere residue of power politics but

might actually have some reasonable claims as an organizing principle for political life.

CHAPTER TWO
GLOBAL GOVERNANCE OR CONSTITUTIONAL GOVERNMENT

1. Frederick Schumann, *The Commonwealth of Man, Power Politics and World Government* (Knopf, 1952) offers many examples from the period. In March 1946, for example, Supreme Court Justice William O. Douglas said, in a public address to a world federalist conference: "Our goal should be a world government representing the peoples of the world, functioning under an international bill of rights through a legislature, judiciary, and executive" (ibid.), p. 435. Two years later, 105 members of the House of Representatives and twenty-two senators sponsored a resolution urging "that it should be a fundamental objective of the foreign policy of the U.S. to support and strengthen the U.N. and to seek its development into a world federation open to all nations with defined and limited powers adequate to preserve peace and prevent aggression through the enactment, interpretation and enforcement of world law" (ibid.), p. 439. Chancellor Robert M. Hutchins of the University of Chicago organized distinguished members of the Chicago faculty as the "Committee to Frame a World Constitution" which continued to publish proposals for such a project over the next several years.

2. The LEXIS electronic inventory of law review articles (predominantly but not exclusively from American publications) contains only three articles using the term before 1990, only fourteen before 1995, but 208 between 1995 and 2000 and 202 between 2000 and the spring of 2002. The LEXIS inventory for "general news" (covering major English-language newspapers) contains one article using the term before 1990, ten between 1990 and 1995, forty-seven from 1995 to 2000, fifty-six from 2000 to the spring of 2002.

3. Curtis A. Bradley and Jack L. Goldsmith, "Customary International Law as Federal Common Law," *Harvard Law Review*, vol. 110 (February 1997), p. 815, offers extensive documentation of how widely established this view has become—and how questionable it is, viewed from the traditional constitutional perspective.

4. *Kadic v. Karadzic*, 70 F.3d 232 (2d. Cir., 1995); *Republic of Philippines v. Marcos*, 806 F.2d 344 (2d. Cir., 1986).

5. *Beanal v. Freeport-McMoRan*, 969 F. Supp. 362 (E.D. La., 1997) (on behalf of workers in Indonesia); *Doe v. Unicol*, 963 F. Supp. 880 (C.D. Cal. 1997) (on behalf of workers in Burma); *Aguinda v. Texaco*, 850 F. Supp. 282 (S.D.N.Y., 1994) (on behalf of workers in Ecuador).

6. *Don Beharry v. Janet Reno*, 98 CV 5381 (January 22, 2002), arguing that federal immigration law must be interpreted to conform with the Convention on the Rights of the Child (CRC), so a non-citizen father, convicted of robbery, could not be deported to his home country (as the law otherwise required) without special hearings to determine "the best interests of the child" (as required by the CRC).

7. The case law of the European Court of Justice on "general principles of law," starting with *Stauder v. City of Elm* (Case 29.69, 1969 ECR 419), sought to fill gaps in the Treaty of Rome. It has no direct counterpart in U.S. law. *Black's Law Dictionary* (subtitled, "Definitions of Terms and Phrases of American and British Jurisprudence, Ancient and Modern"), has been a standard reference work for American lawyers since 1891. As late as the sixth edition of 1990, it had no entry for "general principles of law." The term appeared only in the seventh edition (West Publishing Co., 1999) with a vague reference to practice in international law.

8. Quincy Wright, *The Control of American Foreign Relations* (Macmillan Co., 1922), pp. 95–126, provides a classic account. The Supreme Court has not had the occasion to comment on the continuing force of the old doctrine in relation to international institutions. But in *Printz v. United States* 521 U.S. 898 (1997), the Court held that federal statutes could not delegate·implementing authority even to agents of state governments within the United States. It is very hard to conceive the logic which would forbid delegation to officials still bound by the U.S. Constitution and still accountable to American voters but then allow delegations of governing authority to international officials operating without either sort of constraint.

9. Robert Keohane, "Ironies of Sovereignty: The European Union and the United States, *Journal of Common Market Studies*, vol. 40 (November 2002), claims disputes about the meaning of sovereignty are not really important in tensions between the EU and the United States. I believe this claim is most unlikely to prove correct in the future and is clearly mistaken as a description of past American policy and prevailing American opinion—at least regarding American obligations to maintain U.S. sovereignty.

10. Bentham explained that, "were it not for the force of custom," the term "law of nations . . . would seem rather to refer to internal jurisprudence." He notes that a French jurist has made "a similar remark" in suggesting that "droit des gens" ought rather to be termed "droit *entre* les gens." "Introduction to the Principles of Morals and Legislation," in Wilfrid Harrison, ed., *A Fragment of Government and Introduction to the Principles* (Basil Blackwell, 1960), ch. 17, par. 25, fn. 1, p. 426.

11. The German term *völkerrecht* can be understood as a direct translation of the Latin term, *ius gentium*, which is the basis for the historic term "law of nations." Perhaps the persistence of *völkerrecht* in German usage reflects the longer persistence of older outlooks in Germany, even in the eighteenth and nineteenth centuries, when Enlightenment doctrines swept over countries more firmly rooted in the west. But there may be more involved. When writers in western countries spoke of the "nation," they had in mind a body of people living within the same state and for whom that state was the authorized voice: so that Bentham could limit "international law" to "mutual transactions between sovereigns" on the assumption that "inter-national" was synonymous with "between sovereigns." In Germany, however, the "deutsches volk" had no clear correspondence with a particular state. In a Germany divided among different states, the persistence of the older term—*völkerrecht* or "law of peoples"—may have reflected longing for a law that somehow recognized peoples rather than states. The term may also

reflect characteristic German impatience with a world of independent states. When a German scholar offered a history of international law after the Second World War, he organized his exhaustive survey into periods, each designated by the supposed hegemonic power of that era—so a "Spanish Age" was followed by a "French Age" and then a "British" and an "American Age." Bentham's assumption—of truly independent states, acting from mutual agreement—is treated as too childish to take seriously. This account does not offer a separate discussion of a "German Age" but presumably it would have been from 1940 to 1944. It was a period when "volk" had great prestige as an organizing concept for German scholars and when ethnic or "racial" categories (as German scholars defined the term) were arranged in hierarchies thought to take precedence over mere claims of states. See Wilhelm G. Grewe, *The Epochs of International Law*, English translation by Michael Byers (W. de Gruyter, 2000). The first edition was completed in Berlin in 1944, but publication was disrupted, as the author reports, by Allied bombing and then by Russian shelling.

12. Hague Convention (IV), "Respecting the Laws and Customs of War on Land," 36 Stat. 2277: "The provisions contained . . . in the present Convention do not apply except between Contracting Powers [that is, states which ratify the convention] and then ony if all belligerents [in a particular conflict] are parties to the Convention" (article 2).

13. A point noticed at the time by legalists. See Hans Kelsen, "The Old and the New League: The Covenant and the Dumbarton Oaks Proposals," *American Journal of International Law*, vol. 39 (January 1945), p. 46: "we may say the [planned UN] organization is to have a political rather than a legal character. This means that its activity is not to be limited too much by strict rules of law but that the Charter shall confer upon the agencies of the new League a great deal of discretion in the exercise of their functions."

14. Paul Hirst and Grahame Thompson, *Globalization in Question* (Polity Press, 1996), p. 49: "the level of integration, interdependence, openness or however one wishes to describe it, of national economies in the present era is not unprecedented. Indeed, the level of autonomy under the Gold Standard up to First World War was much less for the advanced economies than it is today." Among other things, as the authors note, much larger public sectors mean that in a modern economy, a smaller portion of the GNP is available for export or for foreign investment.

15. The United States was one of twenty-one nations that joined in the International Postal Convention of October 9, 1874. The ten-page text appears at 19 Stat. 577. The United States refused to join the International Telegraphic Union (ITU), organized by European states a decade earlier—for fear that government-operated telegraphy services would impose burdensome rules on the commercial American services. Lack of U.S. participation in the original ITU does not seem to have impeded the development of trans-Atlantic telegraphy, however, after the laying of the Atlantic cable. The United States joined the new International Telecommunications Union—out of concern to assure non-interference with radio frequencies—after the Second World War. For the history of international regulation in this area, see George Codding Jr., *The International Telecommunication Union* (E. J. Brill, 1952).

16. Stephen C. Neff, *Friends But No Allies, Economic Liberalism and the Law of Nations* (Columbia University Press, 1990), p. 58, describes several European "enforcement" efforts in the early nineteenth century in Latin America and in the eastern Mediterranean.

17. "New Battle as British Begin Pullout from Sierra Leone," *The Guardian*, June 1, 2000. "News that the deployment was being scaled down . . . was greeted with dismay [by people on the streets in Freetown]: 'We want the British to stay' . . . 'A British vice-president!' followed triumphantly by the final sally [from people in the street]; 'A British president for Sierra Leone!' . . . It is hard to convey the intensity of those who see in the British presence not only a solution to the war but a signal that Sierra Leone is to be included again in the world of prosperity, jobs, good clothes, good living." The French force in Côte d'Ivoire elicited a different reaction: "You should just go back to your country." Matt Bigg, "Troops Hold Back Mob in Ivory Coast Protest," *The Independent* (London), February 1, 2003 (reporting "anti-French riots," featuring burning of the French flag, throwing of stones at French soldiers and calls for attacks on French civilians in the country, after French peacekeepers pressured the Ivorian government to accept a "peace deal" involving power sharing with antigovernment rebels, regarded by protestors as terrorists).

18. On medieval acceptance of rape as a legitimate form of punishment in a just war, see F. Vitoria, "Second Relectio on the Indians, or on the Laws of War Made by the Spaniards on Barbarians," in *De Indis et de iure belli reflectiones*, translated by J. P. Bate (Carnegie Institute, 1917), pp. 163, 185.

19. The Regulations Respecting Laws and Customs of War on Land, adopted at the Hague Peace Conference in 1907, begin with the specification that they apply only to organized military forces—defined at the outset as forces "commanded by a person responsible for his subordinates," marked by "a fixed distinctive emblem recognizable at a distance," organized to "carry arms openly," and conducting their "operations in accordance with the laws and customs of war" (art. 1). The same restrictive definitions were carried over in the Geneva Convention of 1949 on protections for prisoners of war (art. 4). No state would have agreed to provisions which allowed an enemy to rely on guerrilla bands, hiding among civilians and not answerable to an order to surrender from their own ostensible commanders. The courtesies of war were made available only to those who would honor them in kind. For discussion of contemporary dispute over the reach of the Geneva Convention, see Jeremy A. Rabkin, "At War Over the Geneva Convention," *The National Interest*, Summer 2002.

20. M. Weller, "The Reality of the Emerging Universal Constitutional Order," *Cambridge Review of International Studies* (Winter/Spring 1997), p. 40. A more recent and similar argument: David Held, "Law of States, Law of Peoples," *Legal Theory*, vol. 8 (March, 2002), pp. 1–44, which accumulates many citations to other writings in this vein.

21. Described at length in Sandrine Tesner, *The United Nations and Business, A Partnership Recovered* (St. Martin's Press, 2000).

22. "Living with the Enemy," *The Economist*, August 9, 2003. The article says, "An NGO attack can wreak havoc with employee morale and on recruitment. . . . Moreover, when companies make concessions, NGOs often come back

for more," citing complaints of former activists that NGOs try to generate publicity for their own fund-raising rather than build relations of trust with business firms inclined to cooperate.

23. Pierre-Marie Dupuy, "Soft Law and the International Law of the Environment," *Michigan Journal of International Law*, vol. 12 (Winter 1991), p. 420, offers a very astute overview of the trends driving the concept: First the "existence and development of a ramified network of permanent institutions . . . [in which the] 'UN family' of organizations plays the leading role" and connected with that, "the increasingly important function of nongovernmental organizations . . . asuring . . . a dynamic relation between inter-State diplomacy and international public opinion." Second, "the arrival of underdeveloped countries on the international stage" that "having the weight of the majority without the power of the elder countries, have speculated on the utilization of 'soft' instruments, such as resolutions and recommendations of international bodies, with a view toward modifying a number of the main rules and principles of the international legal order." For a parallel account of increasing reliance on "soft law" in the human rights context, see David Forsyth, *Human Rights in International Relations* (Cambridge University Press, 2000), pp. 12–17, emphasizing that agreement to "soft law" is easier to secure than agreement to "hard law."

24. "Notes from the President," *Newsletter*, American Society of International Law, March 1993.

25. One of the most recent and systematic versions of the argument is in Charles Jones, *Global Justice, Defending Cosmopolitanism* (Oxford University Press, 2000).

26. From a very extensive literature belaboring this argument, particularly emphatic versions are: Joseph Camilleri and Jim Falk, *The End of Sovereignty* (Edward Elgar, 1992); H. G. Gelber, *Sovereignty Through Interdependence* (Kluwer Law International, 1997); Jan-Aart Scholtz, *Globalization, A Critical Introduction* (Palgrave, 2000).

27. The refusal of European states to support U.S. resolutions calling for inquiry into Chinese human rights practices—following threats from China to retaliate by cancelling commercial contracts—is described in Henry Steiner and Philip Alston, *International Human Rights in Context* (Oxford University Press, 2d. ed., 2000), pp. 634–40. In 2002, while continuing the refusal of any inquiry toward China, the Commission voted eight resolutions of condemnation of Israel, following seven resolutions of condemnation the previous year. No other state has received more than one condemnation in the same year. The commission has never condemned the tactic of deploying suicide terror attacks against Israeli civilians.

28. M. J. Peterson, "International Fisheries Management," in Peter M. Haas, Robert O. Keohane, and Marc A. Levy, eds., *Institutions for the Earth* (MIT Press, 1993).

29. The argument is developed at length in Thomas Schelling, *Costs and Benefits of Greenhouse Gas Reduction* (AEI Press, 1998). Meanwhile, Bjorn Lomborg points out that, even with flexible provisions for trading of emission rights, the cost of implementing Kyoto would be five times the cost of providing proper water treatment and sanitation for all the world's people—which could prevent 2

million deaths per year and half a billion people becoming ill each year, due to un-safe water. *The Skeptical Environmentalist* (Cambridge University Press, 2001), p. 318. If there is going to be global mobilization on the scale of Kyoto, it is not obvious why it should focus on the priorities of environmentalists in affluent states.

30. The excellent coinage of Noel Malcolm, *Sense on Sovereignty* (Institute for Economic Affairs, London, 1995).

31. A characteristic text of the late 1990s, by a Danish diplomat, with an en-thusiastic preface from the former president of the European Commission, ex-presses the point this way: "the room for maneuver is indeed very small. Are there differences between the policies of John Major and Tony Blair in Great Britain? Between the [1989–1993] Bush administration and the Clinton administra-tion? . . . Internationalism is a strong unifying force regarding domestic policies, for the simple reason that problems to be dealt with become more and more sim-ilar." J. Orstrom Moller, *The End of Internationalism, Or World Governance?* (Praeger, 2000), p. 151. Similarly: "The present juncture presents the first occa-sion since the large Roman and Chinese empires (which administered universal governance in their respective "worlds") to make what we would like to call the big swing in strategy: the swing away from focusing upon conflicts and con-frontations, and instead concentrating upon building cooperation" (ibid.), p. 8. One can see from such effusions why the "unilateralism" of the second Bush ad-ministration has provoked such outrage in Europe. Nations were no longer sup-posed to be capable of making departures from the European consensus, which was supposed to be the emerging consensus for "universal governance."

32. "To become partners in the UN's search for a tripartite governance for-mula, civil society organizations must be confident that the future policy role of the business community will not develop at the expense of their representation and agenda. They must be convinced that they . . . can derive moral authority from the willingness of states and [business] corporations to accept that NGOs speak for the global community." Tesner, *The United Nations and Business*, pp. 57–58.

33. One of the few contemporary writers to grasp the logic of this historic un-derstanding is Alan James, who provides an excellent short summary in "The Practice of Sovereign Statehood in Contemporary International Society," *Political Studies*, vol. 47 (February 1999), p. 457, equating "sovereignty" with "constitu-tional independence . . . a legal, an absolute, and a unitary condition" (ibid.), p. 462.

34. William Blackstone, *Commentaries on the Laws of England*, vol. 1, Intro-duction (University of Chicago Press edition, 1979, facsimile of the first edition, 1765), p. 46.

35. Justice Sandra Day O'Connor, in a book of musings designed to be inof-fensive, used this as her title: *The Majesty of Law, Reflections of a Supreme Court Justice* (Random House, 2003).

36. *Second Treatise*, par. 3. The rest of the sentence specifies the purpose of such government "for regulating and preserving property." The conjunction is shocking to modern sensibilities—capital punishment for mere offenses against property? It is true that Locke's subsequent account of "property" includes the

explanation that "every man has a property in his own person" (par. 27). Still, the earlier formulation, which connects "penalties of death" with "preserving of property" is a stark reminder that even a law for limited ends may need the strongest coercive force because men do not readily agree, even over property.

37. It is striking, however, that the most active campaign for the abolition of capital punishment comes from the European Union and the Council of Europe— that is, from organizations of states which have forfeited much of their sovereignty. It seems to reflect an instinct to lower the status of governmental authority, to diminish the authority of law, to close the distance between an actual state and a mere private constituency. Perhaps it is connected with the hope that guarantees of welfare to all will soften conflicts in society and soften the people in that society.

38. "Politics as a Vocation," translation by H. H. Gerth in *From Max Weber* (Oxford University Press, 1946), p. 78. A fuller exposition can be found in Weber's *Economy and Society*, vol. 1, edited by Guenther Roth and Claus Wittich (University of California Press, 1978), p. 56.

39. The Federal Tort Claims Act (1946) authorizes suits against the federal government only "under circumstances where the United States, if a private person, would be liable to the claimant" 28 U.S.C. sec. 1346b. Liability of foreign governments to tort claims under the Foreign Sovereign Immunities Act (1976) similarly extends to commercial activity conducted by governments but excludes intrinsically "sovereign acts": 28 U.S.C. sec. 1602–08. The case law discloses many complications implicit in the statutory formulas but the underlying concern, as courts see it, is to shield the most distinctively governmental acts from judicial second-guessing. Closely parallel provisions of the British statute are analyzed in Georges R. Delaume, "The State Immunity Act of the United Kingdom," *American Journal of International Law*, vol. 73 (April 1979), p. 185.

40. "A Government which enjoys the habitual obedience of the bulk of the population with a reasonable expectation of permanence can be said to represent the State in question and as such to be entitled to recognition [by other states]." L. Oppenheim, *International Law*, vol. 1, 8th ed., revised by H. Lauterpacht (Longmans, Green and Co., 1955), p. 131.

41. G. L. Haskins, *The Growth of English Representative Government* (University of Pennsylvania Press, 1948): in the "sixteenth and [early] seventeenth centuries as [in] the Middle Ages . . . people were under no compulsion to think of parliament except in terms of what it had been in the beginning, a court of justice" (ibid.), p. 98. C. H. McIlwain, *The Growth of Political Thought in the West* (Macmillan, 1932): "'sovereignty' . . . could not and did not assume its distinct and definite form until 'legislation' itself in its modern sense had become so frequent that it forced itself upon the attention of men, and this 'legislation' is not the medieval 'finding' of a precept whose binding force comes from its supposed conformity to universal reason or to immemorial custom but the modern *making* of a rule recognized to be law only because of the authority of the organ of the state . . . until national law can thus be made, there can be no true 'legislation'; and until there is true 'legislation' of this more modern type, there can be no real conception of legislative sovereignty" (ibid.), p. 390.

42. No. 70, p. 395.

43. Jeremy Waldron, *The Dignity of Legislation* (Cambridge University Press, 1999), provides a particularly insightful exposition of the way in which the idea of legislation (by an elected legislature) is not so much a repudiation of natural law notions of justice as a recognition that people differ in their understandings of these notions: "With the establishment and operation of a legislature, law begins to exist in a new sense. It exists now as 'ours,' as something tangible, something each of us can count on as a *common* point of reference" (ibid.), p. 76. Waldron offers a compelling analysis of Locke's account, in these terms, and shows that it has very close parallels even in Kant's understanding of legislative authority.

44. "Death is not Justice," Council of Europe, Strasbourg, June 2001.

45. The term "subsidiarity" was taken over from internal principles of the Catholic Church—whose organization is not usually described as a model of federalism, though it certainly includes many features of decentralization. It is not equivalent to a constitutional formula because, in itself, "subsidiarity" does not specify which functions ought to be pursued at a local level. It is perhaps more akin to a philosophy than a rule—and in that sense, almost the opposite of a constitutional formula.

CHAPTER THREE
THE CONSTITUTIONAL LOGIC OF SOVEREIGNTY

1. On the canonical status of these three documents, see Richard Cox, ed., *Four Pillars of Constitutionalism* (Prometheus Books, 1998), pp. 26–40, describing the history of their incorporation, as "organic law," in successive codifications of federal law since 1796. The Declaration of Independence, in its penultimate paragraph, speaks of "free and independent states" (rather than "sovereign" states) but then describes the rights of "free and independent" states in terms that follow classic accounts of sovereignty. The Articles of Confederation (Article II) assume the equivalence in providing that each state "*retains* its sovereignty, freedom and independence" except for those powers "expressly delegated to the United States." The text of the Constitution concludes with the formula, "done in the Year of our Lord 1787 and of the Independence of the United States of America the Twelfth." In the Northwest Ordinance, outlining standards for the government of U.S. territory not yet incorporated as states of the Union, drafted in the same year, this formula appears as, "Done by the United States . . . in the year of our Lord 1787 and of their sovereignty and independence the 12th." The different phrasings may reflect this difference in context: the Northwest Ordinance is clearly a sovereign legislative act of the United States government itself, while the Constitution is not "ordained" by the government but by the "people"—whose claim to "sovereign" authority is more ambiguous.

2. Thomas Engeman, Edward Erler, and Thomas Hofeller, *The Federalist Concordance* (University of Chicago Press, 1980): "sovereignty" appears thirty-three times; "sovereign" thirty-six; "sovereigns," fifteen; "sovereignties," nine (total: 93); "freedom," eight; "republic," fifty-nine; "republican," seventy-five; "moral" or "morals," thirteen; "reason," 112.

3. No. 15, edited by Clinton Rossiter, notes by Charles Kesler (Mentor, 1999), p. 78.

4. *Summa Theologica*, Q. 90, A. 4.

5. "For each individual believes of himself that he would by all means maintain the sanctity of the concept of right and obey it faithfully, if only he could be certain all the others would do likewise" but without reliable enforcement, "each individual, despite his good opinion of himself, assumes bad faith in everyone else." "Perpetual Peace," in Hans Reiss, ed., *Kant's Political Writings* (Cambridge University Press, 1970), p. 121.

6. "the serf has a *dominus*; we may prefer to render this by *lord* and not by *master* or *owner*" but "medieval Latin can not express this distinction; if the serf has a dominus, the palatine earl, nay the king of England, so long as he is duke of Aquitaine [hence, nominal vassal of the king of France], has a dominus also." "It is characteristic of the time that rights of sovereignty shade off into rights of property: the same terms and formulas cover them both: the line between them is drawn by force rather than by theory." Frederic Maitland and Frederick Pollock, *The History of English Law Before the Time of Edward I*, vol. 1, revised ed. (Cambridge University Press, 1968), pp. 412, 68.

7. Sydney Painter, *Feudalism and Liberty* (Johns Hopkins University Press, 1961), p. 157.

8. Joseph Strayer, *The Medieval Origins of the Modern State* (Princeton University Press, 1970), p. 83: "The concept of 'foreign affairs' could hardly exist in a Europe that . . . was not quite sure what states were sovereign. For example, a king of France might send letters on the same day to the count of Flanders, who was definitely his vassal but a very independent and unruly one, to the count of Luxembourg, who was a prince of the Empire but who held a money-fief (a regular, annual pension) of the king of France, and to the king of Sicily, who was certainly ruler of a sovereign state but was also a prince of the French royal house. In such a situation one could hardly distinguish internal and external affairs."

9. James Bryce, *The Holy Roman Empire* (Macmillan, 1907), pp. 183–91, documenting episodes in which imperial authority was claimed over "Hungary, Poland, Denmark, France, Sweden, Norway, Iceland, Spain, England, Scotland, Ireland, South Italy and Sicily, Venice, Cyprus and Armenia, the East."

10. Ruston Coulborn, *Feudalism in History* (Princeton University Press, 1956), p. 236.

11. Bernard Guenée, *States and Rulers in Late Medieval Europe*, English translation (Basil Blackwell, 1985), p. 16. "As poems, folktales and prophecies show, during the last quarter of the fifteenth century the idea of empire as a universal organization was alive and well in the popular consciousness." Martin van Crevald, *The Rise and Decline of the State* (Cambridge University Press, 1999), p. 80.

12. The Emperor's Golden Bull of 1356 did establish an electoral procedure for choosing a new emperor—more than four centuries after the founding of the Empire. Even that proved misleading, as the Habsburg family soon established near-hereditary claims on the imperial throne, in circumvention of the scheme for election by prince-electors of the Empire. Popes were indignant when not consulted over the imperial peace agreements ending various wars of religion in the sixteenth

and seventeenth centuries because the relation between the papacy and the Empire remained so obscure.

13. On the "Donation of Constantine," by which the first Christian Emperor was supposed to have confided the western empire to the care of the popes, see Michael Wilks, *The Problem of Sovereignty in the Later Middle Ages* (Cambridge University Press, 1963); though later exposed as a forgery, it was taken seriously in a very serious dispute about which authority—the Pope or the Holy Roman Emperor—was the true successor to the vanished authority of ancient Rome. Sun and moon metaphors still figure in the bull, *Unam Sanctum*, issued by Boniface VIII in 1302 to rebuke the French king and arguing, among other things, that France must accept papal direction (regarding Church revenues) because France remains part of the Holy Empire and the Pope is supreme authority in the Empire. The same metaphor is deployed by Dante's *De monarchia* a decade later to prove the supremacy of the Emperor over the Pope. Other claims about political inheritance by family descent survived still longer: "The young European nations took pride in their Trojan origins which no one contested and their rulers found it a source of powerful arguments." A German writer in the mid-fifteenth century wrote that they "used their Trojan origin to prove that the Germans were the equal of the Romans and superior to the French. . . . Ferdinand and Isabella thought they should encourage the emergence of a newcomer, the Trojan Hispanus," Guenée, *States and Rulers*, p. 60. These arguments seem far less absurd when one recalls that kings based their most immediate claims to rule on legitimate descent from rightful kings and wars were commonly justified as efforts to reclaim a legitimate territorial "inheritance"—as in the Hundred Years War between England and France, where both sides invoked Trojan ancestry as well as more immediate genealogical claims to the French throne.

14. Dante's *De monarchia* invokes a variety of mystical arguments to prove that all the peoples of the world can be assured universal peace and brought to the highest levels of human perfection if they are all ruled by the Holy Roman Emperor. *The Defensor Pacis* ("Defender of the Peace") of Marsilius of Padua, while purporting to trace all political authority to the consent of the people (to show that priests have no inherent claim to rule) still concedes that such authority might encompass the entire world in a single empire (ch. 17).

15. Jean Richard, *The Crusades, c. 1071–c. 1291* (English translation by Cambridge University Press, 1999), pp. 260–70, on the preaching of Crusades, noting the personal incentives employed, such as indulgences wiping out the effects of past sins for participants in Crusades and the application of such doctrines to "crusades" against Christian heretics within Europe; ibid., pp. 38–41, on unsuccessful efforts of popes, emperors and local authorities to protect Jews from attacks by Crusaders on the march in Germany.

16. For example, the holdings of the crusading order of Teutonic knights remained independent until 1525, when Albert of Brandenburg, master of the Order, on the advice of Martin Luther, simply annexed them to his own personal holdings and renamed them the "Duchy of Prussia," van Crevald, *Rise and Decline*, p. 68.

17. McIlwain, *Growth of Political Thought*, p. 390: "Until there is a State, standing prominent before the eyes of men with its reciprocal public relation of

ruler and subject, instead of a mere quasi-private relationship existing between the individual vassal and his overlord, there can be no such organ by which national law can be *made*."

18. Marc Bloch, *Feudal Society* (English translation by University of Chicago Press, 1961), p. 425: "In England there was Parliament; in France, the provincial Estates, always much more frequently convoked and on the whole more active than the States-General. In England there was the common law, almost untouched by regional exceptions; in France, the vast medley of regional customs." Strayer, *Medieval Origins*, p. 45: "It was only because England was a state with a strong sense of its identity that a few hundred men in Parliament could presume to give assent for the whole community. And it was only because the king had sovereign power that the assent of Parliament had any meaning."

19. Strayer, *Medieval Origins*, p. 47. The fact is all the more notable as most "English" nobles were still French-speaking Normans in the thirteenth century, though they had already lost their fiefs in Normandy by the beginning of the century. Despite vast differences in rank and status, common institutions seem to have nurtured a sense of common nationality—and even to have begun to erode differences in rank. Determined to develop a *common* law, royal courts would not enforce land transactions involving serfs without treating the latter as free men and the law made no distinction, in most matters, between freemen and nobles. Maitland and Pollock, *History*, pp. 418–19. Paradoxical as it may seem, England owed its evolving nationality to the completeness of the Norman conquest, which allowed its kings to develop uniquely strong governing institutions, compared with any other territory in medieval Europe. It was the reliability of the royal courts that won them loyalty from those who counted most—the armed nobles. An early illustration of this confidence in English law was the refusal of the king and barons in 1236 to change the English law of inheritance (when the parents of an out-of-wedlock child were subsequently married) to satisfy Church objections: "they were not prepared to agree . . . that the pope knew best when it came to drawing up the rules for succession to landed property in England." J. A. Watt, "Spiritual and Temporal Powers" in J. H. Burns, ed., *Cambridge History of Medieval Political Thought* (Cambridge University Press, 1988), p. 388.

20. C. R. Cheney, *From Becket to Langton, English Church Government* (Manchester University Press, 1956), p. 337, claims that Pope Innocent III actually did expect to "claim direct power in political as well as ecclesiastical matters" from John's submission but faced with more immediate challenges from the Emperor, Innocent did not press these claims and subsequent English kings were not prepared to accept them. Blackstone's account of this "most unparalleled and astonishing" episode, berating the "effrontery" of the Pope and the "meanness" of "the dastardly" King John is in his *Commentaries*, vol. 4, p. 8.

21. van Crevald, *Rise and Decline*, p. 84. Even then, Henry thought it necessary to commission Italian scholars "to produce a whole series of complicated historical fabrications," demonstrating that Henry's imperial title derived from the "ancient fellow Briton, the Roman Emperor Constantine"—though he did not thereby claim rights within the Holy Roman Empire. The Act of Supremacy, repudiating any papal or imperial authority above the king, proclaimed, "this realm of England is an empire"—that is, an empire in itself, not part of the Holy Roman Empire.

22. Even where Protestant princes claimed to rule by "divine right," the claim seems to have been advanced to counter religious claims on behalf of the papacy and the emperor. So the arguments were readily mixed with quite different arguments advanced by Bodin. J. N. Figgis, *Divine Right of Kings* (Cambridge University Press, 1896) gives a more sympathetic account of the modernizing tendencies in the religious theory, with respectful discussion of Bodin's influence (ibid.), pp. 126–29. Julian Franklin, *Jean Bodin and the Rise of Absolutist Theory* (Cambridge University Press, 1973) is a darker account of Bodin's influence.

23. McIlwain, *Growth of Political Thought*, p. 380 (no other theorist had more influence on "thoughtful and moderate men" before mid-seventeenth century). Modern commentators have complained that Bodin's treatise is rambling and disorganized but probably no contemporary reader is competent to sort through the maze of arcane references—from Greek and Latin classics, Hebrew commentaries, medieval glossators on Roman Law to analyses of contemporary politics in a dozen European countries. There is much in this text to distract or confuse a hasty modern reader. But it is known that Bodin took great pains in reworking successive editions and in an age of religious persecution, he had many reasons to choose his words with care. Bodin has often been compared with Montesquieu (who seems to have borrowed Bodin's climate theory among other things) and modern readers have also complained about the disorganized quality of Montesquieu's great work, *The Spirit of the Laws*, while earlier readers saw it quite differently. I do not claim to have penetrated much beyond the surface of Bodin's treatise in my exposition here, but even the surface rewards careful reading.

24. The 1606 translation by Richard Knolles, *Six Books of a Commonweale*, is still the only complete English translation. It was reprinted by Harvard University Press in 1962, with useful notes by Kenneth McRae. Knolles combined the text of the original French edition with a slightly expanded Latin edition, prepared by Bodin himself. Citations in the following notes, marked "K", are to this edition, where paragraphs on each page are indicated with letters. The original French text of 1576 has been reprinted in six volumes (corresponding to the original six "livres") by Fayard (Paris, 1986), under the editorial direction of Christine Fremont, Marie Dominique Couzinet, and Henri Rochais. Citations marked "F", are to pages in this edition, where the numbering begins over again with each new volume. Citations in the following notes will begin with a Roman numeral indicating in which of the six books the passage can be found, then an Arabic number indicating the chapter within that book, followed by page references for each of these editions.

25. The opening sentence of *La république* begins by defining "une république" as "un droit gouvernement de plusieurs mesnages et de ce qui leur est commun avec puissance souveraine"—a lawful or rightful government [of many households and that which they have in common, with a strong sovereign], emphasizing the distinctive quality of *government* rather than the wholeness of the community. As McIlwain notes, this definition is "in many ways the most significant thing in that great work," implying "a very different thing from what Aristotle meant" in defining the polis. *Constitutionalism, Ancient and Modern*, revised ed. (Cornell University Press, 1947), p. 135. "With Bodin, the word 'sovereignty' entered the vocabulary of law and politics, as the word 'state' had done with

Machiavelli." A. P. D'Entreves, *The Notion of the State* (Oxford University Press, 1967), p. 102.

26. III, 1: Senate should have power to advise but not command (K 277, F 42). Bodin takes "counsel" so seriously that he sees more danger in a good prince with evil counselors than in an evil prince with good counselors (III, 1: K 254G, F 8).

27. IV, 6: wrong for princes to administer justice in person (K 507E, F 154); princes judging on their own will be tempted to display too much lenity (K 509D, F 164); where the sovereign's own interests are involved, "it is contrary to the law of nature that the party should be judge also" (K 514F, F 170—also III, 6: K 346F, F 149).

28. II, 1: Polybius mistaken to think king, nobles, and people can share in sovereignty (K 185, F 11); distinguishing "state" from "government of the state" (K 199, F 34); VI, 6 popular "sovereignty" can go with aristocratic "government" (K 785, F 297); justice best administered by men of different classes in magistracy (K 789C, F 297).

29. IV, 1: "an undoubted maxim, that he is master of the state ["republique"] who is master of the force" (K 420H, F 30); V, 5: "he always commands the state ["estat"] that is master of the force" (K 612H, F 160); II, 1: division of sovereignty yields endless strife (K 194, F 160); VI, 5: "if he is master of forces, he is master of the state" [estat] (K 750H, F 243); III, 2: Aristotle misdefines magistrate by failing to focus on "power to command" force (K 278K, F 46).

30. III, 7: internal rule of subordinate corporations, merchant guilds, etc.; III, 5: all offices belong to commonwealth (K 330K, F 125); governing power not properly connected with ownership of land (K 331, F 125–26); I, 9: feudal rights must be subordinate to sovereign, so if held of different sovereigns, one only must be primary (K 123E, F 247); VI, 3: taxes should apply to nobility, as in England (K 669D, F 79–80—but the French edition is not so clear regarding favorable contrast to English practice, compared with that in France).

31. I, 9: French kings always resisted papal control (K 145–47, F 281–83); French kings not obligated to the Emperor (K 134–35, F 265); marginal note by translator, Knolles: "the majesty of the emperor too much impugned by this French author" (K 150).

32. II, 5: right to overthrow tyrants (K 219E, F 71); I, 1: obligations to keep promises and respect laws of war apply to other sovereigns, but not to robber bands (K 2F, F 28).

33. *Methodus ad facilem historiarum cognitionem*, first published in 1566: English translation by Beatrice Reynolds, *Method for the Easy Comprehension of History* (Columbia University Press, 1945), p. 168: "all kingdoms of all peoples, empires, tyrannies and states are held together [in dealings with each other] by nothing but the rule of reason. . . . But since this dominion of reason constrains no one, one state cannot actually be forged out of all peoples." Regarding this "rule of reason" for dealings between states, it is telling that, in the *République*, Bodin several times praises wars undertaken by one sovereign to liberate subjects of a tyrant. II, 5: "it is magnifical ["tres belle et magnifique"] to take up arms to defend a people against a tyrant, as Moses did" (K 220K, F 72); V, 6: a wise prince can win "immortal praise and reputation" as Hercules did by intervening to protect subjects of "intolerable tyranny" elsewhere (K 632E, F 214); V, 5:

contrary to Cicero's claim, "just war" is not only to recover one's own, since "none is more just than to defend the lives of innocents" (K 601D, F 137); on the other hand, Bodin notes that free peoples are better at defending their territory and government—V, 6: "we may not think ever to keep that people in subjection which has lived in liberty, if they be not disarmed" (K 615B, F 166).

34. VI, 4: "if the prince be subtle and wicked, he will plant a tyranny; if he be cruel, he will make a butchery of the commonwealth; or a brothel house if he be licentious," etc. etc. (K 714K, F 177–78).

35. The nine "marks" of sovereign power (I, 10): 1) power to make laws; 2) power to declare war and conclude peace; 3) power to appoint higher magistrates, such as judges; 4) power to hear last appeals; 5) power to grant pardons; 6) power to demand ultimate or primary fealty of feudal lords; 7) power to coin money; 8) power to regulate weights and measures; 9) pre-emptive rights of taxation. All of these powers are, in one way or another, assigned to the federal government in the U.S. Constitution. Legislation, declarations of war, regulation of the coinage and of weights and measures are all among the powers of Congress enumerated in Article I, Sec. 8. Even the seemingly anachronistic feudal power appears in Article I, Sec. 9 ("no person holding any office . . . [under the United States] shall, *without the consent of Congress*, accept any . . . title, of any kind whatsoever, from any King, Prince or foreign State." The appointment power is shared between the president and Senate, while appellate powers are vested in the Supreme Court and the pardon power in the president—though judges and the president might be impeached by Congress for abusing these powers.

36. I, 8: sovereign bound by constitutional norms establishing sovereign power (K 95A, F 197); sovereign bound by own promise if received specific benefit for it in contract (K 92K, F 194); III, 7: in meeting of Estates General, Bodin successfully resisted king's plan to have joint committee speak for whole body, since each estate must separately vote and improper to override ancient constitution (K 370–71, F 188–89).

37. II, 2: first governments were "lordly" ["seigneuriales"] (K 200G, F 35); only in Muscovy and Turkey today (K 201C, F 37); elsewhere "every subject has true property in his own things" (K 201E, F 37); "men free borne and lords of their own goods . . . would easily rebel [against threat to reduce them to lordly rule] being noble hearts ["coeurs genereux"] nourished in liberty" (K 204H, F 42).

38. VI, 4: "chiefly established to . . . forbid theft" which is also "commanded by the word of God who will have every man to enjoy the property of his own goods" (K 707D, F 160–61); I, 8: "it is not in the power of any prince in the world at his pleasure to raise taxes upon the people, no more than to take another man's goods from him" (K 97A, F 201); III, 7: praises regular parliaments in England (K 384K, F 207).

39. III, 4: obligation to "law of nature and of God" ["loy de Dieu et de nature"] (K 312–313, F 97–98); magistrate should resign rather than enforce measures against "laws of God and nature" (K 318I, F 105); IV, 2: precept of "the great God of Nature" ["grand Dieu de nature"] (K 449C, F 72).

40. I, 5: "Christian princes" ended slavery from "fear" of revolts (K 39E, F 99).

41. For example, I, 3: divorce should be permitted because authorized in Hebrew Bible (K 18I, F 59); VI, 6: "eye for an eye" not to be taken literally but as basis for monetary compensation, according to Talmudic interpretation (K 781B, F 291).

42. Friedrich Meinecke thus classified Bodin "among the first opponents of Machiavellism in France" (*Der idee der staatsrason*, 1925; English translation as *Machiavellism*, Yale University Press, 1957), ch. 2. But Bodin's actual view of Machiavelli was certainly more complex. Roger Chauvire notes the text of the *République* frequently parallels arguments and prescriptions in Machiavelli's *Discourses* but without acknowledgment: "Quand il le nomme, c'est pour le contredire; quand il l'imite, il n'en sonne mot." *Jean Bodin, auteur de la république* (Librairie Ancienne Honore Champion, 1914), p. 194, n. 4. In the *Methodus*, Bodin offered this curious appraisal: "Machiavelli wrote many things about government—the first, I think, for about 1,200 years after barbarism had overwhelmed everything. [His sayings] are on the lips of everyone, and there is no doubt but that he would have written more fully and more effectively and with a greater regard for truth, if he had combined a knowledge of the writings of ancient philosophers and historians with experience" (ibid.), p. 153. The 1,200-year interval neatly excludes almost all Christian thought. The notion that Machiavelli lacked "knowledge of ancient historians" can hardly be taken as serious criticism, given that Machiavelli's most extended work, the *Discourses on Livy*, is, after all, a commentary on an ancient historian. Nor does Bodin, himself, seem at all partial to "ancient philosophers." Chauviré sums up the affinity this way: "Ce gout du succes, du possible, et l'utile que nous trouverons tout a l'heure en Bodin, le rapprochement si pousse qu'il etablit entre l'interet et la justice, tout cela sent la politique florentine" (ibid.), p. 197. The least one can say is that Bodin did not seem to think this enough. Bodin's continual emphasis on "the law of nature," for example, stands in sharp contrast with Machiavelli's silence on natural law and Bodin is far more respectful of "God's law." But Bodin's natural law is not that of Thomas or Cicero.

43. Harvey Mansfield, *Taming the Prince* (Free Press, 1989), pp. 153–54.

44. All of Bodin's works were placed on the Vatican "Index" of prohibited works in 1628. In Bodin's lifetime, it was rumored that his mother was a Jewish exile from Spain and the claim has been advanced, down to the twentieth century, as a known fact—though it is not. Compare the "Bodin" entries in *Catholic Encyclopedia* (Robert Appleton Co., 1907: "probably of Jewish origin") with *Encylopedia Judaica* (Macmillan Co., 1971: "baseless supposition that his mother was of Jewish origin"). Chauviré, *Jean Bodin*, pp. 15–22, seems to have been the last scholar to investigate the confusing contemporaneous claims, biased at first by the eagerness of Catholic critics to associate Bodin with foreign influences and then (on the part of those refuting rumors about his ancestry) with eagerness to claim him for France. Chauvire discounts the Spanish ancestry claims but he regards as conclusive evidence the fact that Bodin studied with Carmelites in his youth—which may not be very conclusive, since the Carmelites, in fact, had many connections with Spanish Jews or Marranos. Lord Burghley, operating an intelligence network for Queen Elizabeth, received a report that Bodin had identified himself to an English visitor as a secret Protestant. Bodin seems to have been im-

prisoned for over a year during a period of anti-Huguenot persecution (McRae's introduction, *Six Books*, p. A7). Yet Bodin asked to be buried in a Catholic cemetery and Church authorities did not object. Paul Rose, *Bodin and the Great God of Nature, the Moral and Religious Universe of a Judaizer* (Librarie Droz, Geneva, 1980) rests on a rather idiosyncratic equation of "judaizing" with reliance on precepts from the Hebrew Bible (even when the reliance is clearly selective). Similarly, the secret conversion claim in Christopher Baxter, "Jean Bodin's Daemon and his Conversion to Judaism," published in Horst Denzer, ed., *Verhandlungen der internationalen Bodin Tagung in Munchen* (Beck, 1973) posits a "conversion" that involves no actual communication with an actual Jewish community and therefore no observance of required rituals.

Near the end of his life, Bodin prepared an extended work, the *Colloquium heptaplomeres de rerum sublimium arcanis abditis*, in which a Catholic, a Zwinglian, a Lutheran, a Muslim, a Jew, a skeptic, and a freethinker debate the merits of various religions in a manner reminiscent of Yehuda Ha-Levi's medieval *Kuzari*. Though known to Grotius, Leibniz, and others in its manuscript form, the *Heptaplomeres* was not published in its entirety until the mid-nineteenth century. An English translation by Marion Daniels Kuntz is now available (*Colloquium of the Seven about Secrets of the Sublime*, Princeton University Press, 1975). As Chauviré records, some readers have supposed that Bodin identified with the Jewish participant, who is certainly shown to be the most learned in biblical sources. Others think Bodin favored the freethinker. The Catholic, who is host to the discussions, seems generous and hospitable to all but somewhat detached, while the Protestants seem most irritable and dogmatic. They all part in friendship—but agree never to take up such debates or discussions again. Some scholars have recently argued that Bodin was not the actual author of the Heptaplomeres but it was rather a later author, pretending to be Bodin. Whether or not this is so, it is still telling that discerning readers for more than two centuries were quite prepared to think the work was actually written by Jean Bodin. See Karl Friedrich Faltenbacher, *Magie, religion und wissenschaften im colloquium heptaplomeres* (Darmstadt, Wissenschaftlic he Buchgesellschaft, 2002).

45. "Forthright advocate": George Sabine, *History of Political Theory* (Holt & Co., 1937), p. 401; III, 7: expulsion of Jews from France and Spain by monarchs seeking to "enrich themselves" (K 383B, F 205); IV, 7: will not say which religion is best (K 537A, F 206), but coerced religion only promotes atheism (K 539C, F 207); IV, 5: better to have many sects than two (K 540F, F 208).

Bodin also published a denunciation of witchcraft, *De la demonomanie des sorciers* (1580), which Sabine (*History*, p. 401), like others, sees as contradicting Bodin's general position on religious toleration. An original edition of the *Demonomanie* is available in the rare book collection at Cornell University. It is an odd work in many ways—for example, in continual appeals to the authority of Maimonides, who (when one tracks down the references) actually denies that sorcerers do have any occult powers. But Bodin was hardly unique in favoring broad toleration in matters of religion, while urging the suppression of claims to manipulate nature with occult or demonic powers. Thomas Jefferson proposed a revision of Virginia's criminal code which included "whipping, not to exceed fifteen stripes" for all "attempts to delude the people . . . by exercise of the pretended arts of witchcraft, conjuration, enchantment or sorcery." As Ralph Lerner notes, "with its elaborate and ancient supporting citation in Anglo-Saxon, Latin, Old French, and English, this is no merely routine copying of Virginia precedent." *The Thinking Revolutionary* (Cornell University Press, 1987), p. 75. Lerner cautiously suggests that Jefferson feared claims to occult powers would threaten the supremacy of civil authority (ibid.), p. 76, and the same may be true for Bodin. Or more broadly, Bodin may have feared that claims to occult powers threatened the most basic premises of a political structure built on predictable, recurring human patterns; see L. Strauss, *The Political Philosophy of Hobbes* (University of Chicago Press, 1952), pp. 86, 91, 94, for suggestions regarding Bodin's anticipation of characteristic Enlightenment notions regarding the foundations of modern natural law.

46. VI, 4: small states encourage tyranny (K 721, F 192); I, 6: against Aristotle's notions, as slighting centrality of sovereignty (K 50-51, F 118–19); but see VI, 5: "natural people" of a country easily stirred to resentment and revolt against "foreign princes" (K 750H-I, F 243).

47. III, 8: nobility originally based in violence and murder and no one definition of true nobility would now be accepted by all nobilities of different nations (K 389B, but not in the Fayard edition); I, 6: Aristotle wrong to see nobles as more fully citizens (K 53C, F 123).

48. Reynolds, *Method*, ch. 9, "Tests by which to Test the Origins of People," p. 362: "all men for a long time have been so fused in migrations and also in teeming colonial populations, as well as in wars and captivity, that none can boast about the antiquity of their origin and the great age of their race except the Jews"—and the exception, too, may be intended as a discouragement to such "boasts," since it contradicts a number of other Bodinian tenets, as Reynolds notes in her introduction, p. 24.

49. I, 7: commercial treaties even with enemies (K 74-I, F 161); VI, 2: "in my opinion it is more seemly . . . to be a merchant than a tyrant and for a gentleman to traffic than to steal" (K 660H, F 60); VI, 4: God has scattered resources in different nations to encourage peaceful exchange (K 708H, F 162).

50. John Neville Figgis, *Political Thought from Gerson to Grotius* (Cambridge University Press, 1907; reprinted by Harper Torchbooks, 1960), p. 145.

51. Initially published in 1568 as *La Réponse de Maistre Jean Bodin Advocat en la cour au paradoxe de Monsieur de Malestroict*; then republished in 1578, as *Discours de Jean Bodin sur le rehausement et diminution des monnoyes*, enlarged with extensive extracts from *Six livres de la république* (VI, 3, on the same subject). An English translation of the expanded edition, by Henry Tudor and R. W. Dyson, has recently appeared as *Response to the Paradoxes of Malestroit* (Thoemmes Press, 1997), with an extended introduction indicating the importance of the work in the history of economic theory. H. W. Spiegel, *The Growth of Economic Thought*, revised ed. (Duke University Press, 1983) pp. 89–92, assesses Bodin's place in the history of economics, concluding with the remark that Bodin's account "com[es] close to enunciating what was to become one of the central ideas of modern times—the idea of progress."

52. *République*, VI, 3 (K 687C, F 117) is particularly emphatic on this point: "a prince may not make any false money, no more than he may kill or rob."

53. Tudor and Dyson, *Response to the Paradoxes of Malestroit*, p. 68: complaining about "monopolies of merchants, artisans and labourers when they unite to fix the prices of goods or to enhance their daily wage" and "normally cover themselves with the veil of religion"; p. 85: "Plato and Lycurgus forbade trade with foreigners . . . yet, if I am not greatly mistaken, both would have done better to permit trade, as Moses wisely did, thus showing that he was a greater leader than those two. For the light of virtue . . . increases in brightness the more it is shared. Yet we cannot pride ourselves so much in our virtue as to assume that foreigners will not be able to equal us." (But *République*, III, 8, K: 399 reports biblical prophets and Church fathers denounced merchants); p. 86: "God has with admirable foresight . . . distributed His favours in such a way that there is no country in the world so well provided for as not to lack many things . . . in order to maintain all the subjects of His commonwealth in friendship, or at least to prevent them from making war for any length of time, since they always have to do business with one another"; p. 87: "They say that when trade flourishes everything in the country becomes dearer" but "the imports, which replace the goods exported, lower the price of what would otherwise be scarce"; p. 89: prohibiting exports to keep down prices for the poor only causes "the goods which may not be exported . . . [to] remain on the hands of the owners and merchants of the kingdom . . . and the [native] workmen and the poor die of hunger": p. 93: prohibitions on import of luxuries do not work so long as the nobles and the royal court enjoy them, "for there is nothing more pleasant or more agreeable to man than what is prohibited, when he who makes the law contravenes it"; p. 102: "For if money, which ought to govern the price of everything, is changeable and uncertain no one can know what he has: contracts will be uncertain, charges, taxes, wages, pensions and fees will be uncertain . . . the prince cannot, without incurring the infamy of a counterfeiter, alter the weight of his coin to the prejudice of his subjects."

54. Sabine, for example, who does not always display great imagination, sees Bodin as a forerunner of Locke: "Without much exaggeration Bodin might be said to make the possession of property simply a natural right, somewhat after the fashion of Locke" and like Locke was committed to "modernizing and secularizing of the ancient theory of natural law, in order to find if possible an ethical and yet a not merely authoritarian foundation for political power." Yet Sabine also sees Bodin as a forerunner of Hobbes, displaying an underlying "confusion" in that the "two sides [of Bodin's philosophy]—constitutionalism and centralized power—were not really drawn together" (*History*, p. 413). Jean-Fabien Spitz, *Bodin et la souverainété* (Press Universitaires de France, 1998) depicts Bodin as a defender of constitutional limits but on the basis of medieval traditions. A recent work, by Scott Gordon, *Controlling the State: Constitutionalism from Ancient Athens to Today* (Harvard University Press, 1999) presents Bodin's theory of sovereignty (and indeed all theories of sovereignty) as opposed to "constitutionalism" because, in Gordon's view, constitutionalism is fundamentally about the separation of powers (ibid., ch. 2). Yet Gordon himself acknowledges "the continuous development of constitutionalism is a comparatively recent phenomenon, traceable no further than to 17th Century England" (ibid.), p. 358. He does not make any effort to account for this interesting fact—that the "continuous development

of constitutionalism" only emerged after the development of clear theories of sovereignty.

55. *République*, IV, 6 (K 517B, F 177).

56. Among other things, Bodin studied legal institutions of many countries to escape from the usual dependence of legal analysts on Roman Law digests. Julian Franklin, *Jean Bodin and the Sixteenth Century Revolution in the Methodology of Law and History* (Columbia University Press, 1963), describes some of the ambition behind this comparative study—the fruits of which are on display in the *République*. At the same time, Bodin tried to discern the influence of climate and terrain on culture and politics, developing a theory that has often been compared with Montesquieu's. Bodin rejects any notion that men are simply prisoners of their environment but he does try to show that different countries are likely to develop different patterns of law and government, even when they have access to the same learning. *République*, V, 1.

57. I, 5: Turks are only modern people to measure nobility by virtue rather than birth (K 44H: Knolles seems to have relied on the Latin text here, as the French is not so explicit); IV, 7: Turkish king tolerates all other faiths but observes his own with "more devotion" than any other ruler (K 537E, F 207).

58. Frederick Pollock, *Introduction to the History of the Science of Politics* (Beacon Press, 1960, reprinting 1911 revised ed. by Macmillan: original edition, 1896), p. 57.

59. See "The Readie and Easy Way to Establish a Free Commonwealth," *Areopagitica and Other Political Writings of John Milton* (Liberty Fund, 1999), p. 429, for an extended paraphrase of Bodin's *République*, III, 1; p. 443 for "one united and entrusted Sovrantie". Milton's title may have been intended to remind alert readers of Bodin's *Methodus ad facilem*, since it follows Bodin's "method" in surveying models from the ancient world to show what is most feasible in the modern world. Milton refers directly to "Bodin, the famous French writer" in his 1641 pamphlet, "The Reason of Church Government Urged Against Prelaty," where Bodin ("though a papist") is invoked in support of Milton's argument for separating Church authority from government (*Milton's Prose Works* [H. J. Bohn, 1883, vol. 2, p. 490]).

60. Pollock, *Science of Politics*, p. 47.

61. John T. Scott, "The Sovereignless State and Locke's Language of Obligation," *American Political Science Review* (March 2000), notes that the term "sovereignty" almost never appears in Locke's *Second Treatise*, though it appears with some frequency (and almost always in disparaging terms) amidst Locke's attack on Filmer's arguments for absolutism in the *First Treatise*. The implied reservation is worth noting: the specter of rebellion is always hovering in the background of Locke's account, a perpetual limit on claims to ultimate sovereignty. The article is particularly valuable in collecting illustrations from a long-running scholarly dispute about whether the "ultimate sovereign" is the legislative power or the people or the individual—to which Scott is persuasive in arguing that there is no "ultimate" sovereign. But the point should not be exaggerated. Richard Cox, *Locke on War and Peace* (Oxford University Press, 1960), pp. 109–10, notes that what Locke concedes to be "marks of sovereignty" in the *First Treatise* (pp. 129, 131—following Filmer's adoption of Bodinian formulas) reappear in

almost the same terms as attributes of "the supreme power" in the *Second Treatise* (pp. 83, 88). Cox makes a strong case for a rather conventional or Bodinian view of sovereignty in Locke (*Locke on War and Peace*, pp. 108–70).

While Locke speaks of different agents or forces as "supreme" in different contexts, all the claimants to "supremacy" are internal to the same community. And there are good reasons why Locke speaks so emphatically as he often does about the "supremacy" of government within a properly constituted commonwealth. If individuals can too readily appeal from the authority of civil law to the law of nature—thereby making the legislative power less than "supreme"—they have not, after all, given up their natural power to execute the law of nature, though Locke himself insists the surrender of such private power to punish (or to judge, on behalf of others) is the precondition for the establishment of civil society (*Second Treatise*, par. 128). On the other hand, if every act of the legislative power is seen as a direct expression of popular will, so that the people are literally self-governing, there is no security for private rights, as the individual is entirely submerged in the collectivity. My exposition in the text is not offered as a refutation of Scott's interpretation of Locke. My intention is simply to highlight those elements in Locke's account which allowed his successors to speak of "sovereignty" and "Locke" in the same breath.

62. On Locke as the forerunner of international human rights movement, see Louis Henkin, Gerald Neuman, Diane Orentlicher, and David Lecbron, *Human Rights* (Little, Brown, 1998), pp. 22–27. On Locke as forerunner of supranational governance, see Michael Doyle, *Ways of War and Peace* (W. W. Norton, 1997), p. 225. On why Doyle's view is highly implausible, see Cox, *Locke on War and Peace*, ch. 5 and pp. 190–92.

63. "Letter on Toleration," in David Wooton, ed., *John Locke, Political Writings* (Mentor, 1993), pp. 424–26.

64. There is some ambiguity in this passage about whether it is "the community" or its individual members whose "self-preservation" is "fundamental, sacred and unalterable": In the course of the *Second Treatise*, Locke uses equally emphatic language when speaking of the community's authority and when speaking of the individual's rights—and he often, as here, seems to run them together. The rights of the individual are secured by an organized community. So, Locke insists in various passages that private property predates civil society (pp. 27, 35), that protecting this property is the purpose of entering into civil society (pp. 3, 88, 95, 120, 124, 139)—and then he says, in other passages, that the rights of property are determined by civil society (pp. 38, 45, 50).

65. *République* IV, 3: better to wait for a tyrant to die a natural death—unless he has children (K 475C, F 108-09); III, 5: always wrong for private citizens to resist magistrates with force, even when wronged, except to resist wrongful death sentence (K 338F, F 136); citing Roman rather than Christian examples to show "it is more necessary for private men to obey, respect and honor the magistrates, for the defense of the commonwealth and of the civil society" ("pour tuition des Republiques et soietez des hommes") (K 340I, F 140).

66. On the notion of shared language as a basis for nationality, see Jeremy A. Rabkin, "Grotius, Vattel and Locke: An Older View of Liberalism and Nationality," *Review of Politics* (Spring 1997), pp. 307–9. Scott, reviewing similar passages in

the *ECHU*, makes the sensible suggestion that the power of language communities is a constraint on sovereign power. One could equally say, however, that it is a safeguard for the "supreme power" of the national government against outside powers, competing for popular support within the community: *we* "understand" each other. But trade across boundaries does not require much in the way of common understandings: exchange has been "made practicable out of the bounds of society, and without compact, only by putting a value on gold and silver and tacitly agreeing in the use of Money" (*Second Treatise*, par. 50).

67. Locke thus asserts that "society" cannot exist without government: "the laws" are—or rather, "by their execution" are—"the bonds of the society," so "when that totally ceases . . . the people become a confused multitude, without order or connection" (*Second Treatise*, par. 219). But revolution seems to rest on the opposite premise: When government abuses its rightful powers, "the people are at liberty to provide for themselves by erecting a new legislative" (par. 220). The seeming contradiction might be resolved, as Leo Strauss pointed out, by thinking of such direct action by the people as feasible only in brief moments of revolutionary convulsion, between the rejection of one government and the establishment of its successor. *Natural Right and History* (University of Chicago Press, 1953), p. 232. Still, the tension between Locke's different claims here reminds us that, without the constraints of law, "the people" cannot readily act as a united force. This may mean that successful revolutions depend on prior experience in being governed together—and perhaps long and extensive experience. In this, as in other things, Locke's abstract account seems to rely on the actual history of England.

68. *Commentaries on the Laws of England*, vol. 1, Introduction, sec. 2, p. 49.

69. Ibid., vol. 1, ch. 1, pp. 120, 125.

70. Ibid., vol. 1, Introduction, sec. 2, p. 48.

71. Ibid., pp. 49, 51–52: the ellipses excises the cautious, parenthetical remark, "(who perhaps carries his theory too far)."

72. Ibid., vol. 4, ch. 4, p. 54.

73. Ibid., vol. 4, ch. 4, p. 57.

74. Ibid., vol. 4, ch. 8, pp. 108–9.

75. Jefferson compares the migration of English colonists to America with the medieval migration of Saxons to England, which brought no claim of "superiority or dependence" from the Saxon homelands—and if it had, the English, having "too firm a feeling for their rights," would have refused to "bow down the sovereignty of their state before such visionary pretensions." In accepting Britain's military aid against French incursions, "these states [the American colonies] never supposed . . . that they thereby submitted themselves to her [Britain's] sovereignty." So enactments of the British Parliament are "foreign to our [American] constitutions and unacknowledged by our laws," while the king is merely the "mediatory power between the several states of the British empire" or "the link connecting the several parts of the empire." Merril D. Peterson, ed., *Thomas Jefferson, Writings* (Library of America, 1984), pp. 105–6, 115, 107.

Almost half of the itemized complaints against the king in the Declaration of Independence concern royal interference with colonial legislatures—on the apparent assumption that these bodies should have had total or near total "supremacy" all along. On Jefferson's reading of Bodin, see "Jefferson as Reader of Bodin," in J. P. Mayer, *Fundamental Studies on Jean Bodin* (Arno Press, 1979), which reproduces a few pages from Jefferson's personal copy of Bodin (now in the Library of Congress), showing Jefferson's markings in the margin, including his highlighting of a passage on the binding authority of the law of God and nature (ibid.), p. 25.

76. "Cincinnatus V," New York Journal, November 29, 1787, "Commentaries on the Constitution," in John Kaminski and Gaspare Saladino, eds., *Documentary History of the Ratification of the Constitution (DHRC)*, vol. 14 (State Historical Society of Wisconsin, 1983), p. 308.

77. "The Impartial Examiner," *Virginia Independent Chronicle*, February 20, 1788, *Documentary History*, vol. 8, p. 392.

78. "Genuine Information, XII," *Baltimore Maryland Gazette*, February 8, 1788, *Documentary History*, vol. 16, p. 91.

79. Max Farrand, *Records of the Federal Convention of 1787* (Yale University Press, 1937, 1966); vol. 1, p. 331 (Wilson); vol. 1, p. 323 (Hamilton); vol. 1, p. 328 (King).

80. Speech at Pennsylvania Ratifying Convention, December 11, 1787: "The sovereignty rests with the people. In them consists the supreme power." *Documentary History*, vol. 2, p. 570. In the July 4th Oration in 1788, Wilson spoke of the ratification process as "the most dignified ["spectacle"] that has yet appeared on our globe . . . a WHOLE PEOPLE exercising its first and greatest power—performing an act of SOVEREIGNTY, ORIGINAL and UNLIMITED" (original emphasis), *Documentary History*, vol. 17, p. 244.

81. Farrand, *Records*, vol. 3, p. 112; even before the Convention, Benjamin Rush, in a published article, echoed the claim that the "people of America have mistaken the meaning of the word sovereignty: hence each state pretends to be *sovereign*. In Europe, it is applied only to those states which possess the power of making war and peace—of forming treaties and the like. As this power belongs only to congress, they are the only *sovereign* power" (original emphases). But he went still further: "It is often said that 'the sovereign and all other power is seated *in* the people.' This idea is unhappily expressed. It should be—'all power is derived *from* the people.' They possess it only on the days of their elections. After this, it is the property of their rulers, nor can they [the people] exercise or resume it, unless it is abused. It is of importance to circulate this idea, as it leads to order and good government" (original emphasis), *Documentary History*, "Commentaries," vol. 12, p. 47.

82. James Madison, "Sovereignty," in Gaillard Hunt, ed., *Writings of James Madison* (Phila, J. B. Lippincott & Co., 1867), vol. 4, p. 390.

83. No. 15, p. 76.

84. No. 16, p. 84.

85. No. 15, pp. 76–77, 78.

86. No. 16, p. 84.

87. No. 17, p. 88.

88. No. 2, p. 6: "a people descended from the same ancestors, speaking the same language, professing the same religion, attached to the same principles of government, very similar in their manners and customs, and who, by their joint

counsels, arms and efforts, fighting side by side throughout a long and bloody war, have nobly established their general liberty and independence."

89. No. 17, p. 87.

90. No. 19, pp. 98, 100, 101; Bodin's account is in *République*, I, 7 (K 75–79, emphasizing sovereignty of individual cantons because they retain the armed forces of the confederacy: Bodin goes on to discuss the Achaen League of ancient Greece and the Holy Empire, the three main confederacies discussed in *The Federalist*, No. 19.

91. No. 30, p. 159.

92. No. 62, pp. 348–49.

93. Hamilton was still more explicit on this point at the Convention: "It had been said that respectability in the eyes of foreign Nations was not the object at which we aimed; that the proper object of republican Government was domestic tranquility & happiness. This was an ideal distinction. No Governmt. cd give us tranquility & happiness at home, which did not possess sufficient stability and strength to make us respectable abroad." Farrand, *Records*, vol. 1, 466–67.

94. "Special Message to Congress," July 4, 1861 in *Abraham Lincoln, Speeches and Writings, 1859–1865* (Library of America, 1989), pp. 256, 259–60: the first ellipsis excludes Lincoln's qualification of the claim that "no one of our states ever was a sovereignty" with the acknowledgement of the special case of Texas, briefly an independent republic before joining the Union.

95. Art. I, Sec. 9. Unlike the prohibition on domestic titles of nobility, the international prohibition allows for exceptions with the consent of Congress. The Framers seem to have envisaged the need to accommodate certain innocent diplomatic gestures. But the location of this clause, amidst prohibitions on Congress rather than authorizations of federal power, emphasizes the general prohibition rather than the innocent exceptions. It did not appear at all in earlier drafts (see, Farrand, *Records*, vol. 2, pp. 169, 183, 389) and was evidently regarded as a natural extension of the preceding prohibition on titles of nobility.

96. See, for example, A. V. Dicey, *Introduction to the Study of the Law of the Constitution* (Liberty Classics, 1982, reprinting 8th ed., 1915), p. 81 ("the legal sovereignty of the United States resides in the States' governments as forming one aggregate body represented by three-fourths of the several States"). For the earlier version, see John Austin, *Jurisprudence*, 4th ed. (Cockroft, 1875), p. 268 (emphasizing the Supreme Court).

97. The Constitution itself, Article VI, Sec. 3, requires that legislators and officials of state governments, as well as their federal counterparts, "be bound by oath to support this Constitution" and a federal statute prescribes a minimal version of this oath: "I solemnly swear that I will support the Constitution of the United States" (4 USC sec. 101). But the prescribed oath for new citizens requires a pledge to "support and defend the Constitution and the laws of the United States against all enemies, foreign and domestic; to bear true faith and allegiance to the same; and to bear arms on behalf of the United States when required by the law" (8 USC sec. 1448). The oath required of those in "the civil services or uniformed services" of the United States government follows this more elaborate formula (5 USC sec. 331).

98. Some modern historians of the medieval period have emphasized that

modern ideas of freedom owe much to the feudal nobility. Sydney Painter, for example, notes that the social obligations of a feudal lord "imposed little restraint on him. The church could control him far less than it could other men. Even the state recognized him as especially privileged. Naturally, the status of the noble was the envy of other classes. Essentially the rights and liberties for which the middle and lower classes struggled through the seventeenth, eighteenth and nineteenth centuries were those enjoyed by the nobles in the Middle Ages . . . the legal and political institutions which secured this freedom in western Europe and America were those forged by the feudal aristocracy" *Feudalism and Liberty*, p. 257. See, to the same effect, Walter Ullmann, *The Individual and Society in the Middle Ages* (Johns Hopkins University Press, 1966), p. 96 ("In general, . . . it did not need particular acumen at a later stage to envisage feudally practiced rights and duties of a member of the feudal community as natural rights and duties of the individual citizen. . . . through its becoming legalized, the feudal system had fostered the idea of individual freedoms which were protected by law.") Sovereignty doctrines may have aimed, originally, at humbling the feudal nobility, but, in allowing for a looser community than an ancient republic, they also allowed for a kind of generalization or broadening of the independent spirit of nobles. The institutions of representative government—not requiring personal involvement or personal responsibility for government—are symptomatic of the difference between modern and ancient republics. Representative assemblies, as *The Federalist* takes pain to note, were unknown in ancient republics. (See No. 9, p. 40 where medieval institutions are described as "modern" because they are not ancient.)

CHAPTER FOUR
THE ENLIGHTENMENT AND THE LAW OF NATIONS

1. James Madison, "Examination of the British Doctrine which Subjects to Capture A Neutral Trade not Open in Time of Peace," in Hunt, ed., *Writings of James Madison*, vol. 2, p. 234. Some years later, Chief Justice Marshall thanked his court reporter for supplying extracts from Grotius to elucidate cases on naval seizures on the high seas: "Old Hugo Grotius is indebted to you for your defence of him and his quotations. You have raised him in my estimation to the rank he deserves." Letter to Henry Wheaton, March 24, 1821, quoted in Wheaton, *Elements of International Law*, 6th ed. Henry (Little, Brown, 1857), p. liv.

2. Calvin DeArmond David, *The United States and the First Hague Peace Conference* (Cornell University Press, 1962), p. 166. A. D. White elaborates at some length in his memoirs, *The Autobiography of Andrew Dickson White* (Century Co., 1906), vol. 2, pp. 291, 326–32, noting also that he commissioned a portrait of Grotius (p. 320) which he subsequently donated to the Cornell Law School.

3. Quotations in the text are from the translation by Francis W. Kelsey (Clarendon Press, 1925).

4. Francisco Suarez, *Defensio fidei Catholicae et Apostolicae adversus Anglicanae sectae errores* ("Defense of the Catholic and Apostolic Faith in Refutation of the Errors of the Anglican Sect," 1613), in James Brown Scott, ed., *Selections*

from Three Works (Clarendon Press, 1944), English translation by Gwladys L. Williams, Ammi Brown, and John Waldron. On papal powers to depose kings, see book 3, ch. 23, pp. 685–704. On objections to world government, *De Leqibus, Ac Deo Legislatore*, book 3, ch. 2, pp. 374–77. *De triplici virtute theologica: De charitate*, ch. 5, pp. 825–26.

5. In the Prolegomena to *De jure* (sec. 57), Grotius protests: "I have refrained from discussing topics which belong to another subject, such as those that teach what may be advantageous in practice. For such topics have their own special field, that of politics . . . Bodin, on the contrary, mixed up politics with the body of law with which we are concerned."

6. Richard Tuck, *Natural Rights Theories* (Cambridge University Press, 1979), p. 79, emphasizes the point.

7. Michael Zuckert, *Natural Rights Republic* (Princeton University Press, 1994), ch. 4, 5.

8. Arthur Nussbaum, *Concise History of the Law of Nations* (Macmillan, 1954), p. 110.

9. Heinrich Rommen, *The Natural Law* (Liberty Fund, 1998, original edition, 1947), p. 64.

10. Richard Tuck, *Rights of War and Peace* (Oxford University Press, 1999), pp. 94–108, offers a particularly ruthless Grotius.

11. It would be more accurate to say that Grotius follows the lead of some medieval thinkers in this view. As Grotius himself notes, many earlier Christian thinkers took the opposite view—that there is no generalized power to punish wrongdoers in other places. Book 2, ch. 20, par. 4, citing the "contrary view held by Vitoria, Vazquez, Azor, Molina and others, who in justification of war seem to demand that he who undertakes it should have suffered injury either in his person or his state or that he should have jurisdiction over him who is attacked" (p. 506).

12. Should one emphasize the latitude in this right to punish or its restrictions? Richard Tuck, emphasizing the latitude, depicts Grotius as an apologist for Dutch colonial conquests and a quite ruthless approach to statecraft. According to Tuck, "Grotius endorsed for the state the most far-reaching set of rights to make war which were available in the contemporary repertoire" of philosophic arguments (*Rights of War and Peace*, p. 108). In Tuck's view, later readers have been misled by slight revisions in the text of *De jure*, which Grotius introduced in the 1631 edition, so that "a theory about minimal natural sociability, based on a general view of the role of self-interest in the natural world, appeared to later readers to be based instead on a different view, and one which was closer to traditional notions of both human sociability and divine law." Nonetheless, he notes, many readers in the seventeenth century did sense that Grotius had drifted quite far from traditional natural law views and therefore read him as not very different from Hobbes (ibid., pp. 102, 144–46). Thomas Pangle and Peter Ahrensdorf, *Justice Among Nations* (University of Kansas Press, 1999), concludes that "Grotius's primary goal was not so much to push the law of nations toward the natural law as to restore the law of nations on its ancient Roman, sound if brutal, principles. His enterprise as a whole suggests that in his eyes, the greatest problem of his epoch is that Christian fanaticism and political moralism have obscured the

ancient law of nations and as a consequence have plunged Europe into ever wider and more limitless wars of punitive indignation and crusading religious fervor" (ibid.), p. 177. Yet he also says that "if Grotius's teaching were to be arraigned as testimony for Hobbes, his witness would be inadvertant or unwilling," as there is a moral "chasm that separates him from the teaching that was to be published a few years later by Hobbes" (ibid.), p. 174. How one regards this dispute may depend, in part, on how one thinks about Hobbes.

13. Nussbaum, *Concise History*, p. 112. Grotius's acknowledgment of the rights of neutrals was what made him important for Madison's study.

14. See Tuck, *Rights of War and Peace*, pp. 106–8.

15. Neff, *Friends But No Allies*, p. 33, describes the frustration of Cornelius Bynkershoek, judge of a Dutch prize court, at the overriding of traditional claims of war by new treaties. Bynkershoek's treatise protests that "the interests of the mercantile class and the mutual needs of peoples have almost annulled the laws of war relating to commerce." *Quaestionum Juris Publici*, book 1, ch. 3, in translation by Tenney Frank (Clarendon Press, 1930), p. 30.

16. *De jure naturae et gentium*, translated by C. H. and W. A. Oldfather (Clarendon Press, 1934), book 8, ch. 5, sec. 18; ch. 6, sec. 5.

17. Ibid., book 8, ch. 6, par. 14.

18. Nussbaum, *Concise History*, p. 150.

19. Quotations in the text from the translation by Charles G. Fenwick (Carnegie Institution, 1916).

20. Nussbaum, *Concise History*, p. 163, reports that twenty-three English-language editions of Vattel had been published by the early twentieth century (thirteen of them American), compared with twenty-one editions in the original French. Vattel seems to have known his audience: The original French edition, though actually printed in the Netherlands, was presented as having been published in England.

21. John Bassett Moore, *The Principles of American Diplomacy* (Harper & Bros., revised ed., 1918), p. 23, salutes the editor, Charles William Frederick Dumas for having (apart from the American diplomats, Adams, Franklin, and Jay) "rendered services more important than any other man" in advancing the "American cause" in Europe during the revolution. He was a Swiss native who spent most of his career working in the Netherlands, where he helped arrange loans for the rebellious colonies, publicized proceedings of the Continental Congress, and wrote articles on behalf of the American cause. His edition of Vattel contained "copious notes."

22. Nussbaum, *Concise History*, p. 158.

23. Pangle is most severe: "Edifying in tone while morally indulgent in substance, apparently rigorous yet intellectually easygoing or evasive, Vattel managed to produce an amiably eclectic combination of essentially incompatible philosophies, whose profound antagonisms were hidden by a veneer of earnest or well-meaning moralism" *Justice Among Nations*, p. 178. Madison, while acknowledging Vattel's "great merit," scolds that "Vattel is, however, justly charged with failing too much in the merit of a careful discrimination; and sometimes with delivering maxims, which he either could not reconcile or does not take pains to explain" "Examination," p. 249.

24. At the end of the nineteenth century, John Westlake's highly regarded treatise, *Chapters on the Principles of International Law* (Cambridge University Press, 1894), p. 76, saluted Vattel's treatise for describing international law with unprecedented "fullness" and "from the point of view of a man well-versed in affairs. . . . Its reputation was therefore as well deserved as it was immediate, and it must remain of lasting importance in the study of international law." Fifty years later, J. L. Brierly still acknowledged Vattel as a writer who "has probably exercised a greater permanent influence than any other writer on international law and his work is still sometimes cited as an authority in international controversies." *The Law of Nations*, 4th ed. (Clarendon Press, 1949), pp. 37–38.

25. *Lectures on Jurisprudence* (Oxford University Press, 1978), pp. 548–49 (from Lecture "Report" of 1766). Smith notes that "prisoners of war are now as well treated as other people" and in the war with France, "they generally treated our wounded prisoners better than their own wounded soldiers" but "there is no nation which pushes this point of gallantry farther than we do." He attributes respect for enemy soldiers to the chivalrous impulse encouraged by the Crusades—toward fellow Christians. But respect for enemy property he sees as "more from motives of policy than humanity" since naval warfare continues to practice ruthless confiscation of enemy property. "Why this distinction? It is the interest of the general not to rob the peasants, because it would be difficult to march an army carrying all its provisions thro' the country of the enemy. But by engaging them to stay he is supplyed without any other expedient. By this means, war is so far from being a disadvantage in a well cultivated country that many get rich by it."

26. "Regulations Respecting the Law and Customs of War on Land," art. 10: "Prisoners of war may be set at liberty on parole . . . and in such cases they are bound, on their personal honor, scrupulously to fill . . . the engagements they have contracted."

27. The six months grace period for merchants to clear their stock in the event of war between the home state and the host state was included, for example, in the first American treaty, a commercial treaty with France, signed in 1778. European states sometimes allowed trade to continue through the duration of a war, even among belligerent states themselves. Neff, *Friends But No Allies*, p. 35.

28. Included as "The State of War" in Jean-Jacques Rousseau, *The Social Contract and Other Later Political Writings*, translated by Victor Gourevitch (Cambridge University Press, 1997). Extracts quoted in text appear at pp. 162–63. French original, Oèvres Completes, III, 608.

29. "The State of War," in Rousseau, *Social Contract*, pp. 162, 163.

30. Ibid., p. 163.

31. Letter to Thomas Jefferson, October 24, 1787 (explaining and justifying provisions in the proposed new constitution), Madison, *James Madison, Writings*, p. 149. Substantially the same argument appears, of course, in *The Federalist* No. 10 (though without the interesting allusion here to "theoretic writers"— presumably of special interest to Jefferson, then serving as ambassador in Paris).

32. Book IV, ch. 9 (Gourevitch, ed., p. 152). Pierre Hassner, "Rousseau and the Theory and Practice of International Relations," in Clifford Orwin and Nathan Tarcov, eds., *The Legacy of Rousseau* (University of Chicago Press, 1997) offers

a very insightful survey of the difficulties getting from the kind of state sketched in the *Social Contract* to any binding version of international law.

33. "Extrait du Projet de Paix Perpetuelle de M. L'Abbé de Saint-Pierre," pp. 365–87, and "Jugement Sur La Paix Perpetuelle," pp. 388–96, C. E. Vaughan, ed., *The Political Writings of Jean Jacques Rousseau* (John Wiley & Sons, 1962). Rousseau insists that the project is not "chimerique" and if it is not likely to be executed that is because "les hommes sont insenses, et que c'est une sort de folie d'etre sage au milieu des fous," p. 387. "Realisez sa République européenne durant un seul jour, c'en est assez pour la faire durer eternellement: tant chacun trouverait par l'experience son profit particulier dans le bien commun."

34. Madison, "Universal Peace" in *James Madison, Writings*, p. 505.

35. David Hume, "Of the Balance of Power," in Eugene Miller, ed., *Essays, Moral, Political, and Literary* (Liberty Press, 1985), pp. 337, 341.

36. "Of the Balance of Trade", ibid., p. 308, and "Of the Jealousy of Trade," in ibid., p. 327.

37. "Of the Rise and Progress of the Arts and Sciences," ibid., p. 119, original emphasis.

38. "Of Refinement in the Arts," ibid., p. 273.

39. Ibid., pp. 273, 277.

40. Reiss, *Kant's Political Writings*, p. 103.

41. Ibid., p. 114. Kant describes the pacifying effects of commerce at more length in "Idea for a Universal History," pp. 50–51.

42. Ibid., pp. 99–102. Kant gives a highly formal definition of "republican government," which does not seem to require even universal suffrage or regular elections and seems entirely compatible with an executive power vested in a hereditary monarch. For example, the Germany of Kaiser Wilhelm II, which was principally responsible for the First World War, would have satisfied Kant's definition of a "republican government" as indeed would the government of Bismarck's Prussia, which provoked and prosecuted wars with Denmark, Austria, and France within less than a decade.

43. Ibid., p. 113.

44. Ibid., p. 105: "Cosmopolitan Right . . . limited to universal hospitality." Pufendorf argues against the Spanish jurist Francisco Vitoria, who defended Spanish incursions into the New World as "natural communication": "[W]hoever wishes to lay upon others such a requirement for hospitality, ought surely be rejected as too severe an arbiter." *De jure naturae*, book 3, ch. 3, pp. 364–65.

45. To the contrary, among the "Preliminary Articles for Perpetual Peace" is a stipulation that no state should "interfere in the constitution and government of another state," Reiss, *Kant's Political Writings*, p. 96. Kant nowhere indicates that this is suspended for the wider federation in dealings with individual states.

46. Ibid., p. 104.

47. "There is only one rational way in which states coexisting with other states can emerge from the lawless condition of pure warfare. Just like individual men, they must renounce their savage and lawless freedom, adapt themselves to public coercive law, and thus form an international state which would necessarily continue to grow until it embraced all the peoples of the earth. But since this is not the will of the nations, according to their present conception of international

right . . . the positive idea of a world republic cannot be realised. If all is not to be lost, this can at best find a negative substitute in the shape of an enduring and gradually expanding federation likely to prevent war," (ibid.), p. 105. As Pangle notes, Kant's expressions of hope for ultimate peace are compatible with "quite a few world wars" along the way, since Kant acknowledges that republics may "backslide" into despotism and efforts at agreement collapse into anarchy, Pangle and Ahrensdorf, *Justice Among Nations*, p. 318, n. 85.

48. No. 51, Rossiter, ed., p. 324.

49. Madison, *James Madison, Writings*, p. 505. Madison then goes on to propose that, as a check on war, republican governments limit military expenditures to what can be financed through taxes—a proposal which is strikingly parallel to Kant's fourth "preliminary article for perpetual peace": "No national debt shall be contracted in connection with the external affairs of the state," p. 95. It may not be irrelevant that, at the time he published his own article on "Peace," Madison was a leader of the party questioning the constitutional propriety of a federal bank. As president, Madison presided over a disastrous war, for which the United States was quite unprepared. In his second term, Madison reversed his previous position and supported the rechartering of the Bank of the United States—so that the federal government could borrow money more easily.

50. Farrand, *Records*, vol. 1, p. 19: Speech of Randolph, May 29.

51. Federalist No. 2, by John Jay, is entitled "Concerning Dangers from Foreign Force and Influence." The next three papers each bear the title, "The Same Subject Continued."

52. Farrand, *Records*, vol. 2, pp. 614–15, September 14.

53. John Kaminski and Gaspare Saladino, eds., *Documentary History of the Ratification of the Constitution (DHRC)*, vol. 10 (State Historical Society of Wisconsin, 1993), p. 1388 (speech of Mr. Grayson at Virginia Ratifying Convention, June 19, 1788).

54. Ibid.

55. Ibid., p. 1384, June 18, 1788.

56. Ibid., p. 1392, speech of Francis Corbin, Virginia Ratifying Convention, June 19.

57. Ibid., pp. 1395–96.

58. *DHRC*, vol. 17 (May–September 1788), p. 346 (compilation of proposed amendments from seven states, urging, among other things, stipulations that treaties not be allowed to override state constitutions, nor to invalidate federal legislation, nor to expand the jurisdiction of the federal courts).

59. "Camillus," in H. C. Lodge, ed., *Works of Alexander Hamilton*, vol. 5 (G. P. Putnam's Sons, 1885), p. 30.

60. Joseph Story, *Commentaries on the Constitution*, vol. 3, sec. 1502 (Hilliard, Gray, 1833, reprinted by DaCapo Press, 1970), p. 356.

61. James Kent, *Commentaries on American Law*, vol. 1, 14th ed. (Little, Brown, 1896), p. 21 ("Lecture 2").

62. Ibid., pp. 2–3 ("Lecture 1").

63. *Elements of International Law*, part 1, sec. 15, par. 2; part 1, sec. 14. Originally published in London as well as Philadelphia, Wheaton's treatise was soon published in French translation (by the author) and went through several subsequent

European editions. The quoted definition appears almost word for word in Madison's "Examination," too, though without attribution in either place: it probably has a common source but I have not been able to locate it. Despite his subsequent career as an American diplomat, Wheaton's name is most familiar to American lawyers from his years as "Reporter of the Supreme Court" from 1816 to 1827—as the case reports from those years still bear his name (abbreviated in standard form citations as "Wheat").

64. H. W. Halleck, *International Law or Rules Regulating the Intercourse of States in Peace and War* (D. Van Nostrand, 1861), ch. 2, sec. 8, p. 86. At the outset of the Civil War, Halleck commissioned the first U.S. army manual on the "laws of war" and served as military commander of the Western District, directing operations of Grant and Sherman in Tennessee.

65. "Opinion on the French Treaties," April 28, 1793 (memorandum written for President Washington, while acting as Secretary of State) in Peterson, ed., *Thomas Jefferson, Writings*, p. 423.

66. "Since all Princes and Rulers of Independent Governments all through the world are in a State of Nature, 'tis plain the World never was, nor ever will be, without Numbers of Men in that State. I have named the Governors of Independent Communities, whether they are, or are not, in League with others: For 'tis not every Compact that puts an end to the State of Nature between Men, but only this one of agreeing together mutually to enter into one Community and make one Body Politick". *Second Treatise*, par. 14. Note Locke's parenthetical claim "nor ever will be," implying that a "body politic" embracing the whole world is impossible or at least extremely unlikely.

67. Krasner, *Sovereignty*, ch. 6.

68. Nussbaum, *Concise History*, p. 136.

69. Charles Fairbanks, "The British Campaign Against the Slave Trade," in Marc F. Plattner, *Human Rights in Our Time* (Westview, 1984) pp. 30–68. Fairbanks served as deputy assistant secretary of state for Human Rights in the Reagan administration and offers useful contrasts between this highly effective nineteenth-century campaign and its dismal, late twentieth-century counterparts.

CHAPTER FIVE
DIPLOMACY OF INDEPENDENCE

1. The text of the U.S. Constitution, for example, concludes with the affirmation that it was "done" in the year 1787, which it identifies as the "twelfth" year of "the independence of the United States"—dating independence to 1776, when the United States declared itself independent, rather than to 1778, when its independence was recognized by France or to 1783, when its independence was formally affirmed by Britain. The Constitution assumes a world in which the legal status of independence follows from an independent act.

2. Talleyrand, having found refuge in the United States at the height of the Teror in Paris, subsequently described "the Americans" as "devoured by pride, ambition and cupidity" and, as French foreign minister under the Directory, proposed schemes to limit American expansion. In his first years as Napoleon's foreign

minister, in the midst of efforts to "pacify Europe," Talleyrand aimed at "the creation of an empire in the New World" (that is, a new French empire) which seemed "the more sure of success because, in the reactionary spirit of the time, he commanded the sympathy of all Europe in checking the power of republicanism in it's last refuge." Henry Adams, *History of the United States During the Administrations of Thomas Jefferson* (Library of America, 1986 reprint of revised edition of 1903), pp. 240, 243. The unexpected expense involved in French efforts to "pacify Europe" then prompted a complete change in French policy toward the United States—not for the first or last time.

3. No. 11, p. 55.

4. Congress proved the point by eliminating all funding for U.S. operations in Vietnam. The tragedy that ensued may raise doubts about the wisdom of the action but only underscores the ultimate legal claim of Congress to have the last word.

5. A proposal to reduce the required ratification vote to a simple majority was voted down—with all states opposing except one. Farrand, *Records*, vol. 2, pp. 548–49. W. Stull Holt, *Treaties Defeated by the Senate* (Johns Hopkins University Press, 1933; reprinted by Peter Smith, 1964), pp. 1–13, offers a useful review of the Founding debates on the treaty power, "When the Constitution was being debated in the states, one of the most frequent complaints about its treaty-making provisions was that two-thirds of the members of the Senate present was too small a number to prevent abuse of the great power involved." Citing Jonathan Elliot, ed., *The Debates in the State Conventions on the Adoption of the Federal Constitution*, 2d. ed., revised edition (J. B. Lippincott, 1881), III, pp. 331–65, 499–516.

6. Edward S. Corwin, *The President, Office and Powers* (New York University Press, 1954), pp. 178–81, offers a useful overview of the arguments on each side.

7. "Charters" (*National Gazette*, January 19, 1792), Madison, *James Madison, Writings*, p. 504.

8. *The Federalist*, No. 22, pp. 117–18.

9. Farewell Address, James D. Richardson, ed., *A compilation of the Messages and Papers of the Presidents* (Government Printing Office, 1897), vol. 1, p. 214.

10. "Foreign Influence," *Aurora General Advertiser*, January 23, 1799, Madison, *James Madison, Writings*, p. 595.

11. Jefferson, first Inauqural Address, Richardson, *Messages and Papers*, vol. 1, p. 322.

12. See Adams, *History of the United States*, pp. 301–2, noting that had "either of Jefferson's predecessors" instructed American diplomats to negotiate such an alliance with England "the consequence would have been an impeachment of the President, or direct steps by Virgina, Kentucky and North Carolina . . . tending to a dissolution of the Union."

13. Adams, *History of the United States* p. 1014: The British raiding force "burned the Capitol, the White House, and the Department buildings because they thought it proper, as they would have burned a negro kraal or a den of pirates. Apparently they assumed as a matter of course that the American government stood beyond the pale of civilization; and in truth a government which showed so little capacity to defend its capital, could hardly wonder at whatever treatment it received."

14. James Monroe, Seventh Annual Message, December 2, 1823, Richardson, ed., *Messages and Papers*, vol. 2, p. 787.

15. Dexter Perkins, *A History of the Monroe Doctrine* (tittle, Brown, 1963, original text in 1941), reports that collaboration with Britain was definitely considered—and then definitely rejected (pp. 38–49). Perkins also notes that Monroe resisted temptations to make a moral appeal to the moral claims of republican government. Instead, as Perkins sees it, "Monroe rested his opposition to European intermeddling in Spanish America on the danger to the 'peace and safety' of the United States. In so doing, he took a strong position from both a legal and a moral view. He was basing American policy on the right of self-preservation, a right that is and always has been recognized as fundamental in international law" (p. 45).

16. Letter of Mr. Webster, secretary of state, to Mr. Hulsemann (Austrian foreign minister), December 21, 1850, reprinted in Francis Wharton, ed., *Digest of International Law of the United States* (Government Printing Office, 1886), vol. 1, pp. 188–94 (quoted passages at pp. 191–93).

17. Sixth Annual Message, December 1, 1834, Richardson, ed. *Messages and Papers*, vol. 2, p. 1326.

18. Letter to Wilson Cary Nicholas, September 7, 1803, Peterson, ed., *Thomas Jefferson, Writings*, p. 1140.

19. For example, while allowing Louisiana to draw up a civil code modeled on French practice, Jefferson insisted that it be published in English and that courts in Louisiana operate in English. George Dargo, *Jefferson's Louisiana* (Harvard University Press, 1975).

20. *Dred Scott v. Sandford*, 19 Howard 393 (1857). Andrew McLaughlin, *Constitutional History of the United States* (Appleton-Century, 1936), p. 768, pronounced it "an amusing and entertaining fact" that the Court should seek in this way to "defend the rights of freemen" in the context of a larger defense of slavery.

21. See Robert L. Beisner, *Twelve Against Empire, The Anti-Imperialists, 1898–1900* (McGraw Hill, 1968). Civil service reform champion, Carl Schurz, for example, warned that the addition of "millions of persons belonging partly to races far less good-natured, tractable and orderly than the negro is would exacerbate American race problems" and down the road the country would cease to worry about "a few thousand immigrants from Italy, Russia and Hungary" as it tried to cope with "Spanish-Americans, with all the mixture of Indian and negro blood, and Malays and other unspeakable Asiatics, by the tens of millions," p. 27. E. L. Godkin, editor of *The Nation* warned that imperial acquisitions would entail "the admission of alien, inferior, and mongrel races to our nationality" while "our population" at home remained "unassimilated," p. 76.

22. The most important case in the series was *Downes v. Bidwell*, 182 U.S. 244 (1901), approving a special tariff for Puerto Rico, despite the prohibition in Art. I, Sec. 9 against giving "any preference . . . in regulation of commerce or revenue to the ports of one state over those of another." The majority opinion found it "doubtful if Congress would ever assent to the annexation of territory upon condition that its inhabitants, however foreign they may be to our habits, traditions and modes of life, shall become at once citizens of the United States." The opinion

emphasized that past annexations, while stipulating that inhabitants of the affected territories would become citizens, had been undertaken by treaties which expressly indicated this intention (implying that it did not go without saying) and even then left the details to subsequent determination by Congress (pp. 279–80). On the other hand, it appealed to "certain principles of natural justice inherent in the Anglo-Saxon character which need no expression in constitutions or statutes to give them effect or to secure dependencies against legislation manifestly hostile to their real interests" (p. 280). A concurring opinion, endorsed by three justices, emphasized that "even in cases where there is no direct command of the Constitution which applies, there may nevertheless be restrictions of so fundamental a nature that they cannot be transgressed, although not expressed in so many words in the Constitution" (p. 291). Subsequently, in *Dorr v. U.S.*, 195 U.S. 138 (1904), the Court approved non-jury trials for the Philippines, but then held, in *Weems v. United States*, 217 U.S. 349 (1910), that extreme forms of punishment, left over from Spanish rule, could not be tolerated in the American administration of criminal justice in the islands. Alaska, by contrast, was held to be an "incorporated territory" in which the right of trial by jury could not be waived, given the status which Congress had accorded to this territory at the time of annexation (*Rassmussen v. United States*, 197 U.S. 516 [1904]). Hawaii was held not to be an "incorporated territory" so the guarantees of the Fifth and Sixth Amendments would not apply (*Hawaii v. Mankichi*, 190 U.S. 197 [1903]). The cases are not merely of antiquarian interest. Some of the issues debated in these cases would prove relevant to the complex questions raised by the holding of enemy aliens in such ambiguous settings as the U.S. naval base at Guantánamo, Cuba.

23. *Reid v. Covert*, 354 U.S. 1 (1957): The case concerned American citizens, civilian dependents of American servicemen serving on overseas bases. The reasoning does not apply to American military personnel, for whom the Constitution authorizes military justice. Foreign military personnel might also be subject to American military justice in proper circumstances. It is less clear how the ruling in the Reid case applies to civilians who are non-citizens, particularly when punished in connection with activities taking place outside U.S. territory. The Court's ruling in *U.S. v. Verdugo-Urquidez*, 494 U.S. 259 (1990) held that Fourth Amendment protections against warrantless searches and seizures do not cover foreign nationals (or their personal effects), if apprehended on foreign territory. But the ruling emphasized the initial language of the Fourth Amendment ("the right of *the people* to be secure"), so it is uncertain how far its reasoning may apply to other guarantees in the Bill of Rights.

24. The official compilation of U.S. State Department pronouncements in the late nineteenth century covers policy toward Liberia as an annex to the Monroe Doctrine: "Liberia, although not a colony of the United States, began its independent career as an off-shoot of this country . . . which relationship authorizes the United States to interpose its good offices in any contest between Liberia and a foreign state" (citing statement of Secretary Blaine in 1881). But Secretary Evarts warned that the United States had no legal obligation to "interpose" its "naval forces to preserve order or to compel obedience to law in Liberia." And he subsequently added: "Nor should the United States minister in Liberia interfere with the government thereof by obtruding political advice." Francis Wharton, *Digest*

of International Law of the United States (Government Printing Office, 1886), sec. 66, p. 445.

25. Michael Morrison, *Slavery and the American West* (University of North Carolina Press, 1997) describes debate over Texas at some length (in overview, pp. 13–38, and in succeeding chapters): Before the slavery issue arose, skeptics, like Henry Clay, focused on the danger of war with Mexico while a few New England protectionists worried about the influx of imports through Texas ports. The best argument for annexationists was that British intrigue would otherwise make future annexation impossible.

26. Until the end of the nineteenth century, no American diplomat even carried the designation of "ambassador" which was regarded as pompous and vaguely tainted by monarchy. John Bassett Moore, *Principles of American Diplomacy*, revised ed. (Harper, 1918), p. 435, American "ministers" operated from rented space. With the Foreign Service Building Act (44 Stat. 403, 1926), Congress committed the United States to a systematic program of building permanent U.S. embassies around the world. There were only sixteen permanent embassies in place at the time and only four in Europe (London, Paris, Oslo, Prague). John Mabry Mathews, *American Foreign Relations, Conduct and Policy* (Century Co., 1928), p. 292.

27. Secretary Clay's instructions, dated May 8, 1826, emphasized that the "Congress" was to be regarded only as a diplomatic body without any powers of legislation: It was not to be "an amphictyonic council, invested with power finally to decide controversies between American states or to regulate in any respect their conduct." Clay also noted that while Americans "preferred to all other forms of government . . . their own confederacy," they would allow "no foreign interference" in their own affairs, so they must be "equally scrupulous in refraining from all interference in the original structure or subsequent interior movement of the governments of other independent states," Moore, *Principles*, pp. 371, 375. Even so, congressional critics worried that the Congress "would be called upon to consider plans of international consolidation which would commit the United States to a more hazardous connection with the fortunes of other countries than was desirable," ibid., p. 376.

28. Moore, *Principles*, p. 371.

29. Ibid., p. 386.

30. Moore, *Principles*, p. 45: "Jefferson, always perspicacious in his deductions from fundamental principles, expounded with remarkable clearness and power the nature and scope of neutral duty." Moore then records the approving comments of W. E. Hall, "one of the most eminent of English publicists" at the end of the nineteenth century, who saw Jefferson's standards as generally "identical with the standard of conduct which is now adopted by the community of nations" (pp. 46–47).

31. Madison, "Examination," *James Madison, Writings*, vol. 2, p. 230.

32. But not everyone accepted that legal arguments alone could prevail. John Randolph still denounced Madison's effort as "a shilling pamphlet against eight hundred British ships of war." Adams, *History of the United States*, p. 679.

33. Madison's "Examination" concludes with the argument that British admiralty courts must not presume to judge various commercial responses to necessities

of war since such "questions" are "in their nature . . . improper to be decided by any judicial authority whatever" (pp. 389–90).

34. *The Paquete Habana*, 175 U.S. 677 (1900).

35. It was the French delay in paying the sums awarded by this arbitration that prompted President Jackson's threat to seize French property and his explanation of that threat, cited earlier in the text. When the French government protested the vehemence of Jackson's statement to Congress, the American ambassador in Paris explained that foreign governments had no right to complain about the tone which an American president might use when not addressing those governments directly but simply conveying his views to the U.S. Congress. "The President, as the chief executive power, must have a free and entirely unfettered communication with the coordinate powers of [the U.S.] Government . . . no foreign power has a right to ask for explanations of anything that the President, in the exercise of his functions, thinks proper to communicate to Congress, or of any course he may advise them to pursue . . . the right [of foreign governments to complain about such internal presidential statements] will never be acknowledged and any attempt to enforce it will be repelled by the undivided energy of the nation." Letter of Mr. Livingston to the Duke de Broglie, April 25, 1835. Reprinted in Richardson, ed., *Messages and Papers*, vol. 2, pp. 1397–1403 (quoted passages at pp. 1397–398).

36. Arbitration of the Maine border was provided in the Treaty of Ghent, ending the War of 1812. The question was submitted to the king of the Netherlands as a neutral arbitrator. The king proposed a boundary. The Senate rejected the recommendation, on the grounds that the king had exercised discretion to propose an equitable compromise. The arbitration agreement, as the Senate conceived it, had not authorized proposals for compromise but had sought a judgment on the merits, given the available evidence. Direct negotiations between the United States and Britain ultimately secured mutual agreement, in 1842, on boundary lines—less favorable to the United States, as it turned out, than those proposed by the king. The Senate may not have foreseen this outcome, but its rejection of the initial arbitration result reflected characteristic concerns: the Senate did not want to entrust broad discretion to third parties.

37. "To vest in an outside commission the power to say finally what the treaty means by its very general and indefinite language is to vest in that commission the power to make for us an entirely different treaty from that which we supposed ourselves to be making." S. Doc. 98, p. 6, *Congressional Record* 47: 3935 (1911), quoted in Wright, *Control*, p. 111.

38. On these early efforts, Calvin DeArmond Davis, *The United States and First Hague Peace Conference* (Cornell University Press, 1962), pp. 29–35.

39. The reasons for American skepticism are instructive. The State Department instructions to the American delegates explained the American cautions as follows: "It is doubtful if wars are to be diminished by rendering them less destructive, for it is the plain lesson of history that the periods of peace have been longer protracted as the cost and destructiveness of war have increased. The expediency of restraining the inventive genius of our people in the direction of devising means of defense is by no means clear and considering the temptations to which men and nations may be exposed in a time of conflict, it is doubtful if an international agreement to this end would prove effective" (ibid., p. 79).

40. Moore, *Principles*, p. 64, which dismisses the constitutional argument as groundless, though symptomatic of American wariness.

41. *The Autobiography of Andrew Dickson White* (Century Co, 1906), vol. 2, pp. 352–53.

42. Calvin DeArmond Davis, *The United States and the Second Hague Peace Conference* (Duke University Press, 1975), pp. 354–57, on Wilson's distaste for the prewar traditions of the Hague Peace Conference: Wilson remarked to close associates that the Hague conferences "blazed a trail . . . but it ended in fog overhead and in bog underfoot. The whole business was wish-washy—though well-meant, of course. . . . Now we are met here for hard-and-fast agreements, for binding stipulations, for commitments, and it is my task to see that no nation or group of men holds out on us" (ibid., p. 355). Conversely, "nearly all members of the Senate went on record as advocating some international organization. A periodic conference and a permanent court would have been enough. The League with its quasi-legislative bodies was a far more elaborate organization than they wished" (ibid., p. 356). As Lloyd E. Ambrosius says (*Woodrow Wilson and the American Displomatic Tradition* [Cambridge University Press, 1987], p. 119), Wilson was specifically attracted to Geneva's traditions, through Calvin and Scottish "covenenters"—and it was Wilson who chose the name "Covenant" for the treaty provisions organizing the League.

43. Ambrosius, *Woodrow Wilson*, p. 4, notes that in Woodrow Wilson, *Constitutional Government of the United States* (Columbia University Press, 1908), pp. 77–78, Wilson had said that when the president negotiates a treaty, the United States is "virtually committed" and the Senate would have no practical alternative but ratification, so "One of the President's greatest powers is control, which is very absolute, of the foreign relations of the nation." It required a great deal of inattention to make this claim in 1908.

44. F. P. Walters, *A History of the League of Nations* (Oxford University Press, 1952), vol. 1, p. 259 (on response to inquiry from Canada).

45. On the French treaty, Elihu Root cautioned Lodge, "it seems to me that it is desirable to accompany the opposition which you are making to the vague and indefinite commitments of the League Covenant with an exhibition of willingness to do the definite specific things which are a proper part of true American policy, and which are necessary to secure the results of the War upon which America has expended so much life and treasure." Lodge agreed: "I am in favor of the French treaty . . ." But another Republican senator noted, "Wilson is doing nothing whatever to urge the Senate to pass the French-American Treaty which he promised to France" because he preferred to keep French pressure on Republicans to approve the League. Lodge subsequently blamed Wilson for not supporting the French treaty: "The treaty has received no support from the President and I have not even been able to find out whether he would allow the Democrats to vote for it." Ambrosius, *Woodrow Wilson*, pp. 212–14.

46. Robert H. Ferrell, *American Diplomacy, A History*, revised ed. (W. W. Norton, 1969), pp. 565–68 (noting Kellogg's recognition of the "justly admired axiom of diplomacy . . . that the more signatories to an agreement the less binding it becomes").

47. Gaddis Smith, *The Last Years of the Monroe Doctrine* (Hill and Wang, 1994), p. 33.

48. The first proposed amendment to the League, offered by the Senate Foreign Relations Committee, would "so amend the text as to secure a vote in the assembly of the league equal to that of any other power." The Committee explained: "If other countries like the present arrangement, that is not our affair; but the Committee failed to see why the United States should have but one vote in the assembly of the league when the British Empire has six." The complaint was not quite so silly as it now seems. Canada, Australia, South Africa, and New Zealand had all been dragged into the European war in 1914 because existing arrangements left the British government with constitutional authority to declare war on their behalf. India, which was not even self-governing in domestic affairs, was admitted to the League as an independent member. Still, it is telling that as late as 1919, Republican senators were not willing to assume that Britain and the United States would generally be taking the same positions in international councils. On concern over dominions—when release of a letter to the Canadian prime minister from Wilson, Clemenceau, and Lloyd George, acknowledged that dominions could sit on the Council as well as in the Assembly, see Ambrosius, *Woodrow Wilson*, pp. 194–95.

49. Speech in the Senate, August 12, 1919, reprinted in H. C. Lodge, *The Senate and the League of Nations* (Scribners, 1924), pp. 390–91. Of course, it turned out to be rather important who ruled the Hedjaz when the Wahabis won the internal fighting, established a new kingdom of Saudi Arabia and then found themselves sitting on the world's largest reserves of petroleum. But there are still questions about whether American troops should be committed to the defense of the ruling dynasty there.

50. Speech on the League of Nations, delivered in the U.S. Senate, 1919, reprinted by Bobbs-Merrill, pp. 30, 36. Borah also derided the supposed protection from the provision requiring unanimous consent among League members for any decision: "Has not every division and dismemberment of every nation which has suffered dismemberment taken place by unanimous consent for the last three hundred years? Did not Prussia and Austria and Russia by unanimous consent divide Poland? Did not the United States and Great Britain and Japan and Italy and France divide China and give Shantung to Japan? Was that not a unanimous decision? Close the doors on the diplomats of Europe, let them sit in secret, give them the material to trade on, and there always will be unanimous consent. . . . Mr. President, if you have enough territory, if you have enough material, if you have enough subject peoples to trade upon and divide, there will be no difficulty about unanimous consent" (ibid., pp. 10–11).

51. Lasa Oppenheim, *The League of Nations and Its Problems* (Longmans, Green and Co., 1919), pp. 13, 21.

52. Ibid., pp. 22–23.

53. Oppenheim expressed a certain optimism on this score, characterizing the World War as "at bottom . . . a fight between the ideal of democracy and constitutional government, on the one hand, and autocratic government and militarism on the other." A League established by the victors would, naturally, be dominated

by nations holding to the "ideal of democracy and constitutional government." But he did not think these could be conditions for membership.

54. Lodge, Speech, p. 394; Reservation 3, reprinted in *Senate and the League*, p. 174.

55. Moore, *Principles*, pp. 407–8, offers nearly contemporaneous reactions from a former State Department legal advisor (and acting secretary) who was highly skeptical: "opening the door to constant foreign intrusions into internal affairs."

56. Pitman Potter, "Inhibitions upon the Treaty-Making Power of the United States," *American Journal of International Law*, vol. 28 (July 1934), p. 456, reports the objection of the American delegates, H. M. Robinson and Samuel Gompers, including the concern that to "permit a foreign body to conclude a treaty binding upon the United States would be equivalent to delegating the power of making treaties in the measure of the provisions of the treaty in question."

57. The concern about the impact of "mere advisory opinions" was mocked at the time by foreign critics and subsequent historians. For example, C. Howard-Ellis, *The Origin, Structure and Working of the League of Nations* (George Allen & Unwin, 1928), p. 392, attributed U.S. refusal to participate in the League's Court of Justice to a "peculiar derived sense of politics" in America "especially in the phrase 'European politics and diplomacy,' the words convey a shuddering sense of tattered and whiskered foreigners stealthily conferring in corners on how to put one over on pure-hearted, rich and guileless Uncle Sam." The book does offer a useful survey of British legal scholars on the status of advisory opinions, some of whom expressed sympathy for U.S. concerns (pp. 396–404). Eighty years later, even European states voted against the resolution of the UN General Assembly in December 2003, seeking an "advisory opinion" from the International Court of Justice on Israel's security fence, on the understanding that even an "advisory opinion" could exacerbate regional tensions and prove an obstacle to peace negotiations.

58. Denna Frank Fleming, *The United States and the World Court* (Russell & Russell, revised ed., 1968), pp. 52–67 (failure of Hughes efforts), pp. 117–37 (FDR's failure in 1935).

59. See Stephen C. Neff, *The Rights and Duties of Neutrals* (Manchester University Press, 2000), pp. 188–90, on replacement of "non-belligerency" for "neutrality" in American policy after 1939, with such measures as amendment of neutrality legislation to authorize discriminatory arms embargoes (helping one side only).

For contemporary criticism, see Edwin Borchard, "The Attorney General's Opinion on Exchange of Destroyers for Naval Bases," *American Journal of International Law*, vol. 34 (October 1940), pp. 690–97; and Borchard, "War, Neutrality and Non-Belligerency," *American Journal of International Law*, vol. 35 (October 1941), pp. 618–25.

60. Ruth B. Russell, *A History of the United Nations Charter* (Brookings Institution, 1958), ch. 9, 10.

61. Smith, *The Last Years of the Monroe Doctrine*, pp. 40–55.

62. Reservation 3 reserved to "the United States itself exclusively the right to

decide what questions are within its domestic jurisdiction" and insisted that the United States could not be obliged to submit such questions to "arbitration."

63. But skeptics warned at the time that ratification of the Charter must not be understood as delegating presidential war powers to the Security Council, since such delegation would be unconstitutional: Edwin Borchard, "The Charter and the Constitution," *American Journal of International Law*, vol. 39 (October 1945), p. 767. The article notes that wartime pronouncements had insisted that an international peacekeeping forum would not extend into internal political matters: "The policy of non-intervention in other peoples' affairs is and must be the first principle of sound doctrine. Unless this is the settled practice of nations, there can be no principle of sovereign equality among peace-loving states and probably no permanent peace at all." (Department of State Bulletin, November 27, 1943, p. 386).

64. Fleming, *United States and the World Court*, p. 195.

65. Smith, *Last Years of Monroe Doctrine*, pp. 35–64, notes the impulse to mobilize support in Latin America against Soviet threats at the outset of the Cold War was closely paralleled by prewar mobilization against German and Japanese threats. In both eras, the first impulse was to rally nations in the U.S. neighborhood, rather than in Europe—because there was more support for this approach in Congress, as it was more in keeping with traditional U.S. policy. Stephen C. Schlesinger, *Act of Creation, The Founding of the United Nations* (Westview Press, 2003) reports that leading countries in Latin America also insisted that the Charter of the United Nations must allow U.S. regional security guarantees to operate independently of outside—that is, European, especially Russian—preferences (pp. 65–66, 175–91).

66. Sec. 8(a): "Authority to introduce United States Armed Forces into hostilities or into situations wherein involvement in hostilities is clearly indicated by the circumstances shall not be inferred . . . (2) from any treaty heretofore or hereafter ratified unless such treaty is implemented by legislation specifically authorizing the introduction of United States Forces into hostilities," 87 Stat. 555 (1973), 50 U.S.C. sec. 1548.

67. Louis Fisher, *Presidential War Power* (University of Kansas Press, 1995), ch. 7.

68. *Restatement of the Law of Foreign Relations of the United States* (Second) (American Law Institute, 1965), sec. 120, Reporters Note, p. 378. Court precedents on congressional power in domestic affairs "suggest that Congress can authorize the President to make an executive agreement relating to any matter of international concern."

69. Bruce Ackerman and David Golove, "Is NAFTA Constitutional?" *Harvard Law Review*, vol. 108 (1995), p. 801.

70. George Reedy, quoted in Robert Caro, *The Years of Lyndon Johnson, Master of the Senate* (Knopf, 2002), p. 529.

71. See Natalie H. Kaufman, *Human Rights Treaties and the Senate: A History of Opposition* (University of North Carolina Press, 1990).

72. Among the proponents of this amendment were leaders of the American Bar Association and leading scholars of international law. See George Finch, "The Need to Restrain the Treaty Making Power of the United States Within

Constitutional Limits," *American Journal of International Law*, vol. 48 (January, 1954), p. 57. Finch was a former editor of the *AJIL*. See also, Frank Holman, *The Year of Victory* (Argus Press, 1955), p. 4, warning against proposals to "use the United Nations and the treaty process as a lawmaking process to change the domestic laws and even the Government of the United States . . . along socialistic lines." Holman was a past president of the American Bar Association and a former law school dean. A recent book on international human rights characterizes proponents of the Bricker amendment as "Nationalists" who "championed the supremacy of the U.S. Constitution compared with treaty law"—evidently on the supposition that human rights advocates (or non-"Nationalists") would favor the subordination of the Constitution to treaty law. David Forsythe, *Human Rights in International Relations*, p. 42.

73. Louis Henkin, "U.S. Ratification of Human Rights Conventions: The Ghost of Senator Bricker," *American Journal of International Law*, vol. 89 (April 1995), p. 341, complains about the result.

74. *BNA Trade Reporter*, June 2002.

75. See, as a notable example, *Printz v. United States*, 521 U.S. 898 (1997), where the majority opinion spars with dissenters over the correct interpretation of Madison's argument in *The Federalist*, No. 44—and not as pedantic embellishment in footnotes but as a central point in the argument on each side.

CHAPTER SIX
A WORLD SAFE FOR EUROGOVERNANCE

1. The phrase seems to have been popularized by the philosopher Jürgen Habermas (see, for example, "Toward a Cosmopolitan Europe," *Journal of Democracy*, vol. 14 (October 2003), p. 99, but has been invoked in numerous speeches by the German foreign minister.

2. See Marlene Wind, *Sovereignty and European Integration* (Palgrave, 2001) for extensive discussion of implications for international relations of the European experience, with extensive bibliography of recent literature.

3. The term is not restricted to critics. See, e.g, the rather sympathetic explanation of the practice in L. Neville Brown and Tom Kennedy, *The Court of Justice of the European Communities*, 4th ed. (Sweet & Maxwell, 1994), pp. 308–11, noting the "dynamic character of the Treaties as laying down programmes for the future" means that "it is not the function of the Court to rediscover the intention of the parties in the manner which is traditional for interpreting treaties in international law." As one ECJ justice put it: "It is useless to look at such pointers [in the records of the treaty negotiations or in parliamentary ratification debates] . . . interpretations based on the original situation would in no way be in keeping with a Community law oriented towards the future." H. Kutscher, "Methods of Interpretation as Seen by a Judge of the Court of Justice," *Judicial and Academic Conference, September 27–28 1976*, vol. 1 (1976).

4. The classic account is J.H.H. Weiler, "The Transformation of Europe," *Yale Law Journal*, vol. 100 (June 1991), emphasizing "constitutionalization" of the original treaty by independent action of the ECJ.

5. It was not unusual for international treaties to be invoked by private litigants in national courts—but in such cases the treaty would, of course, be interpreted according to the understanding of national courts. Nor was it unusual for disputes between governments to be submitted to international arbitration—but in such cases, an international tribunal would merely pronounce on the international obligations of the government involved, without creating rights or duties for individuals that could be enforced in domestic courts. What was unprecedented was the potent combination of these practices, allowing a private individual to invoke, in national courts, the interpretations rendered by an international tribunal. What made it particularly potent, as it turned out, was the readiness of national courts to accept and implement ECJ doctrine in subsequent cases.

6. ECJ Case 6/64 [1964], ECR 585, CMLR 425. The ECJ announced the doctrine in this case, but did not insist on applying it: In allowing Italian courts to find that the law could, after all, be consistent with the Rome treaty in the circumstances of this case, the ECJ avoided a direct confrontation over the supremacy of European law. In proclaiming the authority to override national statutes, the ruling invited comparison with the U.S. Supreme Court's celebrated decision in *Marbury v. Madison* (proclaiming judicial authority to treat congressional enactments as invalid)—and it insulated its ruling from resistance with the same evasive tactic employed by the *Marbury* court (which used the doctrine of judicial review in such a way as to avoid deciding Marbury's claim on the merits, giving Secretary of State Madison no direct way to repudiate the ruling). Constitutional review of legislation was a new practice in Europe in the 1960s. Judges at the ECJ seem to have taken notice of how the practice was built up elsewhere—while ignoring the ends to which it was devoted in the United States.

7. *Cassis de Dijon/Rewe Zentral*, Case 120/78, ECR 649. Wind, *Sovereignty and Integration*, pp. 172–73, offers a useful summary of the policy consequences.

8. David Vogel, *Trading Up: Consumer and Environmental Regulation in a Global Economy* (Harvard University Press, 1995).

9. *Van Colson* (1984), on reinterpreting national law to conform with directives; *Marleasing* (1990) authorizing national courts to rewrite national law for this purpose; *Francovich* (1991) on financial awards to parties injured by lack of implementing legislation. The implications of these rulings are helpfully described in Alec Stone Sweet, *Governing with Judges: Constitutional Politics in Europe* (Oxford University Press, 2000), pp. 163–64.

10. *Internationale Handelsgesellschaft mbH v. Einführ-und Vorratsstelle fur Getreide und Futtermittel*, ECJ Case 11/70, ECR 1125.

11. Leslie Friedman Goldstein, *Constituting Federal Sovereignty: The European Union in Comparative Context* (Johns Hopkins University Press, 2001), p. 150, characterizing "open member-state defiance of either ECJ legitimacy or ECJ policies as remarkably rare" which she finds, by comparison to other and older federal systems, to have a "direct correlation" with "the degree to which" modern European society has "internalized the rule of law" (ibid.), p. 158. Among other oddities, Professor Goldstein's analysis assumes that France, for example, even in the first decade of the Fifth Republic—following four previous republics, two monarchies and two empires, all in less than two centuries—had developed much more respect for constitutional order than the early United

States, which just happened to maintain unbroken constitutional continuity (even with the extraordinary challenge of the Civil War). It makes it hard to understand why, if Americans had so little respect for the rule of law in early times, judges and common law standards provided so much of day-to-day government, while France has always required a very extensive administrative and policing apparatus.

12. James L. Gibson and Gregory Caldeira, "Legitimacy of Transnational Legal Institutions," *American Journal of Political Science*, vol. 39 (May 1995), p. 459: "The European Court of Justice does not have an extensive store of good will among ordinary citizens of the European Union. Few people are willing to accept a Court of Justice decision they find objectionable." Similarly, Gregory Caldeira and James L. Gibson, "The Legitimacy of the Court of Justice in the European Union, *American Political Science Review*, vol. 89 (June 1995).

13. Brown and Kennedy, *Court of Justice*, p. 260: "Dissenting judgments cannot be permitted." The authors (one of whom heads the ECJ's "Information Office") are rhapsodic about the benefits: "Undoubtedly, the great advantage of the single, collegiate judgment is to enhance [the Court's] authority. Whatever the hidden reservations or concealed dissents, the judgment moves, syllogistically, to its logical conclusion, to which the appearance of single-mindedness then attaches greater legal certainty . . . the need to prolong deliberation to secure . . . a collegiate judgment . . . helps to produce an agreement (or compromise) which is truly communautaire, that is, one in which all the judges, with their differing viewpoints, bring forward and blend together in the eventual judgment various elements from all the national legal systems" (ibid.), p. 297. While presentations by counsel may be made in any one of the languages of the member states (with simultaneous translation provided for judges), actual deliberations of the judges, among themselves, are in French (ibid., p. 260) which may mean that, in practice, some contributions to this "blending" are less eloquently advanced than others. But the less effective judicial advocates have this consolation: "The absence of individual judgments has also the advantage of not identifying a particular judge with a particular decision. To this extent it is made easier for the Court as a whole to adopt a new departure in its case-law" (ibid.), p. 297.

14. Even the International Court of Justice in the Hague, not exactly a court of towering moral authority, allows its judges to publish dissenting or concurring opinions. Outside ecclesiastical precincts, there are not many examples of courts demanding total submission to the collegiate voice. One of the ECJ's own Advocates General (who act as official legal advisors to the Court) suggested in 1992 "that the time might soon come, with the growing maturity of the Community legal order, when dissenting opinions might be admitted" (ibid., p. 260, quoting Advocate General Sir Gordon Slynn of the UK). More than a decade later, however, the EU's "legal order" has still not attained sufficient "maturity" to accomodate open expressions of dissent by the ECJ.

15. "Snoring while an EU Superstate Emerges?" *The Economist*, May 10, 2003.

16. Roger Scully, "Democracy, Legitimacy and the European Parliament," in Maria Green Cowles and Michael Smith, *The State of the European Union*, vol. 5 (Oxford University Press, 2000); Simon Hix, "Executive Selection in the European

Union," in Karnheinz Neunreither and Antje Wiener, *European Integration after Amsterdam* (Oxford University Press, 2000).

17. James A. Caporaso, "The European Union and Forms of State: West-phalian, Regulatory or Post-Modern?" *Journal of Common Market Studies*, vol. 34 (March 1966), arguing for the last alternative. For one of the few serious efforts to relate the characterization to actual themes in literary theory and social philosophy, see Ian Ward, "The European Union and Post-modernism," in Jo Shaw and Gillian More, *New Legal Dynamics of European Union* (Clarendon Press, 1995).

18. The most exhaustive version of the argument is Andrew Moravcsik, *The Choice for Europe* (Cornell University Press, 1998).

19. Thomas Pedersen, *Germany, France and the Integration of Europe, A Realist Interpretation* (Pinter, 1998).

20. Larry Siedentop, *Democracy in Europe* (Columbia University Press, 2001), p. 221.

21. Vogel, *Trading Up*, p. 97.

22. Bernard Connolly, *The Rotten Heart of Europe* (Faber and Faber, 1995).

23. The product of the "constitutional convention" was entitled—with characteristic ambiguity—a "Treaty Establishing a Constitution for Europe." It was submitted to the Rome meeting of EU heads of state on July 18, 2003 and subsequently made available on the website of the European Commission. Citations in the text are to this document.

24. Ulrich Sedelmeier, "Eastern Enlargement: Risk, Rationality and Role Compliance," in Cowles and Smith, eds., *State of the European Union 2000*, arguing that enlargement has been driven by the self-understanding of the EU as a transnational entity, rather than by definite calculations of advantage by existing member states.

25. Fritz Machlup, *A History of Thought on Economic Integration* (Columbia University Press, 1977), p. 11.

26. Alan Milward, *The European Rescue of the Nation State* (Routledge, 1999).

27. A narrative of the episode, with relevant documents, is provided in Ronald Tiersky, ed., *Euro-skepticism* (Rowman & Littlefield, 2001), pp. 213–25.

28. *Brogan v. United Kingdom*, November 24, 1988, 11 E.H.R.R. 117 (disallowing detention of terror suspects without charge for up to for seven days, rather than the usual two days for other suspects); *Fox, Campbell and Hartley v. United Kingdom*, August 20, 1990, 13 E.H.R.R. 157 (disallowing detention for questioning of suspects previously convicted of terror crimes, when not subsequently charged); *Brannigan v. United Kingdom*, May 26, 1993, 17 E.H.R.R. 594 (disallowing UK's invocation of exemption from the Convention under art. 15 provision for "measures derogating from its obligations" in time of "public emergency," on the grounds that continuing terror attacks in northern Ireland did not qualify as a "public emergency"); *Open Door Counseling and Dublin Women v. Ireland*, October 29, 1992, 15 E.H.R.R. 143 (nullifying Irish law against advertising of abortion services in neighboring countries); *Norris v. Ireland*, October 26, 1988, 13 E.H.R.R. 186 (nullifying Irish laws against homosexual relations); *Lustig-Prean & Beckett v. United Kingdom*, September 27,

1999 (nullifying exclusion of homosexuals from British military services); *Sutherland v. United Kingdom*, 22 E.H.R.R. 22 (1996) (objecting to British law allowing homosexual relations from the age of eighteen while legalizing heterosexual encounters from age sixteen, as denial of equal rights to homosexuals).

29. Ronald Inglehart, co-founder of the Euro-barometer surveys, organized an elaborate world survey of political attitudes in the early 1990s, testing (among other things) support for environmental protection, even when stipulated to impose substantial economic burdens. Italy, France, Belgium—along with less affluent Spain, Portugal, and Ireland—ranked near the bottom in this forty-three nation survey, while the Netherlands and Scandinavian countries were at the top, closely followed by Germany. As a proportion of the national respondents, "high" levels of support for environmental protection were twice as prevalent in the latter countries (at 60 percent) as in the six Catholic countries. "Public Support for Environmental Protection," *PS: Political Science & Politics*, vol. 28 (March 1995), p. 61.

30. Justin Greenwood, *Representing Interests in the European Union* (Macmillan, 1997), p. 181, which concludes, from a survey of specialized studies of EU environmental policy that "of the main influences, economic motives seem to [be] . . . the most important" p. 183.

31. Ibid., p. 186.

32. Greenpeace does not publish detailed accounts of its revenue sources, but does indicate country of origin for donations: more than half its funding in the 1990s came from Germany and Scandinavia.

33. "Parties to Basel Convention Adopt Two-List System for Waste Export," *BNA Environmental Reporter*, March 4, 1998, p. 185, noting that the decision was strongly supported by Greenpeace International, which took the same position as the European governments.

34. Joseph Jupile, "The European Union and International Outcomes," *International Organization*, vol. 53 (Spring 1999), p. 409, shows that interpretation of the original Basel convention became much more aggressive in the mid-1990s, after negotiations among "the parties" (at the time, thirty-five states) were coordinated by the EU (controlling nearly half the votes, as European parties were required to hold to a common EU position).

35. UNDP, *Human Development Report 2001: Making New Technologies Work for Human Development* (Oxford University Press, 2001). Lomborg, *Skeptical Environmentalist*, pp. 342–48, provides a useful overview of the debate.

36. Rick Weiss, "Starved for Food, Zimbabwe Rejects U.S. Biotech Corn," *Washington Post*, July 31, 2002; Elizabeth Neuffner, "Hungry Nations Balk at Gene-Altered Food," *Boston Globe*, August 23, 2002.

37. William Nordhaus, "Costs of Kyoto," *Science*, November 9, 2001.

38. Calculated from figures for 1996 reported in *World Development Report 2000/2001* (published for the World Bank, by Oxford University Press, 2001), Table 10, pp. 292–93. On the eve of the Kyoto conference, Chinese carbon emissions, per capita, were only 14 percent of U.S. emissions. At the time, electric power consumption in China was, on a per capita basis, 6 percent of that in the United States (*2001 World Development Indicators*, World Bank, 2001, pp. 302–4). At that time, the United States had one passenger car for every two people, while China had one car for every 250 people. Figures for 1996 in B. Turner,

ed., *The World Today, 2000* (St. Martins, 2000), p. 187. Meanwhile, China claimed to be operating very close to American levels of energy efficiency (measured by GDP per unit of energy use), so that increasing output without somewhat comparable increases in energy use—and carbon emissions—did not seem likely. *World Development Report, 2000/2001*, Table 10 (1997 figures).

39. Calculated from figures for 1998 in *2001 World Development Indicators*, Table 5.9, pp. 302–4.

40. Ann M. Florini, "Lessons Learned" in Ann M. Florini, ed., *The Third Force, The Rise of Transnational Civil Society* (Carnegie Endowment for International Peace, 2000), p. 229, reports, for example, that the Climate Action Network, one of the most prominent cheerleaders for Kyoto, "owes its origins in significant part" to funding from a German government fund and concludes that the future of such advocacy "will depend in part on the continued willingness of Northern governments and foundations to provide the money" for their activity. "Northern" in this context means governments in western Europe and Canada, assisted by private foundations in the United States.

41. In a press release issued September 16, 2002, Friends of the Earth-Europe called on the European Commission to impose special duties on U.S. goods which were produced with energy-intensive production methods, arguing that such tariffs would be a legal and proper penalty for U.S. failure to ratify the Kyoto Protocol: "The US rejection of the Kyoto Protocol is unfair and puts European business at a disadvantage. With Bush's increasing rejection of international agreements that are essential to protect our environment, Europe should have every right to penalise US goods for the pollution they cause." The statement can be found at <http://www.foeeurope.org/press/AW_16_09_02_SMOsynergy.htm>.

42. A 1992 resolution of the European Parliament (A3-0329/92) called for protective duties against "environmental dumping" by countries which did not conform to international environmental standards. By 1998, MEPs were urging bans on "cheap imports from countries enforcing lower animal welfare standards than the EU." "WTO Rules Must Not Thwart Environment Agreements," *Europe Environment*, No. 524, June 9, 1998.

43. Stanley Hoffmann, *Decline or Renewal: France since the 1930s* (Viking, 1974), p. 72: "Let us remember that the unity movement in Europe was an attempt to create a regional entity, that its origins and dynamics resembled, on the reduced scale of a half-continent, the process Kant dreamed up in his *Idea of a Universal History*." This characterization of the "spirit" of European integration is all the more striking because the actual provisions of the actual Treaty of Rome are so removed from any actual proposals published by Kant. Kant's hopes for a peace federation might be better associated with NATO, in which national militaries in Europe were subordinated to a common command—except the command being American, it had already been repudiated by France.

44. "Europe's Political Architecture," Speech to the Global Panel in The Hague, May 15, 1992, reprinted as Appendix I in Margaret Thatcher, *The Path to Power* (Harper Collins, 1995), quoted passages at p. 614.

45. Original statement, in German, published June 6, 2003 in *FAZ*, with accompanying introductory text by Derrida. English translation by Ludwig von Tranzivan.

46. "Gegen Volkermord und Diktatur," *Berliner Zeitung*, April 12, 2002.

47. "Council Common Position of 20 June 2002," 2002/474/CFSP. The Commission's "action plan to follow-up on the common position" was released—in advance of the Council's action—on May 15, 2002.

48. UN Charter, art. 103: "In the event of a conflict between the obligations of the Members of the United Nations under the present Charter and their obligations under any international agreement, their obligations under the present Charter shall prevail." Only the Security Council was authorized, under the Charter, to impose directly binding "obligations."

49. Henry Kissinger, *Years of Upheaval* (Little, Brown, 1982), p. 708. Kissinger complains that European governments "assumed that we had the power to force Israel to do our bidding; if we hesitated, it must be because we were willing to subordinate European interests to our domestic pressures" (p. 717). In Kissinger's perception, the main opposition to U.S. policy—seeking to resist Soviet-backed clients in the region—was "led by France" while "the Benelux countries, Denmark, Italy were . . . not inclined to challenge our policies on the Middle East. . . . But they also prized the newfound Community political institutions, which put a premium on the appearance of monolithic cohesion. The EC seemed to find political consensus by one of two methods: either a lowest common denominator of vacuity or vagueness, or any policy advocated passionately by one partner that the others who felt less strongly (or might even disagree with mildly) considered themselves obligated to support for the sake of European unity" (p. 731). The EC thus proceeded to launch a "European-Arab dialogue" without consulting the U.S. on its strategic aims (p. 729).

50. The Irish diplomat, Conor Cruise O'Brien noted a few years later that the EEC's "Venice Declaration" was rejected by the PLO as well as by Israel and therefore could not be regarded as much of "a contribution to a comprehensive peace," but European leaders "will not have been disappointed with the results of their efforts" if the Declaration "goes down reasonably well in Riyadh and the Gulf capitals" (that is, in the principal oil-exporting centers). *The Siege* (Simon & Schuster, 1986), pp. 598–99.

51. Fiona Symon, "Europe's Growing Mideast Role," *EU Observer*, February 7, 2002, reports aid of $900 million between 1996 and 2002, more than half of all international aid to the Palestinian Authority.

52. Forsythe, *Human Rights in International Relations*, p. 169.

53. Art. 8, defining "war crimes" includes (par. 2.b.viii) "The transfer, directly or indirectly, by the Occupying Power of parts of its own civilian population into the territory it occupies." The 1949 Geneva Convention on the Protection of Civilians had admonished that an occupying power should not "deport or transfer parts of its own population" into occupied territory (art. 49)—implying coercive resettlement and did not, in any case, include this offense among the "grave breaches" requiring criminal prosecution. The tightening of the provision at the Rome conference was made on the urging of Arab delegations, with support from European states.

54. On continuing friction over German claims for rescinding postwar decrees restricting German settlement in the Sudetenland and in former Prussian territory claimed by Poland in 1945, see "A Spectre Over Central Europe," *The Economist*,

August 17, 2002 ("The Czechs like the Poles . . . feel those who began an appalling war have no claim to revise its effects" but Austrian as well as German politicians are "not willing to draw a line under the past"—that is to relinquish German claims to equal treatment.) German efforts to build a memorial center to recognize the sufferings of Germans in Polish and Czech territory in 1945 added new strains. Bertrand Benoit and Jan Cienski, "Germans and Poles Rake Over Wartime Ashes," *Financial Times* (UK), October 17, 2003.

55. Ian Black, "Patten Faces Battle Over EU Funds for Palestinians," *The Guardian* (UK), February 5, 2003; Ambrose Evans-Pritchard, "Patten 'Blocking Inquiry' into Cash for Arafat," *Daily Telegraph* (UK), February 5, 2003. Patten's defense: "EU Funding to the PA: Commissioner Patten Responds," *europa*, 6 February 2003 (claiming EU funding was monitored by the IMF—which subsequently disclaimed any capacity to monitor PA expenditures). Nearly a year later, the EU's anti-fraud unit was reported to be undertaking an investigation into the diversion of EU funds to terror groups—but only after Belgian police had launched their own investigations. Leonard Doyle, "EU Fraud Office Investigates Aid Diversion to Bombers," *The Independent* (UK), November 27, 2003.

56. Res. 2002/8 of the Human Rights Commission affirmed "the legitimate rights of the Palestinian people to resist Israeli occupation" and in support of this affirmation, invoked a 1982 UN General Assembly resolution on "the legitimacy of the struggle of peoples against foreign occupation" which endorsed "all means of armed struggle." Since there was no word of condemnation against suicide bombings of civilians—and virtually all the bombings had been directed at civilians—the inevitable implication was that the Commission endorsed suicide bombings of Israeli civilians. Both Germany and the United Kingdom cited this implication in explaining their opposition to the resolution.

57. Ian Black, "EU Hits out at Israeli Fence," *The Guardian* (UK), November 18, 2003 (reporting EU protest at refusal of Israel to meet with the EU's official representative to the Mideast, Marc Otte).

58. Janine Zacharia, "Palestinians Support Armed Struggle Even After Statehood-poll," *Jerusalem Post*, October 22, 2003, reports 59 percent of Palestinians believe that Hamas and Palestinian Islamic Jihad should continue their armed struggle against Israel, even if Israel leaves all of the West Bank and Gaza, including East Jerusalem, and a Palestinian state is created.

59. Ambrose Evans-Pritchard, "Patten, the EU Bruiser, Upsets U.S. and Israel," *Daily Telegraph* (UK), May 11, 2002.

60. "Israel's Fair-weather Friend" (Leader), *Daily Telegraph*, June 20, 2002.

61. Daniel Hannan, "Why MEPs Are So Anti-Israeli," *Sunday Telegraph*, April 14, 2002: "The gap between the EU and the English-speaking nations is rarely wider than over the Middle East. Or perhaps it would be more accurate to speak of a gap between Euro-federalists and Euro-sceptics. . . . Israel represents the supreme embodiment of the national principle. . . . The EU, by contrast, is based on the idea that national loyalties are transient, artificial and ultimately discreditable. Simply by existing, Israelis are challenging the intellectual justification for the European project. No wonder they find it difficult to get a hearing in Brussels." The author served at the time as Conservative MEP for South East England.

62. Kim Willsher, "Jews Attacked in French Anti-war Protests, Officials Fear

New Wave of Anti-semitism," *Sunday Telegraph*, April 6, 2003; "France's Realists, Continued," editorial, *The Wall Street Journal*, April 9, 2003.

63. The survey was conducted by Eurobarometer for the European Commission. "Iraq and Peace in the World," Flash EB, No. 151 (October 10–16, 2003), available at <http://www.europa.eu.int/comm/public_opinion/flash/fl151_iraq_full_report.pdf>.

64. Josef Joffe, "Europe's Axis of Envy," *Foreign Policy*, September/October 2002, argues that resentment of the United States and resentment of Israel have been merged in European thinking, from "envy" of states which still retain national identity and can still wield force in self-defense. While Joffe attributes this outlook to postwar European integration, it has obvious parallels with the thinking of German satellite states in western Europe after 1940—during a previous effort at European integration. From this version, it might seem mere coincidence that Jews figured as hate-objects in both eras. The same observer (editor of *Die Zeit*) offered a more pessimistic view fifteen months later: "The Demons of Europe," *Commentary*, vol. 117, no. 1 (January 2004), p. 29.

65. Of course, not everyone was high-minded even in the era of wartime fervor: Deputy Premier Pierre Laval told an American diplomat in 1941 that he "hoped" for a German victory so that "Britain will pay the bill [for initially resisting Germany] and not France." Paxton, *Vichy France*, p. 85.

66. One of the most forthright versions yet to appear in English is Tony Judt, "Israel: An Alternate Future," *New York Review of Books*, October 23, 2003, proposing a binational state of Israel/Palestine under international military control—to reduce motivations for renewed violence against Jews in western Europe.

Chapter Seven
The Human Rights Crusade

1. Michael J. Dennis, "Current Development: The Fifty-Seventh Session of the UN Commission on Human Rights," *American Journal of International Law*, vol. 96 (January 2002), p. 181.

2. The French Declaration of the Rights of Man and the Citizen is no more promising than the American Declaration of Independence, as a grounding for the contemporary idea of an international law of human rights. Article 3 of the French Declaration declares that "all sovereignty resides essentially in the Nation. No body . . . may exercise authority which does not derive expressly therefrom." Article 6 declares that "law is an expression of the general will. All the citizens have a right to concur personally or by their representatives in its formation." Art. 12 declares that the "security of the rights of man and of the citizen necessitate a public force; this force is thus created for the benefit of all [citizens] and not for the special benefit of those to whom it is entrusted." The French Declaration does assert (art. 2) that "the end of every political association is the preservation of the natural and imprescriptible rights of man" but it nowhere suggests that these "rights" can be just as well secured by international committees which disregard the "sovereignty" and the "general will" of a particular society, make no provision for representation of citizens, and wield no "public force." Perhaps the

fact that even when a French "Emperor" dominated much of Europe and claimed to act on behalf of the principles of the French Revolution, he made no provision for assuring individual rights through Europe-wide institutions, says something.

3. Philip Jessup, *A Modern Law of Nations* (Macmillan, 1947), p. 90.

4. Ibid., p. 71. Jessup also contemplated "real legislation enacted by a world parliament composed of representatives not of states but of peoples"—but not right away (p. 91).

5. Nadine Gordimer, "Reflections by Nobel Laureates," in Yael Danieli, Elsa Stamatopoulou, and Clarence Dias, eds., *The Universal Declaration of Human Rights: Fifty Years and Beyond* (Baywood, 1998).

6. Henry Steiner, "Individual Claims in a World of Massive Violations: What Role for the Human Rights Committee?" in Philip Alston and James Crawford, eds., *The Future of UN Human Rights Treaty Monitoring* (Cambridge University Press, 2000), p. 38.

7. Anne F. Bayefsky, ed., *The UN Human Rights Treaty System in the 21st Century* (Kluwer Law International, 2000), pp. 8–9 (article by Jane Connors, "Analysis of the System of State Reporting"), notes that in 1999, two-thirds of all state parties were behind in their reports to the Human Rights Committee and most submitted reports were quite cursory.

8. "Advisory Opinion on Reservations to the Convention on the Prevention and Punishment of the Crime of Genocide," 1951 I.C.J. 15 (1951). The ICJ recognized that the usual practice, requiring the consent of all parties to reservations made by any one party, was "inspired by the notion of contract and is of undisputed value as a principle." But the majority opinion urged a more flexible approach in relation to human rights conventions since "in a convention of this type, one cannot speak of individual advantages or disadvantages to States or of the maintenance of a perfect contractual balance between rights and duties. The high ideals which inspired the Convention provide . . . the foundation and measure of all its provisions. The object and purpose of the Genocide Convention imply that it was the intention of the General Assembly and of the States which adopted it that as many States as possible should participate. The complete exclusion from the Convention of one or more States would not only restrict the scope of its application but would detract from the authority of the moral and humanitarian principles which are its basis." Dissenting justices protested this logic at the time. The majority sought to balance its concern for "inclusiveness" against dangers of fraudulent ratification by insisting that ratification with unilateral reservations should be accepted as a bona fide ratification only if the reservations were not inconsistent with the "object and purpose" of the convention.

9. Belinda Clark, "The Vienna Convention Reservations Regime and the Convention on Sex Discrimination," *American Journal of International Law*, vol. 85 (April 1991), p. 281.

10. Committee Against Torture, Concluding Observations—Saudi Arabia, December 6, 2002. Saudi Arabia protested that such judgments "presumed to impugn the 1,400 year-old religious beliefs of Saudi Arabia. It is not within the Committee's mandate to do so."

11. Oona A. Hathaway, "Do Human Rights Treaties Make a Difference?" *Yale Law Journal*, vol. 111 (June 2002).

12. Louis B. Sohn, "The Human Rights Law of the Charter," *Texas International Law Journal*, vol. 12 (Spring/Summer 1977), p. 129: "The [UN] Charter . . . provisions prevail over all other international and domestic legislative acts. Should a state . . . issue a legislative act or regulation which constitutes a gross violation of human rights, such . . . act would be clearly invalid as contrary to a basic and overriding norm of the [UN] Charter," pp. 131–32. It is notable that Sohn concludes by characterizing "the relationships between industrial employers and their workers" prior to the New Deal as "semi-slavery" and urges that some "way" must be "found to distribute the world's goods more rationally and equitably"—evidently on the assumption that, viewed in this light, American policies of the 1970s might be conceived as reflecting an international consensus which was shared with communist tyrannies of the era.

13. Myres McDougal, Harold Lasswell, and Lung-Chu Chen, *Human Rights and World Public Order* (Yale University Press, 1980), pp. 272–73 (with extensive citation to other legal scholars making similar claims).

14. On Amnesty's reluctance to associate itself with "conservative opinions" warning of genocide in Cambodia (as late as 1977), see Samantha Power, *A Problem from Hell, America and the Age of Genocide* (Basic Books, 2002), pp. 113–14. See also William Korey, *NGOs and the Universal Declaration of Human Rights* (St. Martin's Press, 1984), p. 169 notes that AI, founded in 1961, did not issue a long report on political prisoners in the Soviet Union until 1975 and the organization's "non-involvement" in human rights advocacy for Soviet victims during the 1970s and 1980s "was striking."

15. McDougal et al., *Human Rights and World Public Order*, p. 711.

16. 630 F.2d 876.

17. Harold Koh, "Transnational Public Law Litigation," *Yale Law Journal*, vol. 100 (June 1991), p. 2366.

18. American Law Institute, *Restatement of the Foreign Relations Law of the United States*, Third (American Law Institute, 1987), ch. 7.

19. Michael DeBan, "Amnesty International Seeks Support on Mall," *Rocky Mountain News*, October 26, 2002, describing AI organized "march" in Denver to drum up public support for U.S. ratification of CEDAW—drawing Denver citizens interested in women's rights. A march on behalf of political prisoners in Burma might not have drawn as much interest.

20. CEDAW Committee, "Concluding Observations—Belarus," January 31, 2000, par. 361.

21. *Toonen v. Australia*, "Views of Committee," March 31, 1994, 1 *International Human Rights Reports* 97 (1994).

22. Fr. Robert Araujo, "Sovereignty, Human Rights, and Self-Determination," *Fordham International Law Journal*, vol. 24 (June 2001), p. 1477 protests endorsements of "reproductive rights" and "sexual health" as human rights claims, pressed by western NGOs at UN conferences in the 1990s.

23. Ronald Inglehart and Pippa Norris, "The Truth Clash of Civilizations," *Foreign Policy* (March/April 2003), report survey findings that people in Muslim nations do express support for democracy, but generally reject prevalent western attitudes toward divorce, abortion, gender equality, and gay rights. There would

seem to be much more potential for human rights advocacy to focus on shared values than these most divisive issues.

24. Amnesty International's position paper on Palestinian suicide bomber operations was not issued until July 2002 ("Without Distinction—Attacks on Civilians by Palestinian Armed Groups," AI Index: MDE 02/03/2002)—nearly two years after the onset of the bombing campaign. Its statement insisting on an unlimited right of return for Palestinians (regarding pre-1967 Israel) was issued March 30, 2001: "The Right of Return: The Case of the Palestinians" (MDE 15/013/2001). Human Rights Watch did not bother to issue a report on suicide bombings until November 2002. ("Erased in a Moment: Suicide Bomb Attacks against Israeli Civilians," HRW Index No. 2807, November 1, 2002). It had issued its own affirmation of an unlimited right of return for Palestinians some three years earlier—helpfully couched as a public letter to Chairman Arafat, at the moment when Arafat and Israeli prime minister Barak were trying to salvage peace negotiations for a final settlement. Human Rights Watch admonished Arafat that international human rights law could not permit any compromise on the right of Palestinians to return to the pre-1967 borders of Israel. ("Letter to Chairman Arafat," December 22, 2000, posted at <http://www.hrw.org/press/2000/12/isrpaa/222.htm.)>.

25. Thomas Risse, "The Power of Norms versus the Norms of Power: Transnational Civil Society and Human Rights," in Ann M. Florini, ed., *The Third Force*.

26. Chris McGreal, "UN Human Rights Commissioner Takes Symbolic Stance as Clashes Over Zionism Threaten to Wreck World Meeting," *The Guardian* (London), August 31, 2001 (reporting Robinson protest against NGO pamphlets "equating the Star of David with a swastika"); Tim Butcher, "Norway Offers Hope to Racism Summit After Setback on Israel," *Daily Telegraph* (London), September 3, 2001 (reporting Robinson disavowal of declaration adopted at NGO forum at Durban, accusing Israel of "genocide and ethnic cleansing").

27. A collection of studies published at the end of the 1990s sought to demonstrate the importance of "international norms" in pressing for democratization—but gives most credit to the pressures brought to bear by "international non-governmental organizations" backed by western governments and provides almost no evidence that formal machinery of the UN made any significant difference. Thomas Risse, Stephen C. Ropp, and Kathryn Sikkink, eds., *The Power of Human Rights, International Norms and Domestic Change* (Cambridge University Press, 1999).

28. Twenty years earlier, the UN's Stockholm Conference on the Human Environment had followed the same formula in trying to link Third World preoccupations with the concerns of western environmentalists by wrapping the whole package in the rhetoric of human rights. "Principle 1" in the resulting "Stockholm Declaration" held: "Man has the fundamental right to freedom, equality and adequate conditions of life, in an environment of a quality that permits a life of dignity and well-being and he bears a solemn responsibility to protect and improve the environment for present and future generations. In this respect, policies promoting or perpetuating apartheid, racial segregation, discrimination, colonial

and other forms of oppression and foreign domination stand condemned and must be eliminated."

29. Figures from Tesner, *The United Nations and Business*, p. 46.

30. Boutros-Ghali, "Foreword" in Thomas Weiss and Leon Gordenker, *NGOs, The UN and Global Governance* (Lynn Rienner, 1996), p. 11.

31. Kofi Annan, "Full Implementation and Enforcement of International Law Rooted in Shared Global Values," Speech of February 11, 2000, <http://www.un.org/News/Press/docs/2000/20000211.sgsm7299.doc.html>.

32. Roy Gutman, "Bosnia: Negotiation and Retreat," in Barbara Benton, ed., *Soldiers for Peace, Fifty Years of UN Peacekeeping* (Facts on File, 1996), describes the episode (pp. 201–4) with appropriate emphasis on Dutch passivity in the face of mass murder.

33. See Helen Fein, *Accounting for Genocide* (Free Press, 1979), pp. 286–89; on "social defense" efforts after 1943 to help those seeking to evade forced labor requisitions, contrasted with complete acquiescence to the round-up of Dutch Jews in 1940–42, pp. 265–75.

34. American officials continued to negotiate with Serb militia leaders even after their indictment by the ICTY. When a subsequent peace agreement provided more security for NATO forces in Bosnia, NATO commanders still remained quite reluctant to risk their own troops by going after indicted war criminals. Gary Bass, *Stay the Hand of Vengeance* (Princeton University Press, 2000), pp. 230–41, 248–60.

35. The Serb president who led the opposition to Milosevic and succeeded him in office was a former law professor and translator of *The Federalist*. He had good reasons for thinking the extradition improper, as did the Yugoslav (at that point, essentially Serbian) Supreme Court. Serbia had a firm rule against extraditing its nationals to foreign tribunals, a rule copied, perhaps from Germany and Italy, which also continued to maintain this nineteenth-century national doctrine. In July 1914, following the assassination of Archduke Franz Ferdinand by a Serb nationalist in Sarajevo, the Austrian government made a series of demands on Serbia, almost all of which the Serbian government agreed to meet—except for the demand that suspects be extradited to Austrian courts. The consequence at that time was world war. Bass, *Stay the Hand*, pp. 315–21, provides some details on Serb views ninety years later.

36. Compare Stephen Castle, "Liberation of Kosovo: War Crimes—Milosevic May Be Charged with Genocide," *The Independent* (London), June 19, 1999; Marlise Simons, "Milosevic Will Face Two Trials Instead of One," *The New York Times*, December 12, 2001. For an account of political maneuvers which finally resulted in Milosevic's transfer to the Hague, see Bass, *Stay the Hand of Vengeance*, pp. 311–23.

37. Richard Sezibera, "The Only Way to Bring Justice to Rwanda," *Washington Post*, April 7, 2002, which notes that local courts, with one-tenth of the financing of the international tribunal, had rendered judgments in more than 5,000 cases in the same period—though, no doubt, with much less due process. Bass, *Stay the Hand*, pp. 307–8, notes that Rwandan national proceedings handed down over a hundred death sentences and a comparable number of life-imprisonment sentences in the first four years of operation, during a period when

the UN tribunal had not yet imposed any sentence on anyone, though the most senior offenders had been taken into UN custody: "No one should have expected the Rwandans to be as unconcerned about the punishment of the genocide as the UN was," pp. 307–8.

38. *The U.N. Criminal Tribunals for Yugoslavia and Rwanda: International Justice or Show of Justice*, Hearing before the Committee on International Relations, House of Representatives, 107th Cong, February 28, 2002 (response of Pierre-Richard Prosper, Ambassador-at-Large for War Crimes Issues, responding to questioning from Rep. Jo Ann Davis). The same hearing also includes discussion of procedural irregularities (such as prosecutors withholding exculpatory evidence), assembled by former Justice Department attorney Larry A. Hammond.

39. If these prosecutions were a bid for mention in case books, they succeeded: see Steiner and Alston, *International Human Rights,* 2d. ed., pp. 1187–88, on cases designed to establish that "sexual violence" may "include acts which do not involve . . . physical contact" and that "coercive circumstances need not be evidenced by a show of physical force"—entirely plausible claims for a domestic legal system but not, one might think, of highest priority for .prosecutors faced with an actual pattern of mass murder that had taken the lives of nearly a million people.

40. Article 12 of the Rome Statute provides that the ICC may assert jurisdiction where the perpetrator of a relevant crime is a national of a ratifying state or where the crime was committed on the territory of a ratifying state. It then offers a third basis for jurisdiction—where the state on which the crime occurred has not ratified the ICC Statute but agrees "by declaration lodged with the Registrar [of the Court], [to] accept the exercise of jurisdiction by the Court with respect to the crime in question." So a dictatorship responsible for mass murder in its own territory could exempt its own crimes from ICC prosecution but still arrange for the ICC to investigate questionable military operations of a liberating army which attacked it.

41. Abi-Saab in A. Cassese, ed., *The New Humanitarian Law of Armed Conflict* (Oceana Publications, 1981), p. 250. He does indicate that "Third World representatives in general attached great weight to general principles."

42. The 1948 Convention on the Punishment of the Crime of Genocide directs that those charged with genocide "shall be tried by a competent tribunal of the State in the territory of which the act was committed, or by such international penal tribunal as may have jurisdiction with respect to those Contracting Parties which shall have accepted its jurisdiction" (art. 6)—the last clause indicating that even the drafters of a convention on the punishment of genocide did not envision an international tribunal whose jurisdiction could be imposed without consent. The implication in the ICC Preamble, that universal jurisdiction was already an accepted part of international law, was, in fact, rejected by the International Court of Justice in *Congo v. Belgium* (2001).

43. Original decision: *Regina v. Bow Street Magistrate*, 3 W.L.R. 1456 (1998); subsequent decision: *Regina v. Bow Street Magistrate*, 2 W.L.R. 827 (1999). Where the subsequent decision relies solely on the Convention Against Torture and then only for the brief period after both Chile and the United Kingdom had ratified it, the earlier decision invoked "international law" principles which had

"by the time of the 1973 coup and certainly ever since . . . condemned genocide, torture, hostage taking and crimes against humanity . . . as international crimes deserving of punishment" (opinion of Lord Steyn at 3 W.L.R. 1456 (1998), p. 1506).

44. See Stephen Macedo, ed., *Princeton Principles on Universal Jurisdiction* (Princeton University, Project on Universal Jurisdiction, 2001), p. 49, n. 20, reporting the partial dissent of Lord Browne-Wilkinson from the consensus of other international legal scholars, who endorsed this broad argument for asserting the jurisdiction of all states to arrest and try anyone, from any state, who might be guilty of extreme human rights abuses. Lord Browne-Wilkinson cautioned that such assertions of universal jurisdiction should only be attempted "with the prior consent" of the home state of the accused. Without this limitation, he warned, "zealots in Western states might launch prosecutions against, for example, Islamic extremists for their terrorist activities. It is naive to think that, in such cases, the national state of the accused would stand by and watch the trial proceed: resort to force would be more probable." Lord Browne-Wilkinson was one of the judges who endorsed the arrest and prosecution of Chilean President Pinochet. Chile was not likely to retaliate with terror attacks against Britain. Those who called for his prosecution, it seems, could therefore be regarded as advocates for justice rather than "zealots."

45. Tobias Buck, "Belgium Decides to Repeal Controversial War Crimes Law," *Financial Times*, July 14, 2003.

46. Tom Farer, "Humanitarian Intervention Before and After 9/11: Legality and Legitimacy," in J. L. Holzgrefe and Robert O. Keohane, eds., *Humanitarian Intervention, Ethical, Legal and Political Dilemmas* (Cambridge University Press, 2003), p. 55: "What was there about the pre-9/11 political, moral or intellectual context that drove debate about something far more talked about than done? Part of the answer, I believe, is the challenge that claims on behalf of humanitarian intervention posed to the inherited structure and the associated ideas, values and norms of global order . . . it arguably exemplified and acted as the doctrinal advance guard of the whole constellation of forces confronting the sovereign state's once indisputable claim to be the principal locus of power and loyalty," p. 55.

47. Kofi Annan, *The Question of Intervention: Statements by the Secretary General* (UN Dept. of Public Information, 1999).

48. Ben Russell, "Blair Comes Under Fire Over Graphic Dossier on Saddam's Brutality," *The Independent* (UK), December 3, 2002 ("Amnesty International . . . spokesman said: 'We are concerned about . . . political opportunism.'"). Amnesty International earlier protested that "western leaders" who "invoked . . . the human rights situation in Iraq . . . to justify military action" were engaged in "nothing but a cold and calculated manipulation of the work of human rights activists." Press release, September 26, 2002. As war approached, AI protested that while President Bush "prepares his country for war, [he] has maintained his support for state-sanctioned killing at home"—by allowing a scheduled execution of a convicted murderer in Indiana to go forward. Press release, March 18, 2003. Amnesty International then organized a demonstration outside Parliament "to highlight the human cost of war"—just as the war was getting underway: AI

Press release, March 20, 2003. A flood of AI press releases then protested possible violations of international humanitarian standards in the conduct of the war.

49. Samantha Power, "Force Full," *The New Republic*, March 3, 2003. The reaction might have been anticipated by alert readers of her previous book, *A Problem from Hell*, which castigates American policy for its indifference to mass murder in so many places during the postwar era. The indictment draws its force by ignoring strategic challenges of the Cold War. Mao's millions of victims are unmentioned, as are Stalin's. The sole reference to Stalin notes that he did not support international human rights conventions—which, outside the community of human rights professionals, is not regarded as his worst crime. Did the United States save lives at the time or save future generations by leading the resistance to communism for so many decades? The thought does not cross the threshold of inquiry in this work.

50. John Shattuck, "In Iraq, U.S. Ignores Human Rights Lessons," *Boston Globe*, November 5, 2003, a theme also of the concluding chapter in Shattuck's book, *Freedom on Fire, Human Rights Wars and America's Response* (Harvard University Press, 2003).

51. Jonathan Petre, "Terrorists Can Have Serious Moral Goals, says Williams," *Daily Telegraph* (UK), October 15, 2003.

52. Former Justice Department attorney Lee A. Casey has compiled a list comparing ICC ratifying states with U.S. State Department ratings of human rights abuses: The majority of signatories are classified by the State Department as having serious problems with their own criminal justice systems. "Human Rights Record of the States Parties to the International Criminal Court," a paper posted on the website of the Federalist Society, <http://www.fed-soc.org>.

53. For the first effort to secure ICC prosecution against British officials, see Kevin Hope and Nikki Tait; "Greeks Try to Indict Blair for Iraq War," *Financial Times* (London), July 29, 2003. Subsequent efforts by legal advocates in Britain and other countries: Severin Carrell, "Blair Faces New War Crimes Accusation," *The Independent on Sunday* (London), January 18, 2004 and Sandra Laville, "Iraqi Families to Sue Britain Over Deaths," *Daily Telegraph* (London), March 1, 2004.

54. Martin Gilbert, *Winston Churchill*, Vol. VI: *Finest Hour, 1939–1941* (Henry Holt, 1992), p. 832: Churchill dismissed ICRC monitoring on the grounds that "It would simply result in a committee under German influence or fear . . . Anyhow, we do not want these people thrusting themselves in, as even if Germany offered to stop the bombing now, we should not consent to it. Bombing of military objectives, increasingly widely interpreted, seems at present our main road home."

55. For details on how carefully the architects of the Nuremberg tribunal sought to limit its significance as a precedent, see Rabkin, "Nuremberg Misremembered," *SAIS Review*, vol. 19 (Summer–Fall 1999).

56. Wheaton, *Elements of International Law* part 2, ch. 1, sec. 2, pp. 85–86 (in 6th edition, Boston, 1857).

57. Perhaps it was not entirely about fear of casualties. In an interview with journalist Marléne Schneiper, published in the Swiss newspaper *Tages-Anzeiger*, published November 8, 2003 (and posted, in translation, on the ICRC website,

www.icrc.org), ICRC president Jacob Kellenberger acknowledged that the ICRC had accepted protection from Russian Interior Ministry units for its personnel in Chechnya, after six of the latter were "murdered in cold blood" by Chechen "bandits." But it would "pose a pretty major problem" to accept "an escort of Coalition soldiers" in Iraq. Reference to the "coalition" turned out to be a euphemism in the ICRC understanding. The interviewing journalist immediately asked, "Is creeping absorption by the superpower not a problem already?" Kellenberg answered, by acknowledging the request of the United States to remain in Iraq but then asserted, "The ICRC will not allow itself to be swallowed up by any power. . . . We demonstrate this every day in the 80 countries around the world where we bring help on the basis of neutrality." On an apparently unrelated point, Kellenberg also acknowledged that 50 percent of ICRC operations are in Muslim countries and asserted that in talks with leaders of these countries "I emphasized that it is precisely in our increasingly polarized and extreme world that the ICRC must maintain its independence." In practice, that seems to mean, avoiding any appearance of association with American forces. The relevant criterion seems to be, not how ICRC involvement would be perceived by people in Iraq, but by leaders in other states where the ICRC wants to operate. Some calculus of this sort has frequently led the ICRC to remain silent in the face of mass atrocities. Its commitment to neutrality outweighs its commitment to "humanitarianism"—necessarily so, perhaps, given that a genuine commitment to "humanitarianism" might require choosing sides in particular conflicts. An organization that was steadfastly neutral in the war against Nazi Germany—as the ICRC was—is not going to compromise its "neutrality" in the face of lesser evils.

CHAPTER EIGHT
IS SOVEREIGNTY TRADED IN TRADE AGREEMENTS?

1. "Laying the Foundations for a Fair and Free Trade System," in Gary P. Sampson, ed., *The Role of the World Trade Organization in Global Governance* (UN University Press, 2001).

2. Remarks at University of Chicago Convocation Ceremony, June 12, 1999, calling for "trade agreements that . . . enhance labor standards and environmental protection all across the world" and comparing this vision to efforts "through the New Deal" to "develop a national economy with a human face." Echoes of the slogan of 1960s communist reformers, "socialism with a human face," may have been unintentional.

3. *De jure naturae et gentium* ("On The Law of Nature and of Nations," 1688), book 3, ch. 3, translation by C. H. and W. A. Oldfather (Clarendon Press, 1934), pp. 364–65, replying to arguments of Francisco Vitoria. On the prior claim that protection of a nation's own people is the primary duty of the sovereign: book 8, ch. 6, par. 14, pp. 1305–306 ("it was to enjoy such defense that free men of their own accord set up governments or submitted to them").

4. Ibid., pp. 364–65.

5. Vattel, *Law of Nations*, book 2, ch. 2, sec. 22–24; book 1, ch. 8, sec. 98–99.

6. Ibid., 2, 2, sec. 26–32.

7. Neff, *Friends But No Allies*, pp. 33–34.

8. Adam Smith, *Wealth of Nations*, book 5, ch. 1, first part (in R. H. Campbell and W. B. Todd, eds., Oxford University Press, 1976), p. 707.

9. Paul Bairoch, "European Trade Policy, 1815–1914," in P. Mathias and S. Pollard, eds., *Cambridge Economic History of Europe*, vol. 8 ("The Industrial Economies: The Development of Social and Economic Policies," 1989), pp. 103–26 (on "Colonial trade policies").

10. Carl Srikwera, "Reinterpreting the History of European Integration" in J. Klausen and L. A. Tilly, eds., *European Integration in Social and Historical Perspective* (Rowman & Littlefield, 1997), p. 54.

11. "Instructions to Mr. Anderson, Minister to Colombia," May 27, 1823, reprinted in Jonathan Elliot, ed., *The American Diplomatic Code* (J. Elliot Jr., 1835), pp. 648, 652–53. Adams also urged efforts to secure guarantees of religious toleration for traveling Americans as separation provisions in trade agreements, but acknowledged that such provisions might be difficult in Catholic countries and he did not make their inclusion mandatory. He put religious freedom on the same level as commercial freedom and "natural rights" and "human rights"—but never suggested that the "human rights" of citizens of Latin nations would be the object of American treaties: "We will use our example and persuasion." Adams was an experienced diplomat but also attentive to American principles: The U.S. would not undertake guarantees of citizen rights in another country, because it would not make the rights of U.S. citizens at home dependent on international agreement.

12. Edward Stanwood, *American Tariff Controversies in the Nineteenth Century* (Houghton, Mifflin Co., 1903), vol. 1, p. 11: "The intellectual leaders of the Revolution had seen the injury to the colonies that resulted from the application to them of the principles of the mercantile system. Emancipated from the ideas and traditions of the Old World polity, they were ready to adopt the views which will ever be associated with the name Adam Smith" Yet: "Their dreams were brief, their awakening was painful. They found that they could expect no reciprocity."

13. Keith Whittington, *Constitutional Construction* (Harvard University Press, 1999), pp. 100–106.

14. F. W. Taussig, *The Tariff History of the United States*, 8th revised ed. (Capricorn Books, 1964), thus devotes several chapters to pre–Civil War tariff politics.

15. Arthur Bentley, *The Process of Government, A Study of Social Pressures* (University of Chicago Press, 1908).

16. Moore, *Principles*, p. 160.

17. *Field v. Clark*, 143 U.S. 649 (1892).

18. Taussig surveys the results of the policy, formally adopted in the 1909 tariff law, purporting to "equalize costs of production" by offsetting lower foreign production costs with protective tariffs—which, as he notes, implied the quite perverse "principle" that "the more disadvantageous it is for a country to carry on an industry, the more desperate should be the effort to cause the industry to be established" (*Tariff History*), p. 364. Nonetheless, the Tariff Commission, especially after it was delegated "quasi-legislative powers to modify rates under the

cost-difference principle" adopted "a pedantic procedure" to determine "figures exact to a fraction of a cent"—though its "leading members were actuated in their conclusions by a wish to make protection higher, to shape and interpret cost figures so as to bring about higher duties" (ibid.), pp. 522–23.

19. Harold James, *The End of Globalization, Lessons of the Great Depression* (Harvard University Press, 2001), pp. 9–13, provides a useful survey of pre–First World War "globalization" as exceeding, in some ways, the levels of the 1990s.

20. Kevin H. O'Rourke and Jeffrey G. Williamson (Globalization and History, The Evolution of a Nineteenth Century Atlantic Economy [MIT Press, 1999]) calculate that trade in goods was responsible for less than a third of the wage convergence between the United States and Britain in the period between 1850 and 1914, with immigration accounting for some 70 percent of the convergence (as emigration tightened labor markets in Britain, boosting wages, while immigration slowed wage increases in the U.S.).

21. On the World Economic Conference, Charles Kindleberger, "Commerical Policy Between the Wars," in Mathias and Pollard, eds., *Cambridge Economic History of Europe*, vol. 8 "The Industrial Economies," pp. 185–88.

22. Henry J. Tasca, *The Reciprocal Trade Policy of the United States* (University of Pennsylvania Press, 1938), p. 95, emphasizes NIRA resistance as "a definite factor in retarding the progress of the trade agreements program" since "it would have been inconsistent for the administration on one hand to increase costs of production through codification of industry, then simultaneously increase the competition of foreign products." Administrators of the parallel scheme for boosting agricultural prices under the Agricultural Adjustment Act (AAA) also resisted tariff reduction agreements and the first Administrator of the AAA was made chairman of the interdepartmental coordinating agency for trade—getting into intense disputes with Secretary of State Hull over new tariff reduction agreements, which were not eased when the official (George Peek) was made special trade adviser for the NIRA (ibid.), pp. 82–92. The pace of negotiations for new agreements was considerably hastened after the NIRA fell victim to the Supreme Court in 1935 (ibid.), p. 98.

23. Richard Gardner, *Sterling-Dollar Diplomacy* (Oxford Press, 1956), p. 377, quoting a pamphlet issued by the U.S. Council of the International Chamber of Commerce (a private, business-advocacy group), protesting various provisions in the ITO Charter as making too many concessions to state planners.

24. Gardner, *Sterling-Dollar Diplomacy*, analyzes the American debate on the ITO in detail (pp. 371–78) but also shows that opposition in the British Parliament would probably have killed the new organization, in any case (ch. 27: "End of the ITO").

25. Robert E. Hudec, *The GATT Legal System and World Trade Diplomacy*, 2d. (Butterworth, 1990), p. 57.

26. Quoted in Hudec, *GATT Legal System*, p. 40, from minutes of negotiating session in Geneva, May 30, 1947.

27. For a useful overview, emphasizing the eagerness of Third World countries to extend international authority to compel development assistance—and their inability to do so under actual UN arrangements of that era, see Robert W. Gregg, "The Politics of International Economic Cooperation and Development," in L. S.

Finkelstein, ed., *Politics in the United Nations System* (Duke University Press, 1988).

28. Gardner, *Sterling-Dollar Diplomacy*, p. 367 (remarks by Clair Wilcox, vice chairman of U.S. delegation, replying to demands by Australia, Brazil, and others to retain the right to impose "quantitative restrictions" on imports, at least for developing countries).

29. For a useful sketch of the legal and political concerns motivating the new system, see John H. Jackson, Jean-Victor Louis, and Mitsuo Matsushita, *Implementing the Tokyo Round* (University of Michigan Press, 1984), pp. 145–55.

30. In the version published by the U.S. Government Printing Office, the official NAFTA text runs to 590 pages, with an additional 2,452 pages of "annexes" (most of which are lists of rates and products, sometimes descending to the enumeration of individual entities): *NAFTA, Texts of Agreement, Implementing Bill, Statement of Administrative Action and Required Supporting Statements* (GPO, 1993).

31. The problem was noticed under the earlier U.S.-Canada agreement from which NAFTA was later constructed. James Chen, "Appointments with Disaster: The Unconstitutionality of Binational Arbitral Review under the U.S.-Canada Free Trade Agreement," *Washington & Lee Law Review*, vol. 49 (Fall 1992), p. 1455.

32. The arguments were noticed in *Coalition for Competitive Trade v. Clinton*, 128 F.3d 761 (D.C. Cir. 1997) but jurisdictional issues prevented a decision on the merits.

33. See Jason Gudofsky, "Shedding Light on Article 1110 of the NAFTA, Concerning Expropriations," *Journal of International Business Law,* vol. 21 (Fall 2000), p. 243 (emphasizing wide latitude given to Mexican environmental regulators in early cases).

34. The limited reach of the North American Agreement on Environmental Cooperation was illustrated by one of the first complaints to reach the Environmental Commission. The U.S.-based Biodiversity Foundation filed a protest against a congressional budget rider by which the new Republican majority temporarily rescinded the application of the Endangered Species Act to a particular forest. This measure was designed to authorize logging operations, even though logging had previously been found to threaten an endangered species of owl in that forest. The secretariat for the Environmental Commission held that this special exemption from the Endangered Species Act did not constitute a failure to enforce existing laws but a change in existing laws—since the exemption had been enacted by Congress. (Submission Sem-95-01, Letter from Secretariat dated September 21, 1995.)

35. Paul Stanton Kibel, "The Paper Tiger Awakens: North American Environmental Law After the Cozumel Reef Case," *Columbia Journal of Transational Law*, vol. 39 (2001), argues that the North American Agreement on Environmental Cooperation (NAAEC) has helped to stimulate environmental advocacy in Mexico—but makes no similar claim for the U.S. where environmental advocacy already had a considerable head-start.

36. "United States, Standards on Reformulated Gasoline," WT/DS2/AB/R, AB Report adopted May 20, 1996. As John Jackson comments: "there has been some

dispute about whether [the WTO] was a 'separate regime,' sort of sealed off from normal concepts of international law, but the AB explicitly states that the WTO is part of international law, and it goes on to engage international law principles of treaty interpretation very deeply, referring to the 'Vienna Convention on the Law of Treaties'" *The World Trade Organization: Constitution and Jurisprudence* (Royal Institute of International Affairs, 1998), p. 89. Jackson notes that even the Statute of the International Court of Justice stipulates that rulings of the court will only be binding on the immediate parties to its rulings (art. 59), whereas the Dispute Settlement Understanding that established the WTO's Appellate Body does not include such a restriction. He reports that diplomats attributed this omission to an oversight (p. 87). But the AB seems to be making the most of it. For an extended account of dangers this may pose, see Claude Barfield, *Free Trade, Sovereignty, Democracy* (AEI Press, 2001).

37. Charles Cheney Hyde, *International Law, Chiefly as Interpreted and Applied by the United States*, 2d. ed. (Little, Brown, 1945), pp. 1582–1608, reports an extensive body of precedents, recognizing that arbitration could not be extended to disputes involving "vital interests" or threatening "national independence" or affecting "questions of political nature"—acknowledged even in arbitration schemes designed to ensure peaceful resolution of conflicts such as the Kellogg-Briand treaty and the Locarno Pact. The "Statute" of the International Court of Justice, adopted along with the UN Charter, evaded the problem by allowing states to decide, on a case-by-case basis, whether they would agree to submit cases to the court.

38. For an optimistic view of the process, see Gregory C. Shaffer, *Defending Interests, Public-Private Partnerships in WTO Litigation* (The Brookings Institution, 2001), arguing that the USTR benefits from private interests providing guidance on which market barriers to attack. Shaffer's account presumes that pressure from exporting interests provides a sound basis for U.S. strategy overall—which might be questioned. Jagdish Bhagwati, a longtime defender of free trade, takes a dimmer view of policy pressures exerted by business firms on U.S. negotiators: "multinationals are so keen to get markets . . . they're like salivating dogs, they will make concessions . . . just to get you out of the way. They're a bunch of cynical bastards." Quoted in William Greider, "The Real Cancun," *The Nation*, September 22, 2003, p. 13 (complaining about readiness of U.S. firms to introduce barriers to imports from developing countries, ostensibly in the name of labor rights or environmental protection, to the detriment of economic development in poor countries and consumers in the U.S.).

39. Gregory Shaffer, "The WTO under Challenge: Democracy and Law and Politics of the WTO's Treatment of Trade and Environment Matters," *Harvard Environmental Law Review*, vol. 25 (July 2001), p. 38, attributes the deadlock to differing views among states and constituencies within states.

40. The episode and its background are well described in Robert O'Brien, Anne Marie Goetz, Jan Aart Scholte, and Marc Williams, *Contesting Global Governance, Multilateral Economic Institutions and Global Social Movements* (Cambridge University Press, 2000), pp. 72, 83–84. The ICTFU's position is set out in *International Workers Rights and Trade: The Need for Dialogue* (Brussels, 1996).

41. Kofi Annan, "Help the Third World Help Itself," *The Wall Street Journal*,

November 29, 1999. The secretary general elaborated on this appeal at the Davos conference on world economic affairs in 1999 and in subsequent speeches, described in Tesner, *The United Nations and Business*, pp. 51–53, 174–75.

42. Frances Williams, "Washington Urges WTO to be More Responsive to Environmental Concerns," *The Financial Times* (London), March 16, 1999.

43. "United States-Import Prohibition of Certain Shrimp and Shrimp Products," WT/DS58/AB/R (November 6, 1998).

44. United States—Import Prohibition of Certain Shrimp and Shrimp Products, WT/DS58/AB/RW (November 21, 2001).

45. Yasmin Moorman, "Integration of ILO Core Rights Labor Standards into the WTO," *Columbia Journal of Transnational Law*, vol. 39 (2001), p. 555; Robert Howse, "The WTO and Protection of Workers' Rights," *Journal of Small and Emerging Business Law*, vol. 3 (1999), p. 131, relying on exemptions in Article 20 for measures "(a) necessary to protect public morals; (b) necessary to protect human, animal or plant life or health; (g) relating to the conservation of exhaustible natural resources"; Steve Charnovitz, "The Moral Exception in Trade Policy," *Virginia Journal of International Law*, vol. 38 (Summer 1989), p. 689.

46. The International Commission of Jurists (a UN advisory body) prepared a set of guidelines for implementing the Covenant on Economic and Social Rights in 1997 (the so-called Maastricht Guidelines) which insisted, among other things, that signatory states must "ensure" that the rights enumerated in the Covenant "are fully taken into account in the development of policies and programs" of the WTO. The Guidelines, with commentary, were published in *Human Rights Quarterly*, vol. 20 (Summer 1998), pp. 691–730, quoted passage at p. 725. See also Mary Robinson, "Making the Global Economy Work for Human Rights," in Sampson, *Role of the WTO in Global Governance*.

47. The perspective is defended in Robert Howse, "The Early Years of WTO Jurisprudence," in J.H.H. Weiler, ed., *The EU, The WTO, and the NAFTA* (Oxford University Press, 2000), emphasizing access to WTO "judicial" decision making by non-business interests.

48. Notably, Ernst-Ulrich Petermann, *The GATT/WTO Dispute Settlement System* (Kluver International, 1997). Petermann, a "Legal Advisor to the WTO," sketches a broad vision of a world constitution in which the WTO plays a central role: "through the traumatic experiences of World Wars I and II . . . governments finally learned to accept the need for worldwide constitutional rules (such as the prohibition of the use of force and collective security arrangements in the UN Charter) and their collective enforcement through international organizations (such as the UN and the Security Council). Not only within states but also among states do the limitation of government failures and the supply of 'public goods' depend on agreed procedures and institutions for rule-making, rule-application and rule-enforcement" (pp. 25–26). In a similar spirit, but with more precision, Joost Pauwelyn, "The Role of Public International Law in the WTO," *American Journal of International Law*, vol. 95 (July 2001), p. 535.

49. See, for example, *Mighell v. Sultan of Johore*, 1 Q.B. 149 (1894), dismissing breach of promise suit by jilted lover against the Sultan, on advice from the Colonial Office that Johore was "sovereign" merely enjoying exclusive British "protection" based on treaty.

50. John Yoo, "Constitutionality of Congressional-Executive Agreements," *Michigan Law Review*, vol. 99 (February 2001), p. 757 (emphasizing distinctive character of trade agreements, given congressional power to regulate "commerce with foreign nations").

51. Robert Howse, "Adjudicative Legitimacy and Treaty Interpretation in International Law: The Early Years of the WTO," in J.H.H. Weiler, *The EU, the WTO and the NAFTA, Toward a Common Law of International Trade* (Oxford University Press, 2000) offers a particularly sympathetic account by a Canadian advocate of integrating labor, environmental, and human rights standards into global trade agreements.

52. On the Foreign Sales Corporation tax dispute, see Shaffer, *Defending Interests*, pp. 73–74.

53. Peter Spiro, "The New Sovereignists, American Exceptionalism and Its False Prophets," *Foreign Affairs*, vol. 79 (November/December 2000) sees the process as inevitable: "economic globalization will inevitably bring the United States in line . . . the international community can advance the rule of international law by working against key U.S. actors—most notably corporations" (p. 13). The interests of "corporations" will then exert "constraining" pressure on "anti-internationalist federal policymakers" (p. 14).

54. For a rare survey of constitutional issues, see Scott McBride, "Dispute Settlement in the WTO: Backbone of the Global Trading System or Delegation of Awesome Power?" *Law & Policy in International Business*, vol. 32 (Spring 2001), emphasizing that U.S. government has so far treated WTO rulings as if legally "binding" so that AB acquires authority, in effect, to rewrite U.S. trade law.

55. Kenneth A. Oye, *Economic Discrimination and Political Exchange* (Princeton University Press, 1992).

56. One version is John O. McGinnis and Mark Movsesian, "The World Trade Constitution," *Harvard Law Review*, vol. 114 (December 2000).

57. Visionaries who think otherwise expound their visions in Volker Rittberger, ed., *Global Governance and the United Nations System* (United Nations University Press, 2001), especially R. Higgot, "Economic Globalization and Global Governance: Towards a post-Washington Consensus" and Otfried Hoffe, "A Subsidiary and Federal World Republic."

CHAPTER NINE
AMERICAN INDEPENDENCE AND THE OPINIONS OF MANKIND

1. Jefferson's original phrasing was more consistent with a profession of faith: "We hold these truths to be sacred and undeniable." It seems to have been Benjamin Franklin, the scientist and freethinker, who suggested the change from "sacred and undeniable" to the more rationalist phrase, "self-evident." Carl Becker, *The Declaration of Independence* (1922, reprinted by Vintage Books, 1972), p. 142. Why did the text retain the initial part of the phrase as "We hold"? Perhaps the final phrasing reflects nothing more than the literary compromises that emerged from drafting by committee. But it may reflect the larger impulse toward

intellectual synthesis inherent in the whole project. Nearly a half century later, Jefferson said the Declaration had been "intended to be an expression of the American mind. . . . All its authority rests then on the harmonizing sentiments of the day." Letter to Henry Lee, May 8, 1825, in Peterson, ed., *Thomas Jefferson, Writings*, p. 1501.

2. Even Canada and Australia, which entered the war at Britain's call in 1939, demonstrated their independence. Canada refused to send troops to fight with the British in North Africa between 1940 and 1943, as the defense of Suez was not a Canadian concern. Australia did send troops to the Western Desert in 1940 but then, much to the consternation of the British, insisted on returning them to Australia to cope with the Japanese onslaught at the beginning of 1942. Britain repaid these assertions of independence—with compound interest—when it entered the European Economic Community in 1972, abruptly repudiated its historic economic ties with these traditionally loyal partners in the Commonwealth. The tenuous hold of loyalty, within this once close community of nations, deserves more attention from globalization theorists than it has received.

3. No. 23, p. 121.

4. For example, Samuel Pufendorf, *De officio hominis et civis* ("On the Duty of Man and Citizen"), book 2, ch. 1, par. 6: "the state of nature which really exists . . . now exists between different states." (English translation by Frank Gardner Moore, Carnegie Endowment for International Peace, 1927), p. 90; Locke, *Second Treatise of Government*, par. 14: "where are, or ever were there any men in such a state of nature? . . . it may suffice as an answer at present that . . . all princes and rulers of independent governments all through the world are in a state of nature."

5. Ronald Inglehart, *Modernization and Postmodernization* (Princeton University Press, 1997), pp. 39–45, explains the "postmaterialist" values that have taken the place of religion—and therefore, in this somewhat strange analysis, of older "materialist values." The point seems to be that before "postmodernism," people worried about "security" in several senses.

6. James Rosenau, "Governance, Order and Change in World Politics," in James Rosenau and Ernst-Otto Czempiel, eds., *Governance Without Government: Order and Change in World Politics* (Cambridge University Press, 1992), p. 4.

7. Myres S. McDougal and associates, *Studies in World Public Order* (Yale University Press, 1960), especially the first chapter, "The Identification and Appraisal of Diverse Systems of Public Order."

8. "Legal Education and Public Policy: Professional Training in the Public Interest," *Yale Law Journal*, vol. 52 (March 1943), pp. 203, 206, 209, 219: reprinted as chapter 2 in McDougal and associates, *Studies in World Public Order*.

9. For one notable version, see Robert Keohane, "Sovereignty, Interdependence and International Institutions," in Linda B. Miller and Joseph Smith, eds., *Ideas and Ideals* (Westview Press, 1993), distinguishing "effective" or "operational" sovereignty from "formal sovereignty." Joseph Nye, *The Paradox of American Power, Why the World's Only Superpower Can't Go it Alone* (Oxford University Press, 2002) goes further: "Seen in the light of a constitutional bargain, the multilateralism of American preeminence [by committing the U.S. to international

institutions] . . . reduces the incentives for constructing alliances against us. And to the extent that the EU is the major potential challenger in terms of capacity, the idea of a loose constitutional framework between the United States and the societies with which we share the most values makes sense," (p. 159). It seems unworthy of notice in this soothing account that the United States already has a Constitution and might have constitutional difficulties sharing constitutional authority even with those nations with which "we share the most values." Professor Nye presumably has France and Germany in mind, since those nations have "the most capacity"—and have shown the most inclination—to rally the EU in opposition to U.S. policy. It again seems unworthy of notice in this account that not all Americans share the same readiness to see their country constitutionally yoked to these nations—and the purpose of a Constitution is to prevent the taste of one set of policymakers from committing the nation to a new constitutional structure. Or perhaps there is no difference in this perspective between a "constitutional framework" and a set of approved policy inclinations.

10. Richard Falk, *Religion and Humane Global Governance* (Palgrave, 2001), pp. 25, 29.

11. Ibid., pp. 8, 9, 29.

12. Michael Ignatieff, *Human Rights as Politics and Idolatry* (Princeton University Press, 2001). More indulgently, Brian Simpson, *Human Rights and the End of Empire* (Oxford University Press, 2001) says: "The human rights movement has a quasi religious character and one cannot but be reminded of an analogous problem [to determining the effect of UN human rights treaties]: the difficulty of telling whether prayer really works, which used to worry me as an adolescent," (p. 823).

13. Albert Gore, *Earth in the Balance* (Houghton Mifflin, 2000), pp. 12, 269.

14. Ibid., pp. 305, 306. Numerous other examples of such thinking are surveyed in Robert Whelan, Joseph Kirwan, and Paul Haffner, *The Cross and the Rain Forest, A Critique of Radical Green Spirituality* (Eerdmans, 1996).

15. Heinrich Rommen, *The State in Catholic Thought, A Treatise in Political Philosophy* (B. Herder, 1945), p. 401. Rommen's very cogent exposition, though purporting to expound Thomistic philosophy, draws more heavily on authorities from the era of the Counter-Reformation. He dismisses "Christian emperors of the Middle Ages," for example, as ruling "empires of short duration" (p. 404), leaving out quite a bit of history in that summation.

16. John Courtney Murray, S.J., *We Hold These Truths: Catholic Reflections on the American Proposition* (Sheed and Ward, 1960), p. 195.

17. A point well recognized by Rommen: "There is some reason to suspect that the fight against the term [sovereignty] has a deeper significance, that it is an attempt to do away with authority. . . . When no objective truth but only relative verities are admitted . . . might becomes right, genuine authority is impossible. . . . Then are destroyed the personal and moral elements of authority as a fact, and also its . . . power to bind, to demand obedience [becomes] pure arbitrary power, unless those who obey, obey only themselves in the general will, in an identification of government and governed. But from this it would follow that the majority decides not what is *hic et nunc* just, measured by an ideal of justice, but what shall be accepted as just only because the majority so decides. The concept of authority

is thus dissolved. No one obeys anyone but himself. The consequence must be a new leviathan." Rommen, *State in Catholic Thought*, 409–10.

18. General Comment No. 24 of Human Rights Committee, CCPR/C/21/Rev.1/Add.6, 2 November 1994, reprinted (in relevant part) in Steiner and Alston, *Human Rights in Context*, pp. 1044–47. The official U.S. response (rejecting the claim) is reprinted in 16 *H.Rts.L.J.* 422 (1995). On why the UN view seems plausible to some American legal scholars, see Richard Lillich, "The Growing Importance of Contemporary International Human Rights Law," *Georgia Journal of International and Comparative Law*, vol. 25 (1995–96).

19. As Louis Henkin has put it, "states have few inalienable rights." "Notes from the President," *Newsletter*, American Society of International Law, March 1993.

20. *Atkins v. Virginia*, 536 U.S. 304 (2002).

21. *Lawrence v. Texas*, 123 S.Ct. 2472.

22. The phrase is advanced—with compelling analysis—in Robert Bork, *Coercing Virtue, The Worldwide Rule of Judges* (AEI Press, 2003), p. 137. For one sign of gathering resistance to this trend, at least in the United States, see, H. Res. 568 (108th Cong, 2d Sess.), condemning invocation of foreign precedents for interpreting American law and appealing to the American Declaration of Independence for its claim that American law should be interpreted solely in light of American precedents. Hearings on the resolution were conducted by the House Committee on the Judiciary, Subcommittee on the Constitution, on March 25, 2004.

23. Inaugural Address, 1927.

24. Eisenhower, Second Inaugural Address, 1957 (*Public Papers of the President*, Eisenhower series, vol. 5, p. 64).

25. 536 U.S., p. 348.

26. "The American, taking part in everything that is done in his country, feels a duty to defend anything criticized there, for it is not only his country that is being attacked, but himself; hence one finds that his national pride has recourse to every artifice and descends to every childishness of personal vanity." Alexis de Tocqueville, *Democracy in America*, translated by G. Lawrence (Anchor, 1969), p. 237.

27. The Equal Rights Amendment, prohibiting sex discrimination by government agencies, was twice approved by two-thirds majorities of the House and Senate and by half the state legislatures—and still failed to receive adequate support for adoption, due to an intense mobilization by opponents. This happened in the 1970s, even as the Supreme Court was reading most of the likely implications of the ERA into the existing (and more general) "equal protection" guarantee in the Fourteenth Amendment. Opponents had almost no prominent figures on their side—but were still able to mobilize enough popular support to overcome pressures on remaining state legislatures to ratify. The pattern is hard to imagine in any other western country.

28. Given that law professors have agitated these arguments for over a decade, that cases involving actions overseas have begun to accumulate, the paucity of cases affecting domestic affairs is striking.

29. Andrew Nathan, "China and the International Human Rights Regime," Elizabeth Economy and Michael Oksenberg, eds., *China Joins the World* (Council on Foreign Relations, 1999).

30. "Australia: Rumbles from Down Under," *National Review*, December 3, 2001.

31. Compare "A Historic UN Ruling on Quebec," *The Gazette* (Montreal), April 10, 1993 (criticism of Quebec language laws by UN Human Rights Committee) and "Language Law Violates Helsinki pact," *The Gazette* (Montreal), August 30, 1999 (describing Quebec's rejection of UN criticism, now warning of adverse reaction in a non-UN forum—which also turned out to make no difference in Quebec).

32. No. 9, pp. 39, 40.

33. Even the high-minded argument for universal law offered by John Rawls, *The Law of Peoples* (Harvard University Press, 1999) acknowledges that liberal states have no moral authority to impose their own constitutional norms on illiberal states (sec. 7–8, pp. 59–70) and limits universal human rights claims to little more than the right to be free of slavery and ethnic violence (sec. 10, pp. 78–81). One might see the point of such self-limiting approaches without subscribing to all of the conceptual apparatus presented in Rawls's work.

34. For a survey of complaints against the World Bank and the IMF, see John Micklethwait and Adrian Wooldridge, *A Future Pefect, The Challenge and Hidden Promise of Globalization* (Crown Business, 2000), pp. 175–79. Robert O. Keohane and Joseph S. Nye, "Introduction," in Joseph Nye and John Donahue, eds., *Governance in a Globalizing World* (Brookings Institution, 2000), pp. 31–32, noting the World Bank has been "relatively successful in co-opting NGOs" but acknowledges that they have made the Bank "more beholden" to NGOs. The "green agenda" that has taken hold in the Bank is the target of James Sheehan, *Global Greens, Inside the International Environmental Establishment* (Capital Research Center, 1998).

35. The claim is so often repeated that it is easy to lose sight of how strange it really is. The recent diplomatic history by Brian Simpson, for example, emphasizes that a prime motivation for the more serious human rights sytem established in Europe after the Second World War was the experience of wartime occupation: "those who had experienced occupation knew, though this could not always be said, so taboo laden was the subject, that under German occupation, particularly in France, those who ill treated the population were, not infrequently, their own fellow citizens and their own government . . . the response, particularly from Christian Democratic parties, but also from others, was the limitation of the power of the potential oppressor, which was the nation state." *Human Rights and the End of Empire*, pp. 601–2. People and their governments had behaved horribly to fellow citizens under a transnational European structure. Therefore, to prevent a repetition of such horrors, European peoples and governments must subordinate themselves under a transnational European structure. The logic is hard to follow. What was meant, presumably, was that instead of a Nazi-inspired structure, there ought to be a Christian-inspired structure. But why suppose that higher ideals are easier to achieve in the company of many other people and governments, which may not share those ideals to the same extent? Is a Christian or socialist Germany more likely to worry about the resurgence of anti-Semitic violence in its territory if it remains responsible for its own people—or if it shares

this responsibility with Gaullist France, which has had a determined policy of ignoring such violence in its own cities?

36. Well documented by Caroline Moorehead, *Dunant's Dream, War, Switzerland and the History of the Red Cross* (Harper Collins, 1998), pp. 416–45.

37. For example: T. J. Lawrence, *Principles of International Law*, 7th ed. (McMillan, 1923): "An intervention to put a stop to barbarous and abominable cruelty is a question rather of policy than of law. . . . It is destitute of technical legality but it may be morally right and even praiseworthy to a high degree" (pp. 127–28).

38. Stephen Erlanger and Christopher Wren, "Early Count Hints at Fewer Kosovo Dead," *The New York Times*, November 11, 1999. For appropriately skeptical assessment of the competing human rights claims—noting the vast suffering imposed by NATO intervention and the plausible grounds for initial Serb resistance—see Ignatieff, *Human Rights*, pp. 45–47.

39. Perhaps there is not quite so much agreement even on slavery: Sudan, one of the states where the practice is known to continue, was elected to the UN Commission on Human Rights in 2002 and almost elected to chair the commission. There has been no serious international intervention to stop the practice of slavery in Sudan.

40. Perpetrators of the massacre of Israeli athletes at the Munich Olympics were subsequently released by the German government—after the subsequent hijacking of a Lufthansa jet "forced" the German government to act. German officials later conceded that the hijacking had been coordinated in advance to provide an adequate pretext for the release. It was part of a pattern: "Germany made secret agreements with Palestinian and other international terrorist groups in a desperate bid to keep them away from German borders." Simon Reeve, *One Day in September* (Arcade, 2000), pp. 157–58. When one of the perpetrators of the Olympic massacre was arrested in France in 1977, the government arranged for his prompt release: "The French authorities had been bribing and blackmailing terrorist groups to persuade them to avoid France during their attacks" (ibid., p. 209). As late as 1999, Austrian officials arranged for the prompt departure from the country of Izzat Ibrahim al-Duri, a top henchman of Saddam Hussein, accused of directing the mass murder of Kurds a decade before, when al-Duri was discovered to be taking medical treatment in Vienna and a criminal complaint was filed against him. The Austrian government's action provoked "the consternation of human rights groups." Barbara Crosette, "Dictators Face The Pinochet Syndrome," *The New York Times*, August 22, 1999.

41. The ICC Statute makes many provisions for participation of nongovernmental organizations (or advocates for victims of relevant crimes) to participate in court proceedings. The Statute requires the prosecutor to seek approval of a Pre-trial Chamber of judges when deciding to proceed to prosecution—or when deciding to drop an investigation without attempting a prosecution (art. 53, par. 3b). According to the Court's Rules of Procedure, the prosecutor must give notice to affected advocates when deciding not to prosecute and these advocates may submit counterarguments to the Pre-trial Chamber (Rule 50). Advocates for victims are then authorized to participate in proceedings before the Pre-trial

Chamber on whether to approve the prosecutor's decision to withhold prosecution in a particular case (Rule 92).

42. The generally accepted doctrine in the nineteenth century held that states could not assert any extraterritorial jurisdiction, except over their own citizens travelling abroad—though some states (with approval from commentators) had asserted an exception for acts in other countries directly threatening the security of the home state. Heads of state, like diplomats, were thought to retain special immunities beyond this structure. Lasa Oppenehim, *International Law*, pp. 194–97, 412–14. The U.S. Supreme Court insisted on a still more emphatic doctrine to prevent "sovereign acts" of other states from being challenged (as to legal validity) in U.S. courts: "Every sovereign state is bound to respect the independence of every other sovereign State and the courts of one country will not sit in judgment on the acts of the government of another done within its own territory." *Underhill v. Hernandez*, 168 U.S. 250 (1897) (rejecting tort claim based on abuse of U.S. citizens by rebel forces subsequently recognized as the governing authority in Venezuela).

43. Statement of Lord Browne-Wilkenson, Macedo ed., *Princeton Principles*.

44. Michael Ross Fowler and Julie Marie Bunck, *Law, Power and the Sovereign State* (Pennsylvania State University Press, 1995), pp. 70–80, reviews various accounts of sovereignty as a "basket" of attributes. Particularly telling is the remark of Hans Blix, hearkening to legal realist analysis of the early twentieth century: "As ownership is described as a bundle of rights, sovereignty may perhaps be described as a bundle of competences" (*Sovereignty, Aggression and Neutrality* [Amquist & Wiksell, 1970], p. 11). As a matter of fact, treating property as a "bundle of rights" which can be dismantled at random makes it very difficult to establish effective markets, because the "bundle" was not randomly assembled in the first place.

45. Dissociating responsibilities for border controls from responsibility for security raises questions for EU states that are far from hypothetical in an age when terrorists—or individuals suspected of terror connections—move readily across borders and EU authorities claim the right to override national border controls. See, for example, Philip Johnson, "EU Overrules Britain's Refusal of Entry to Moroccan," *Daily Telegraph* (UK), September 24, 2003.

46. A prominent exception is Louis Henkin, *Foreign Affairs and the Constitution*, 2d. ed. (Oxford University Press, 1996), p. 263: where "legislative" or "regulatory" powers are given to international agencies, they may be "properly seen as implementations of the original reaty establishing the organization and giving it 'regulatory powers' and in consenting to that agreement, the Senate may be said to have consented in advance to any regulations authorized by that agreement." It seems unlikely that the Supreme Court would endorse this reasoning. Even less likely that the Senate would acquiesce to it. But that resistance is the heart of what Europeans call "American unilateralism"—that is, insisting that the United States must be governed by the arrangement of powers set down in the U.S. Constitution.

47. The claim may seem startling but very difficult to avoid, once one considers the problem with any seriousness. Laurence Tribe, *American Constitutional Law*, 3d. ed. (Foundation Press, 2000), p. 646, fn. 16, acknowledges, for example, the

traditional understanding that treaties are "legitimate only for international agreements related genuinely and not just pretextually to foreign relations. . . . The President and Senate could not, for example, circumvent the House of Representatives by creating a fully operating national health care system in the United States by 'treaty' with Canada—although establishment of a joint, binational health care system by a treaty followed by implementing legislation would presumably [sic] be possible." If both houses of Congress approved such implementing legislation, under the normal legislative process, it might not seem to matter whether such a background treaty were in itself constitutional. But as Tribe recognizes, there remains a question whether the existence of a treaty could give Congress broader legislative powers than those enumerated in Article I, Sec. 8. "If, as the Supreme Court has held, the Commerce Clause does not empower Congress to criminalize all gun possession near schools, it is at least arguable that such power could not suddenly arise from a U.S.-Mexico treaty imposing on each of the signatory nations a free-standing duty to make every possible effort to eliminate guns from the vicinity of schools—at least absent findings, for example, about the relationship between guns near schools and cross border drug traffic." Tribe immediately notices the implications of this line of reasoning to human rights conventions and promptly continues with this disclaimer: "In contrast, human rights treaties imposing on all signatory nations a duty to adhere to specified norms of freedom, equality and decent treatment seem closely enough linked to the effective and humane operation of the international order—for example, by establishing norms of sovereign conduct likely to guarantee humane treatment of persons traveling in foreign lands and thereby to foster international travel, commerce and cooperation—that there would seem to be no comparable danger that the treaty power might be used in this context as a pretext to swell Congress's authority beyond the realm of foreign affairs." This analysis hardly answers the challenge. Human rights treaties do not protect foreign travelers in particular. They purport to protect everyone. If it is encouraging to foreign travelers to know that there will be full human rights protection for every citizen in countries to which they travel, it might just as easily encourage foreign travelers to know that guns will be removed from the vicinity of schools in the countries to which they travel. To put the objection more directly: Is it more likely that advocates for U.S. ratification of the Convention on Elimination of Discrimination against Women are concerned about establishing feminist policy preferences—such as government-sponsored day-care facilities—in Saudi Arabia or in the United States? Contrary to Tribe's disclaimer, it seems entirely reasonable to worry about the "danger" that so-called "treaties" regarding "human rights" will "be used as a pretext to swell Congress's authority beyond the realm of foreign affairs."

48. See, for example, extensive reliance on this epithet in William Schulz, *In Our Best Interest, How Defending Human Rights Benefits Us All* (Beacon Press, 2001), pp. 13, 15, 31–33, 47, 64–65, 179–80, 186, 188, 190.

INDEX